THIS IS THE LAST PAGE.

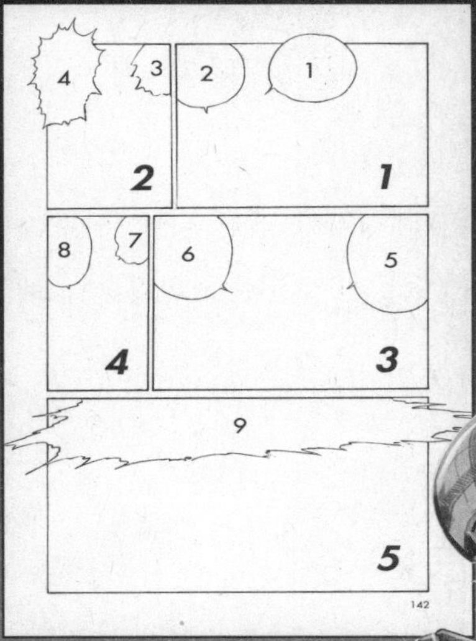

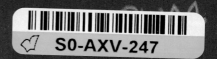

1
2
3
4
1
2
5
6
7
8
3
4
9
5
142

←Follow the action this way.

GOLDEN KAMUY has been printed in the original Japanese format in order to preserve the orientation of the original artwork.

Please turn it around and begin reading from right to left. Unlike English, Japanese is read right to left, so Japanese comics are read in reverse order from the way English comics are typically read. Have fun with it!

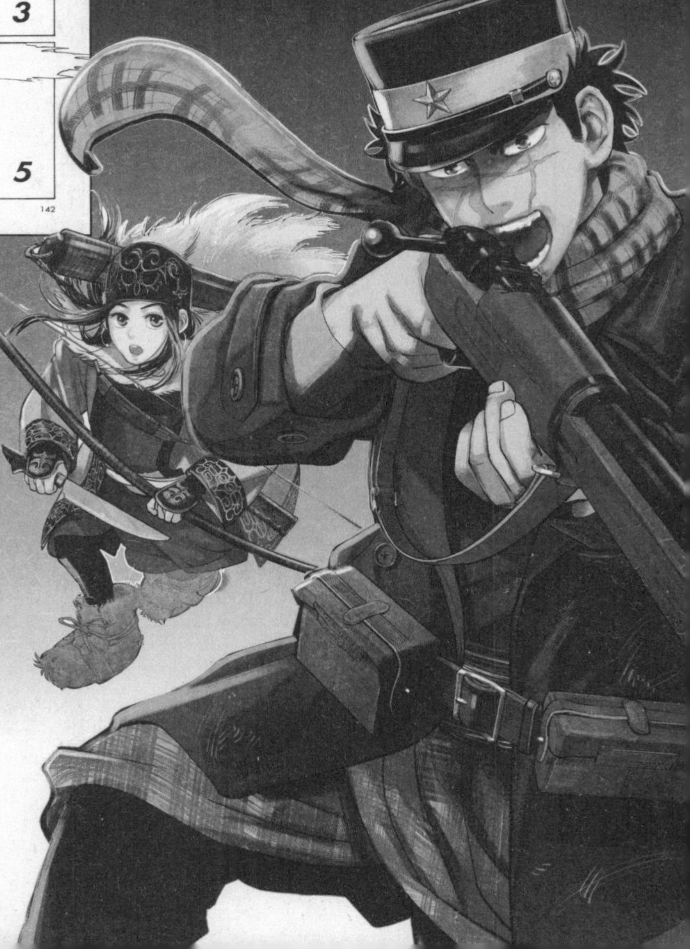

GOLDEN KAMUY

Volume 15
VIZ Signature Edition

Story/Art by Satoru Noda

GOLDEN KAMUY © 2014 by Satoru Noda
All rights reserved.
First published in Japan in 2014 by SHUEISHA Inc., Tokyo.
English translation rights arranged by SHUEISHA Inc.

Translation/John Werry
Touch-Up Art & Lettering/Steve Dutro
Design/Shawn Carrico
Editor/Mike Montesa

The stories, characters and incidents mentioned in this publication are entirely fictional.

Printed in Canada

Published by VIZ Media, LLC
P.O. Box 77010
San Francisco, CA 94107

10 9 8 7 6 5 4 3 2 1
First printing, April 2020

VIZ SIGNATURE

VIZ MEDIA

viz.com

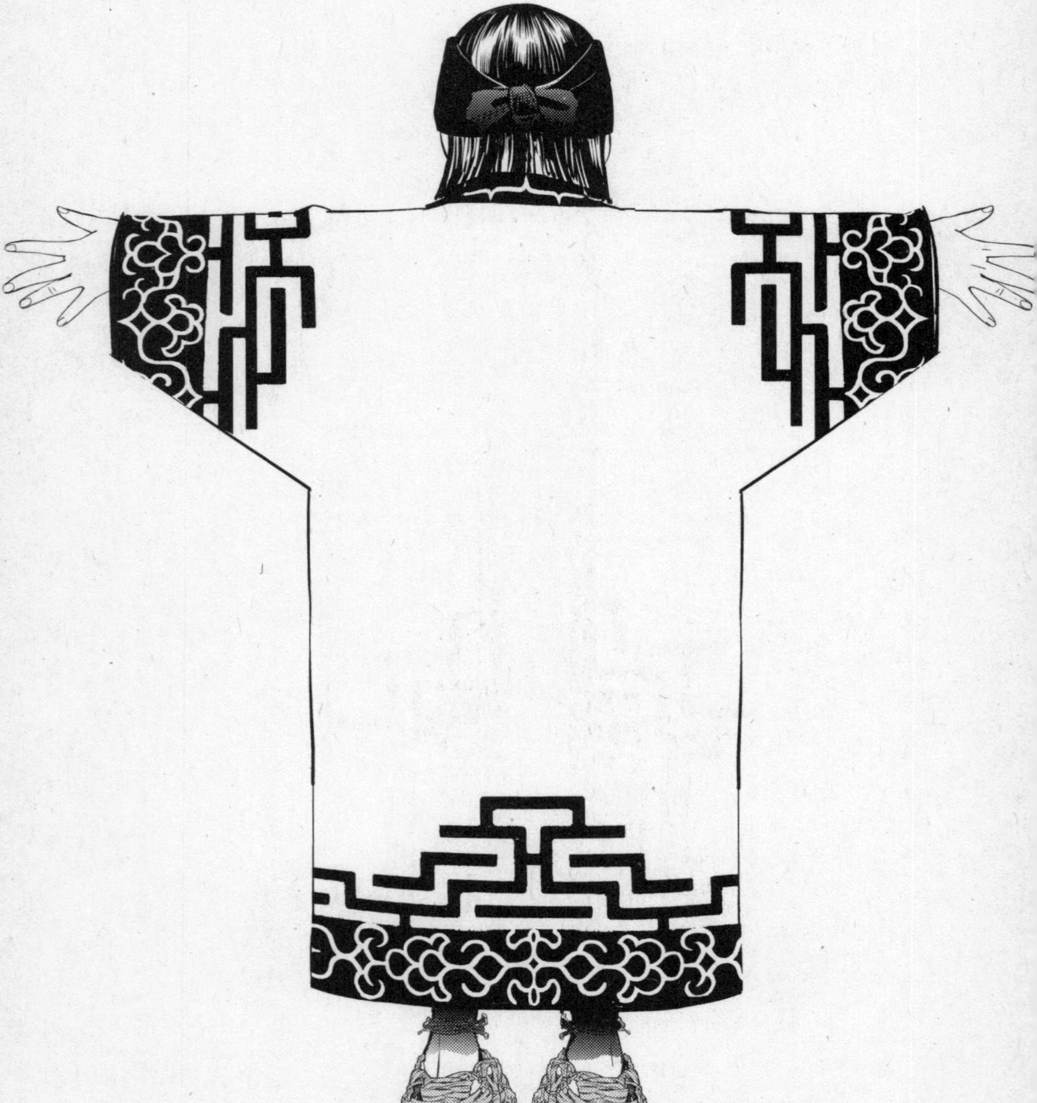

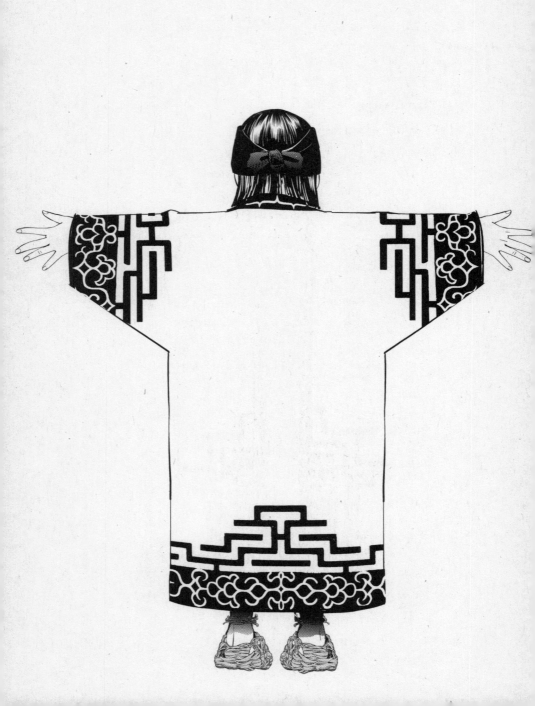

GOLDEN KAMUY 15

Story and Art by Satoru Noda

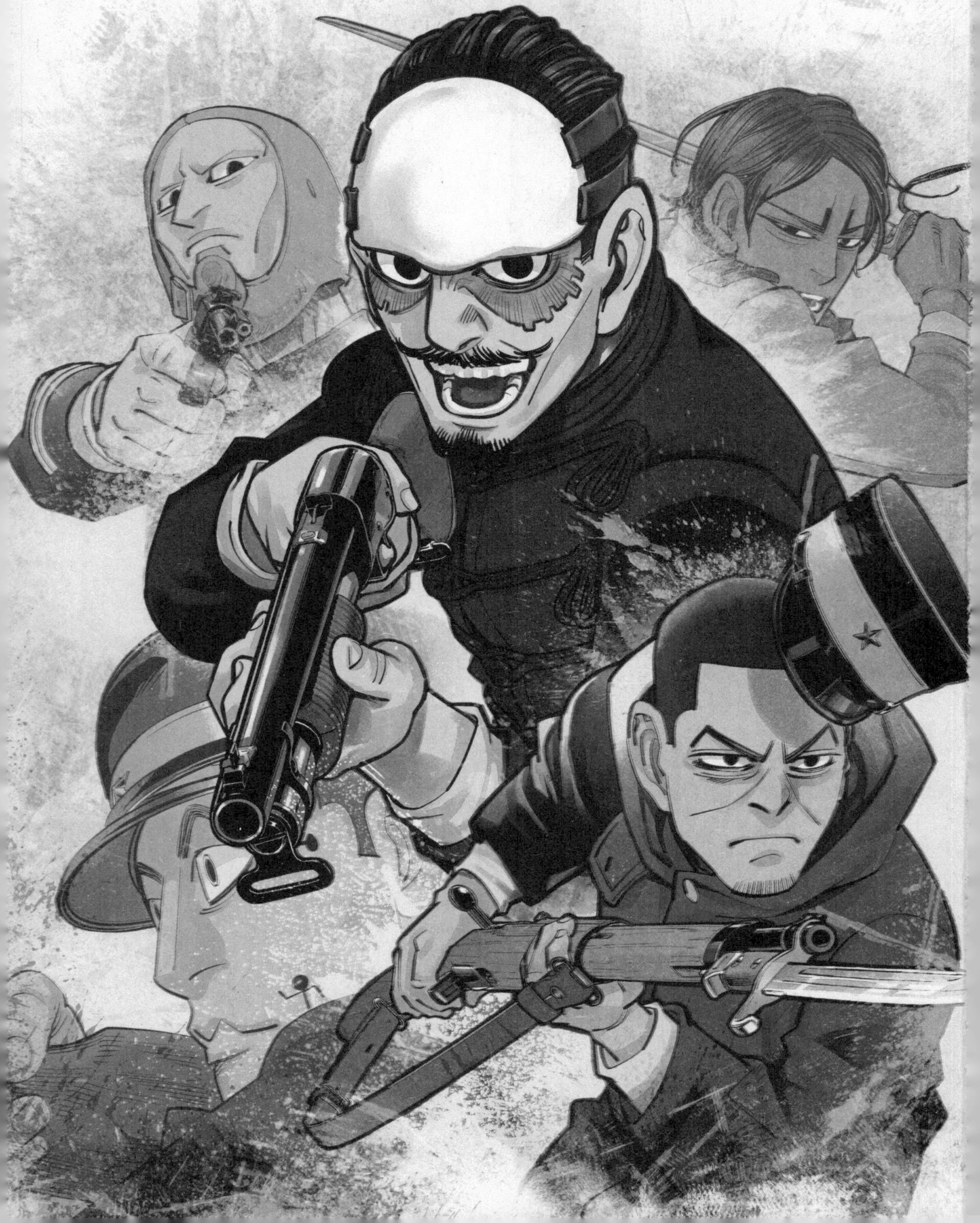

The Story So Far

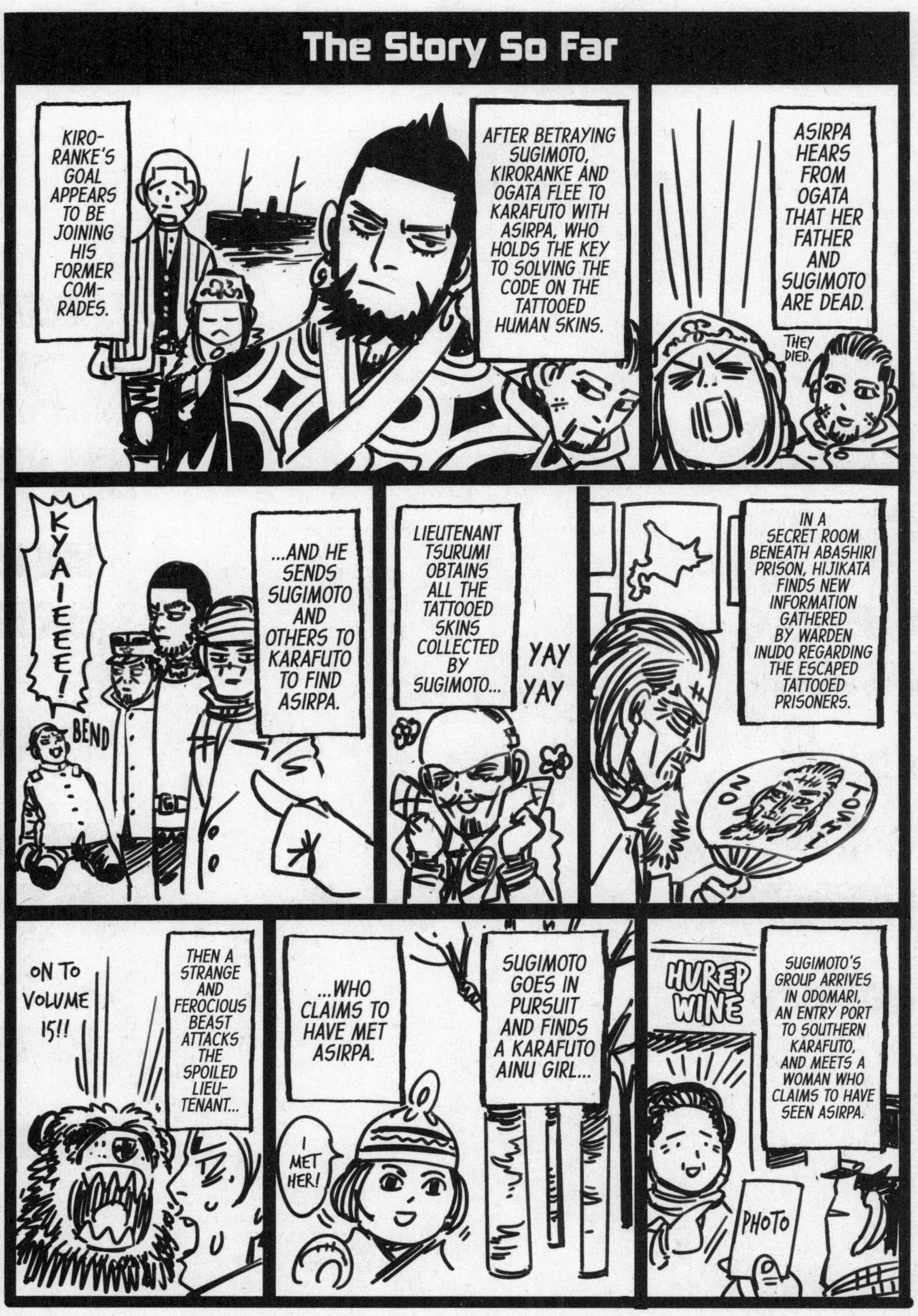

ASIRPA HEARS FROM OGATA THAT HER FATHER AND SUGIMOTO ARE DEAD.
THEY DIED.
AFTER BETRAYING SUGIMOTO, KIRORANKE AND OGATA FLEE TO KARAFUTO WITH ASIRPA, WHO HOLDS THE KEY TO SOLVING THE CODE ON THE TATTOOED HUMAN SKINS.
KIRO-RANKE'S GOAL APPEARS TO BE JOINING HIS FORMER COM-RADES.
IN A SECRET ROOM BENEATH ABASHIRI PRISON, HIJIKATA FINDS NEW INFORMATION GATHERED BY WARDEN INUDO REGARDING THE ESCAPED TATTOOED PRISONERS.
LIEUTENANT TSURUMI OBTAINS ALL THE TATTOOED SKINS COLLECTED BY SUGIMOTO...
YAY YAY
...AND HE SENDS SUGIMOTO AND OTHERS TO KARAFUTO TO FIND ASIRPA.
KYAIEEE!
BEND
SUGIMOTO'S GROUP ARRIVES IN ODOMARI, AN ENTRY PORT TO SOUTHERN KARAFUTO, AND MEETS A WOMAN WHO CLAIMS TO HAVE SEEN ASIRPA.
HUREP WINE
PHOTO
SUGIMOTO GOES IN PURSUIT AND FINDS A KARAFUTO AINU GIRL...
...WHO CLAIMS TO HAVE MET ASIRPA.
I MET HER!
THEN A STRANGE AND FEROCIOUS BEAST ATTACKS THE SPOILED LIEU-TENANT...
ON TO VOLUME 15!!

CONTENTS

ASIRPA TAKES AN INTEREST IN ENONOKA'S *EPIRIKEH* (KARAFUTO *MAKIRI* KNIFE).

Chapter 141: Karafuto Ainu

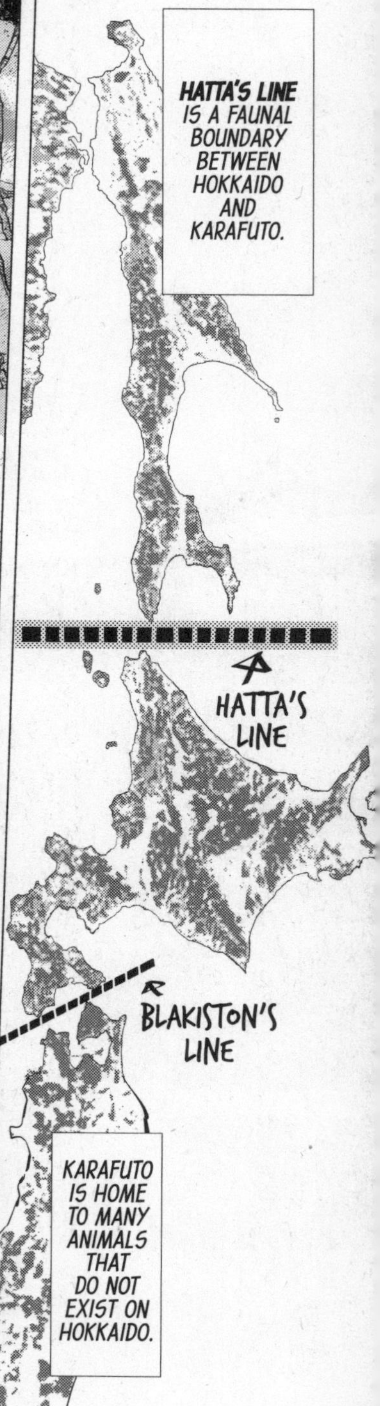
HATTA'S LINE IS A FAUNAL BOUNDARY BETWEEN HOKKAIDO AND KARAFUTO.
HATTA'S LINE
BLAKISTON'S LINE
KARAFUTO IS HOME TO MANY ANIMALS THAT DO NOT EXIST ON HOKKAIDO.

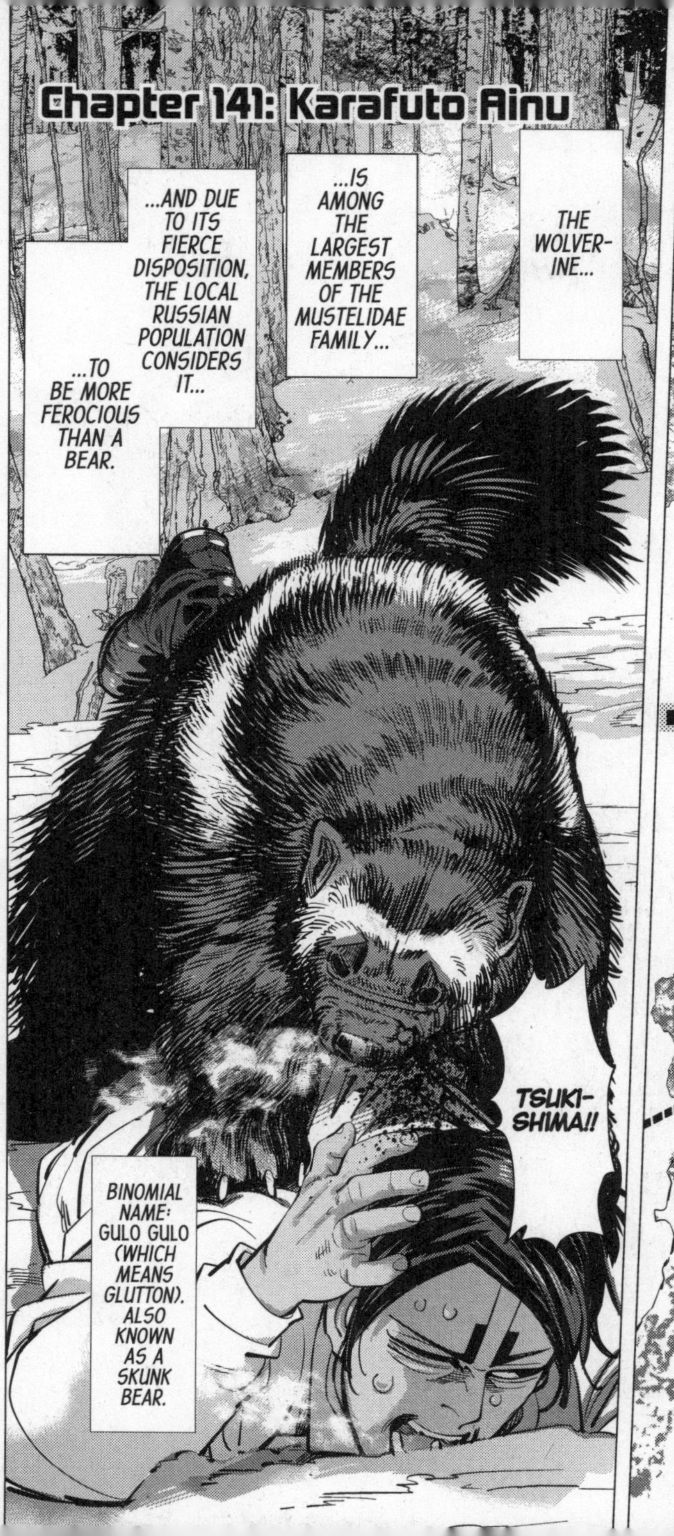
THE WOLVER-INE...
...IS AMONG THE LARGEST MEMBERS OF THE MUSTELIDAE FAMILY...
...AND DUE TO ITS FIERCE DISPOSITION, THE LOCAL RUSSIAN POPULATION CONSIDERS IT...
...TO BE MORE FEROCIOUS THAN A BEAR.
TSUKI-SHIMA!!
BINOMIAL NAME: GULO GULO (WHICH MEANS GLUTTON). ALSO KNOWN AS A SKUNK BEAR.

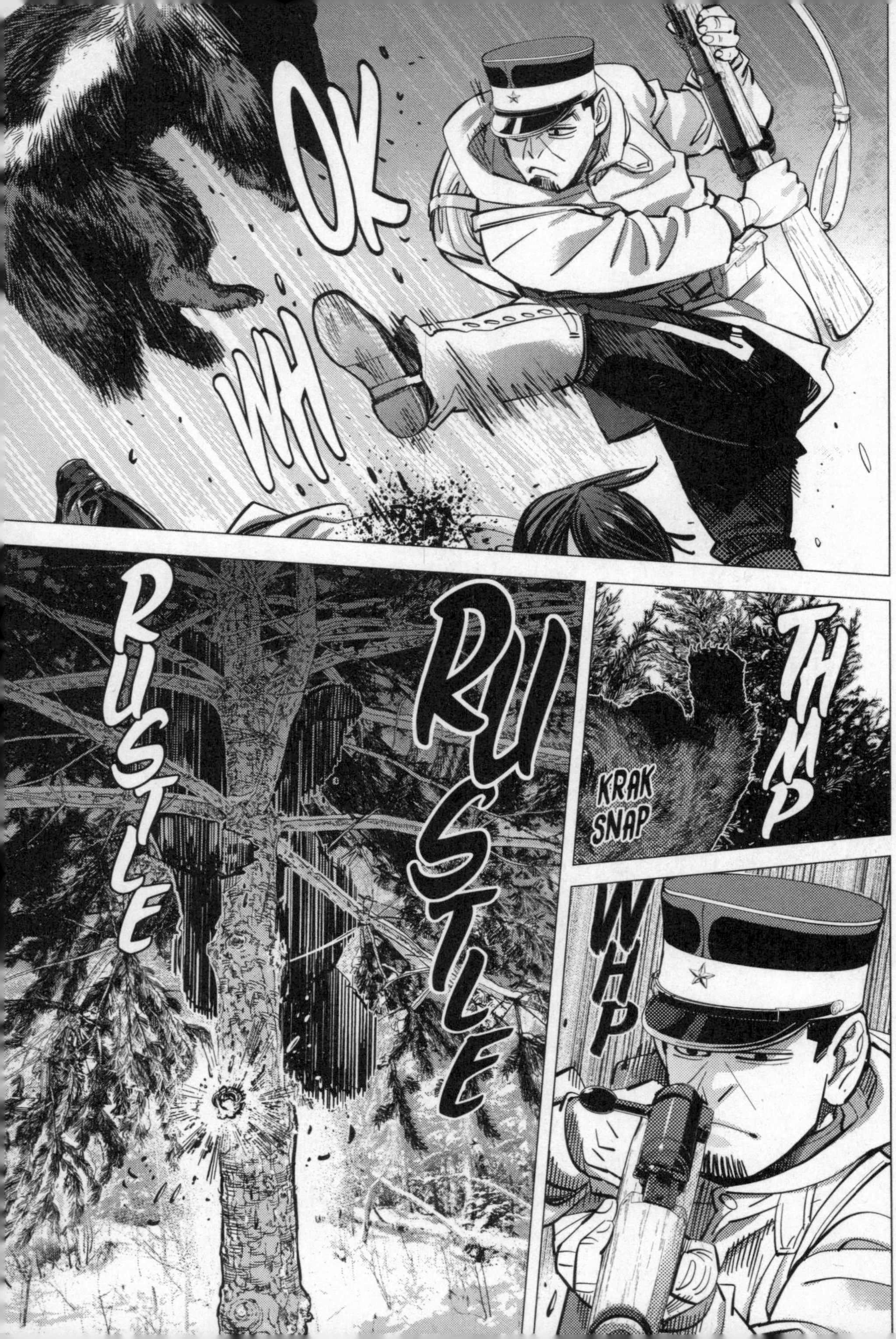

OK
WH
THUMP
KRAK
SNAP
WHP
RUSTLE
RUSTLE

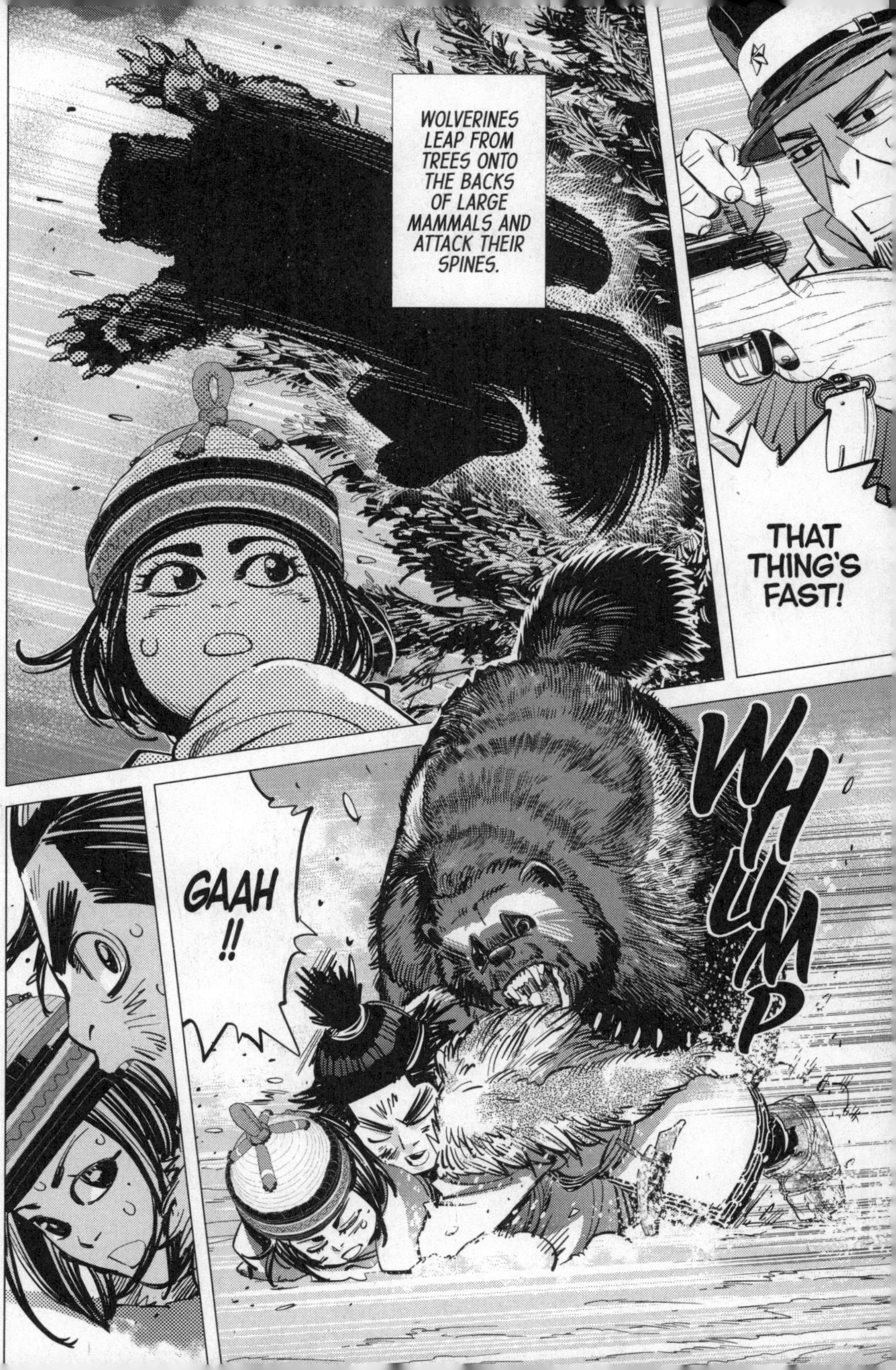
THAT THING'S FAST!
WOLVERINES LEAP FROM TREES ONTO THE BACKS OF LARGE MAMMALS AND ATTACK THEIR SPINES.
WHUMP
GAAH!!

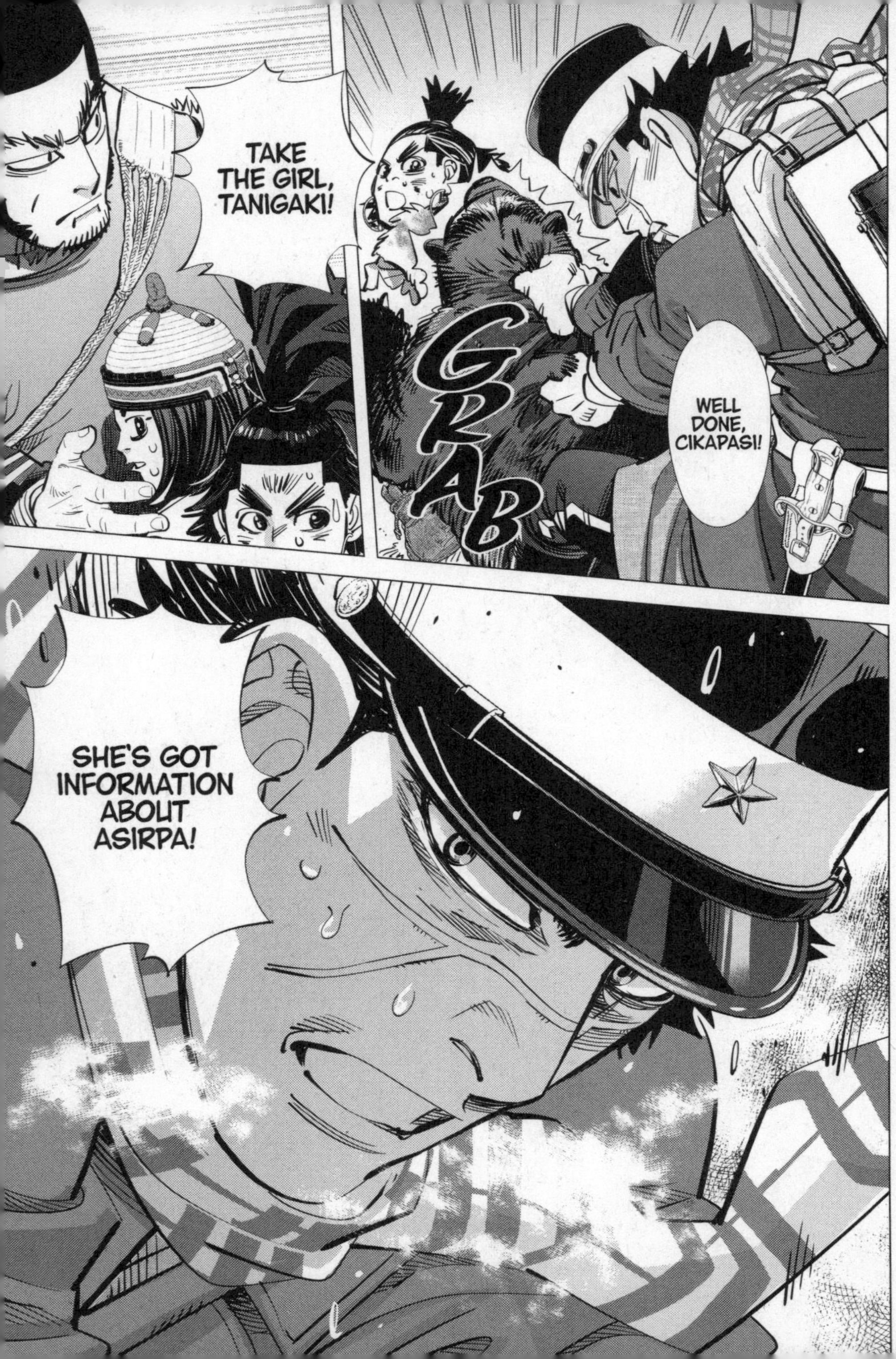
WELL DONE, CIKAPASI!
GRAB
TAKE THE GIRL, TANIGAKI!
SHE'S GOT INFORMATION ABOUT ASIRPA!

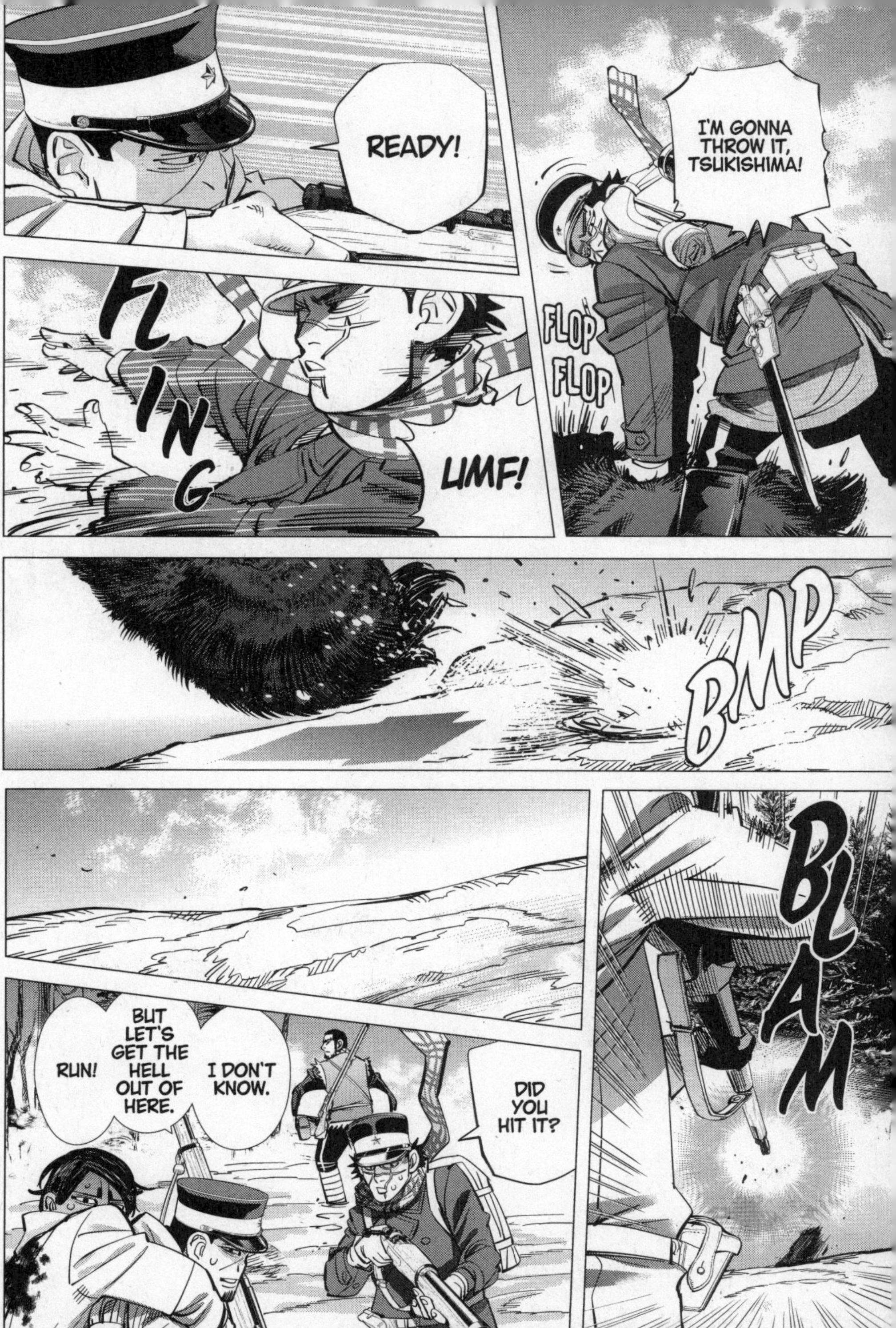
I'M GONNA THROW IT, TSUKISHIMA!
FLOP FLOP
READY!
FLING
UMF!
BMP
BLAM
DID YOU HIT IT?
I DON'T KNOW.
BUT LET'S GET THE HELL OUT OF HERE.
RUN!

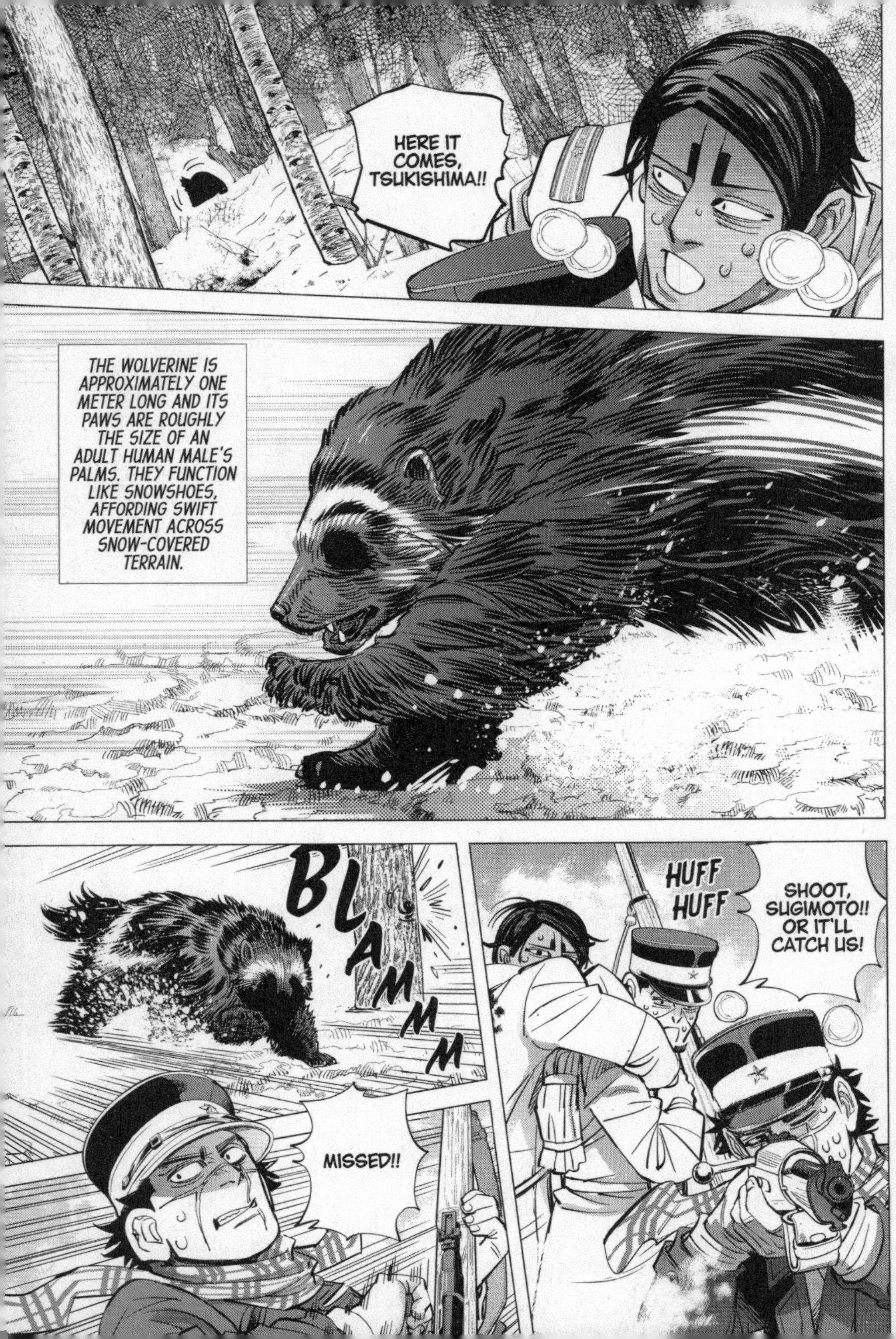
HERE IT COMES, TSUKISHIMA!!
THE WOLVERINE IS APPROXIMATELY ONE METER LONG AND ITS PAWS ARE ROUGHLY THE SIZE OF AN ADULT HUMAN MALE'S PALMS. THEY FUNCTION LIKE SNOWSHOES, AFFORDING SWIFT MOVEMENT ACROSS SNOW-COVERED TERRAIN.
HUFF HUFF
SHOOT, SUGIMOTO!! OR IT'LL CATCH US!
BLAMMM
MISSED!!

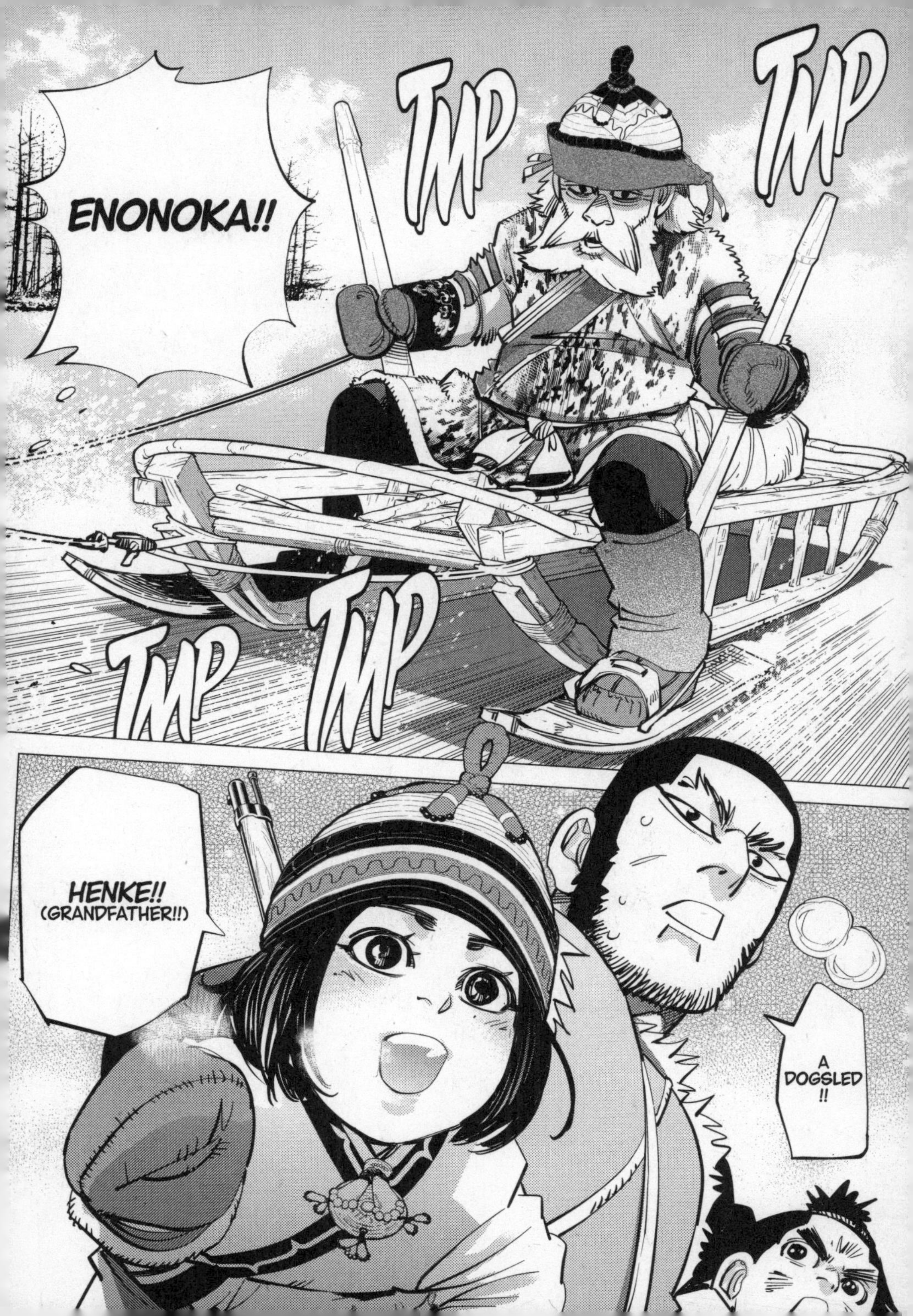
TMP
TMP
ENONOKA!!
TMP
TMP
HENKE!! (GRANDFATHER!!)
A DOGSLED !!

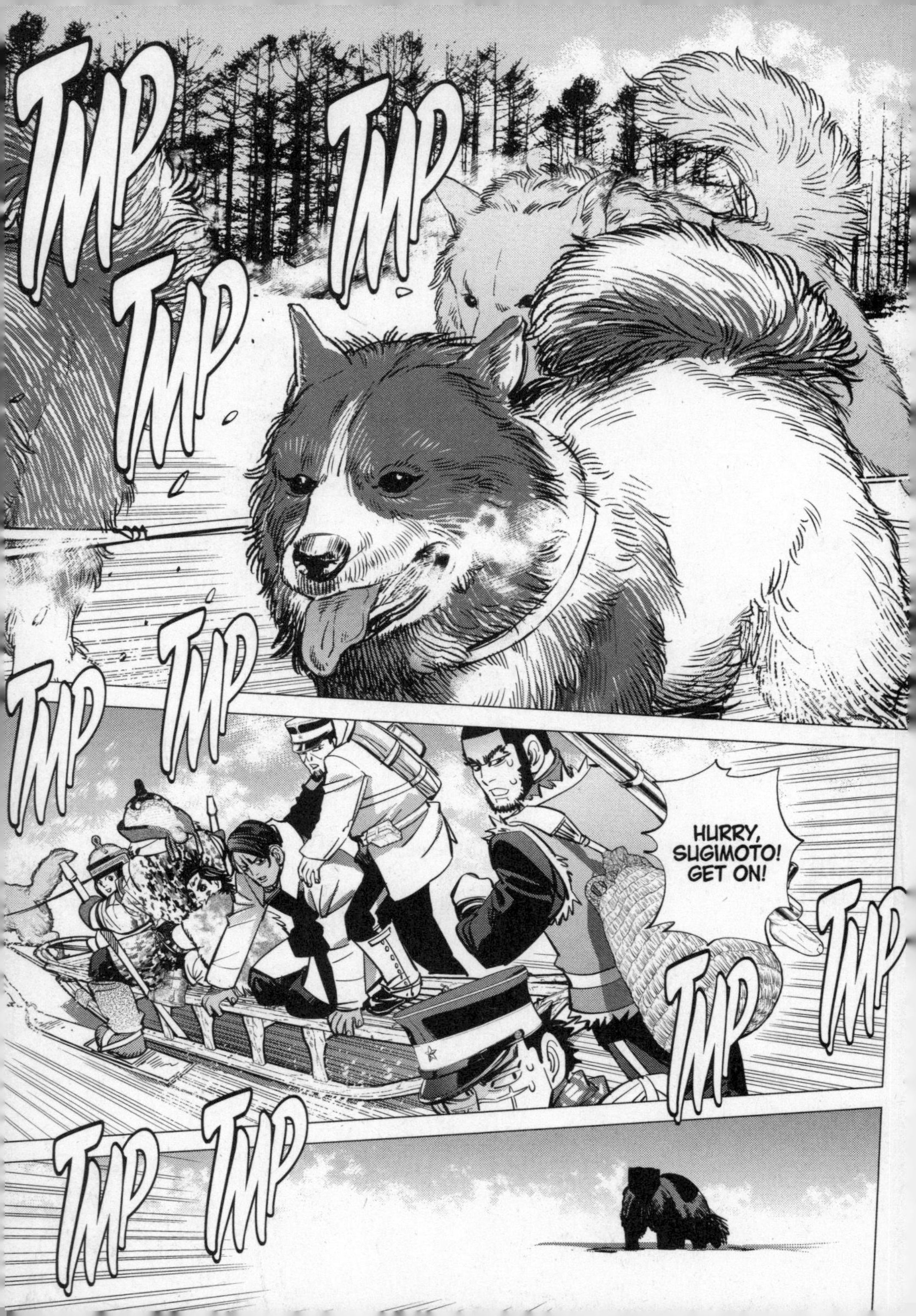
TMP TMP
TMP TMP
TMP TMP
HURRY, SUGIMOTO! GET ON!
TMP TMP
TMP TMP

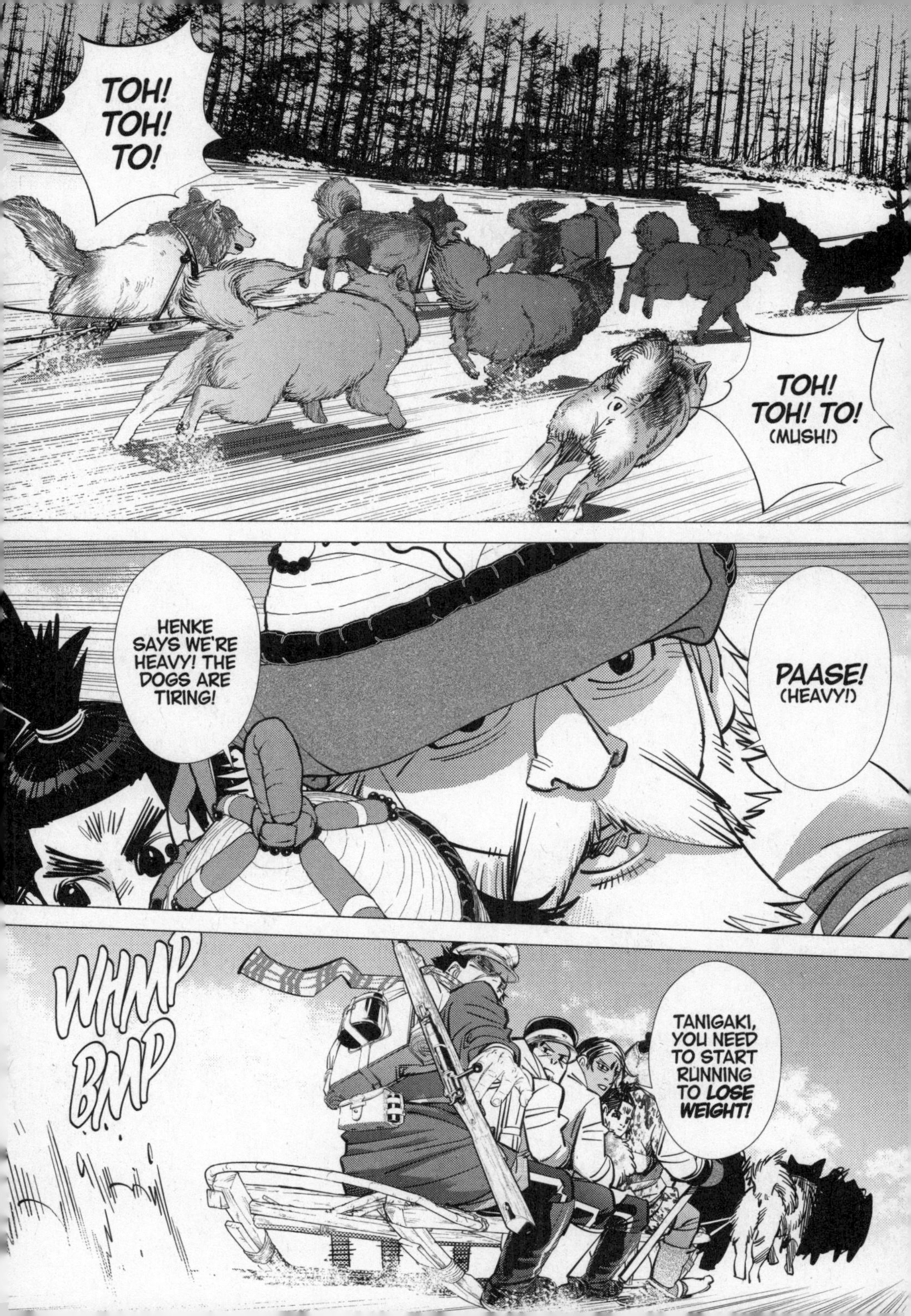
TOH! TOH! TO! (MUSH!)
TOH! TOH! TO!
PAASE! (HEAVY!)
HENKE SAYS WE'RE HEAVY! THE DOGS ARE TIRING!
TANIGAKI, YOU NEED TO START RUNNING TO LOSE WEIGHT!
WHMP BMP

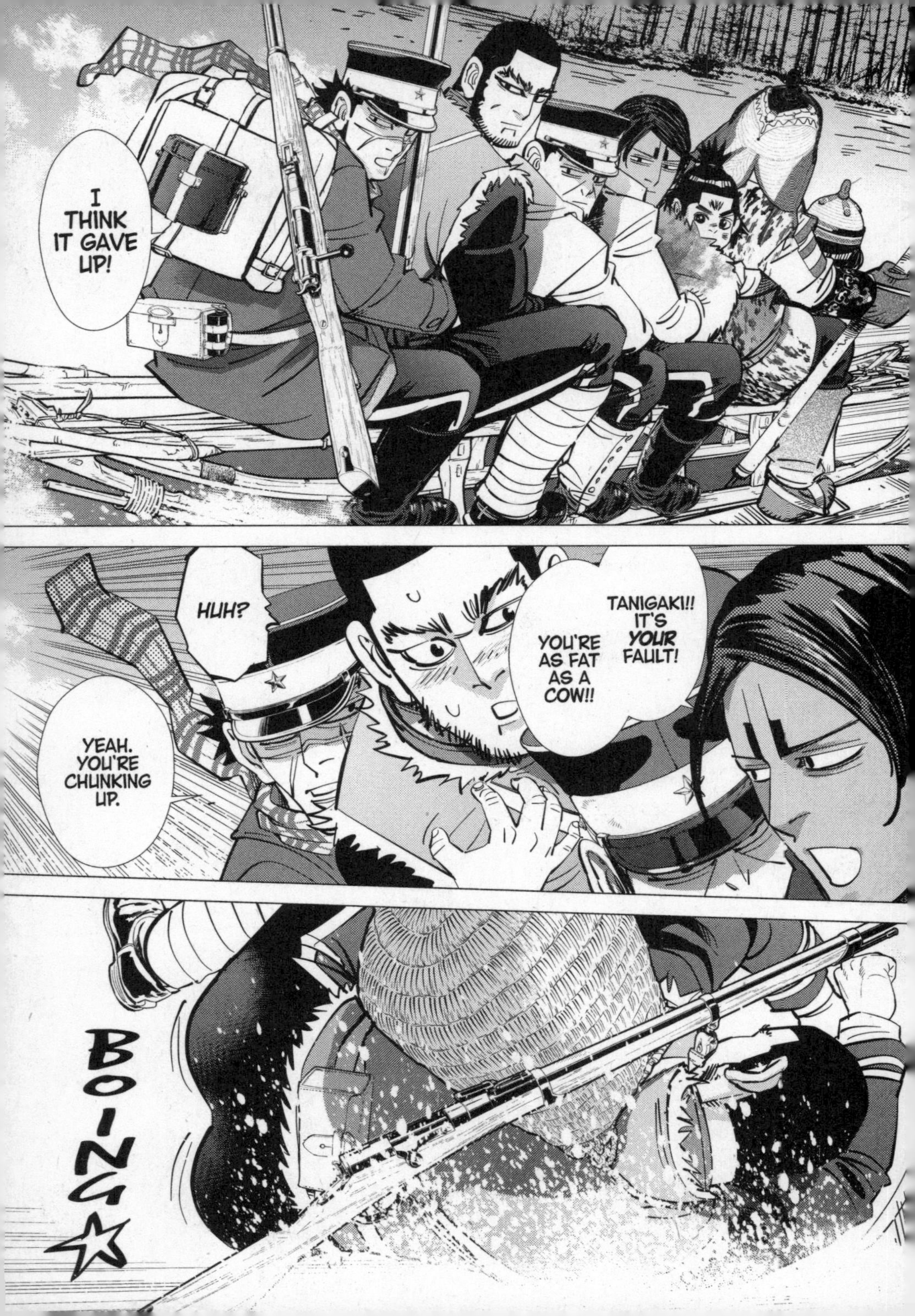
I THINK IT GAVE UP!
TANIGAKI!! IT'S YOUR FAULT!
YOU'RE AS FAT AS A COW!!
HUH?
YEAH. YOU'RE CHUNKING UP.
BOING☆

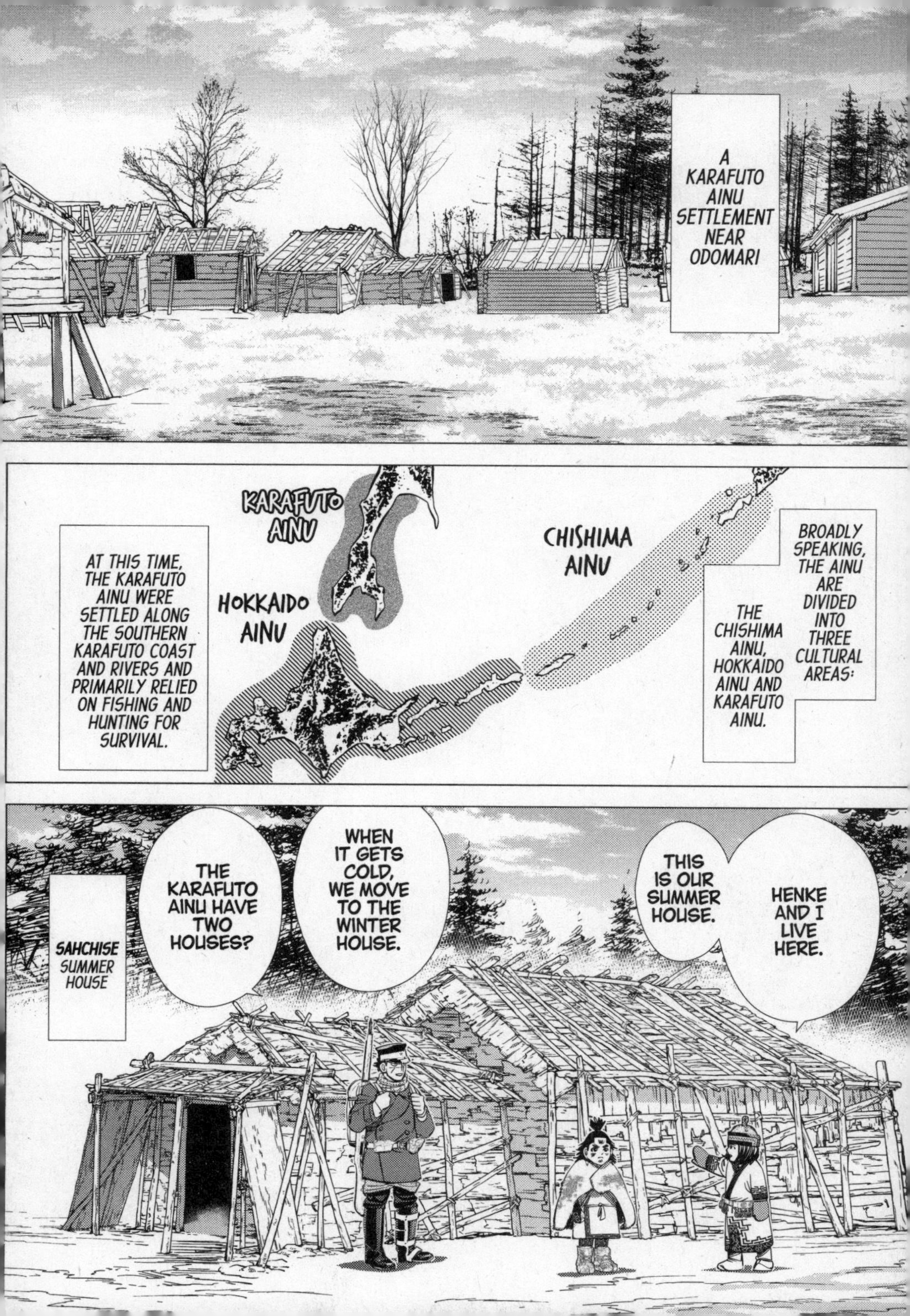
A KARAFUTO AINU SETTLEMENT NEAR ODOMARI
BROADLY SPEAKING, THE AINU ARE DIVIDED INTO THREE CULTURAL AREAS:
THE CHISHIMA AINU, HOKKAIDO AINU AND KARAFUTO AINU.
CHISHIMA AINU
KARAFUTO AINU
HOKKAIDO AINU
AT THIS TIME, THE KARAFUTO AINU WERE SETTLED ALONG THE SOUTHERN KARAFUTO COAST AND RIVERS AND PRIMARILY RELIED ON FISHING AND HUNTING FOR SURVIVAL.
HENKE AND I LIVE HERE.
THIS IS OUR SUMMER HOUSE.
WHEN IT GETS COLD, WE MOVE TO THE WINTER HOUSE.
THE KARAFUTO AINU HAVE TWO HOUSES?
SAHCHISE
SUMMER HOUSE

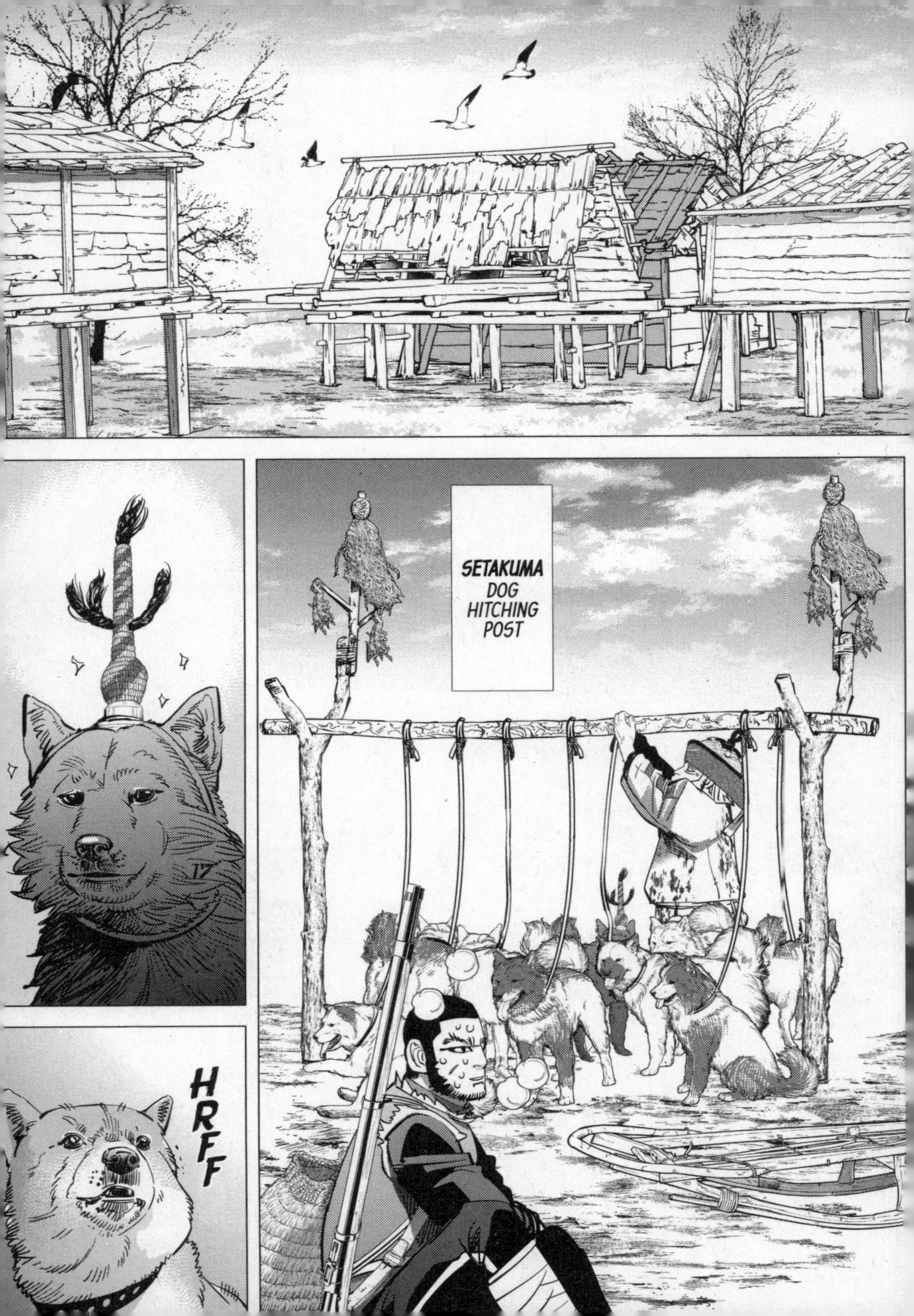
SETAKUMA
DOG
HITCHING
POST
HRFF

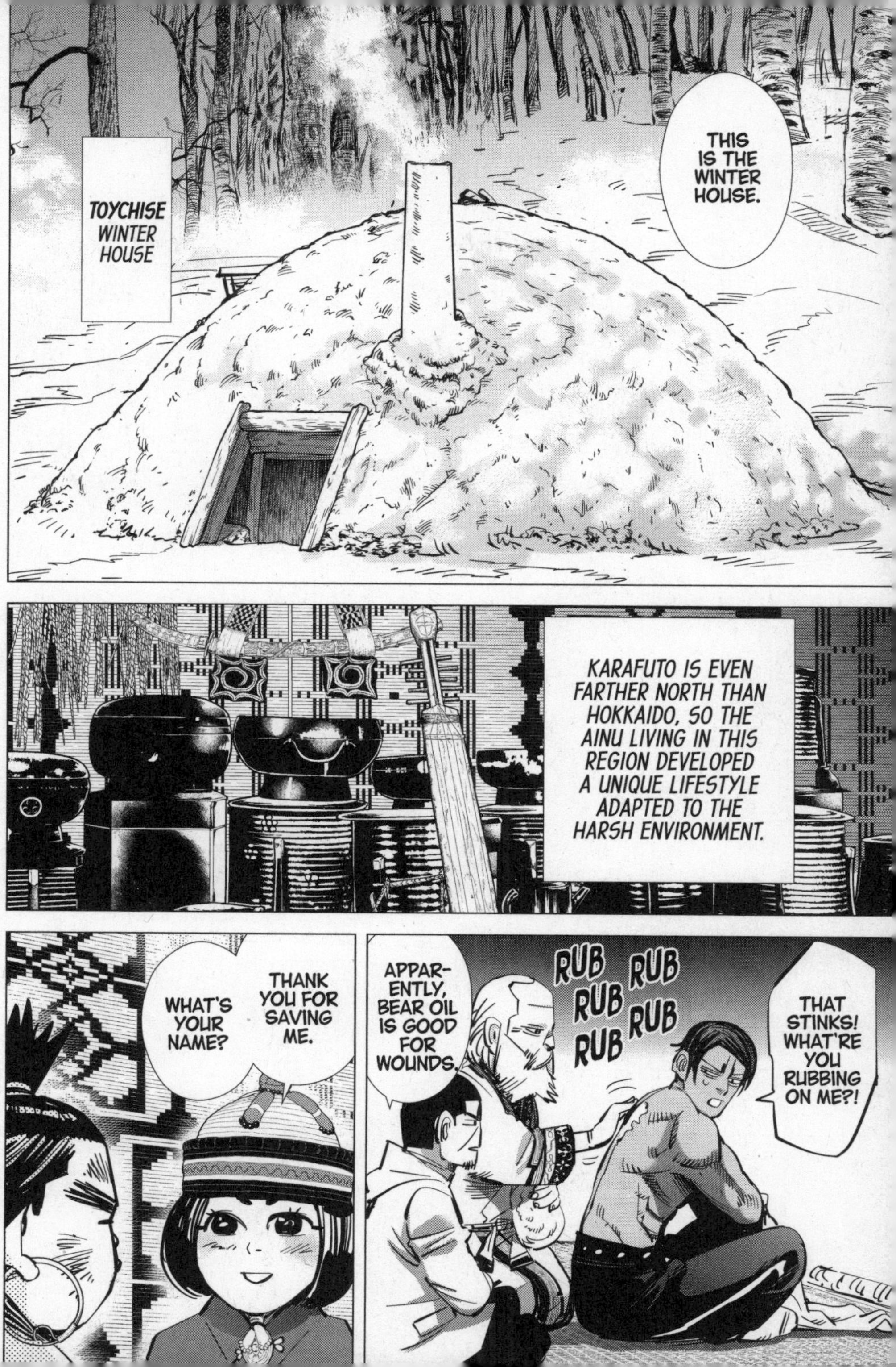
THIS IS THE WINTER HOUSE.
TOYCHISE WINTER HOUSE
KARAFUTO IS EVEN FARTHER NORTH THAN HOKKAIDO, SO THE AINU LIVING IN THIS REGION DEVELOPED A UNIQUE LIFESTYLE ADAPTED TO THE HARSH ENVIRONMENT.
THAT STINKS! WHAT'RE YOU RUBBING ON ME?!
RUB RUB RUB RUB RUB
APPAR-ENTLY, BEAR OIL IS GOOD FOR WOUNDS.
THANK YOU FOR SAVING ME.
WHAT'S YOUR NAME?

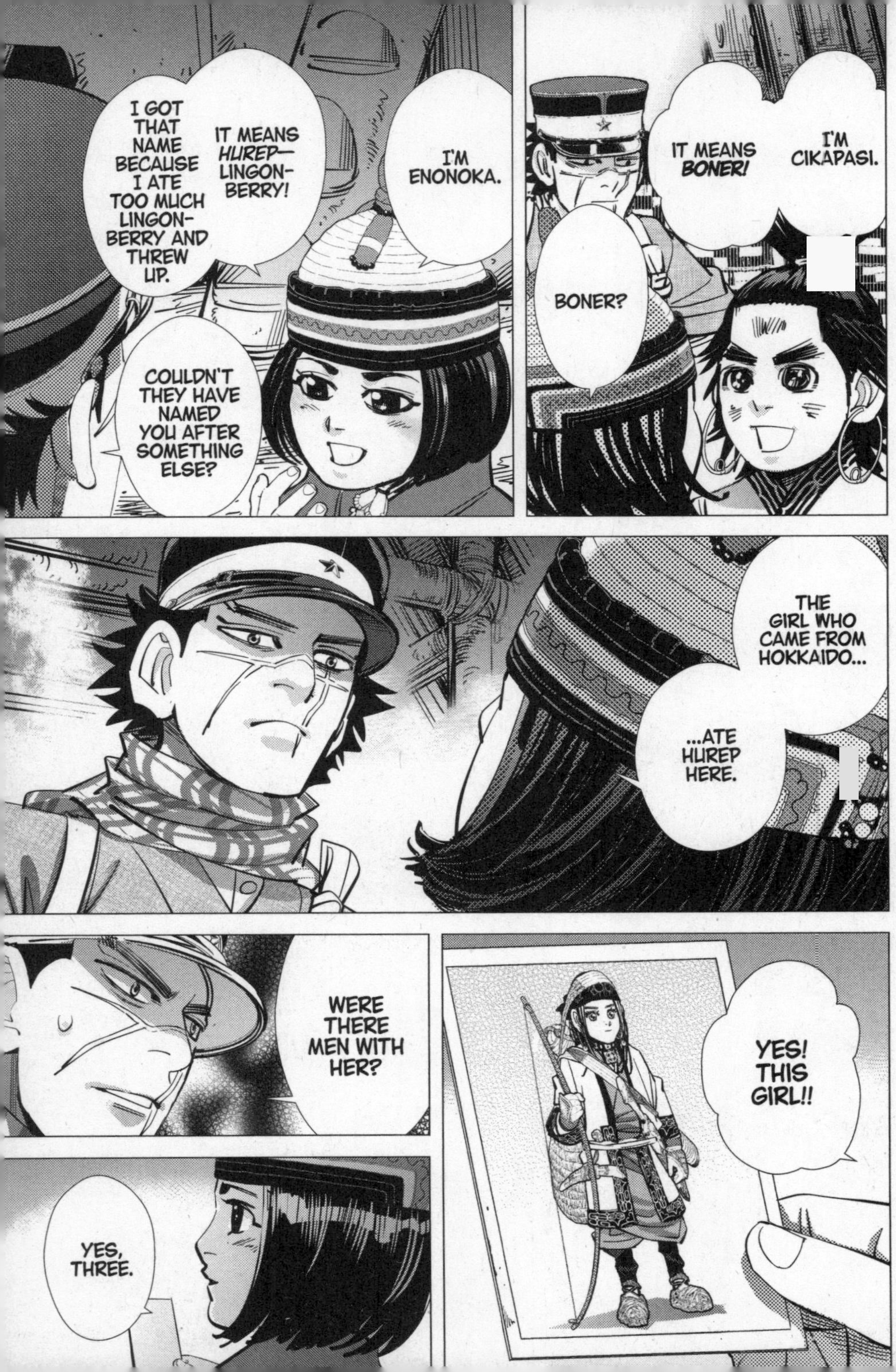
I'M CIKAPASI.
IT MEANS BONER!
BONER?
I'M ENONOKA.
IT MEANS HUREP— LINGONBERRY!
I GOT THAT NAME BECAUSE I ATE TOO MUCH LINGONBERRY AND THREW UP.
COULDN'T THEY HAVE NAMED YOU AFTER SOMETHING ELSE?
THE GIRL WHO CAME FROM HOKKAIDO...
...ATE HUREP HERE.
YES! THIS GIRL!!
WERE THERE MEN WITH HER?
YES, THREE.

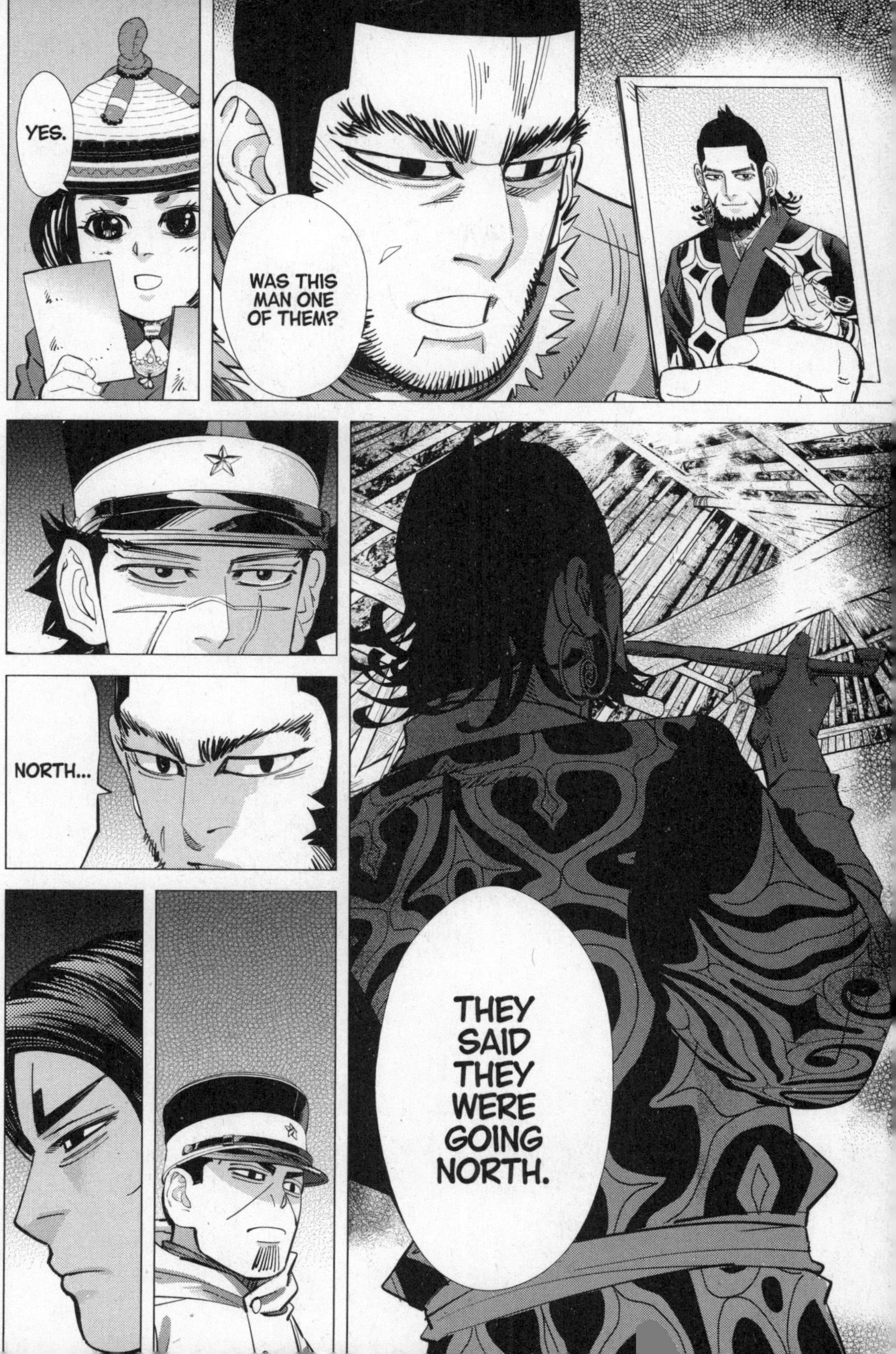
WAS THIS MAN ONE OF THEM?
YES.
THEY SAID THEY WERE GOING NORTH.
NORTH...

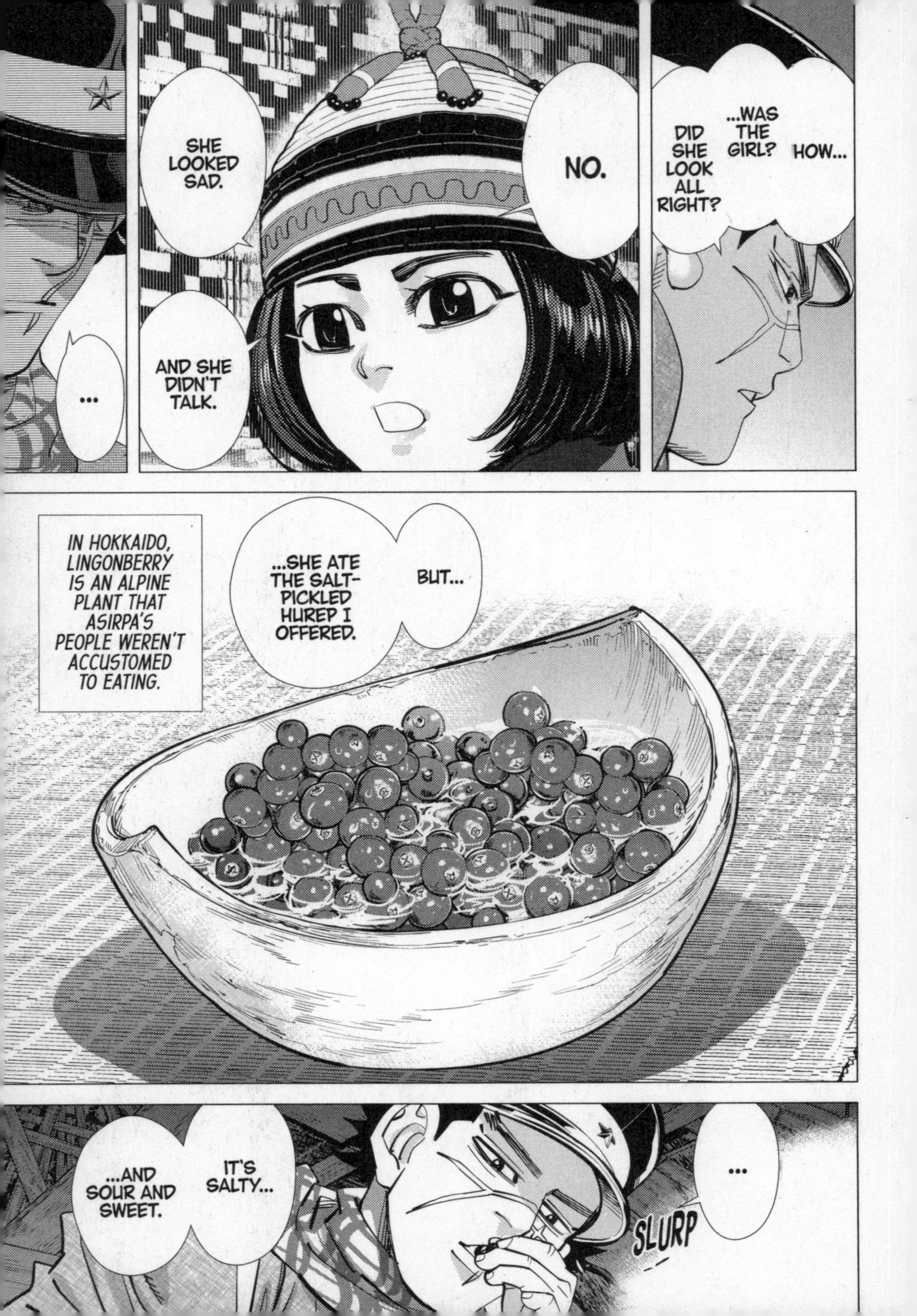
HOW...
...WAS THE GIRL?
DID SHE LOOK ALL RIGHT?
NO.
SHE LOOKED SAD.
AND SHE DIDN'T TALK.
...
BUT...
...SHE ATE THE SALT-PICKLED HUREP I OFFERED.
IN HOKKAIDO, LINGONBERRY IS AN ALPINE PLANT THAT ASIRPA'S PEOPLE WEREN'T ACCUSTOMED TO EATING.
...
SLURP
IT'S SALTY...
...AND SOUR AND SWEET.

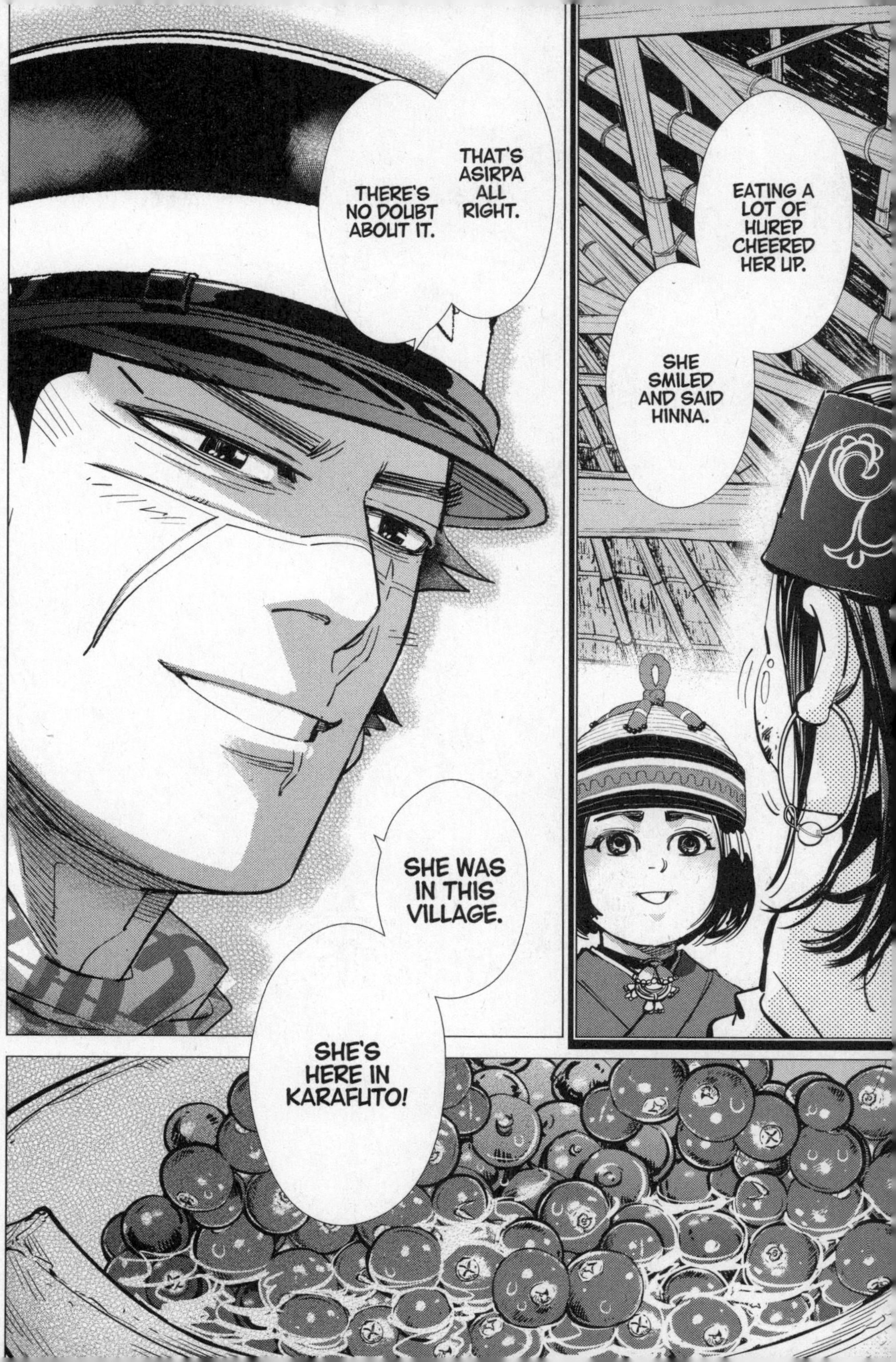
EATING A LOT OF HUREP CHEERED HER UP.
SHE SMILED AND SAID HINNA.
THAT'S ASIRPA ALL RIGHT.
THERE'S NO DOUBT ABOUT IT.
SHE WAS IN THIS VILLAGE.
SHE'S HERE IN KARAFUTO!

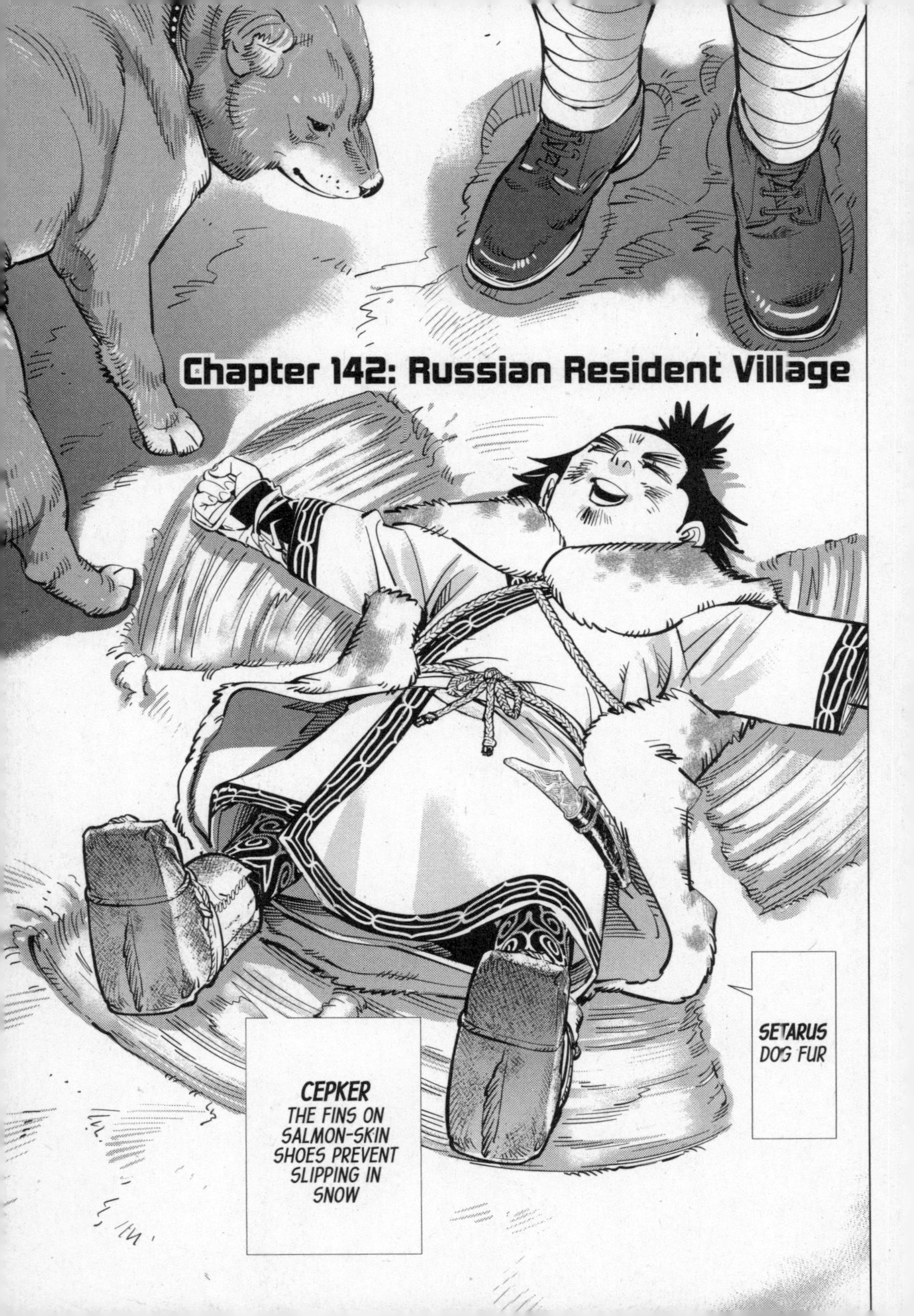
Chapter 142: Russian Resident Village
SETARUS
DOG FUR
CEPKER
THE FINS ON SALMON-SKIN SHOES PREVENT SLIPPING IN SNOW

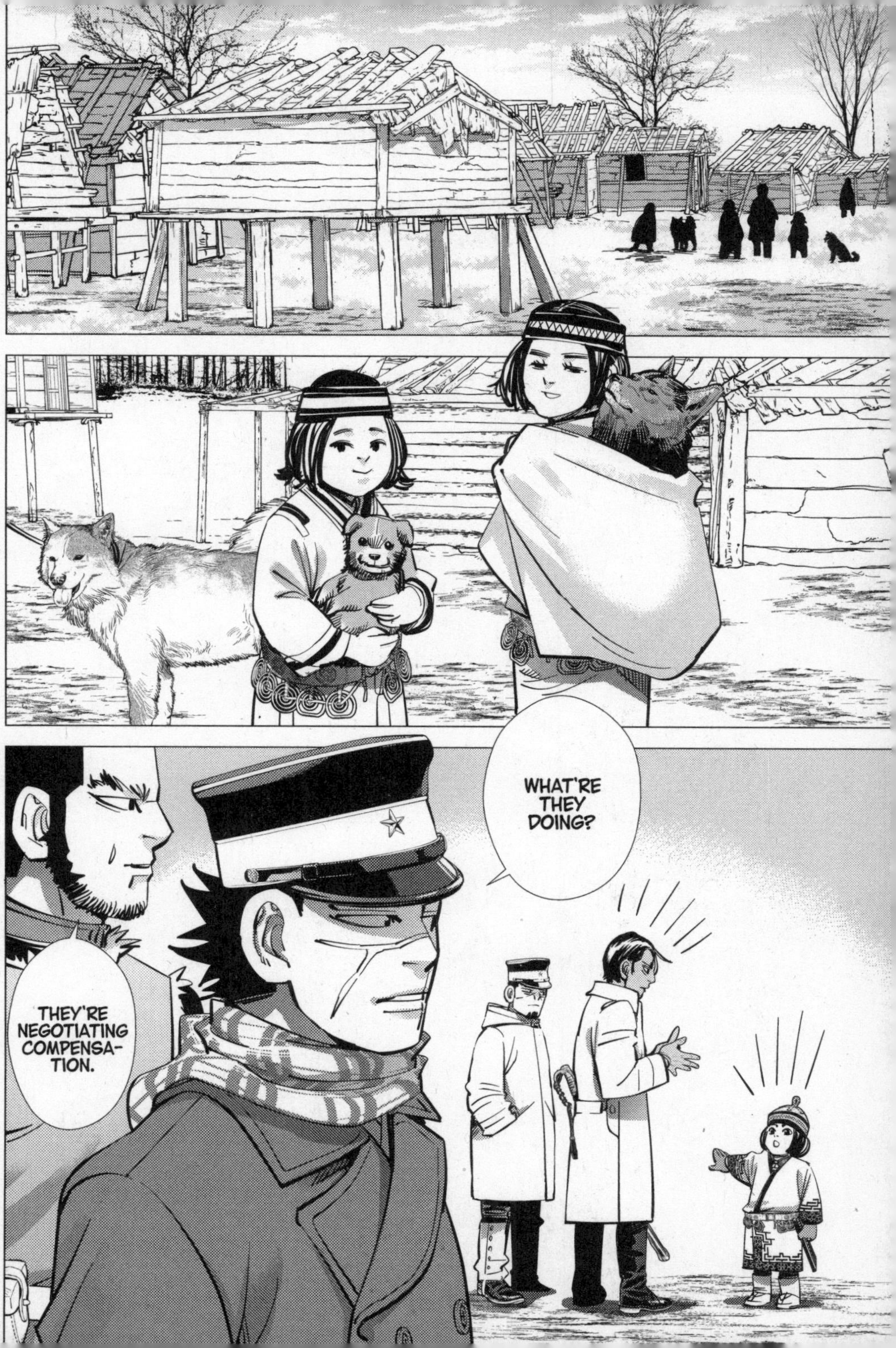
WHAT'RE THEY DOING?
THEY'RE NEGOTIATING COMPENSA-TION.

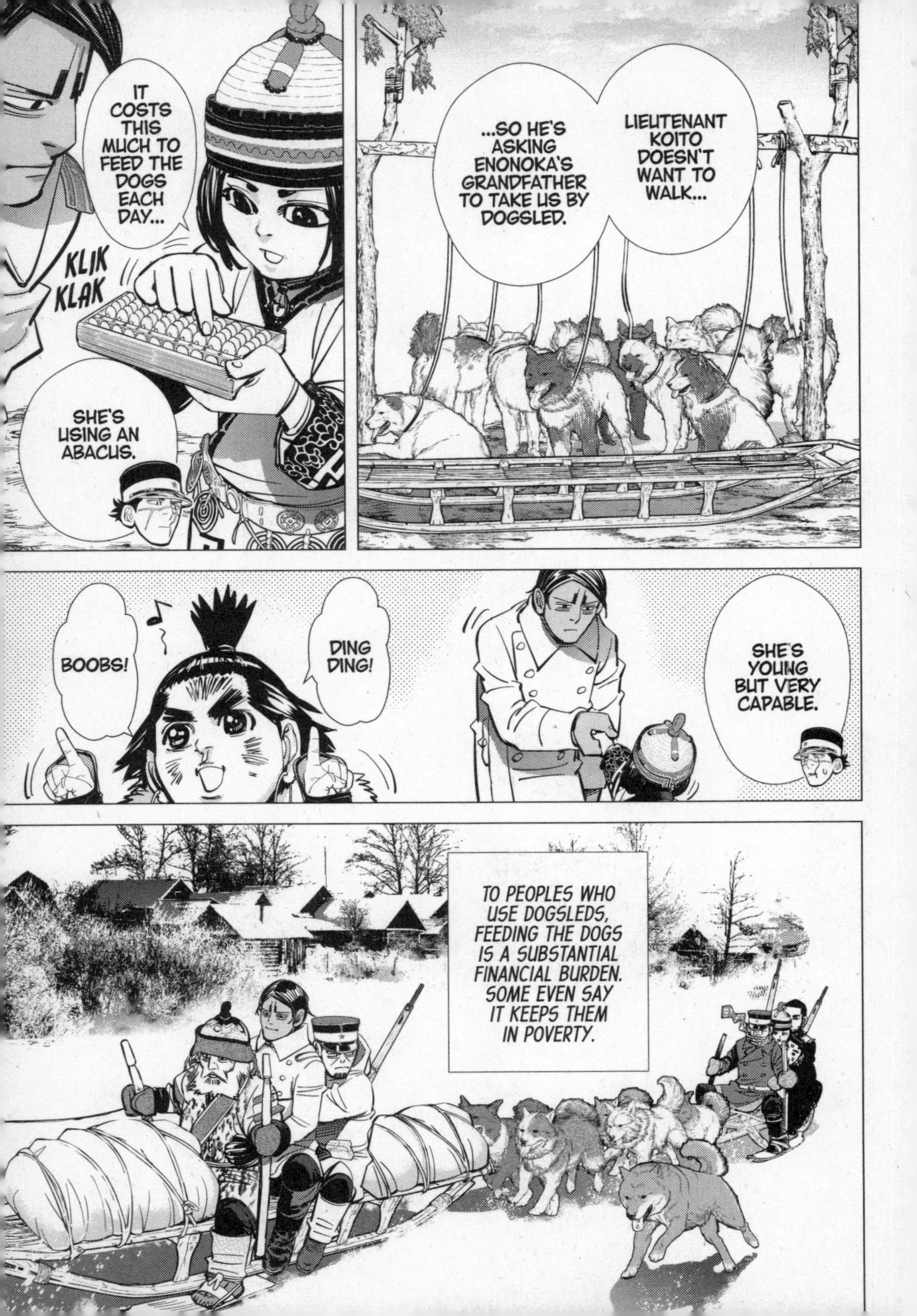
LIEUTENANT KOITO DOESN'T WANT TO WALK...
...SO HE'S ASKING ENONOKA'S GRANDFATHER TO TAKE US BY DOGSLED.
IT COSTS THIS MUCH TO FEED THE DOGS EACH DAY...
KLIK KLAK
SHE'S USING AN ABACUS.
SHE'S YOUNG BUT VERY CAPABLE.
DING DING!
BOOBS!
TO PEOPLES WHO USE DOGSLEDS, FEEDING THE DOGS IS A SUBSTANTIAL FINANCIAL BURDEN. SOME EVEN SAY IT KEEPS THEM IN POVERTY.

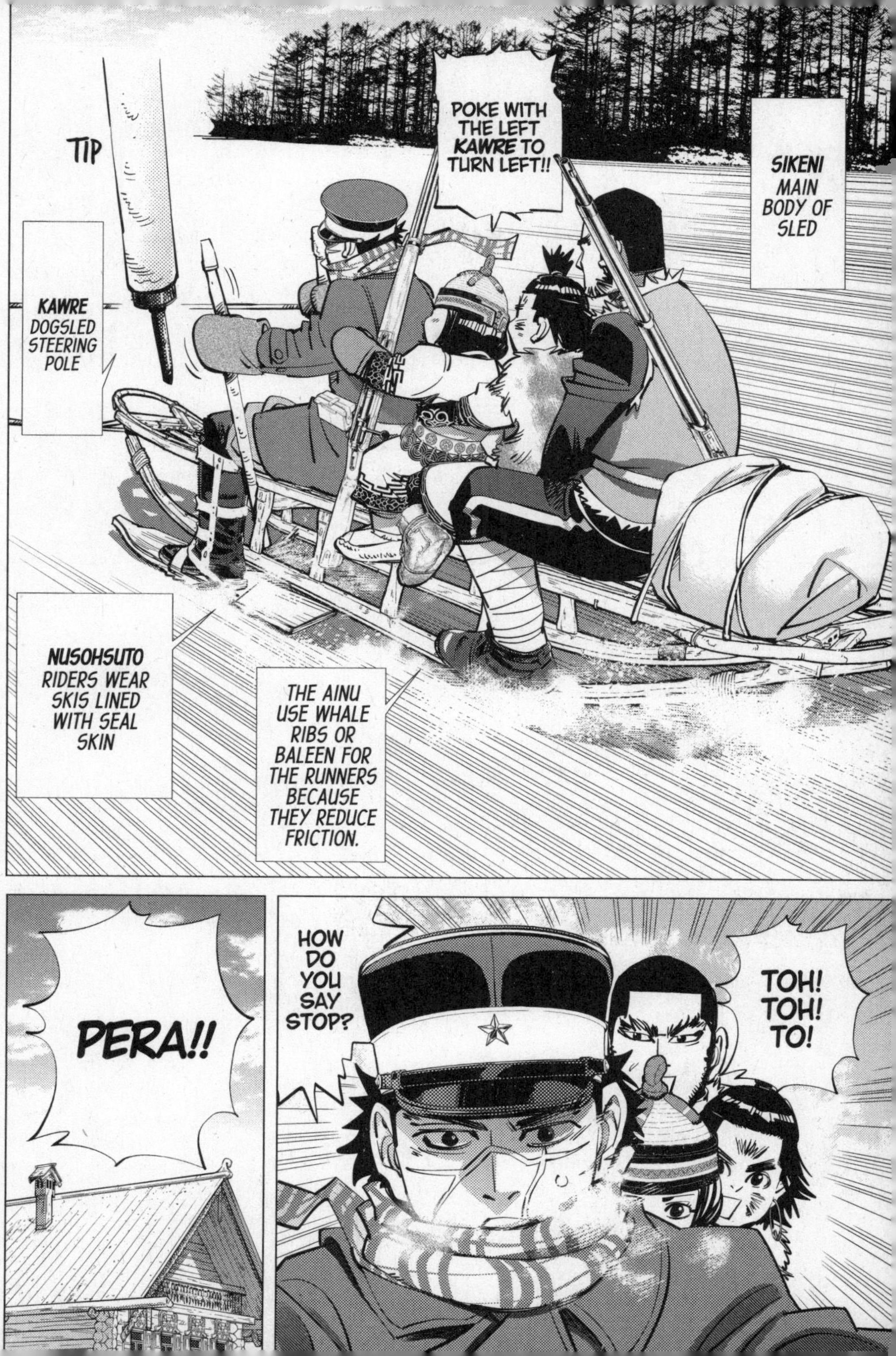
SIKENI
MAIN BODY OF SLED
POKE WITH THE LEFT KAWRE TO TURN LEFT!!
TIP
KAWRE
DOGSLED STEERING POLE
THE AINU USE WHALE RIBS OR BALEEN FOR THE RUNNERS BECAUSE THEY REDUCE FRICTION.
NUSOHSUTO
RIDERS WEAR SKIS LINED WITH SEAL SKIN
HOW DO YOU SAY STOP?
TOH! TOH! TO!
PERA!!

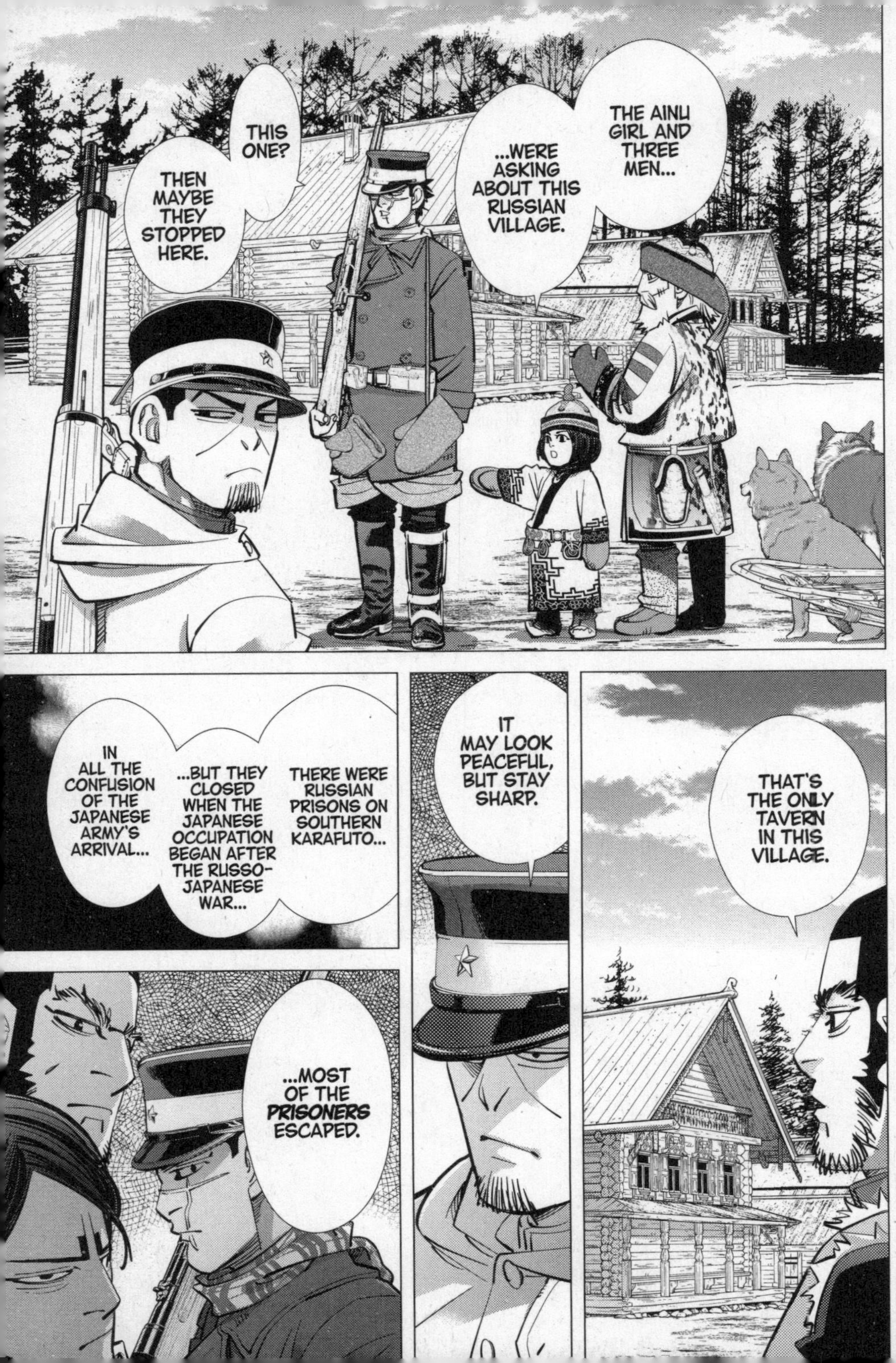
THE AINU GIRL AND THREE MEN...
...WERE ASKING ABOUT THIS RUSSIAN VILLAGE.
THIS ONE?
THEN MAYBE THEY STOPPED HERE.
THAT'S THE ONLY TAVERN IN THIS VILLAGE.
IT MAY LOOK PEACEFUL, BUT STAY SHARP.
THERE WERE RUSSIAN PRISONS ON SOUTHERN KARAFUTO...
...BUT THEY CLOSED WHEN THE JAPANESE OCCUPATION BEGAN AFTER THE RUSSO-JAPANESE WAR...
IN ALL THE CONFUSION OF THE JAPANESE ARMY'S ARRIVAL...
...MOST OF THE **PRISONERS** ESCAPED.

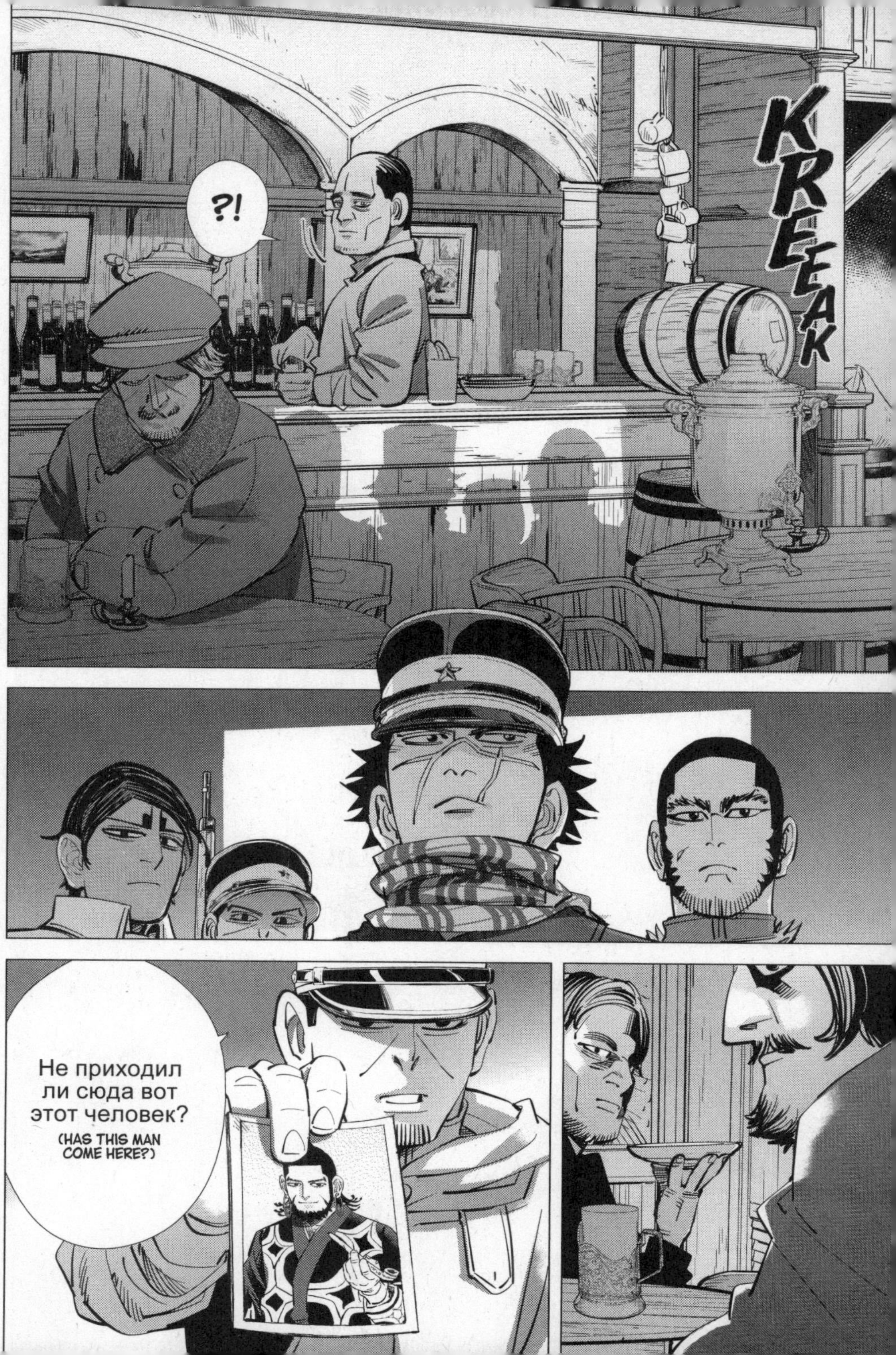
KREEAK
?!
Не приходил ли сюда вот этот человек?
(HAS THIS MAN COME HERE?)

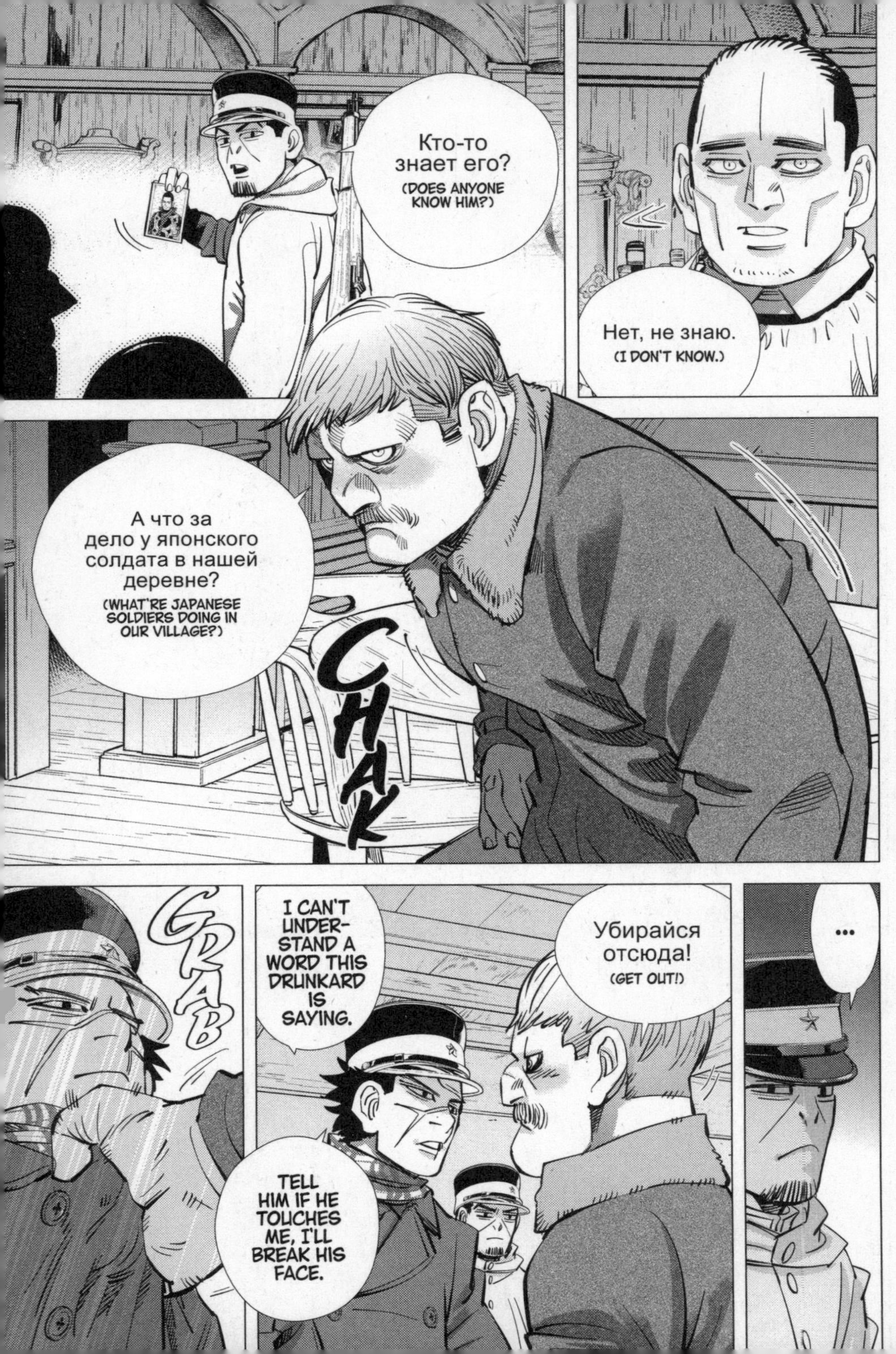

Нет, не знаю.
(I DON'T KNOW.)
Кто-то знает его?
(DOES ANYONE KNOW HIM?)
А что за дело у японского солдата в нашей деревне?
(WHAT'RE JAPANESE SOLDIERS DOING IN OUR VILLAGE?)
CHAK
...
Убирайся отсюда!
(GET OUT!)
I CAN'T UNDERSTAND A WORD THIS DRUNKARD IS SAYING.
TELL HIM IF HE TOUCHES ME, I'LL BREAK HIS FACE.
GRAB

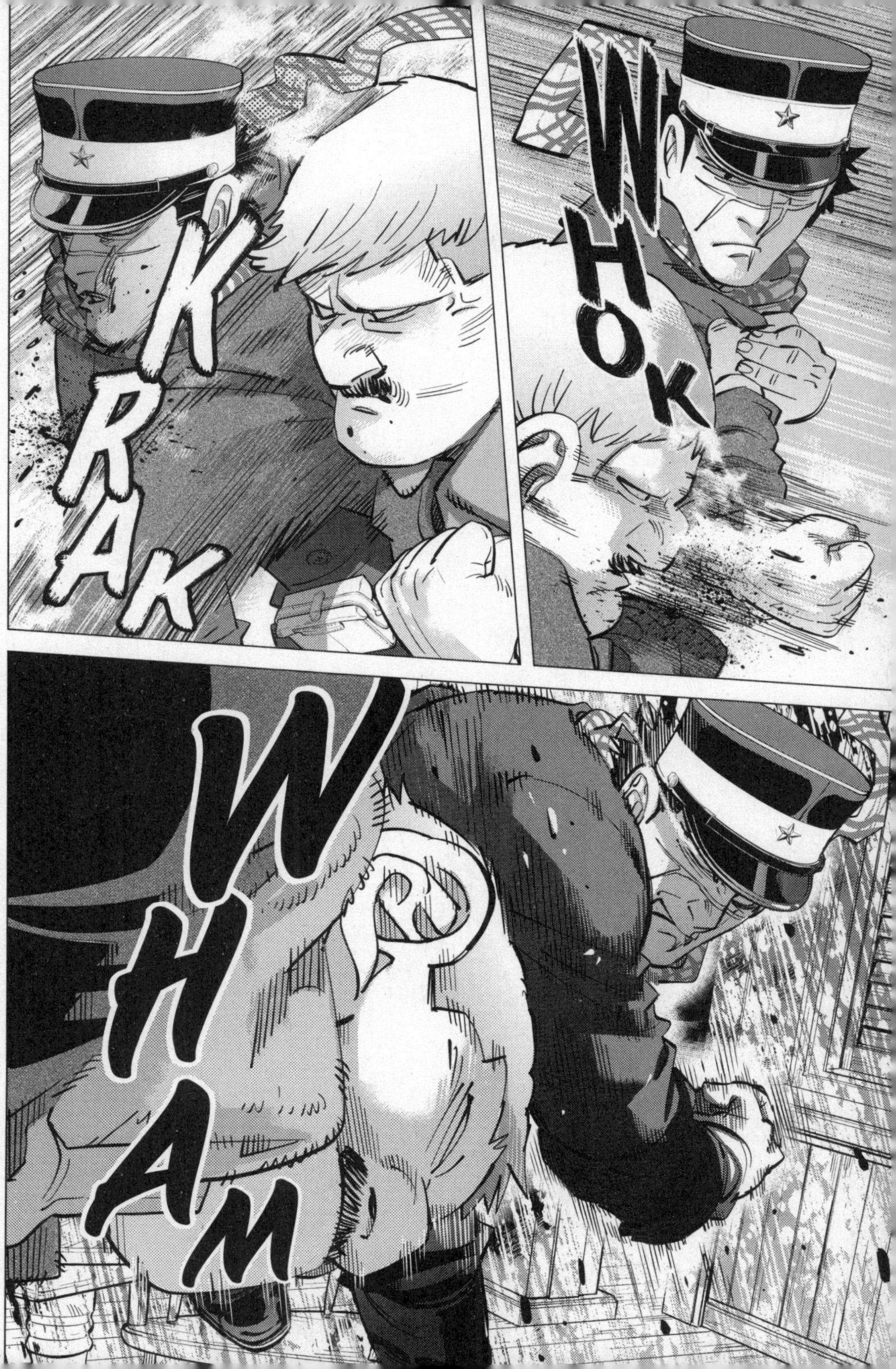
WHOK
KRAK
WHAM

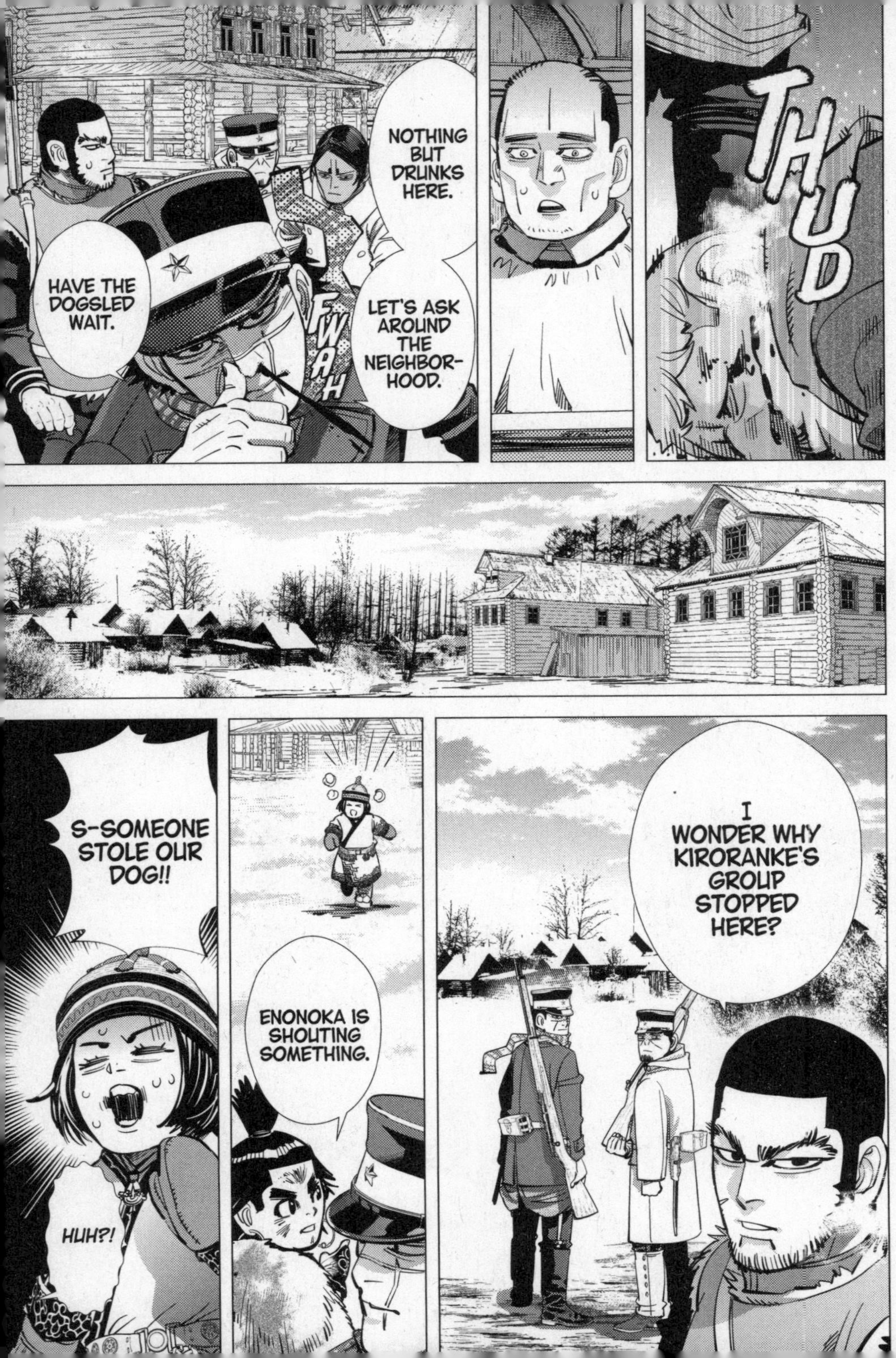
THUD
NOTHING BUT DRUNKS HERE.
LET'S ASK AROUND THE NEIGHBOR-HOOD.
FWAH
HAVE THE DOGSLED WAIT.
I WONDER WHY KIRORANKE'S GROUP STOPPED HERE?
ENONOKA IS SHOUTING SOMETHING.
S-SOMEONE STOLE OUR DOG!!
HUH?!

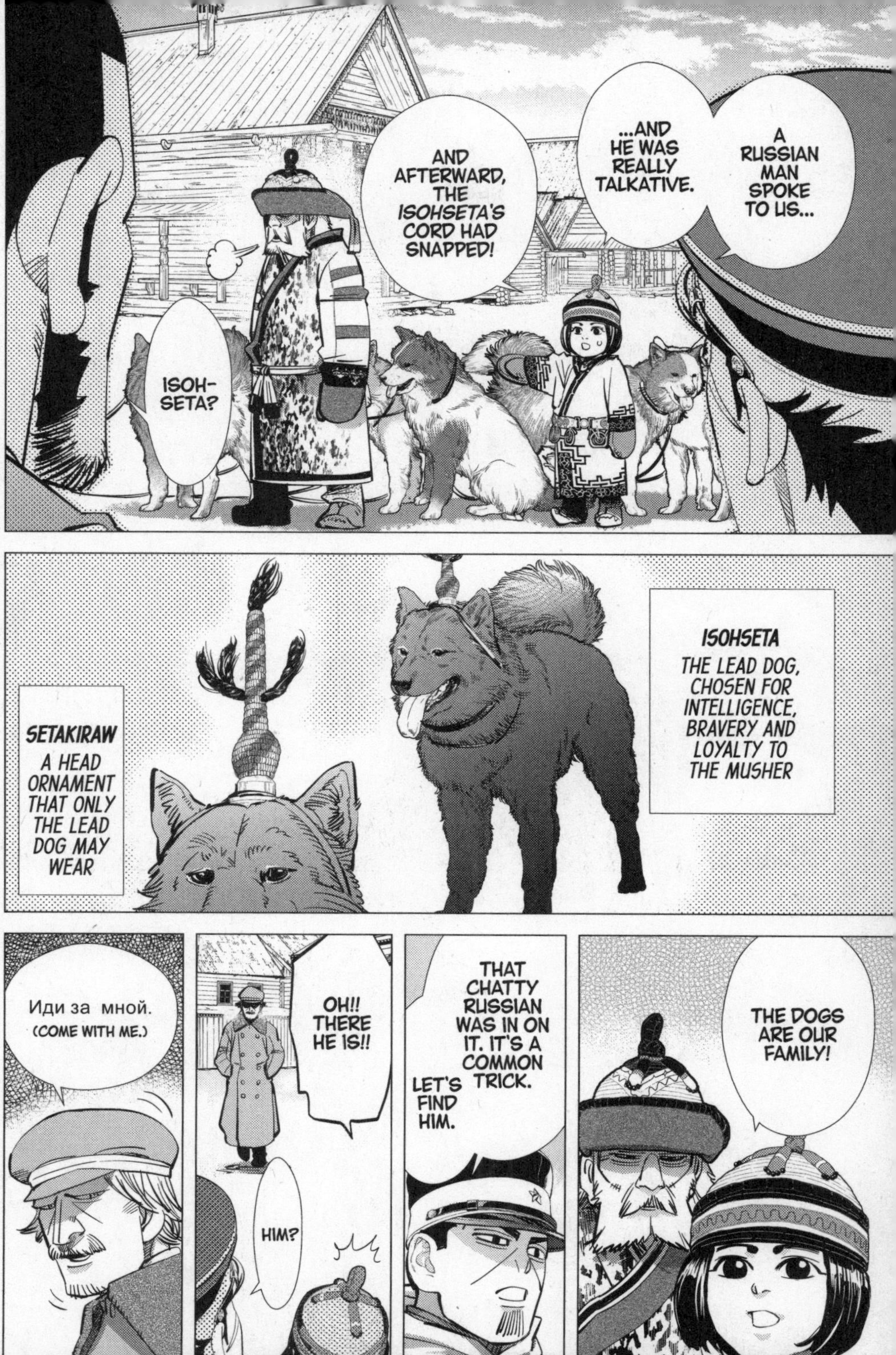
A RUSSIAN MAN SPOKE TO US...
...AND HE WAS REALLY TALKATIVE.
AND AFTERWARD, THE ISOHSETA'S CORD HAD SNAPPED!
ISOH-SETA?
ISOHSETA
THE LEAD DOG, CHOSEN FOR INTELLIGENCE, BRAVERY AND LOYALTY TO THE MUSHER
SETAKIRAW
A HEAD ORNAMENT THAT ONLY THE LEAD DOG MAY WEAR
THE DOGS ARE OUR FAMILY!
THAT CHATTY RUSSIAN WAS IN ON IT. IT'S A COMMON TRICK.
LET'S FIND HIM.
OH!! THERE HE IS!!
HIM?
Иди за мной.
(COME WITH ME.)

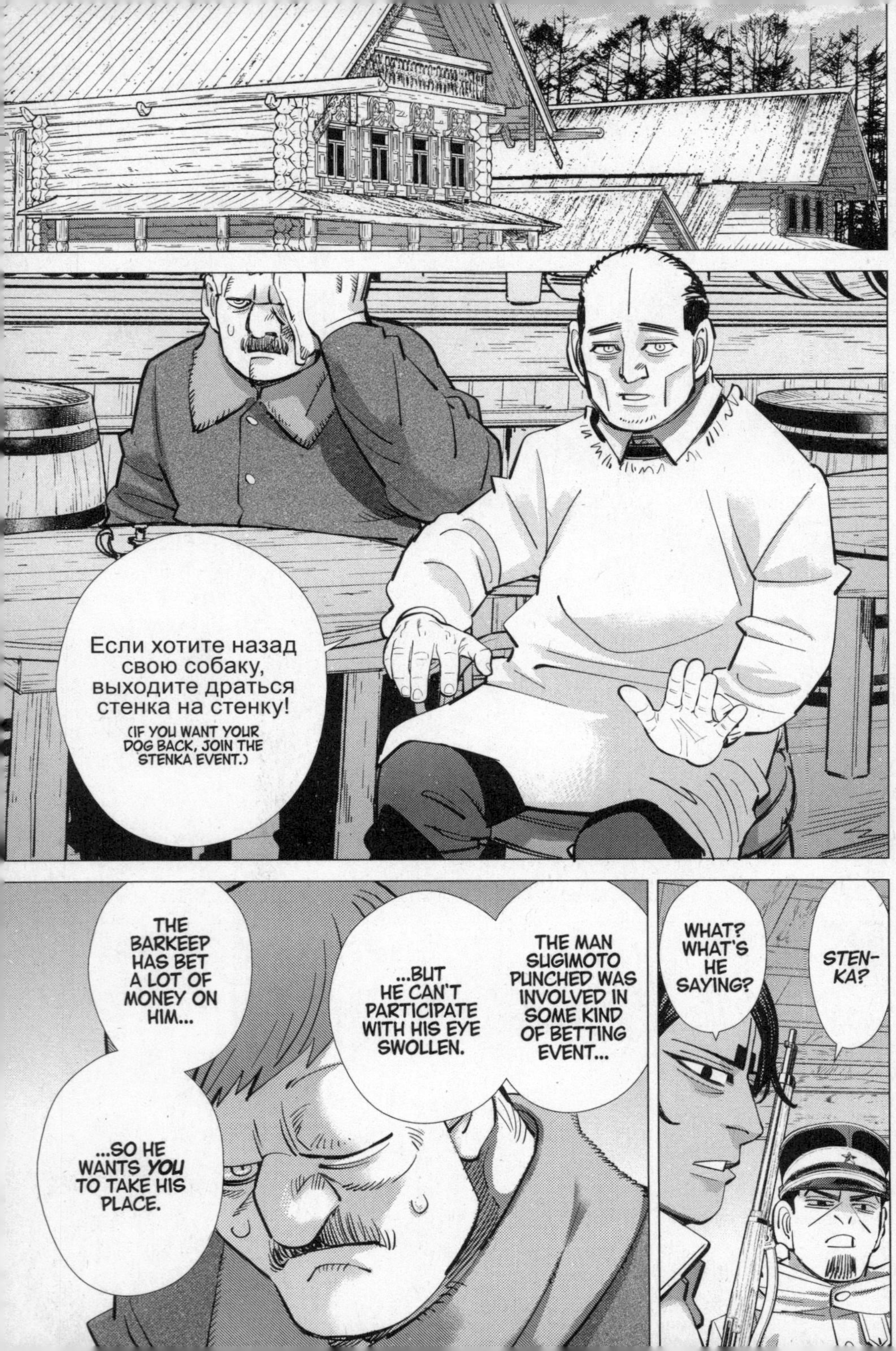
Если хотите назад свою собаку, выходите драться стенка на стенку!
(IF YOU WANT YOUR DOG BACK, JOIN THE STENKA EVENT.)
STEN-KA?
WHAT? WHAT'S HE SAYING?
THE MAN SUGIMOTO PUNCHED WAS INVOLVED IN SOME KIND OF BETTING EVENT...
THE BARKEEP HAS BET A LOT OF MONEY ON HIM...
...BUT HE CAN'T PARTICIPATE WITH HIS EYE SWOLLEN.
...SO HE WANTS *YOU* TO TAKE HIS PLACE.

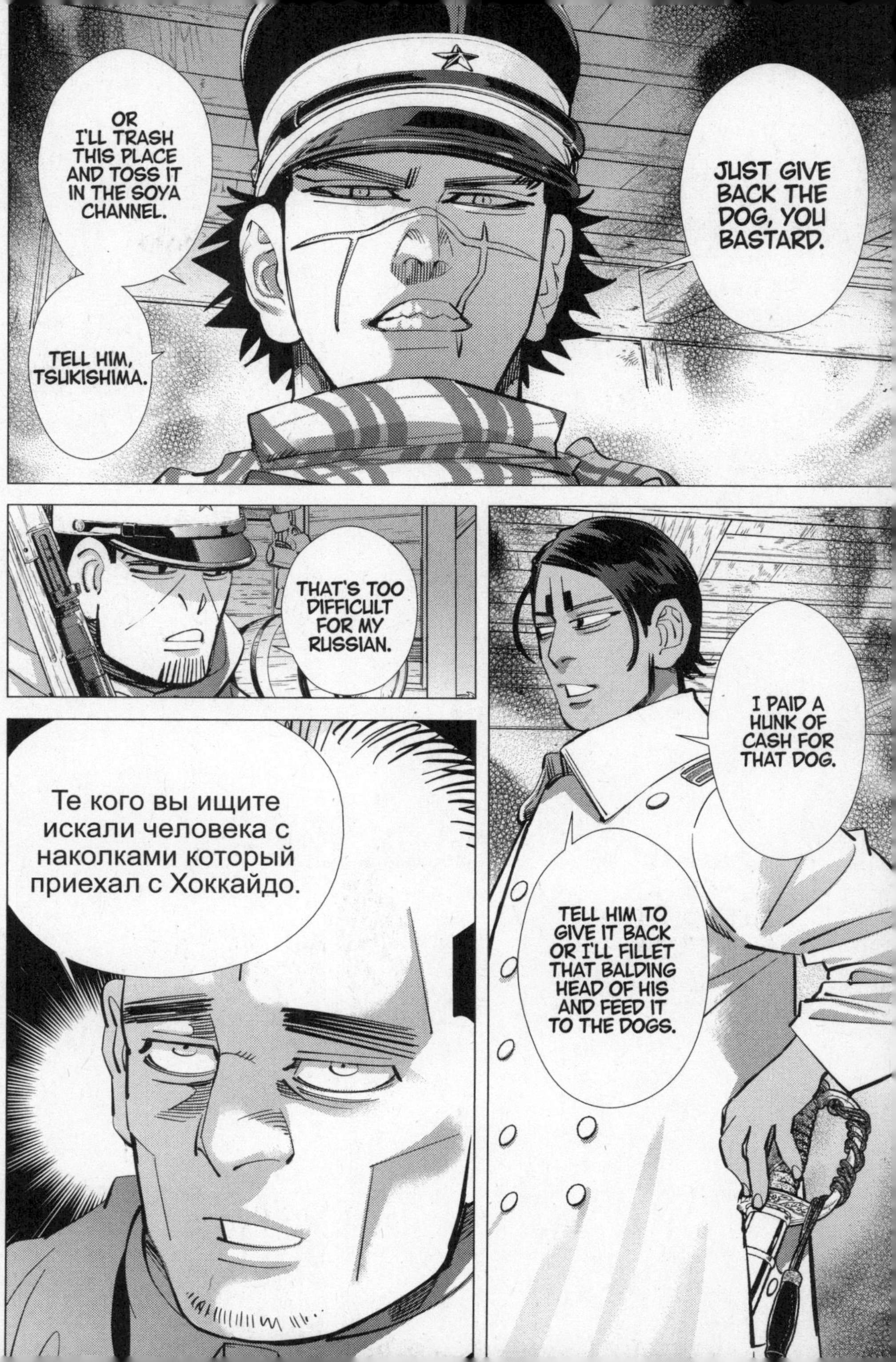
JUST GIVE BACK THE DOG, YOU BASTARD.
OR I'LL TRASH THIS PLACE AND TOSS IT IN THE SOYA CHANNEL.
TELL HIM, TSUKISHIMA.
I PAID A HUNK OF CASH FOR THAT DOG.
TELL HIM TO GIVE IT BACK OR I'LL FILLET THAT BALDING HEAD OF HIS AND FEED IT TO THE DOGS.
THAT'S TOO DIFFICULT FOR MY RUSSIAN.
Те кого вы ищите искали человека с наколками который приехал с Хоккайдо.
...

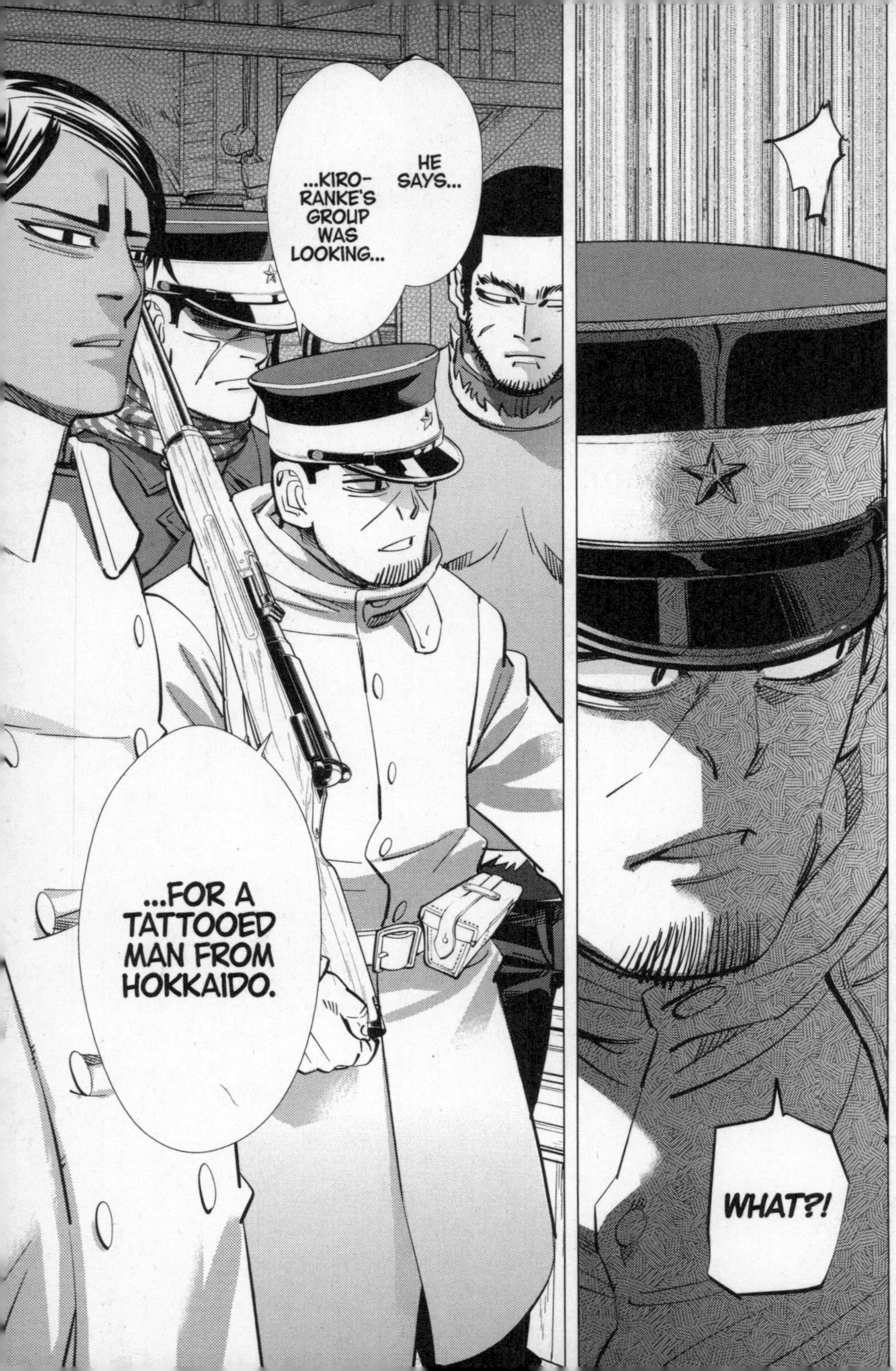
WHAT?!
HE SAYS...
...KIRO-RANKE'S GROUP WAS LOOKING...
...FOR A TATTOOED MAN FROM HOKKAIDO.

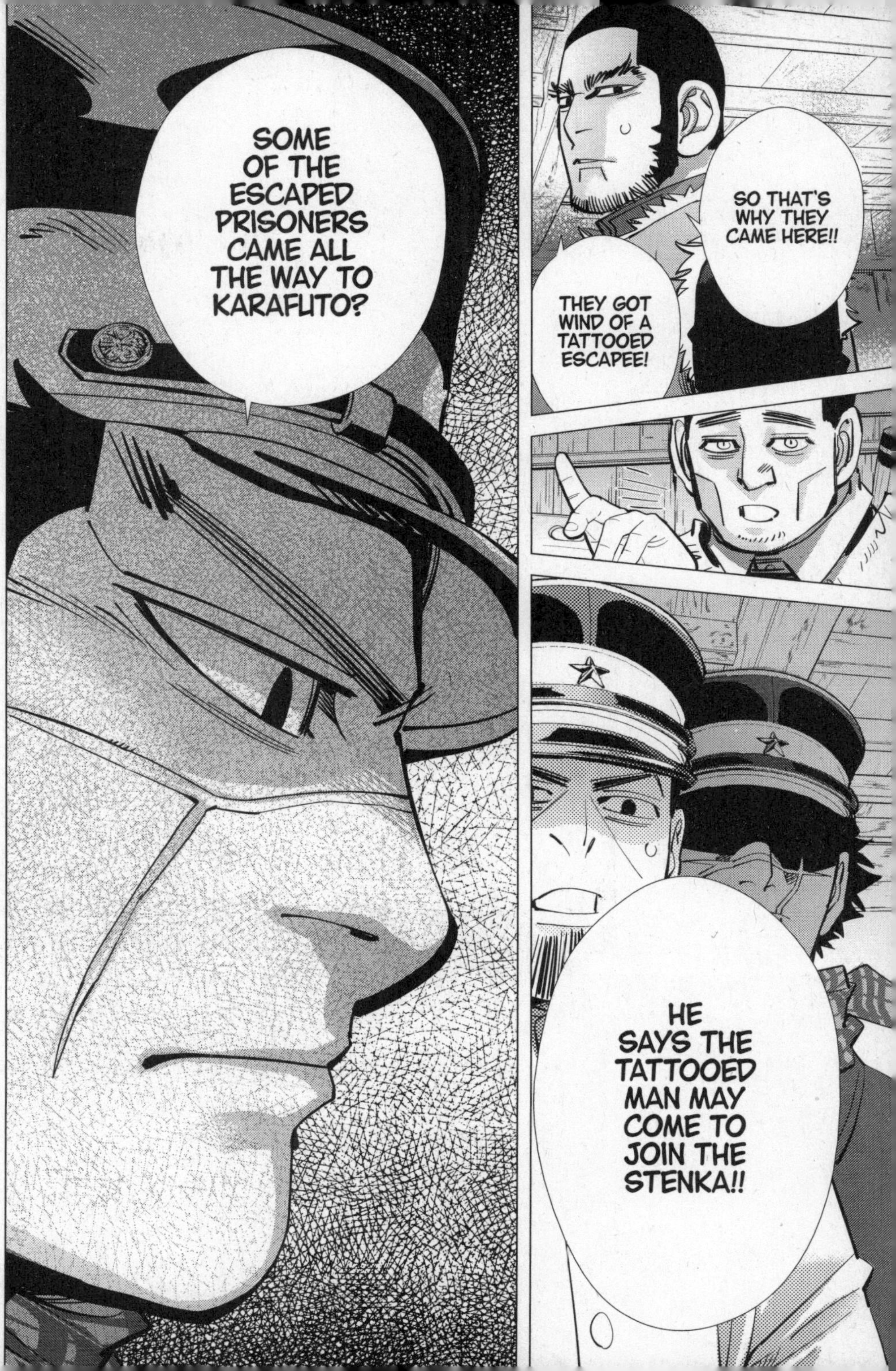
SO THAT'S WHY THEY CAME HERE!!
THEY GOT WIND OF A TATTOOED ESCAPEE!
HE SAYS THE TATTOOED MAN MAY COME TO JOIN THE STENKA!!
SOME OF THE ESCAPED PRISONERS CAME ALL THE WAY TO KARAFUTO?

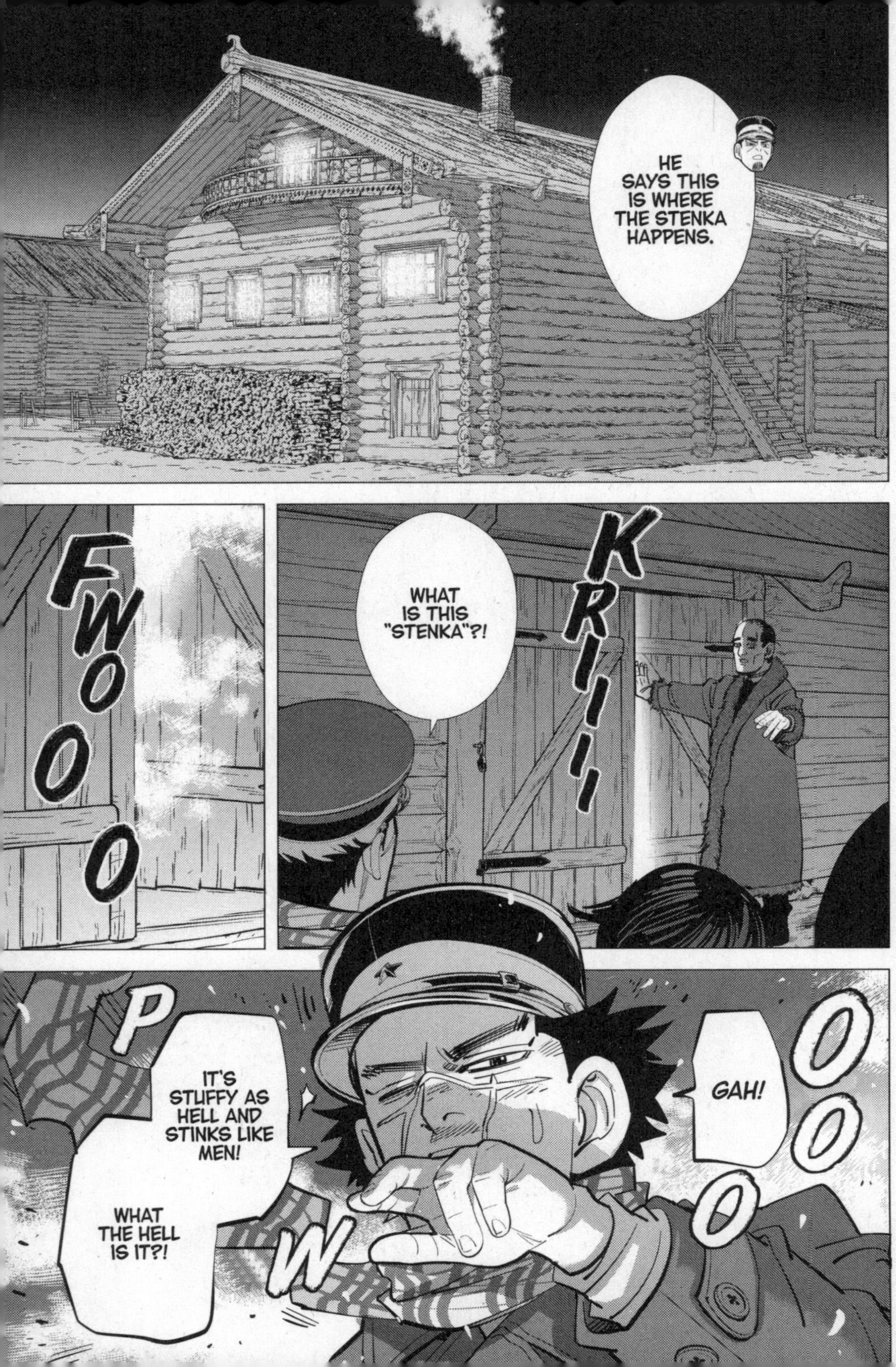
HE SAYS THIS IS WHERE THE STENKA HAPPENS.
KRIIII
WHAT IS THIS "STENKA"?!
FWOOOO
GAH!
OOOO
IT'S STUFFY AS HELL AND STINKS LIKE MEN!
WHAT THE HELL IS IT?!
PW

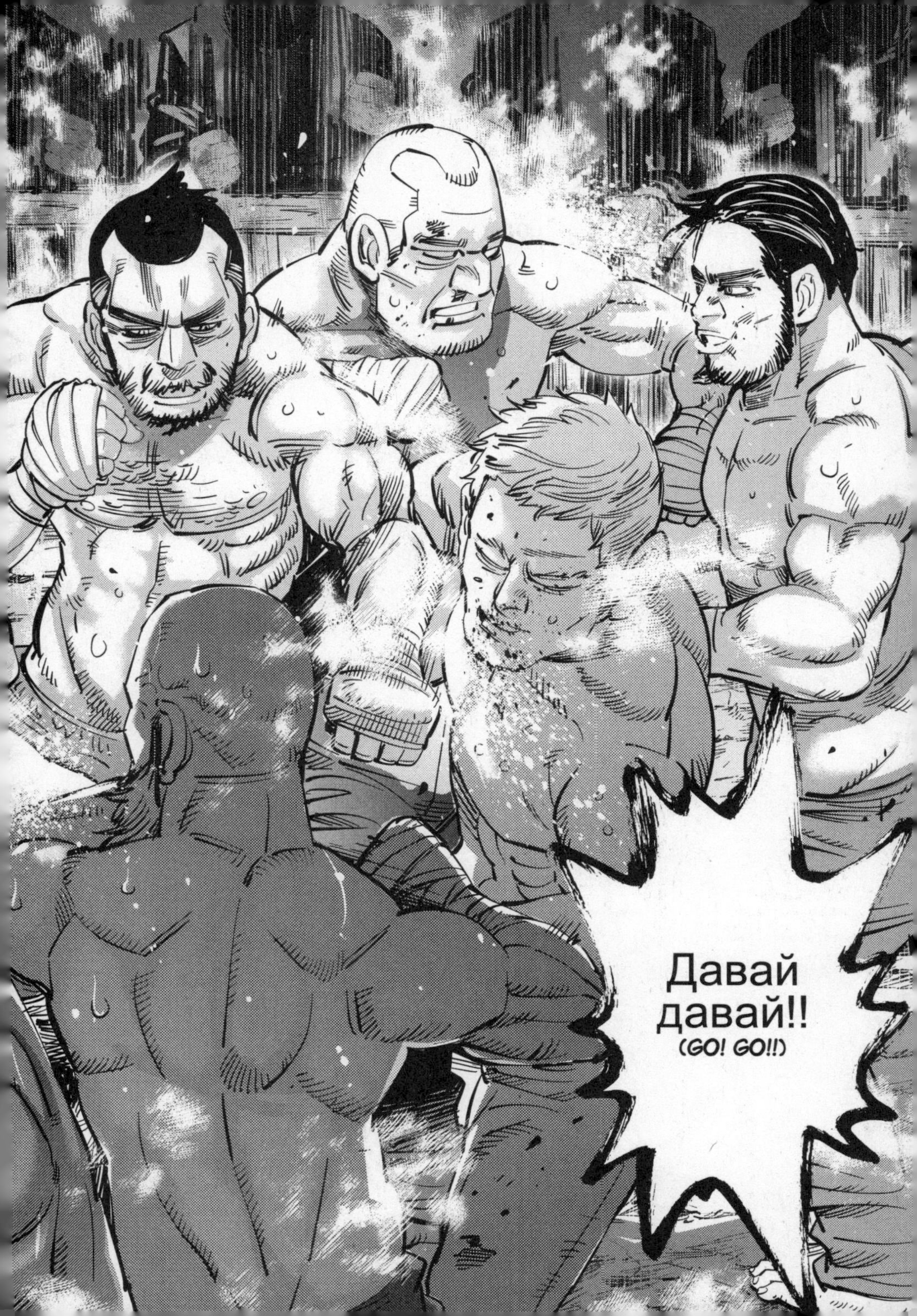
Давай
давай!!
(GO! GO!!)

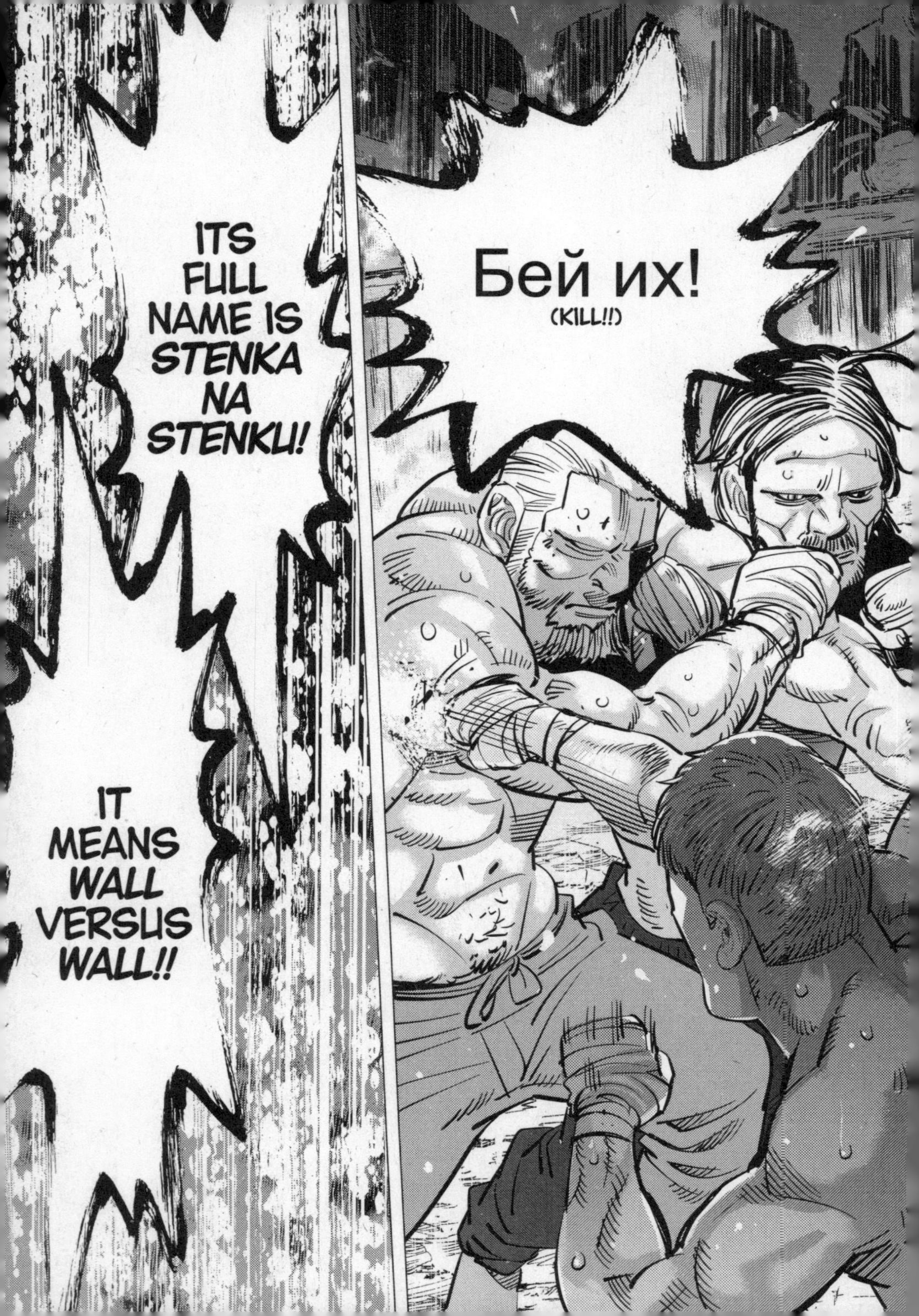
Бей их!
(KILL!!)
ITS FULL NAME IS STENKA NA STENKU!
IT MEANS WALL VERSUS WALL!!

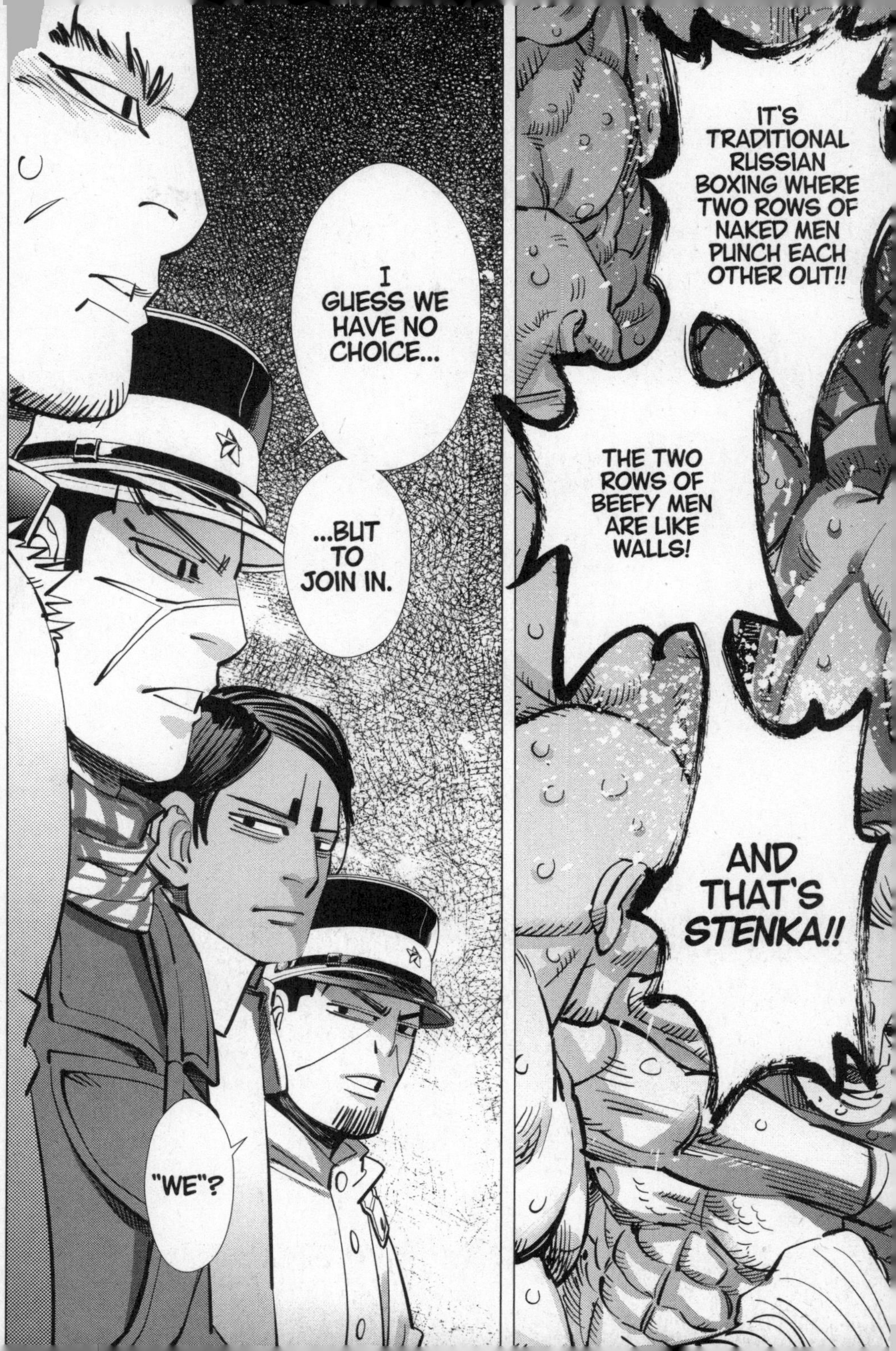
IT'S TRADITIONAL RUSSIAN BOXING WHERE TWO ROWS OF NAKED MEN PUNCH EACH OTHER OUT!!
THE TWO ROWS OF BEEFY MEN ARE LIKE WALLS!
AND THAT'S STENKA!!
I GUESS WE HAVE NO CHOICE...
...BUT TO JOIN IN.
"WE"?

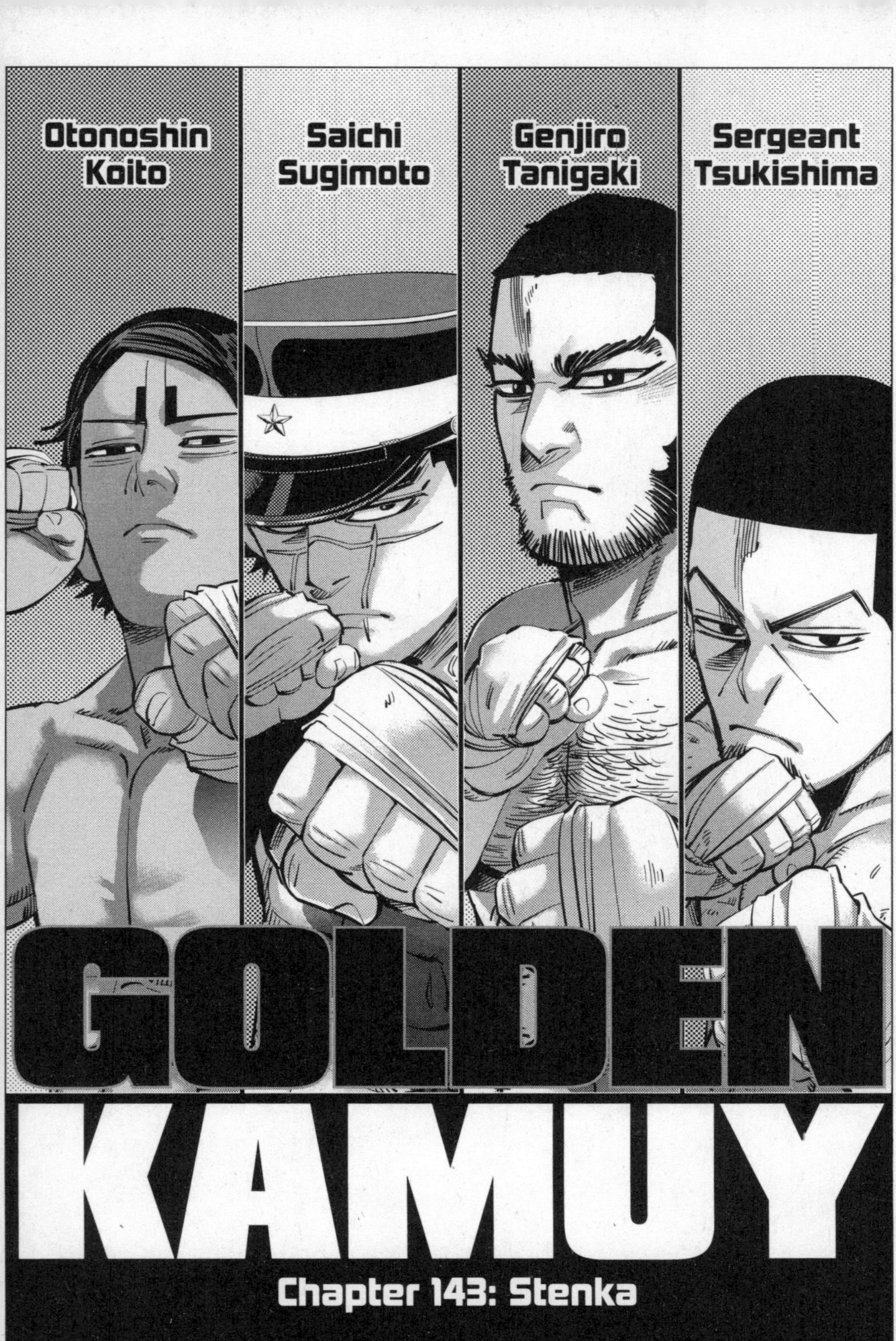

Sergeant Tsukishima
Genjiro Tanigaki
Saichi Sugimoto
Otonoshin Koito
GOLDEN KAMUY
Chapter 143: Stenka

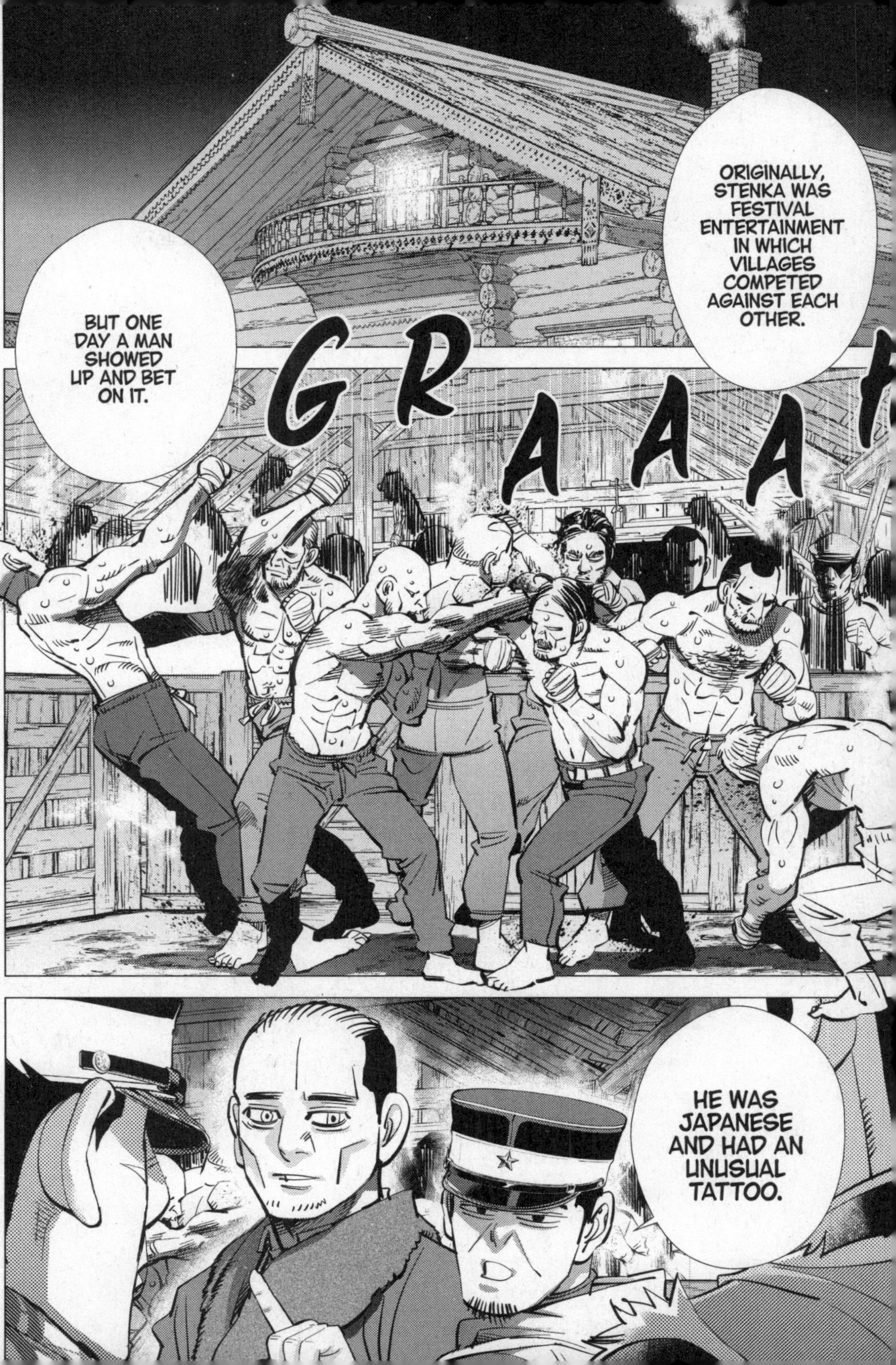
ORIGINALLY, STENKA WAS FESTIVAL ENTERTAINMENT IN WHICH VILLAGES COMPETED AGAINST EACH OTHER.
BUT ONE DAY A MAN SHOWED UP AND BET ON IT.
GRAAA
HE WAS JAPANESE AND HAD AN UNUSUAL TATTOO.

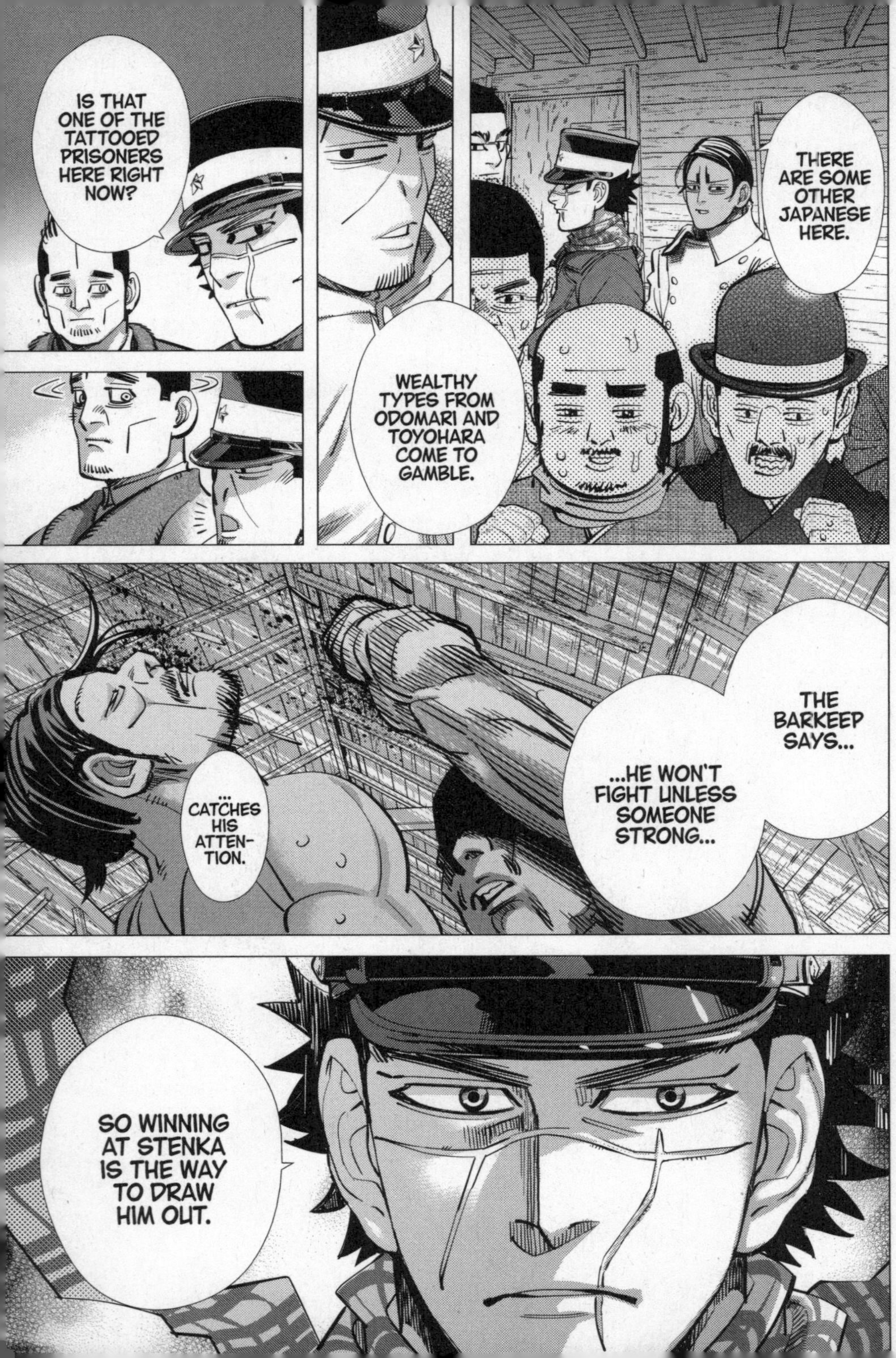
THERE ARE SOME OTHER JAPANESE HERE.
WEALTHY TYPES FROM ODOMARI AND TOYOHARA COME TO GAMBLE.
IS THAT ONE OF THE TATTOOED PRISONERS HERE RIGHT NOW?
THE BARKEEP SAYS...
...HE WON'T FIGHT UNLESS SOMEONE STRONG...
...CATCHES HIS ATTENTION.
SO WINNING AT STENKA IS THE WAY TO DRAW HIM OUT.

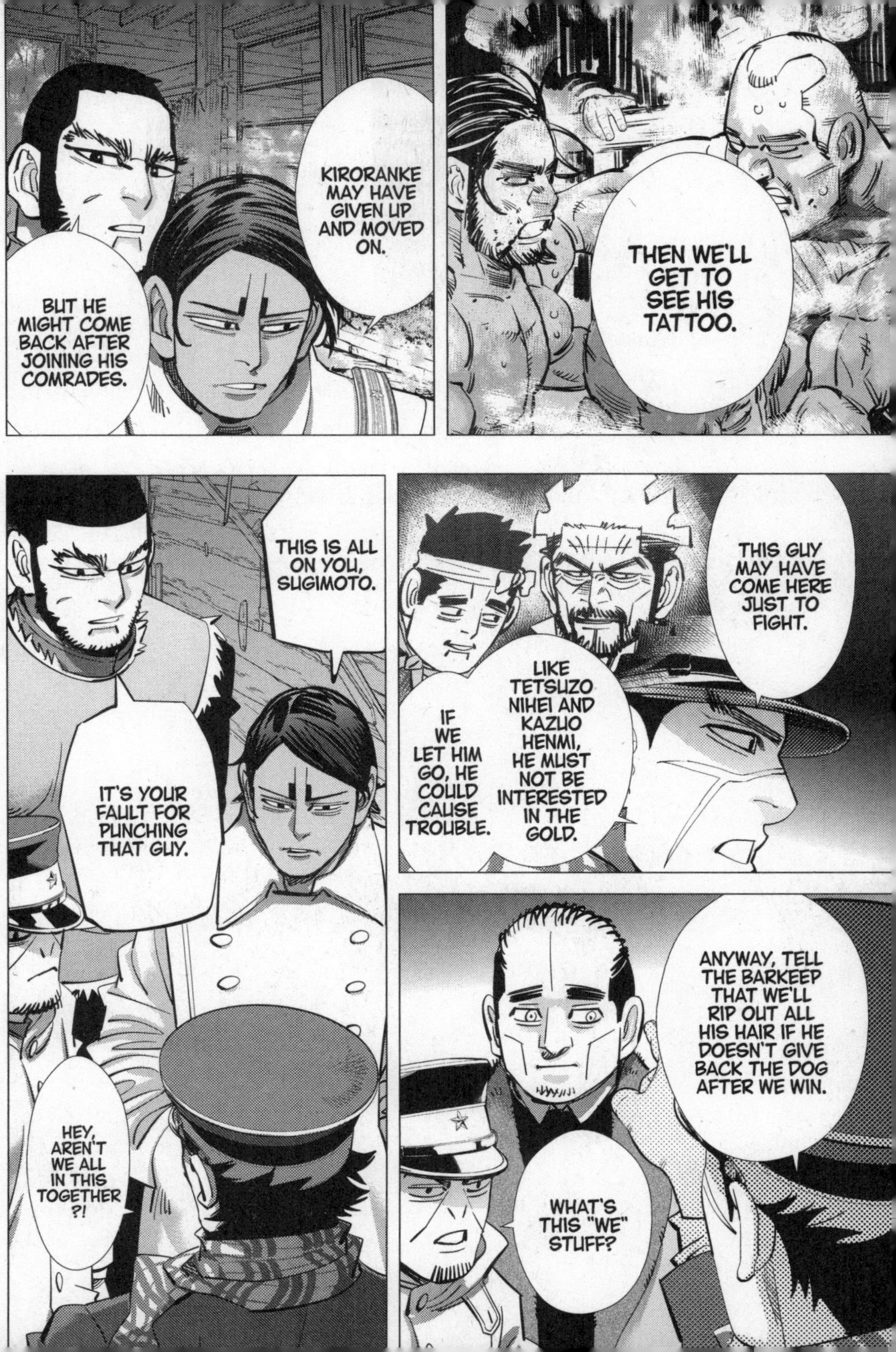
THEN WE'LL GET TO SEE HIS TATTOO.
KIRORANKE MAY HAVE GIVEN UP AND MOVED ON.
BUT HE MIGHT COME BACK AFTER JOINING HIS COMRADES.
THIS GUY MAY HAVE COME HERE JUST TO FIGHT.
LIKE TETSUZO NIHEI AND KAZUO HENMI, HE MUST NOT BE INTERESTED IN THE GOLD.
IF WE LET HIM GO, HE COULD CAUSE TROUBLE.
ANYWAY, TELL THE BARKEEP THAT WE'LL RIP OUT ALL HIS HAIR IF HE DOESN'T GIVE BACK THE DOG AFTER WE WIN.
WHAT'S THIS "WE" STUFF?
THIS IS ALL ON YOU, SUGIMOTO.
IT'S YOUR FAULT FOR PUNCHING THAT GUY.
HEY, AREN'T WE ALL IN THIS TOGETHER?!

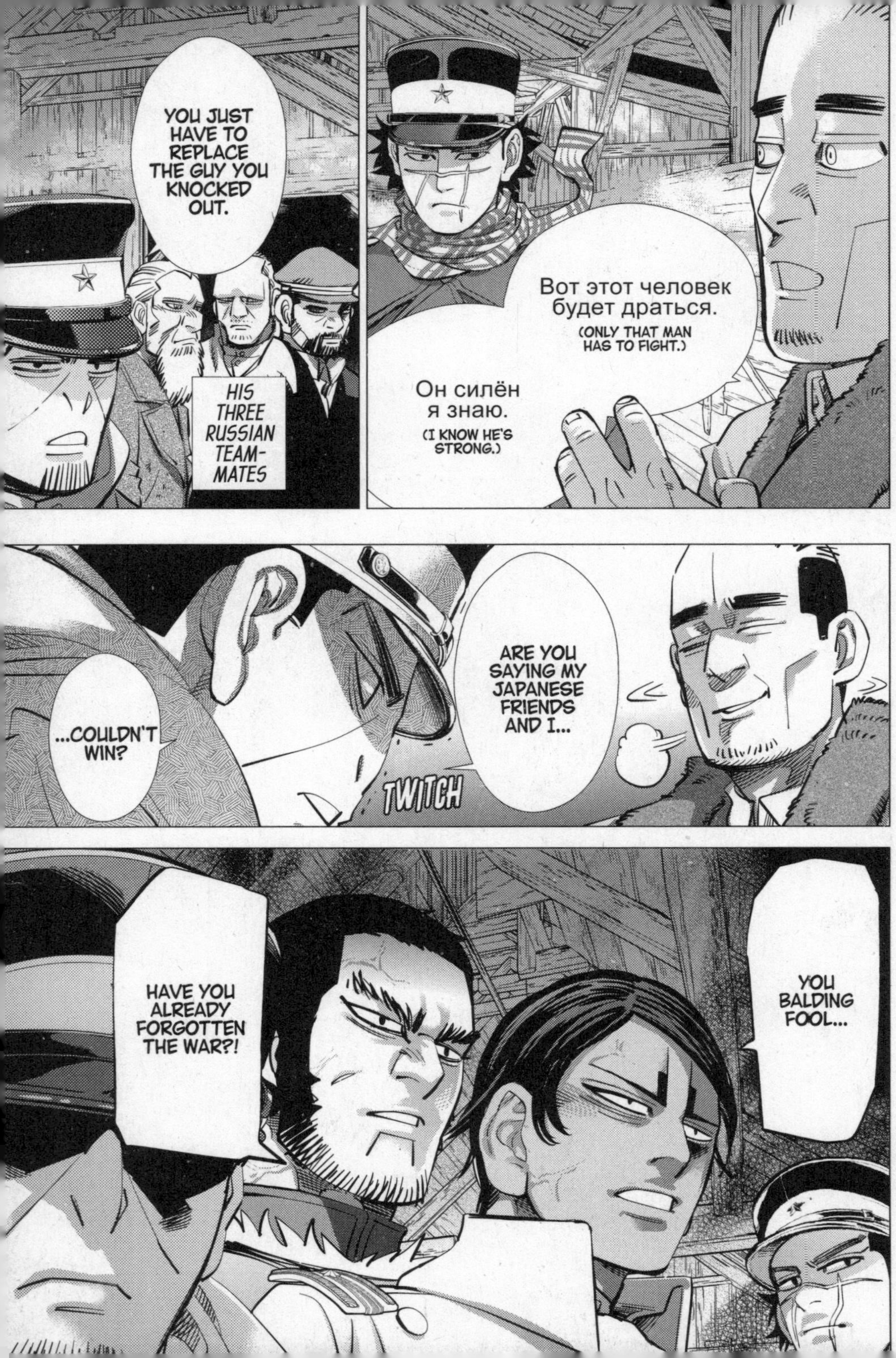
Вот этот человек будет драться.
(ONLY THAT MAN HAS TO FIGHT.)
Он силён я знаю.
(I KNOW HE'S STRONG.)
YOU JUST HAVE TO REPLACE THE GUY YOU KNOCKED OUT.
HIS THREE RUSSIAN TEAM-MATES
ARE YOU SAYING MY JAPANESE FRIENDS AND I...
TWITCH
...COULDN'T WIN?
YOU BALDING FOOL...
HAVE YOU ALREADY FORGOTTEN THE WAR?!

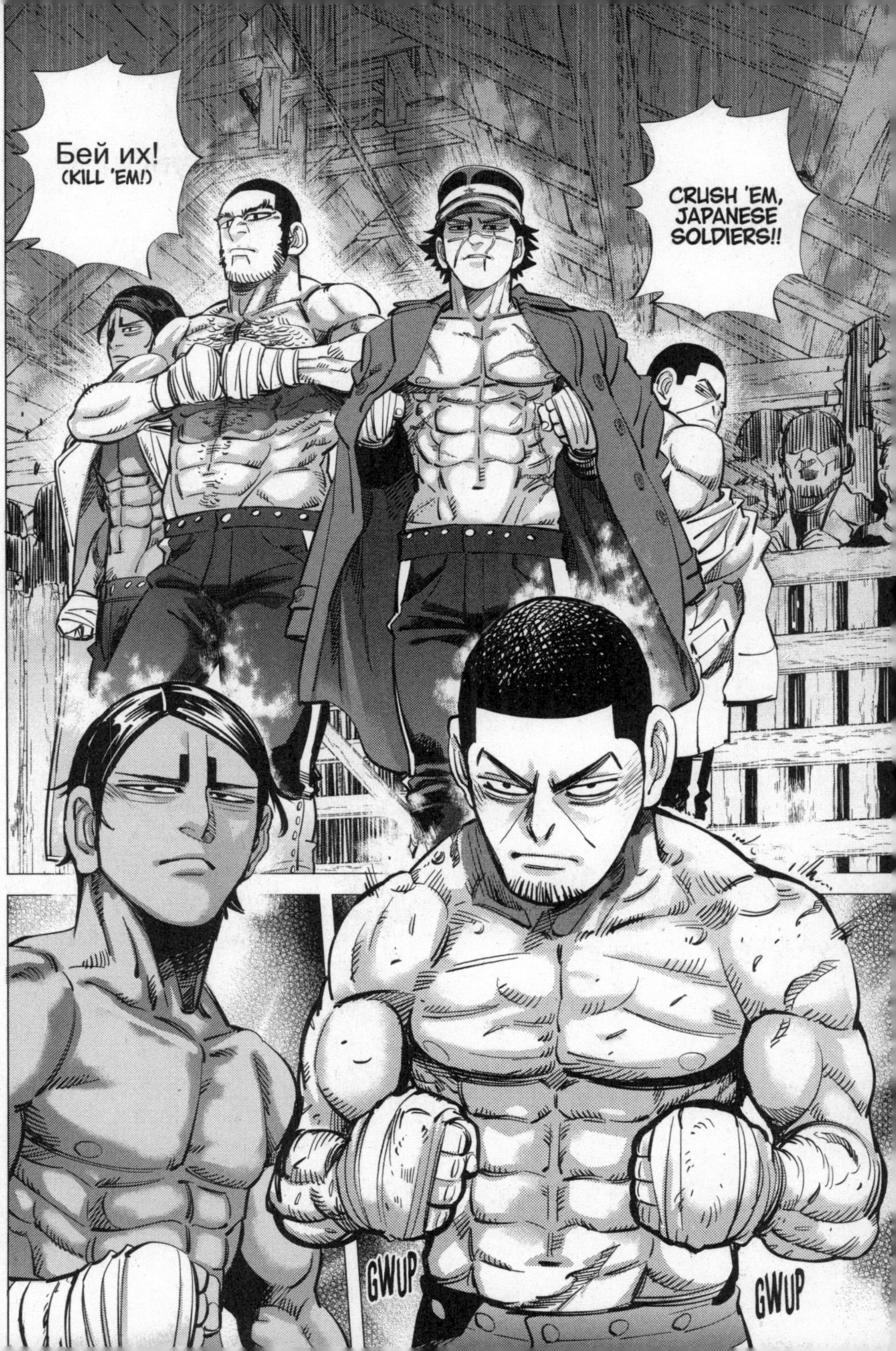
CRUSH 'EM, JAPANESE SOLDIERS!!
Бей их!
(KILL 'EM!)
GWUP
GWUP

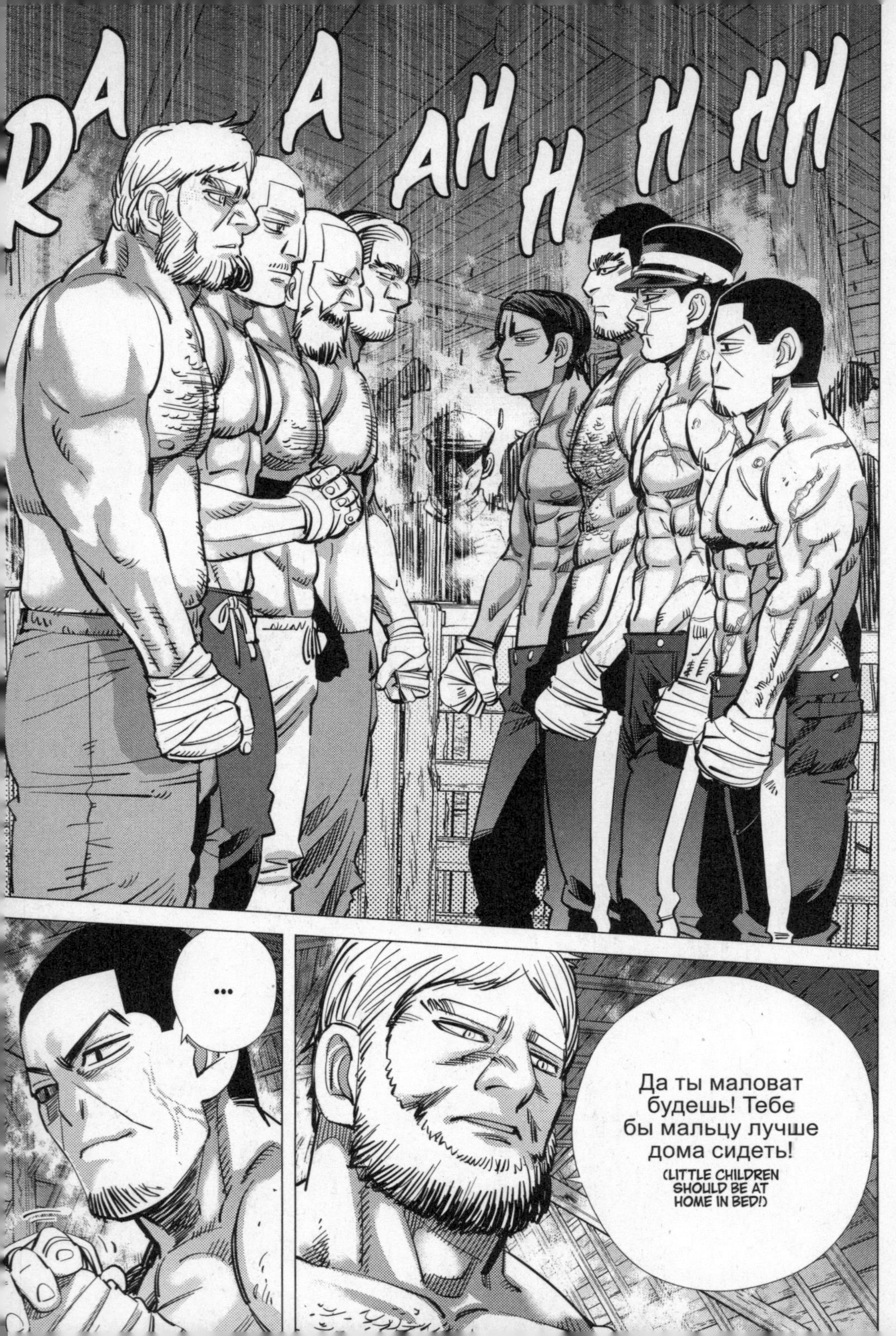
RAAAHHHHHH
Да ты маловат будешь! Тебе бы мальцу лучше дома сидеть!
(LITTLE CHILDREN SHOULD BE AT HOME IN BED!)
...

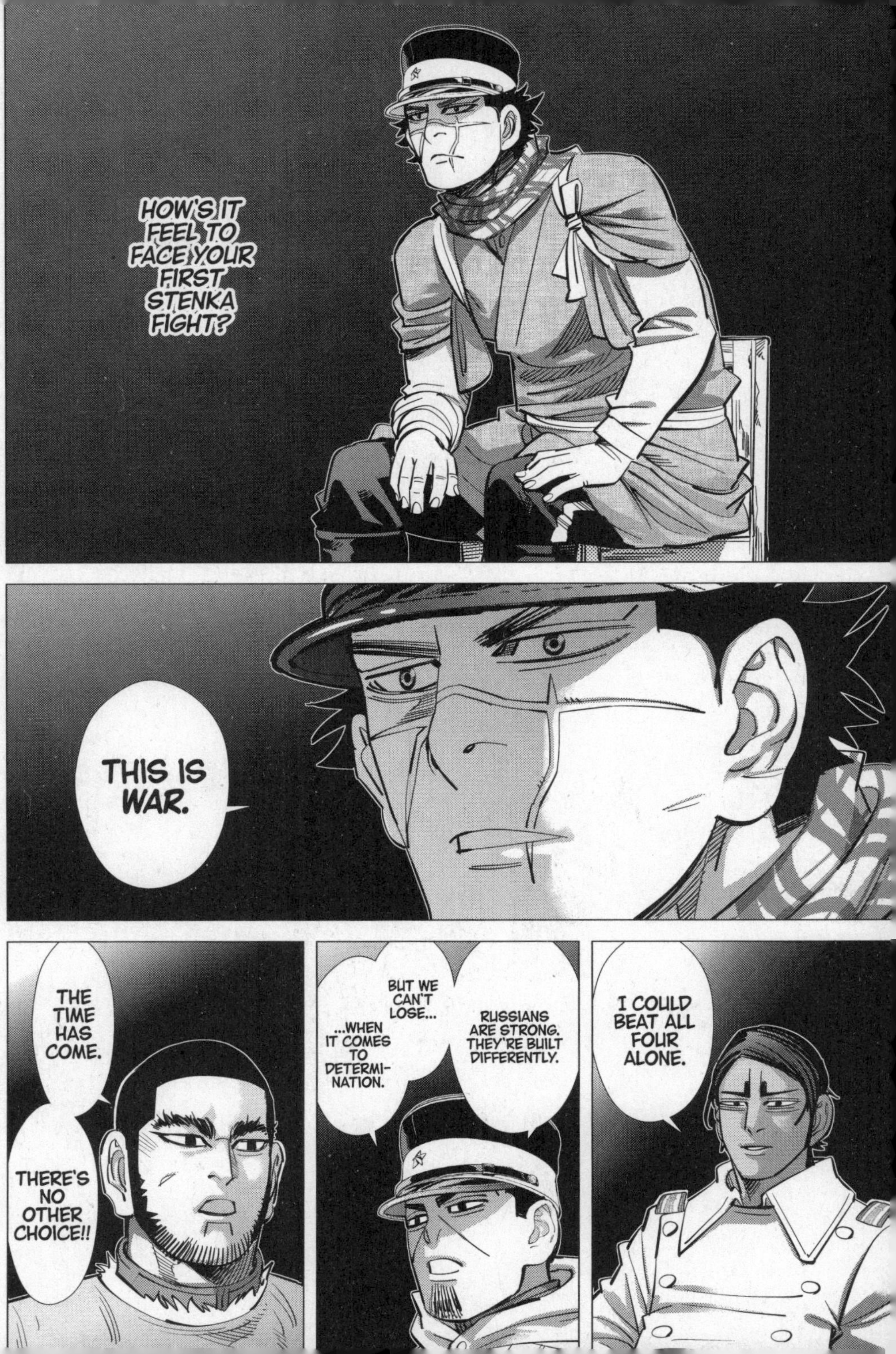
HOW'S IT FEEL TO FACE YOUR FIRST STENKA FIGHT?
THIS IS WAR.
I COULD BEAT ALL FOUR ALONE.
RUSSIANS ARE STRONG. THEY'RE BUILT DIFFERENTLY.
BUT WE CAN'T LOSE...
...WHEN IT COMES TO DETERMI-NATION.
THE TIME HAS COME.
THERE'S NO OTHER CHOICE!!

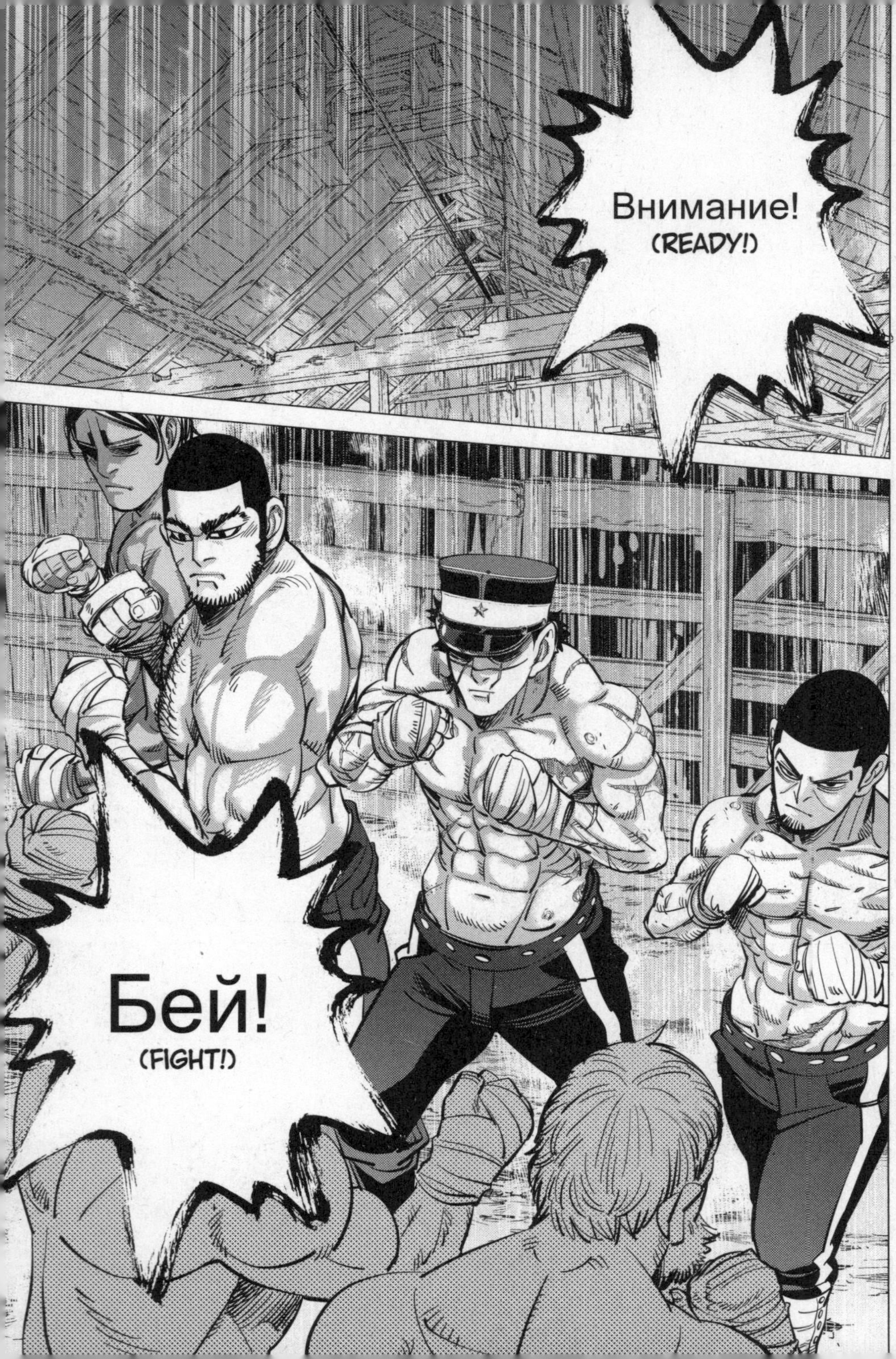
Внимание!
(READY!)
Бей!
(FIGHT!)

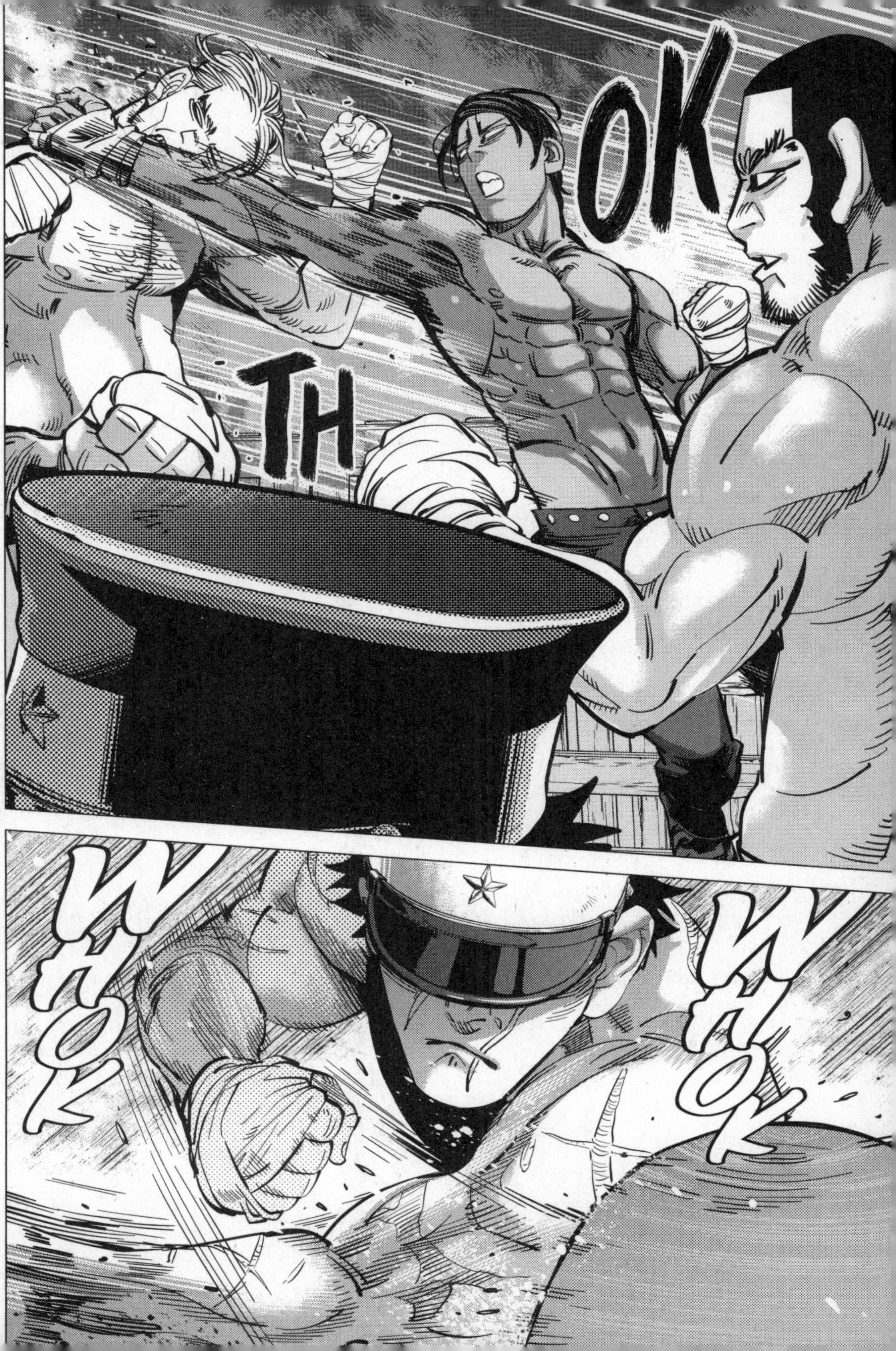
TH
OK
WHOK
WHOK

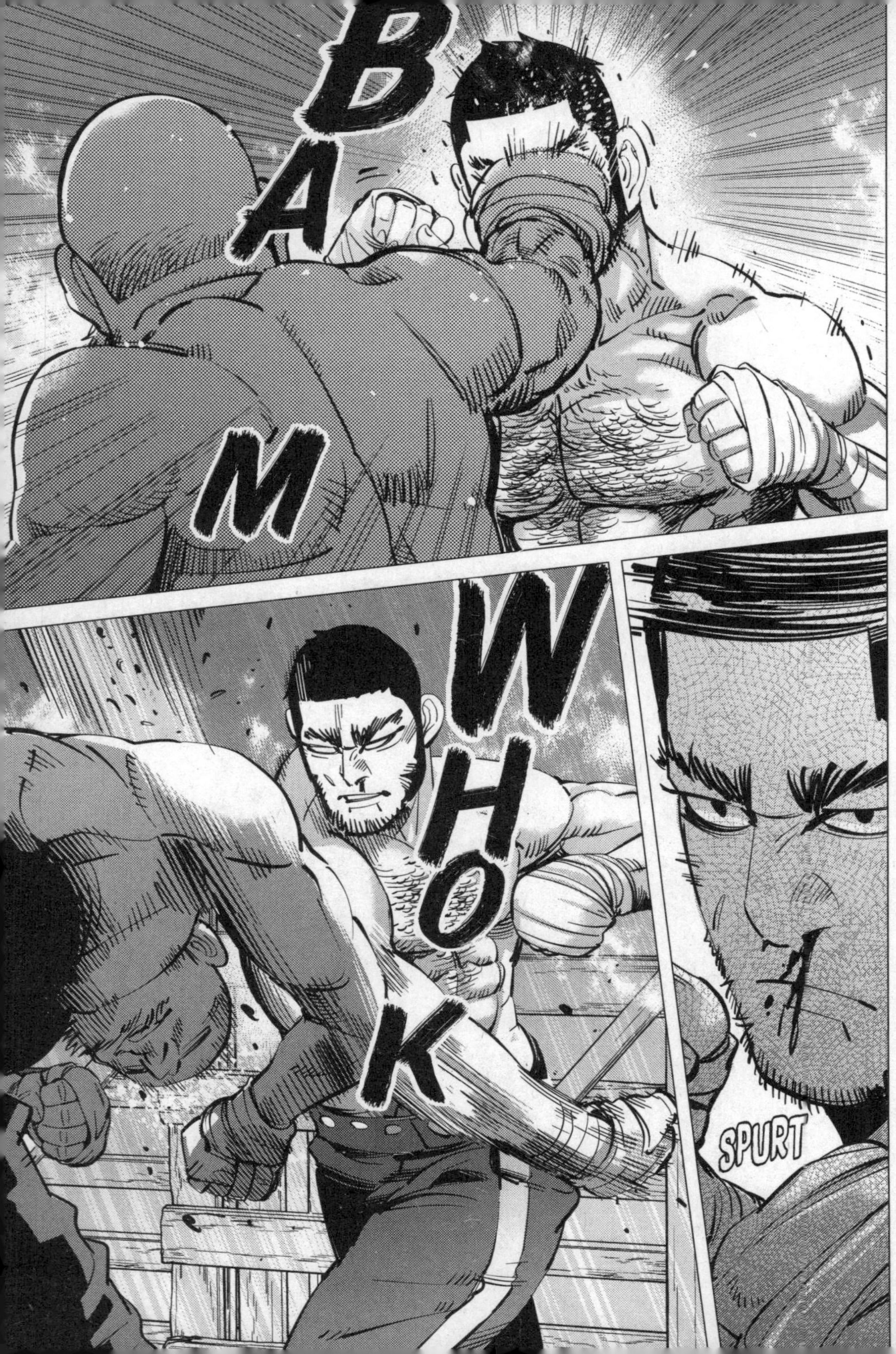
BAM
SPURT
WHOK

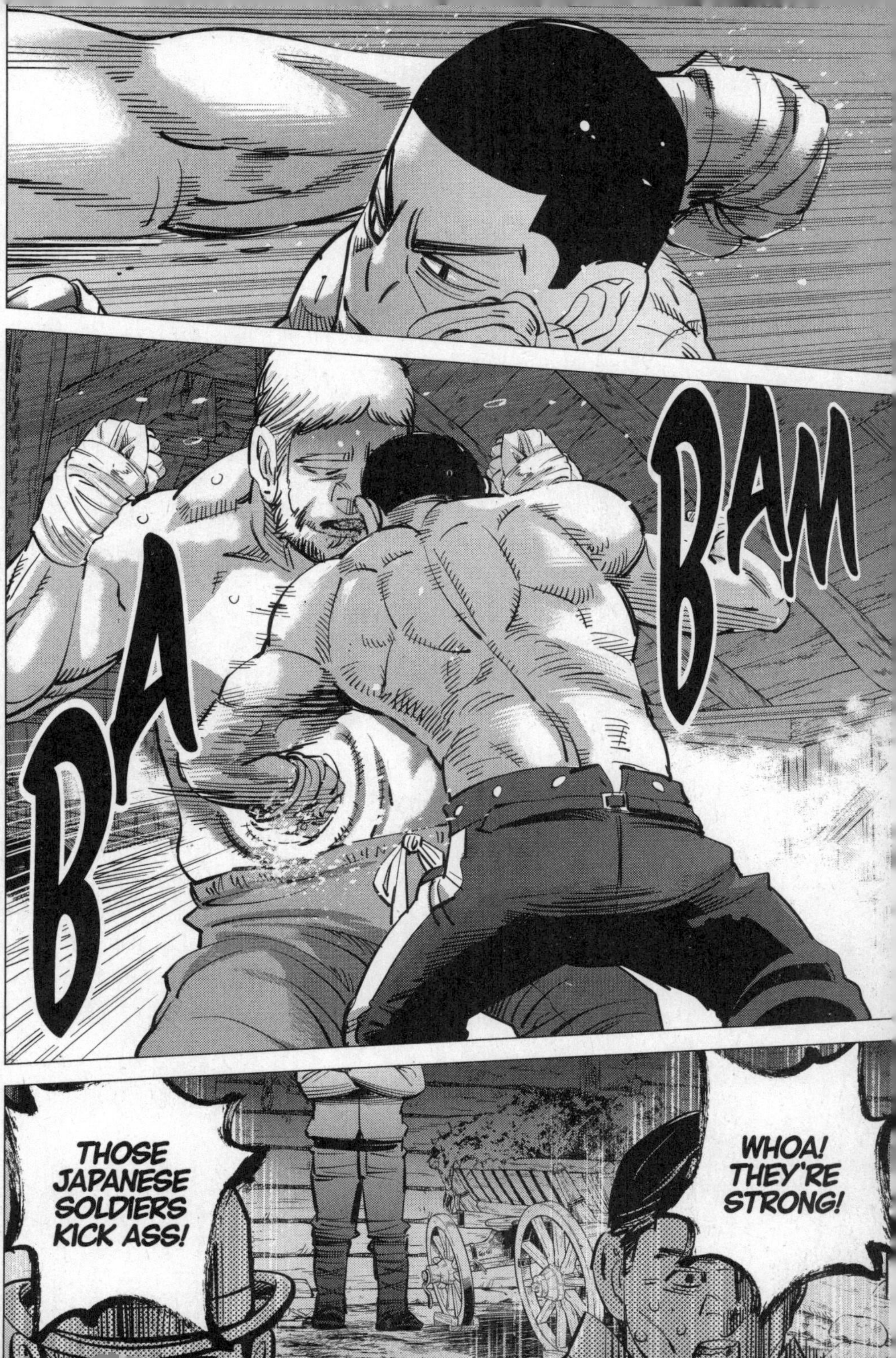
BAM
BA
WHOA! THEY'RE STRONG!
THOSE JAPANESE SOLDIERS KICK ASS!

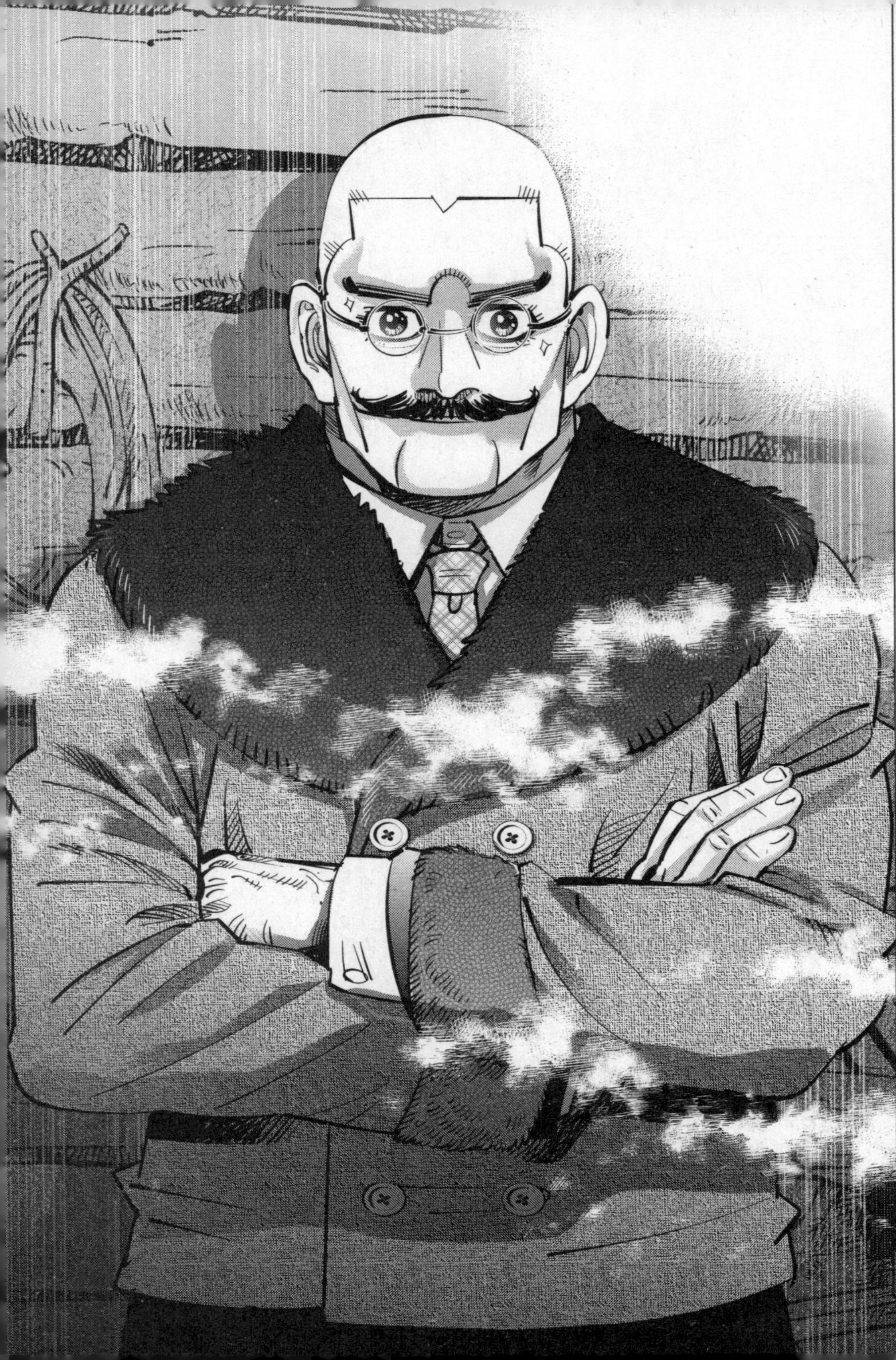

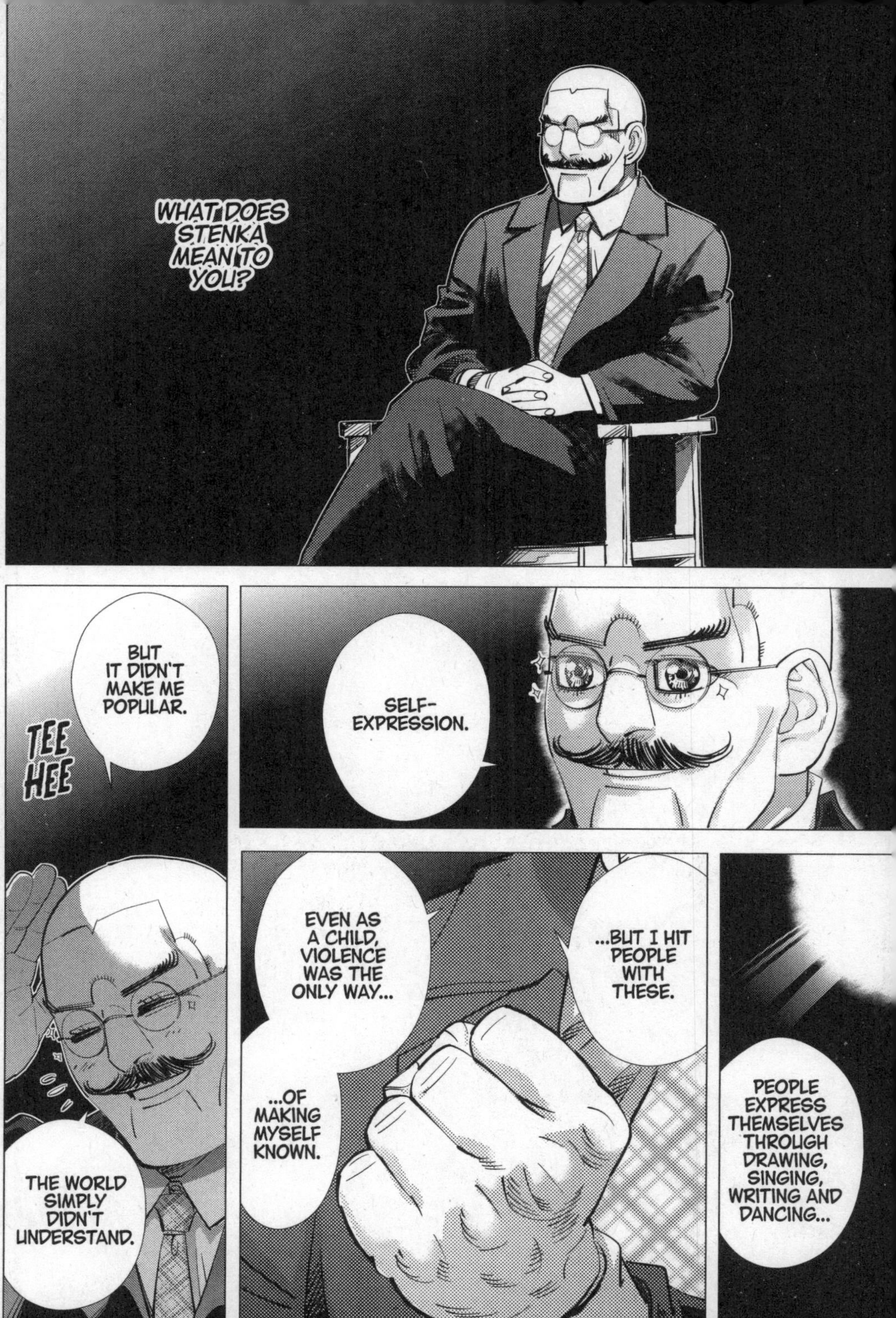
WHAT DOES STENKA MEAN TO YOU?
SELF-EXPRESSION.
PEOPLE EXPRESS THEMSELVES THROUGH DRAWING, SINGING, WRITING AND DANCING...
...BUT I HIT PEOPLE WITH THESE.
EVEN AS A CHILD, VIOLENCE WAS THE ONLY WAY...
...OF MAKING MYSELF KNOWN.
BUT IT DIDN'T MAKE ME POPULAR.
TEE HEE
THE WORLD SIMPLY DIDN'T UNDERSTAND.

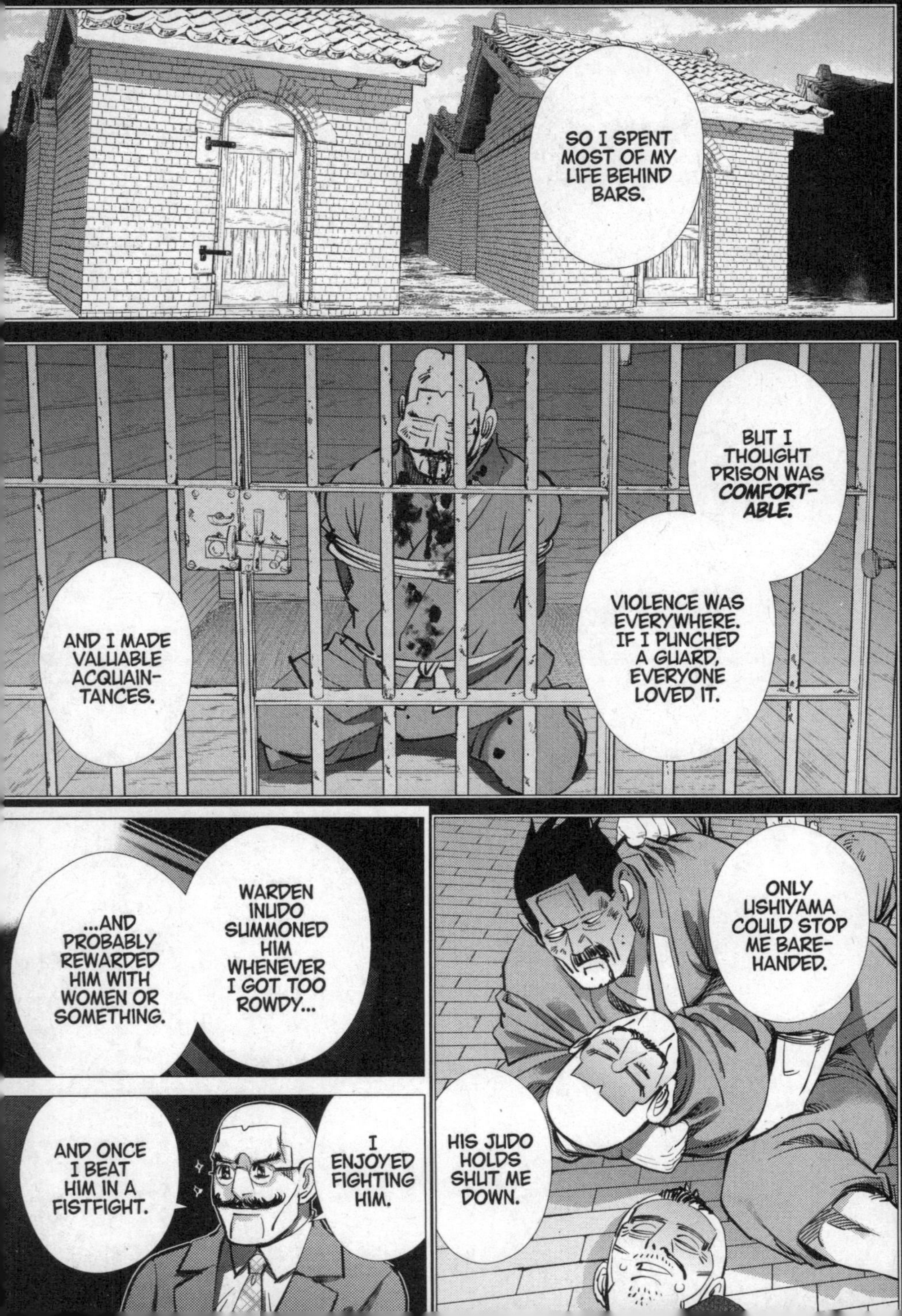
SO I SPENT MOST OF MY LIFE BEHIND BARS.
BUT I THOUGHT PRISON WAS COMFORTABLE.
VIOLENCE WAS EVERYWHERE. IF I PUNCHED A GUARD, EVERYONE LOVED IT.
AND I MADE VALUABLE ACQUAINTANCES.
ONLY USHIYAMA COULD STOP ME BAREHANDED.
HIS JUDO HOLDS SHUT ME DOWN.
WARDEN INUDO SUMMONED HIM WHENEVER I GOT TOO ROWDY...
...AND PROBABLY REWARDED HIM WITH WOMEN OR SOMETHING.
I ENJOYED FIGHTING HIM.
AND ONCE I BEAT HIM IN A FISTFIGHT.

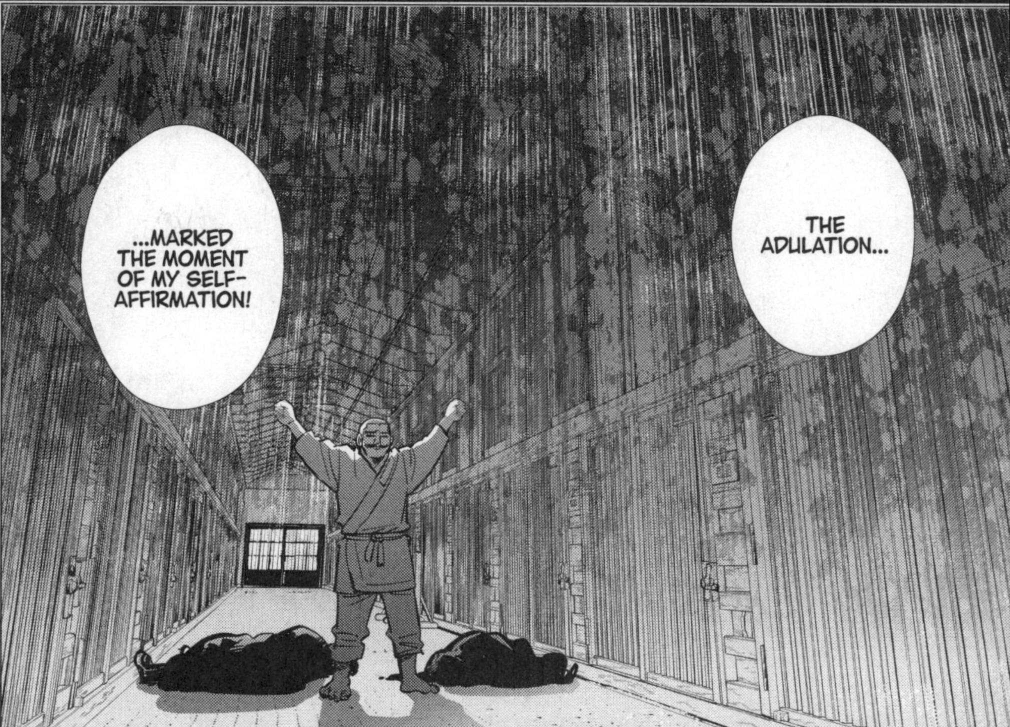
THE ADULATION...
...MARKED THE MOMENT OF MY SELF-AFFIRMATION!

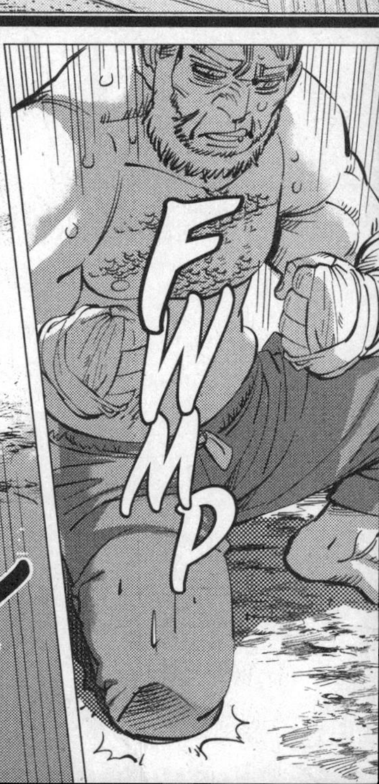
FWMP

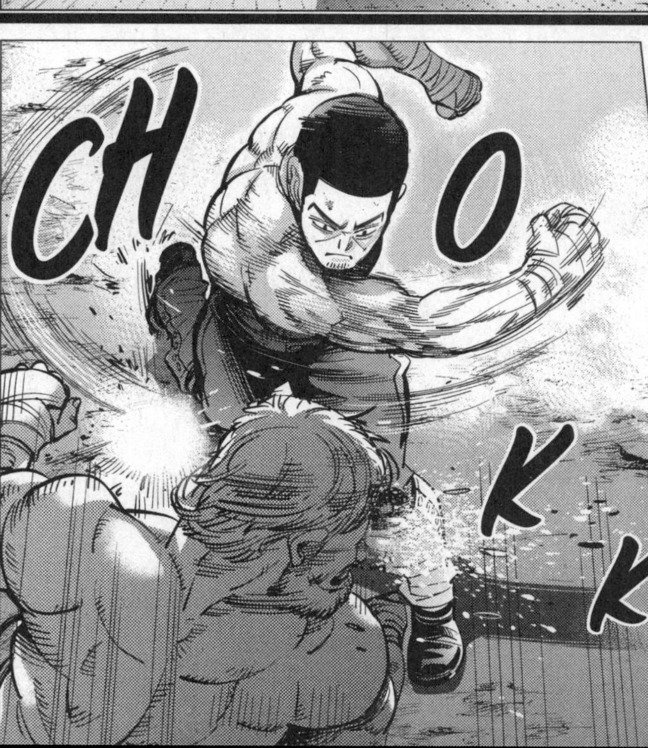
CHOKK

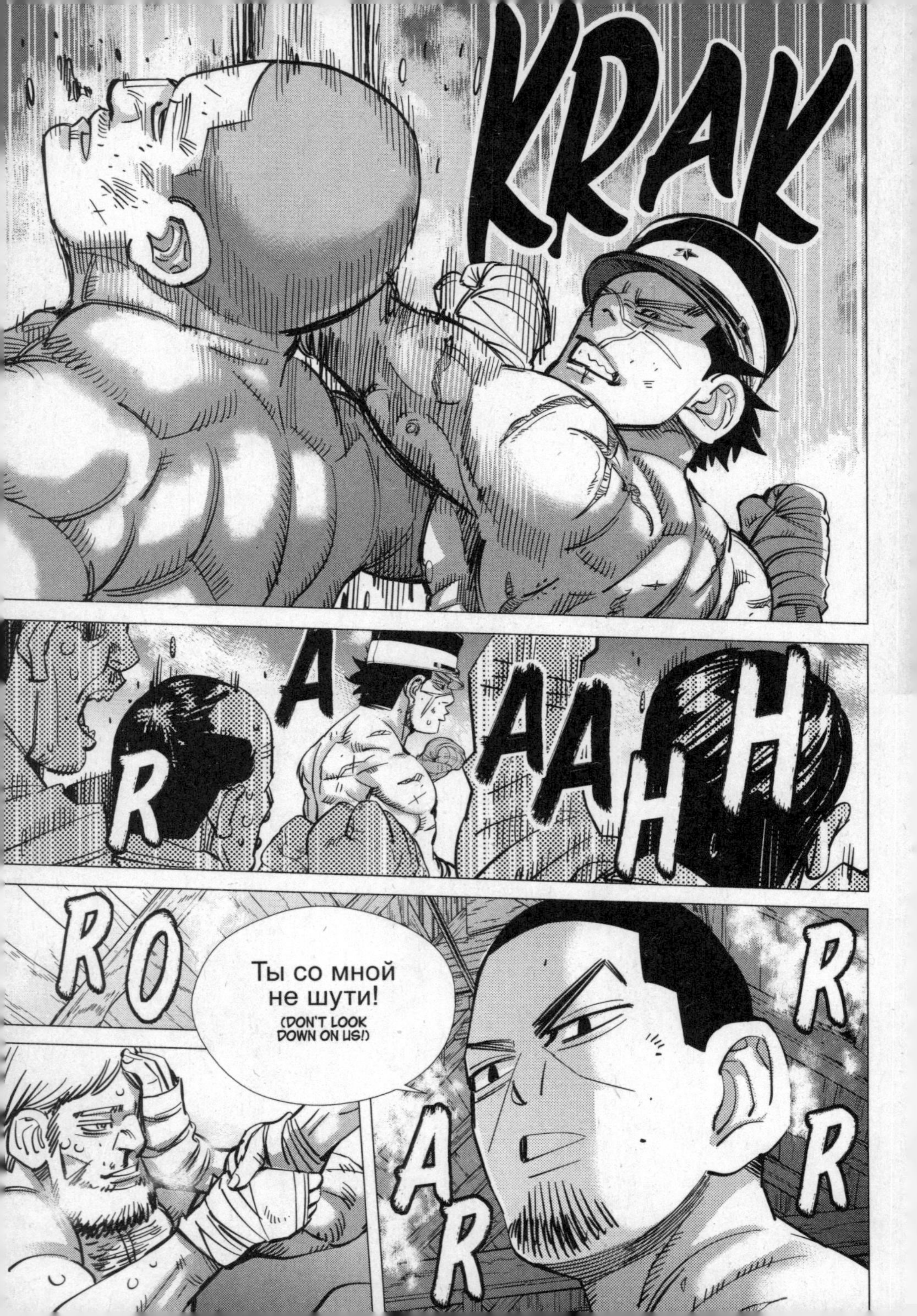
KRAK
R A AAHHH
RO
R
R
A
R
Ты со мной не шути!
(DON'T LOOK DOWN ON US!)

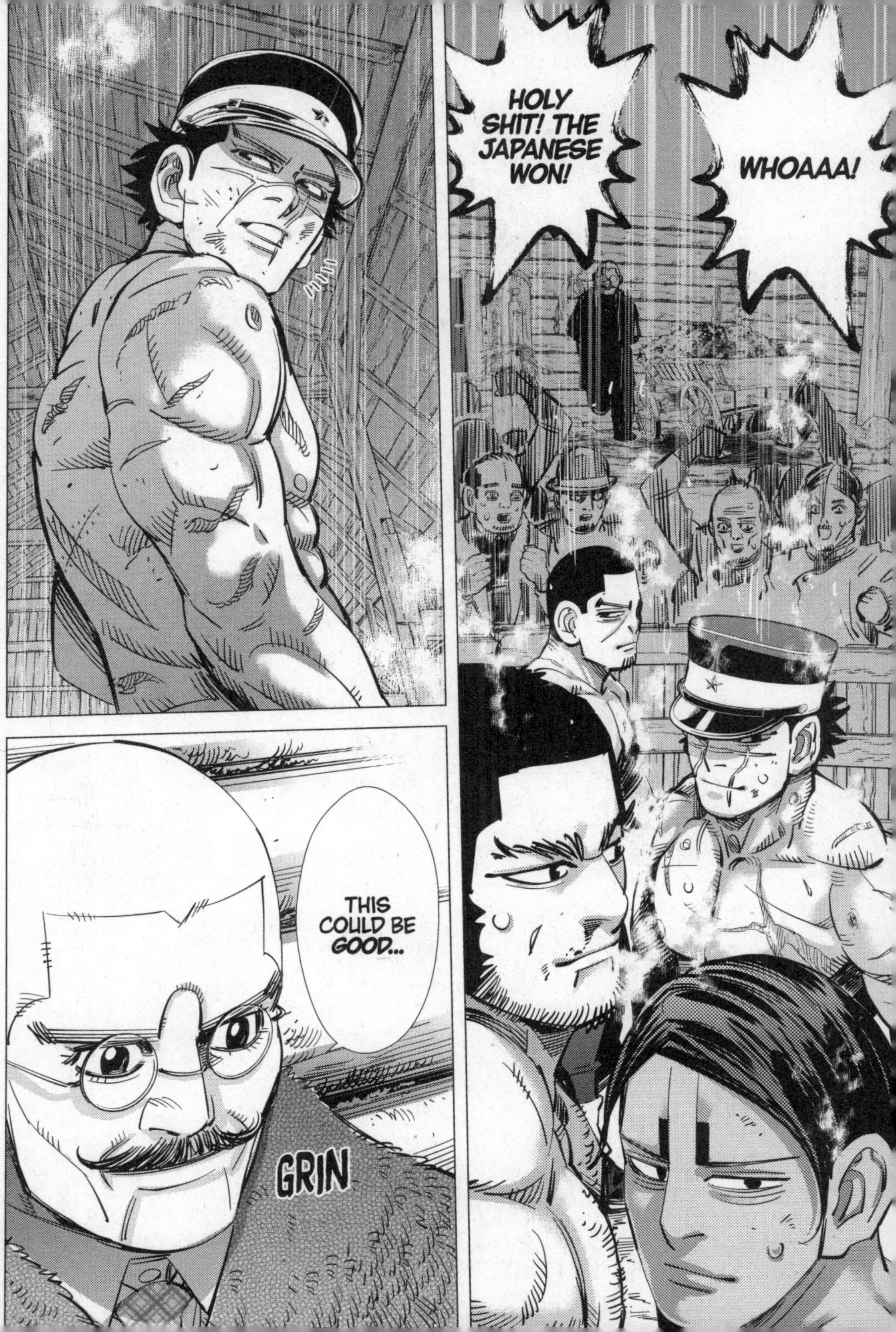
WHOAAA!
HOLY SHIT! THE JAPANESE WON!
THIS COULD BE GOOD...
GRIN

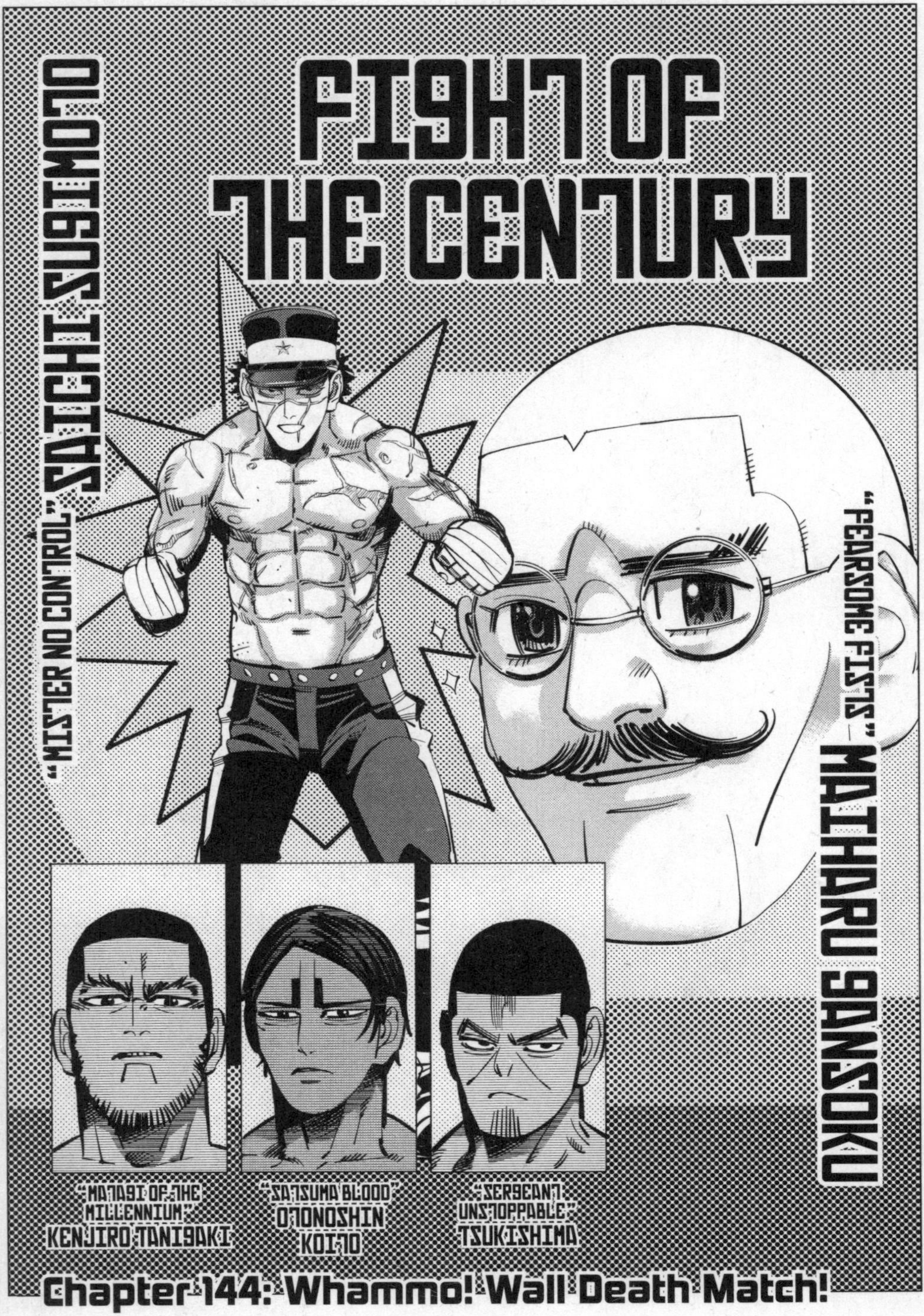
FIGHT OF THE CENTURY
"MISTER NO CONTROL" SAICHI SUGIMOTO
"FEARSOME FISTS" MAIHARU GANSOKU
"MATAGI OF THE MILLENNIUM" KENJIRO TANIGAKI
"SATSUMA BLOOD" OTONOSHIN KOITO
"SERGEANT UNSTOPPABLE" TSUKISHIMA

Chapter 144: Whammo! Wall Death Match!

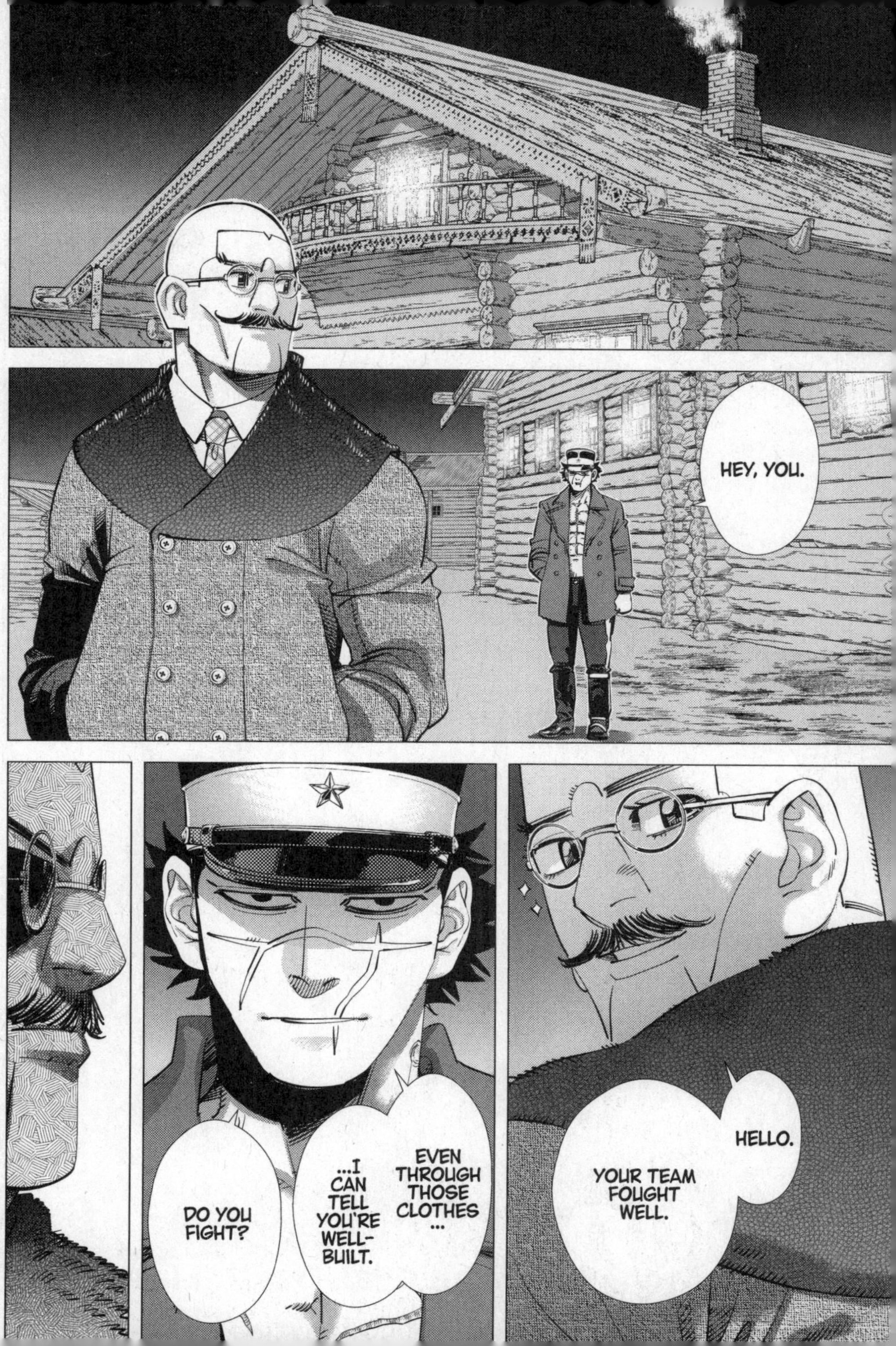
HEY, YOU.
HELLO.
YOUR TEAM FOUGHT WELL.
EVEN THROUGH THOSE CLOTHES ...
...I CAN TELL YOU'RE WELL-BUILT.
DO YOU FIGHT?

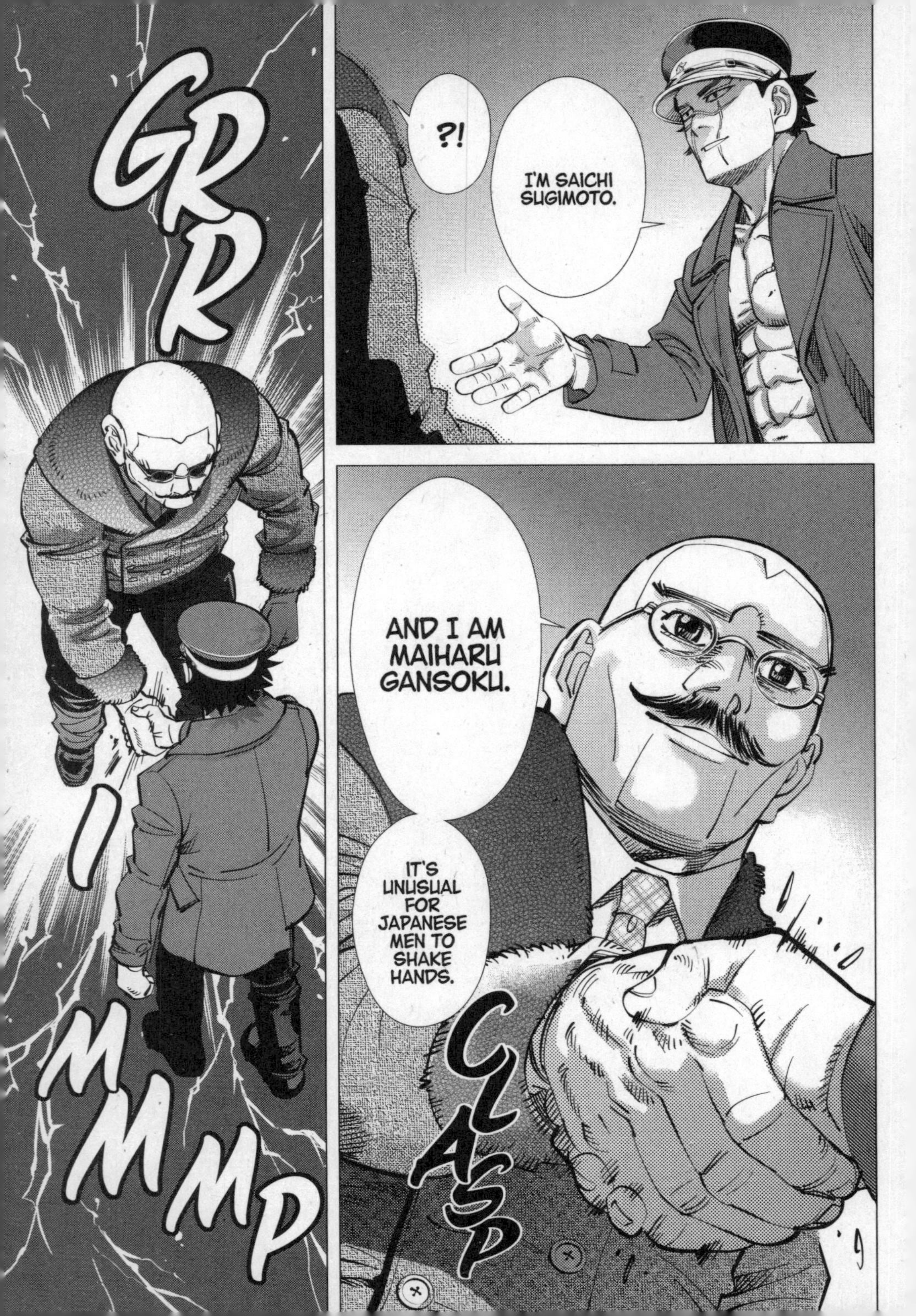
I'M SAICHI SUGIMOTO.
?!
AND I AM MAIHARU GANSOKU.
IT'S UNUSUAL FOR JAPANESE MEN TO SHAKE HANDS.
CLASP
GRRIMMMP

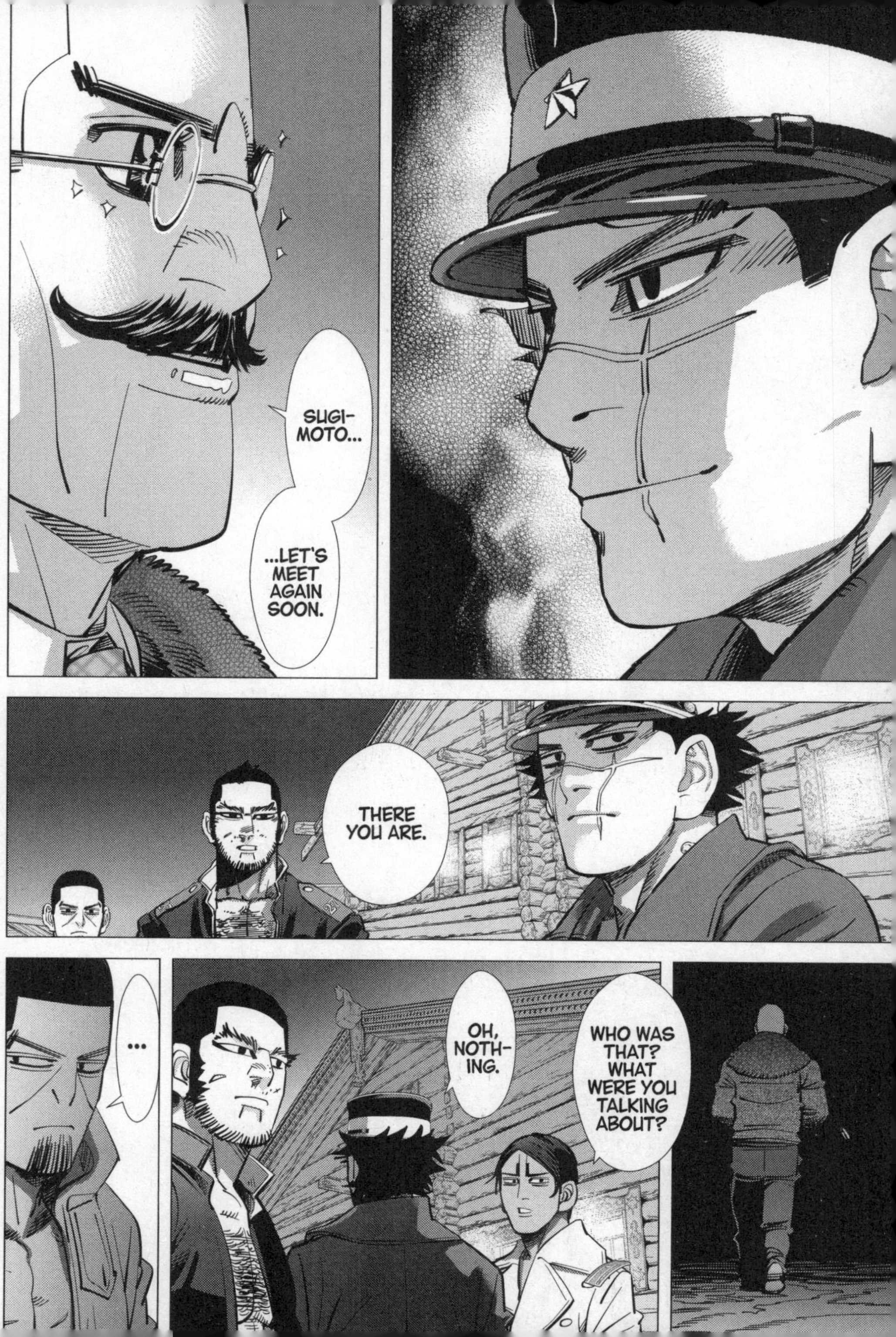
SUGI-MOTO...
...LET'S MEET AGAIN SOON.
THERE YOU ARE.
WHO WAS THAT? WHAT WERE YOU TALKING ABOUT?
OH, NOTH-ING.
...

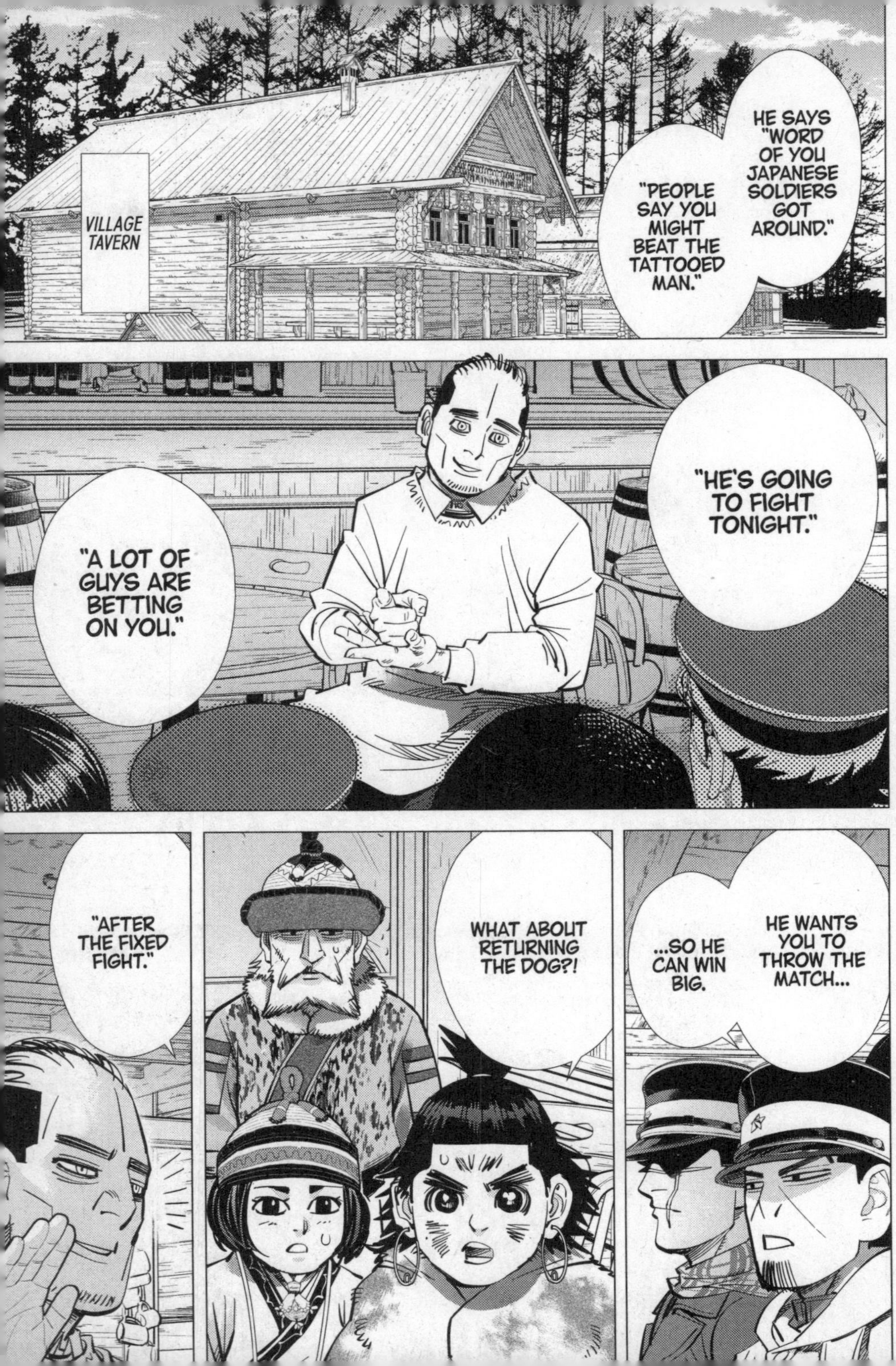
HE SAYS "WORD OF YOU JAPANESE SOLDIERS GOT AROUND."
"PEOPLE SAY YOU MIGHT BEAT THE TATTOOED MAN."
VILLAGE TAVERN
"HE'S GOING TO FIGHT TONIGHT."
"A LOT OF GUYS ARE BETTING ON YOU."
HE WANTS YOU TO THROW THE MATCH...
...SO HE CAN WIN BIG.
WHAT ABOUT RETURNING THE DOG?!
"AFTER THE FIXED FIGHT."

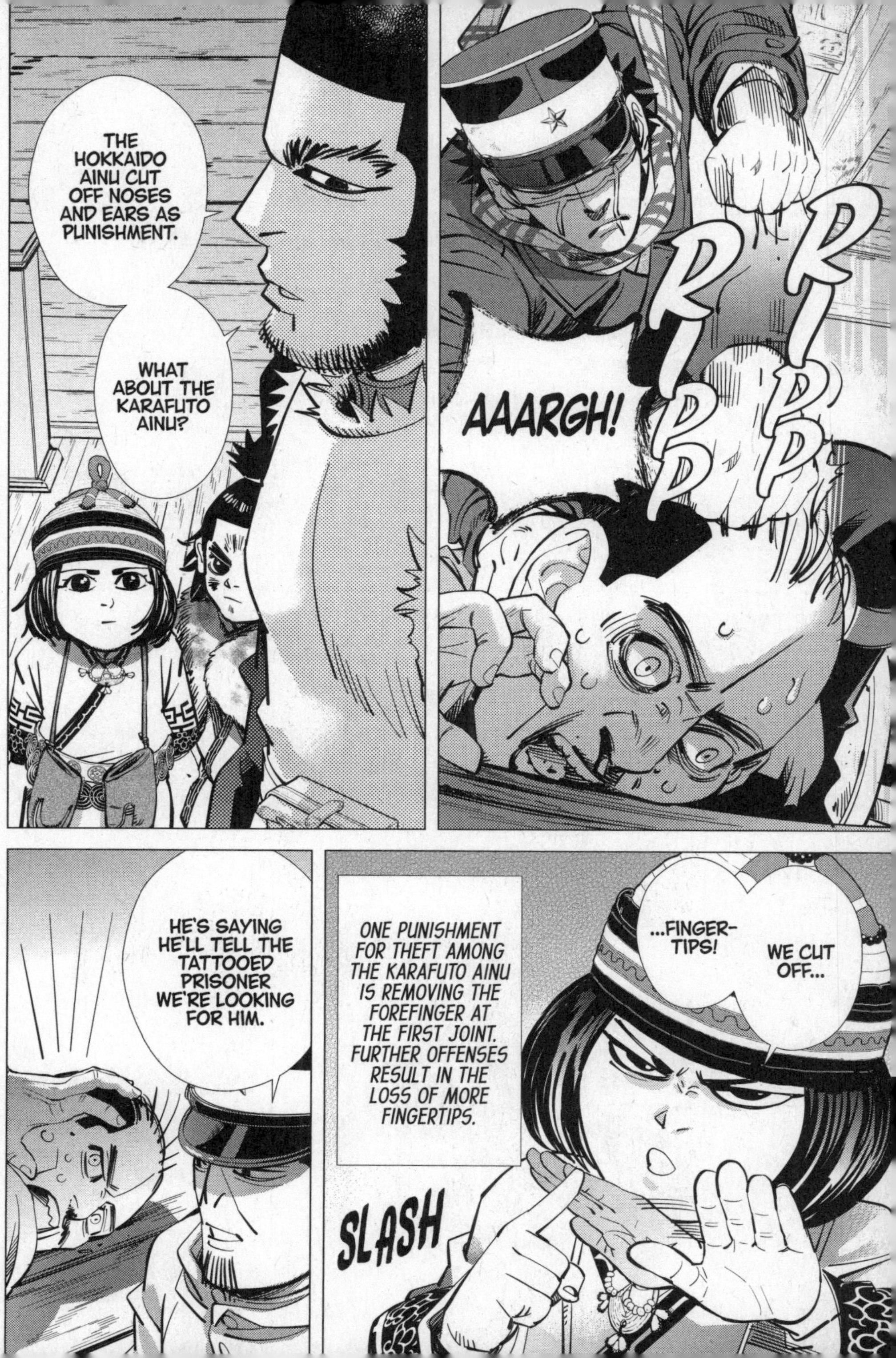
RIPP
RIPP
AAARGH!
THE HOKKAIDO AINU CUT OFF NOSES AND EARS AS PUNISHMENT.
WHAT ABOUT THE KARAFUTO AINU?
ONE PUNISHMENT FOR THEFT AMONG THE KARAFUTO AINU IS REMOVING THE FOREFINGER AT THE FIRST JOINT. FURTHER OFFENSES RESULT IN THE LOSS OF MORE FINGERTIPS.
WE CUT OFF...
...FINGER-TIPS!
SLASH
HE'S SAYING HE'LL TELL THE TATTOOED PRISONER WE'RE LOOKING FOR HIM.

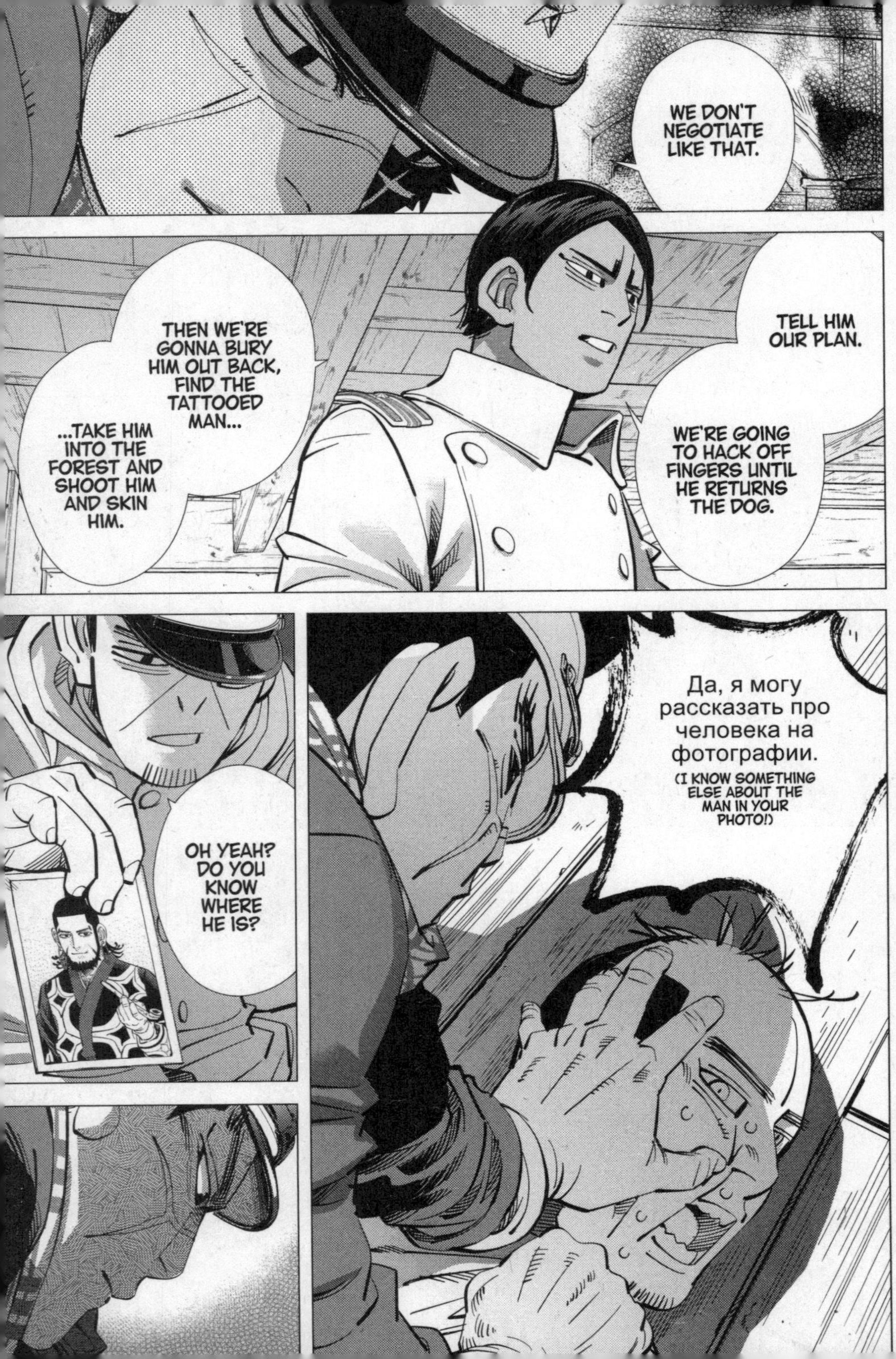
WE DON'T NEGOTIATE LIKE THAT.
TELL HIM OUR PLAN.
WE'RE GOING TO HACK OFF FINGERS UNTIL HE RETURNS THE DOG.
THEN WE'RE GONNA BURY HIM OUT BACK, FIND THE TATTOOED MAN...
...TAKE HIM INTO THE FOREST AND SHOOT HIM AND SKIN HIM.
Да, я могу рассказать про человека на фотографии.
(I KNOW SOMETHING ELSE ABOUT THE MAN IN YOUR PHOTO!)
OH YEAH? DO YOU KNOW WHERE HE IS?

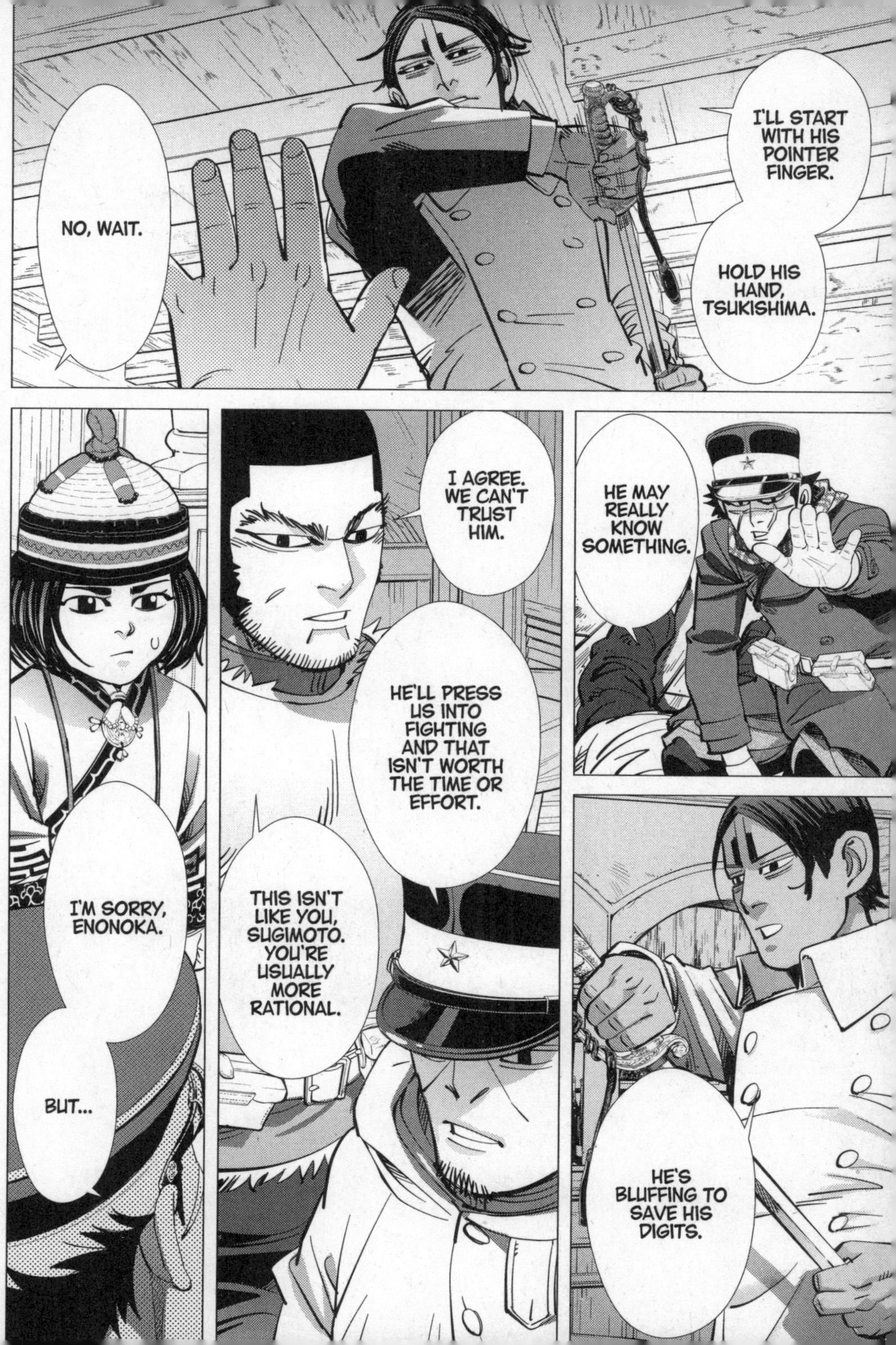
I'LL START WITH HIS POINTER FINGER.
HOLD HIS HAND, TSUKISHIMA.
NO, WAIT.
HE MAY REALLY KNOW SOMETHING.
HE'S BLUFFING TO SAVE HIS DIGITS.
I AGREE. WE CAN'T TRUST HIM.
HE'LL PRESS US INTO FIGHTING AND THAT ISN'T WORTH THE TIME OR EFFORT.
THIS ISN'T LIKE YOU, SUGIMOTO. YOU'RE USUALLY MORE RATIONAL.
I'M SORRY, ENONOKA.
BUT...

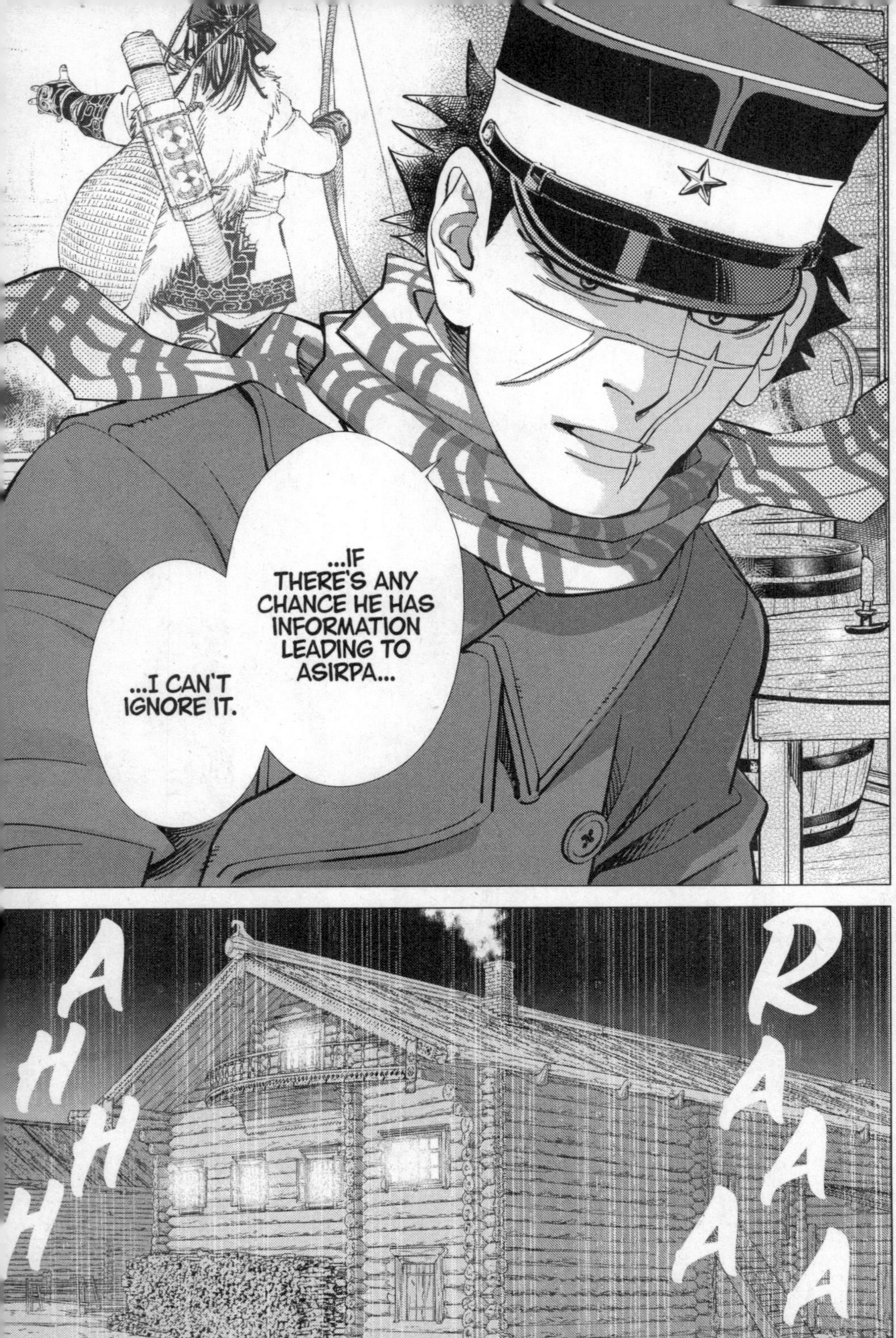
...IF THERE'S ANY CHANCE HE HAS INFORMATION LEADING TO ASIRPA...
...I CAN'T IGNORE IT.
RAAAAA
AHHH

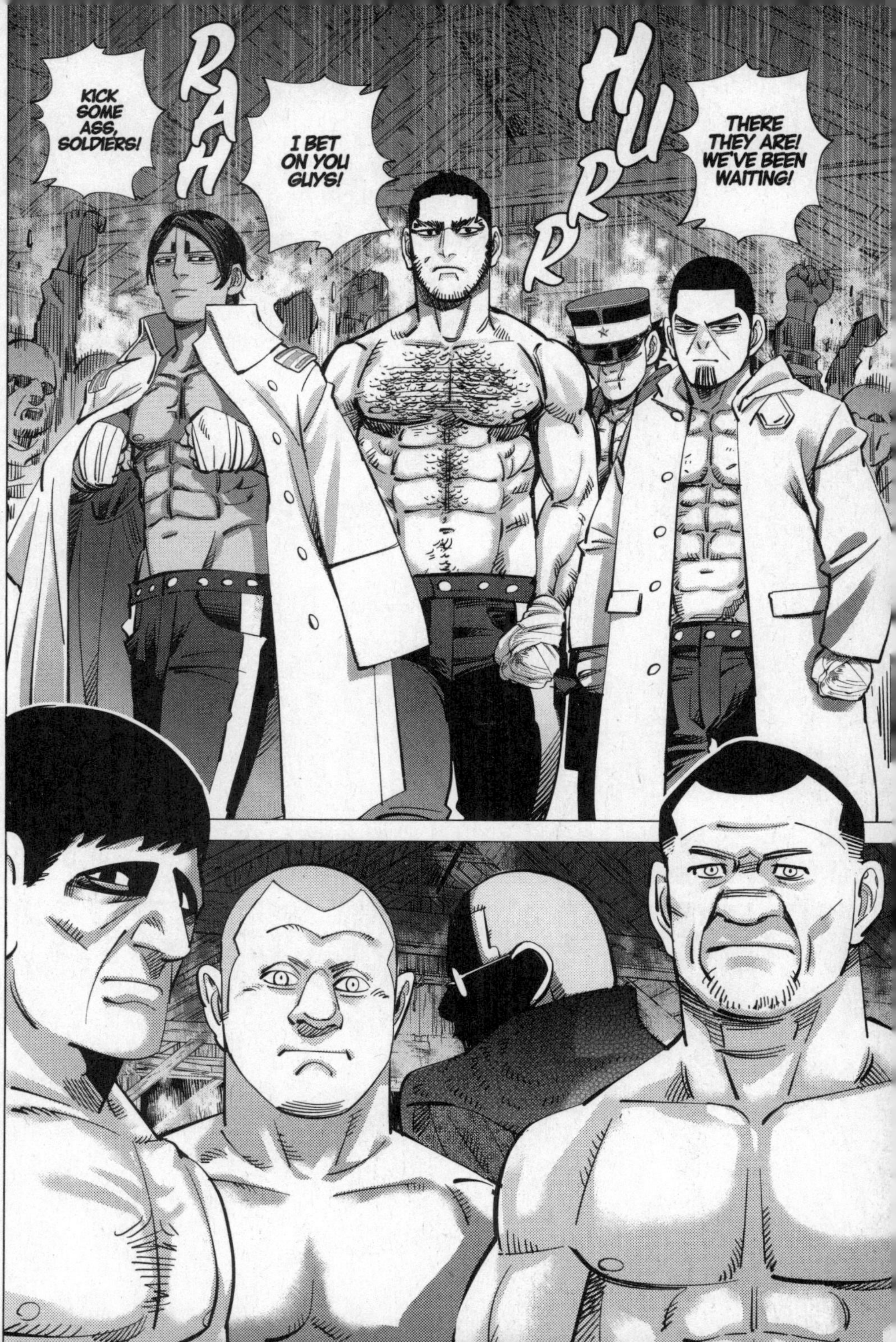
THERE THEY ARE! WE'VE BEEN WAITING!
HURRR
I BET ON YOU GUYS!
RAH
KICK SOME ASS, SOLDIERS!

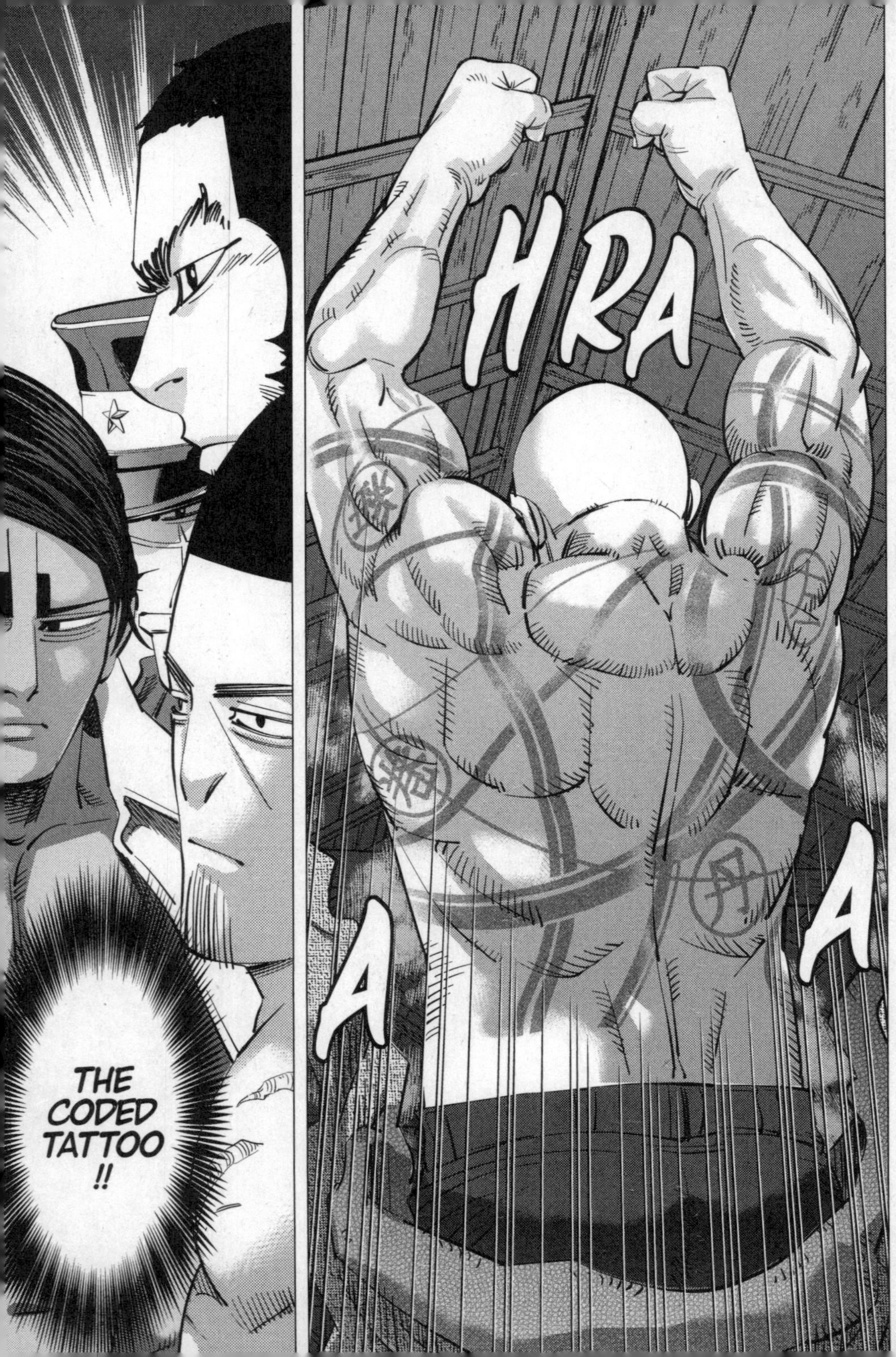
HRAAA
THE CODED TATTOO !!

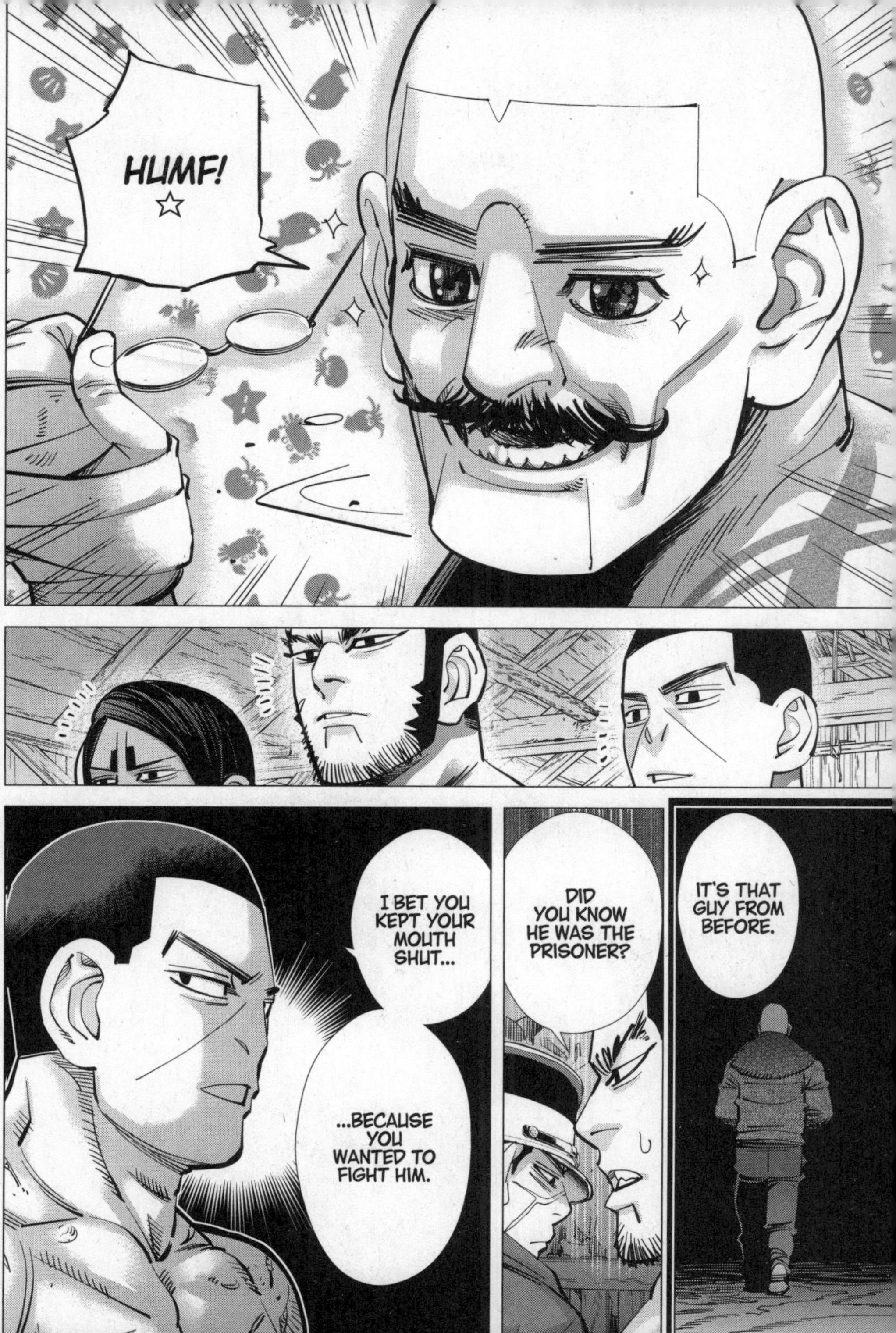
HUMF! ☆
IT'S THAT GUY FROM BEFORE.
DID YOU KNOW HE WAS THE PRISONER?
I BET YOU KEPT YOUR MOUTH SHUT...
...BECAUSE YOU WANTED TO FIGHT HIM.

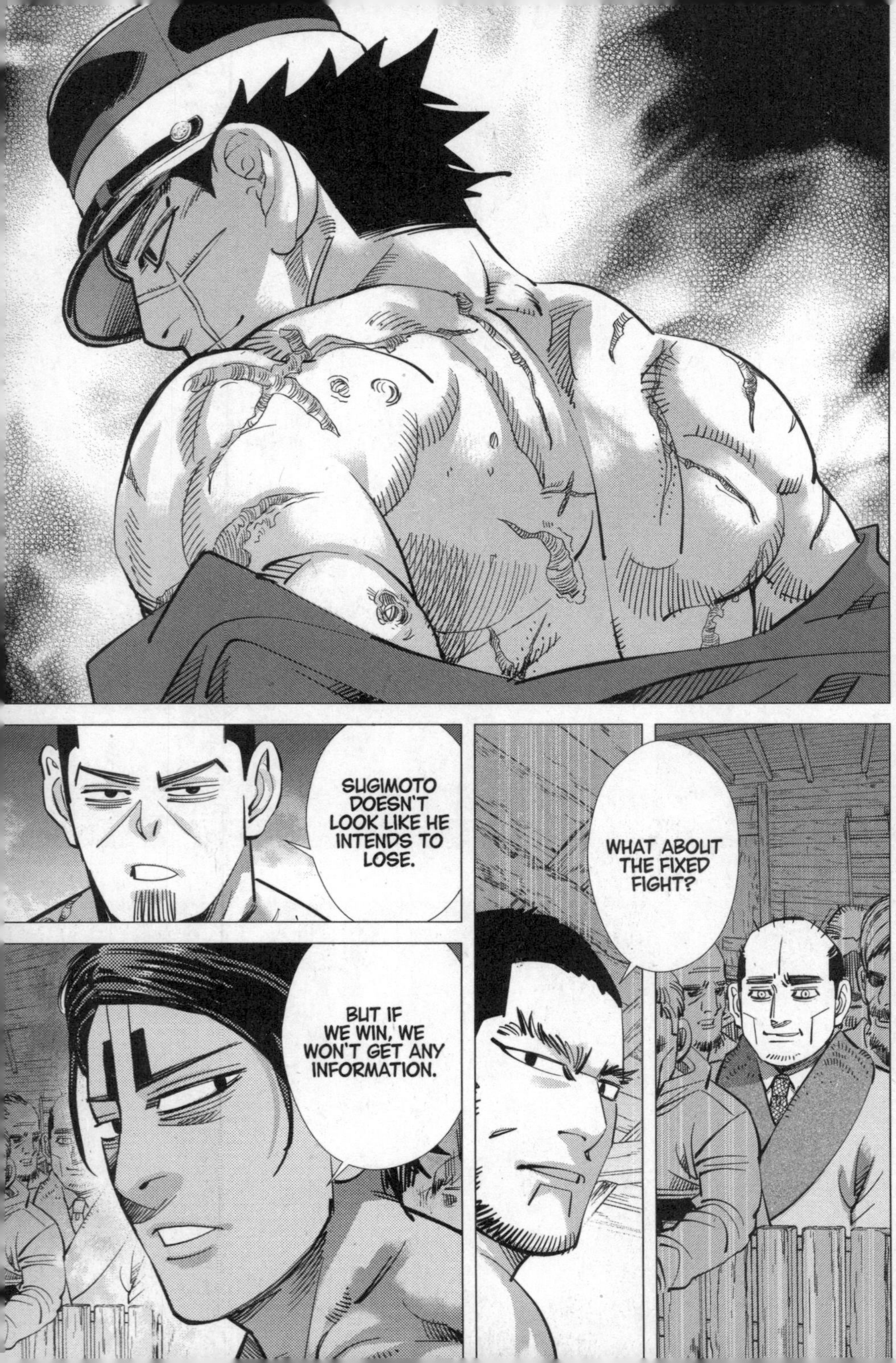
WHAT ABOUT THE FIXED FIGHT?
SUGIMOTO DOESN'T LOOK LIKE HE INTENDS TO LOSE.
BUT IF WE WIN, WE WON'T GET ANY INFORMATION.

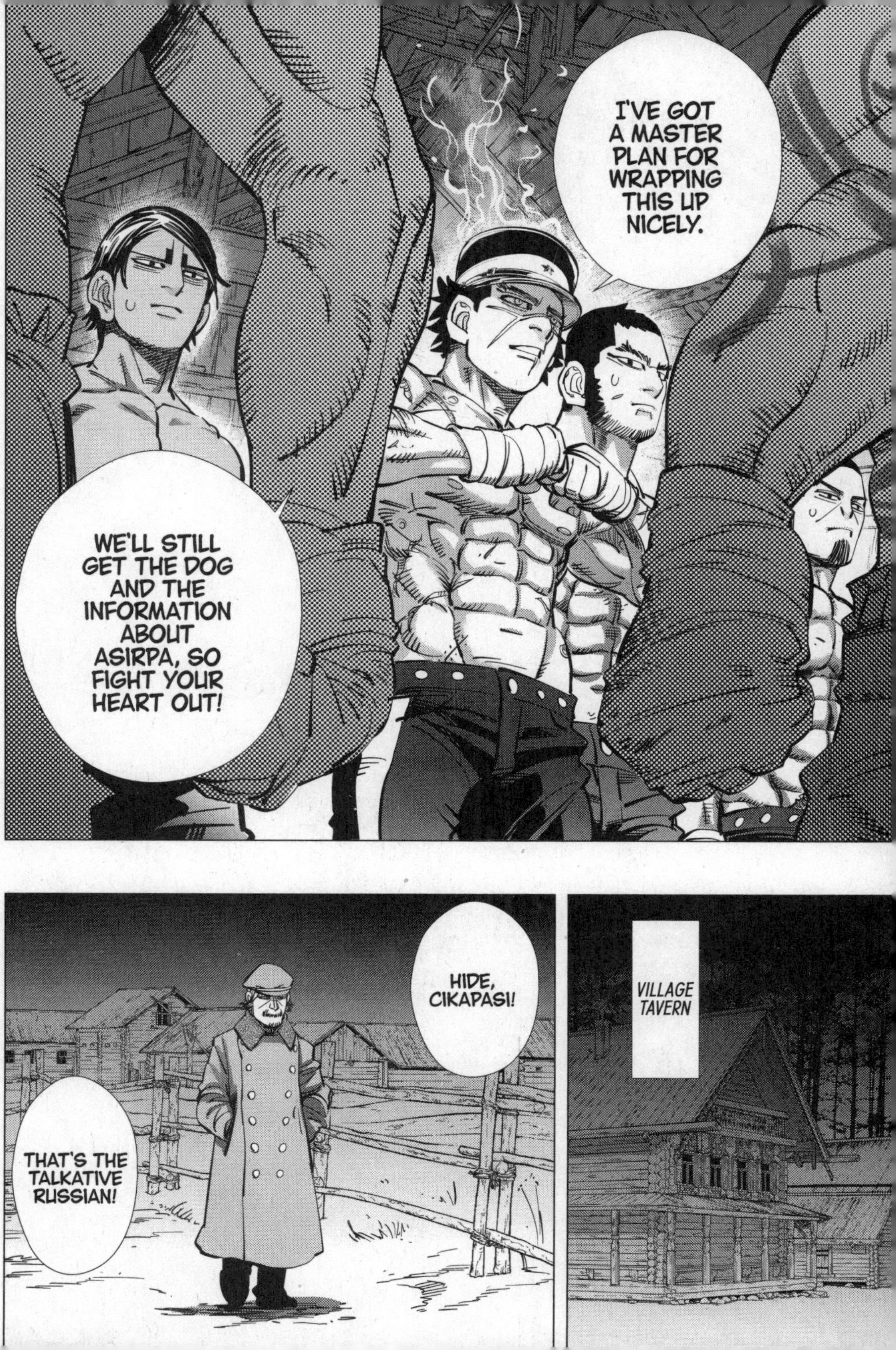
I'VE GOT A MASTER PLAN FOR WRAPPING THIS UP NICELY.
WE'LL STILL GET THE DOG AND THE INFORMATION ABOUT ASIRPA, SO FIGHT YOUR HEART OUT!
VILLAGE TAVERN
HIDE, CIKAPASI!
THAT'S THE TALKATIVE RUSSIAN!

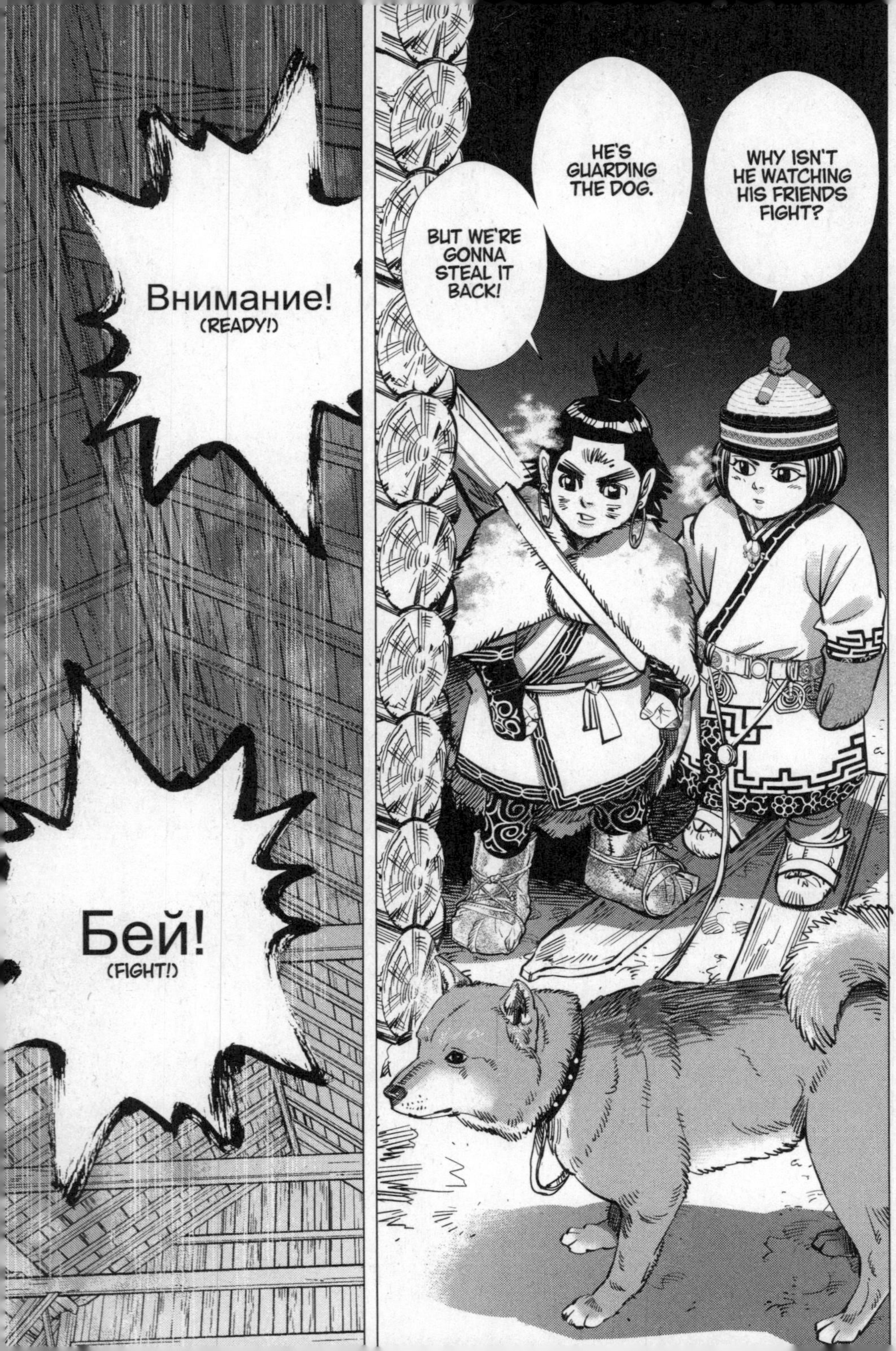
WHY ISN'T HE WATCHING HIS FRIENDS FIGHT?
HE'S GUARDING THE DOG.
BUT WE'RE GONNA STEAL IT BACK!
Внимание!
(READY!)
Бей!
(FIGHT!)

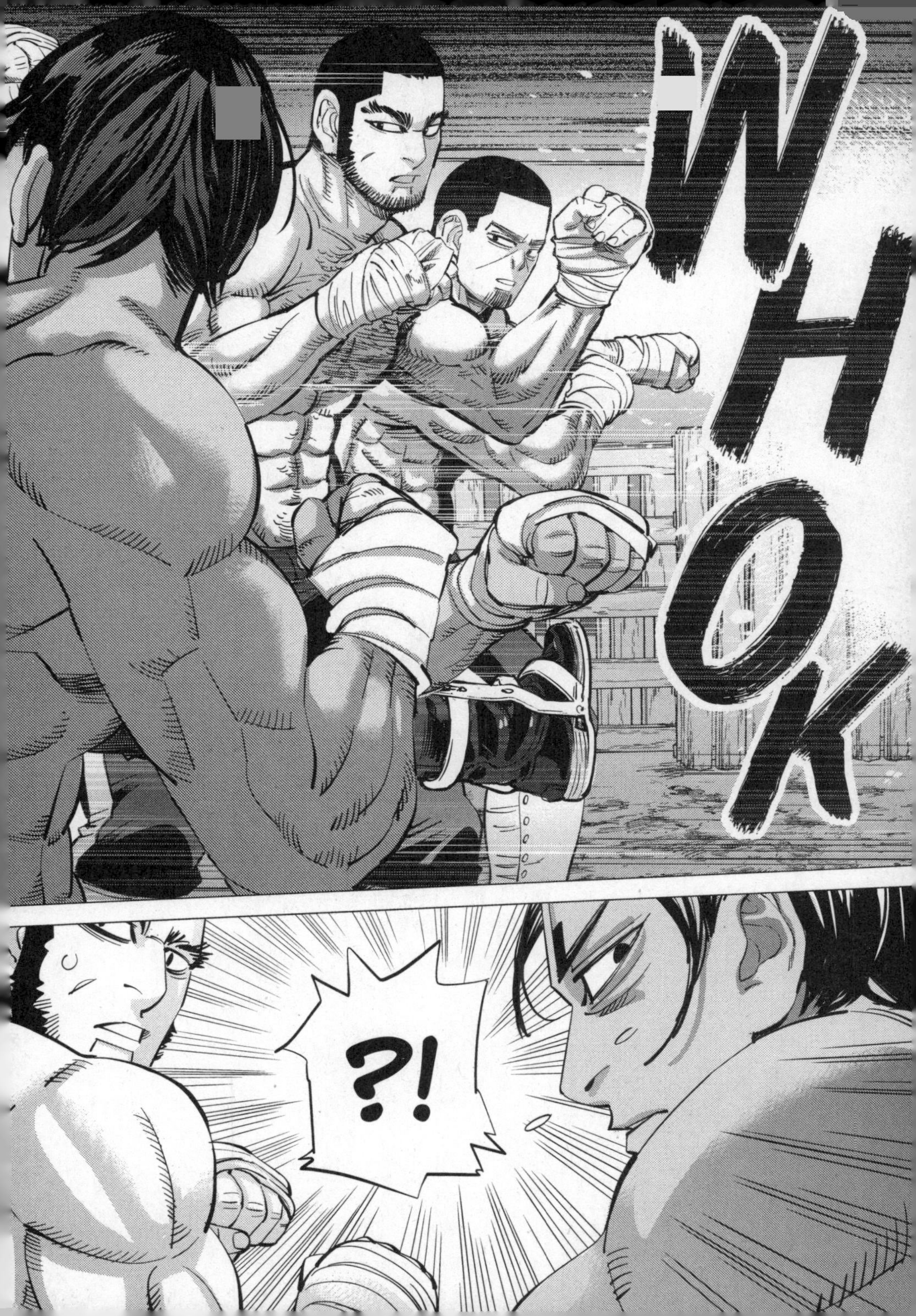
WHOK
?!

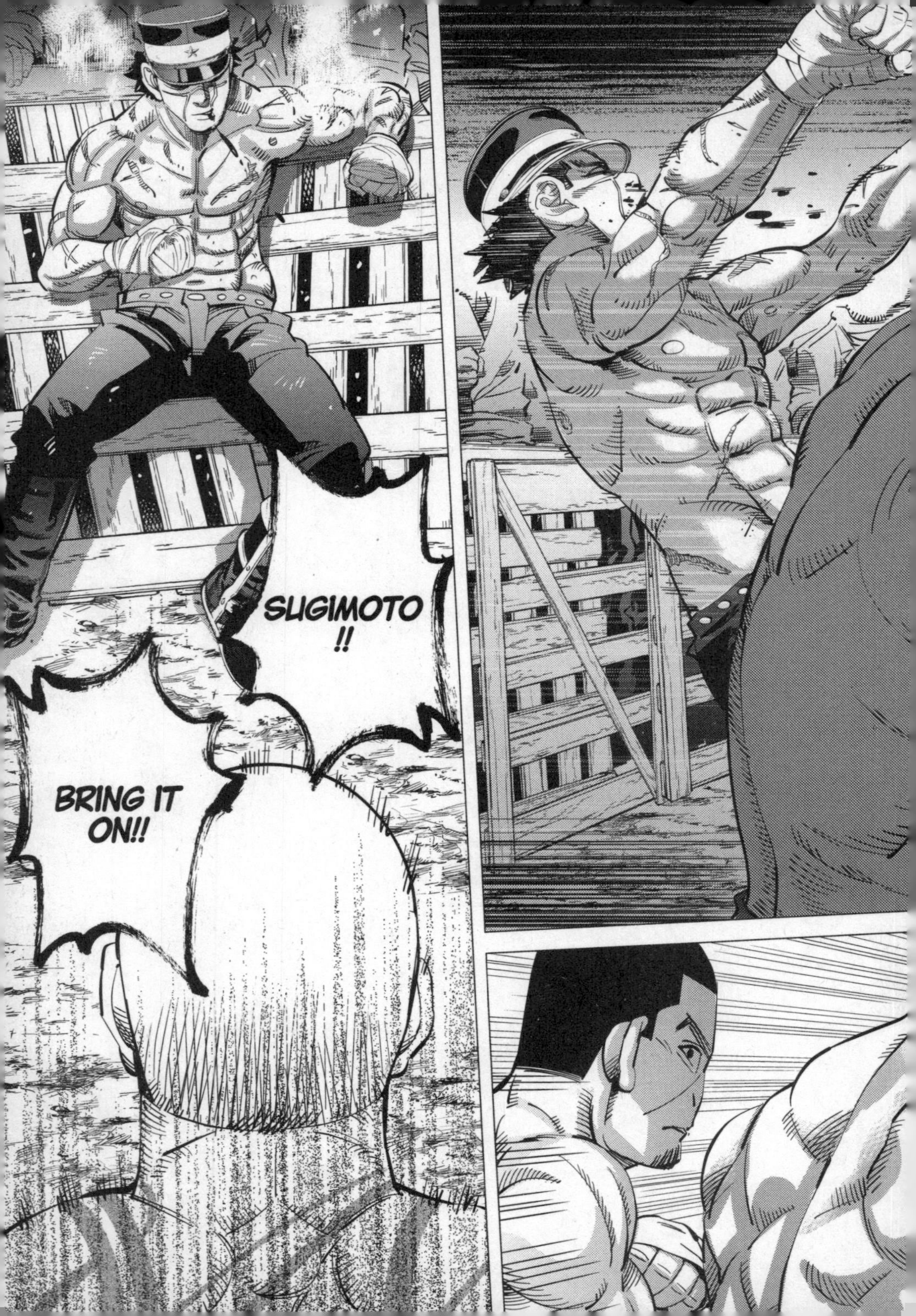
SUGIMOTO !!
BRING IT ON!!

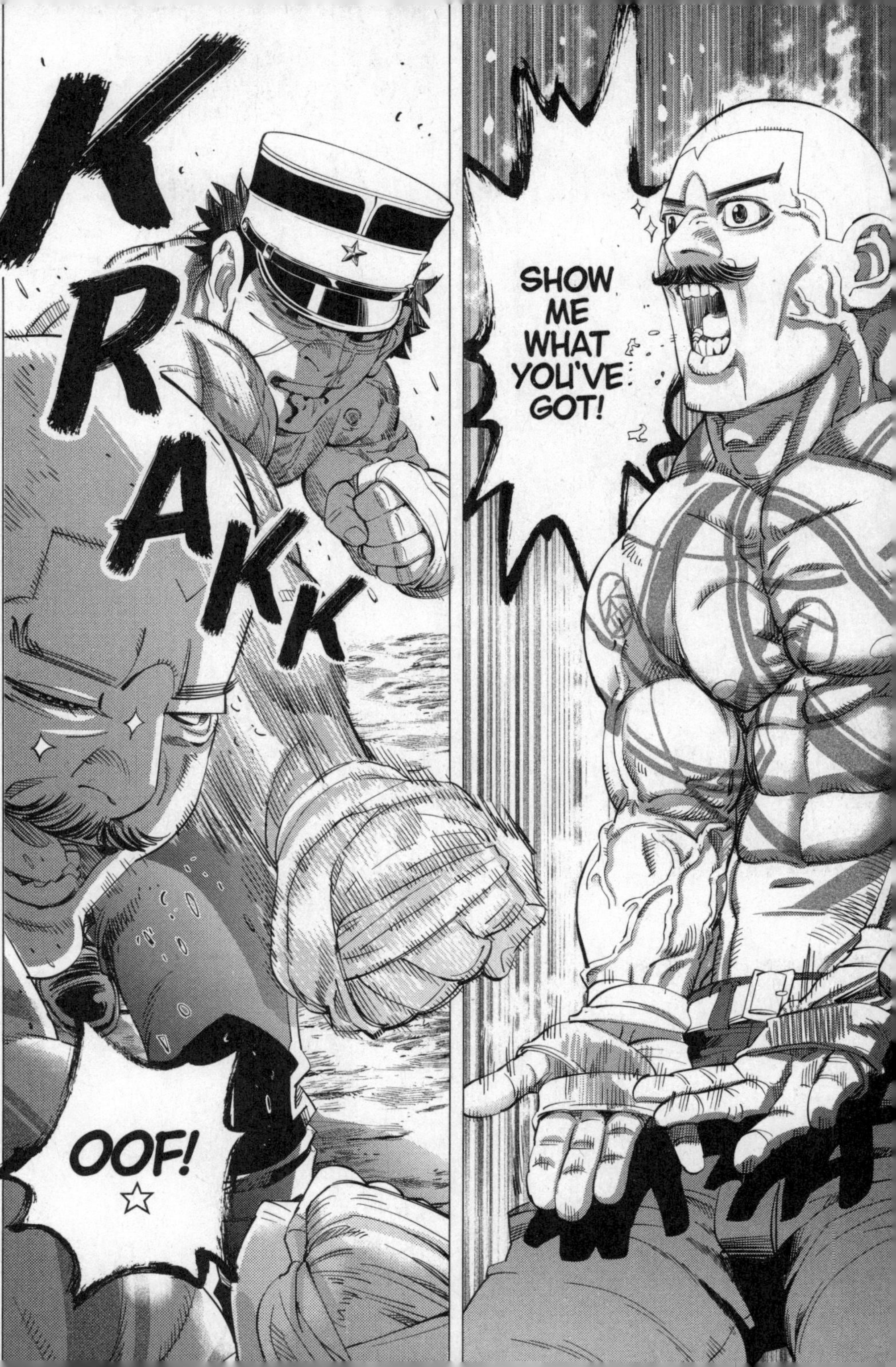
SHOW ME WHAT YOU'VE GOT!
KRAKK
OOF! ☆

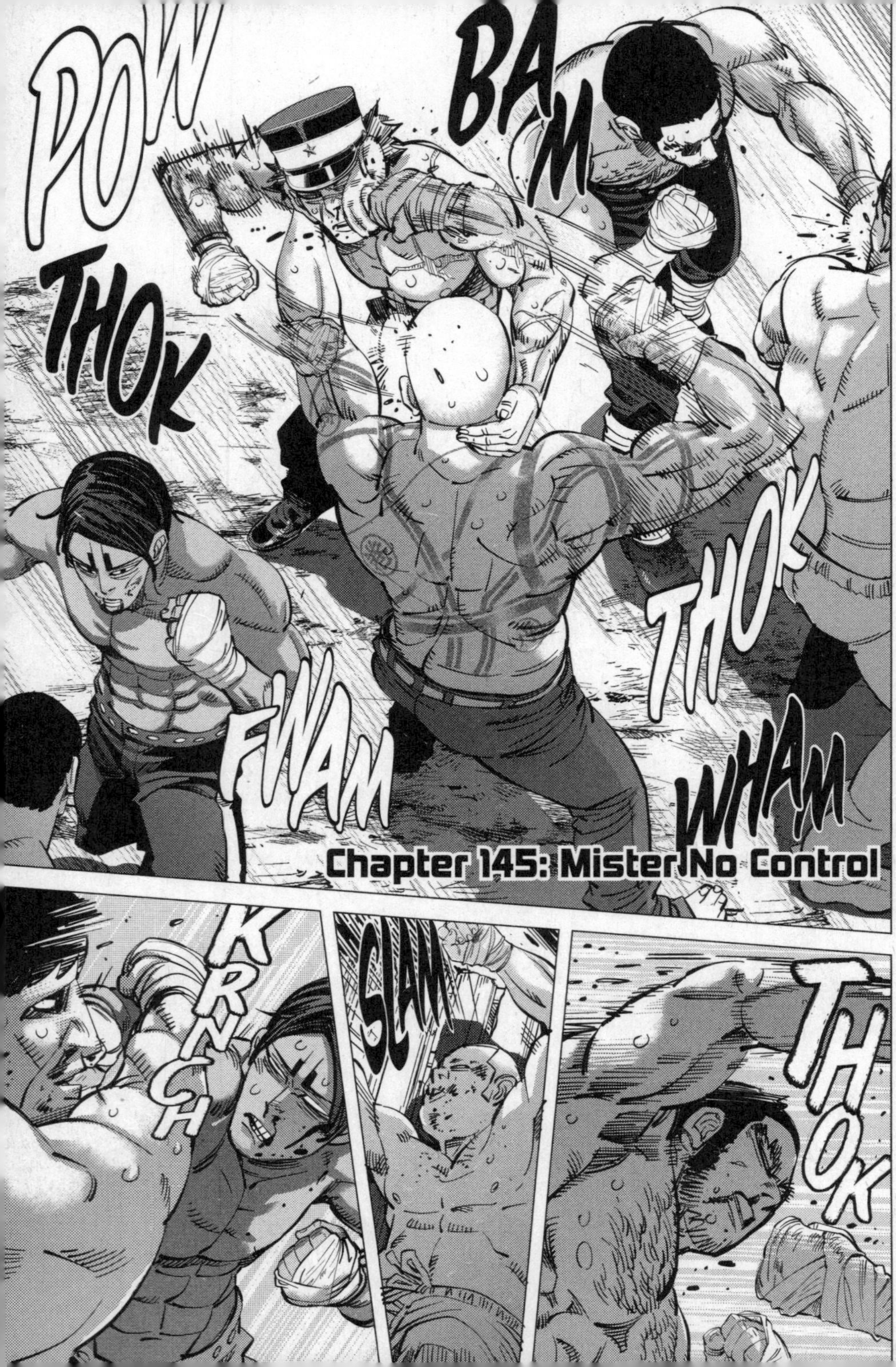
BAM
POW
THOK
THOK
WHAM
FWAM
Chapter 145: Mister No Control
THOK
SLAM
KRNCH

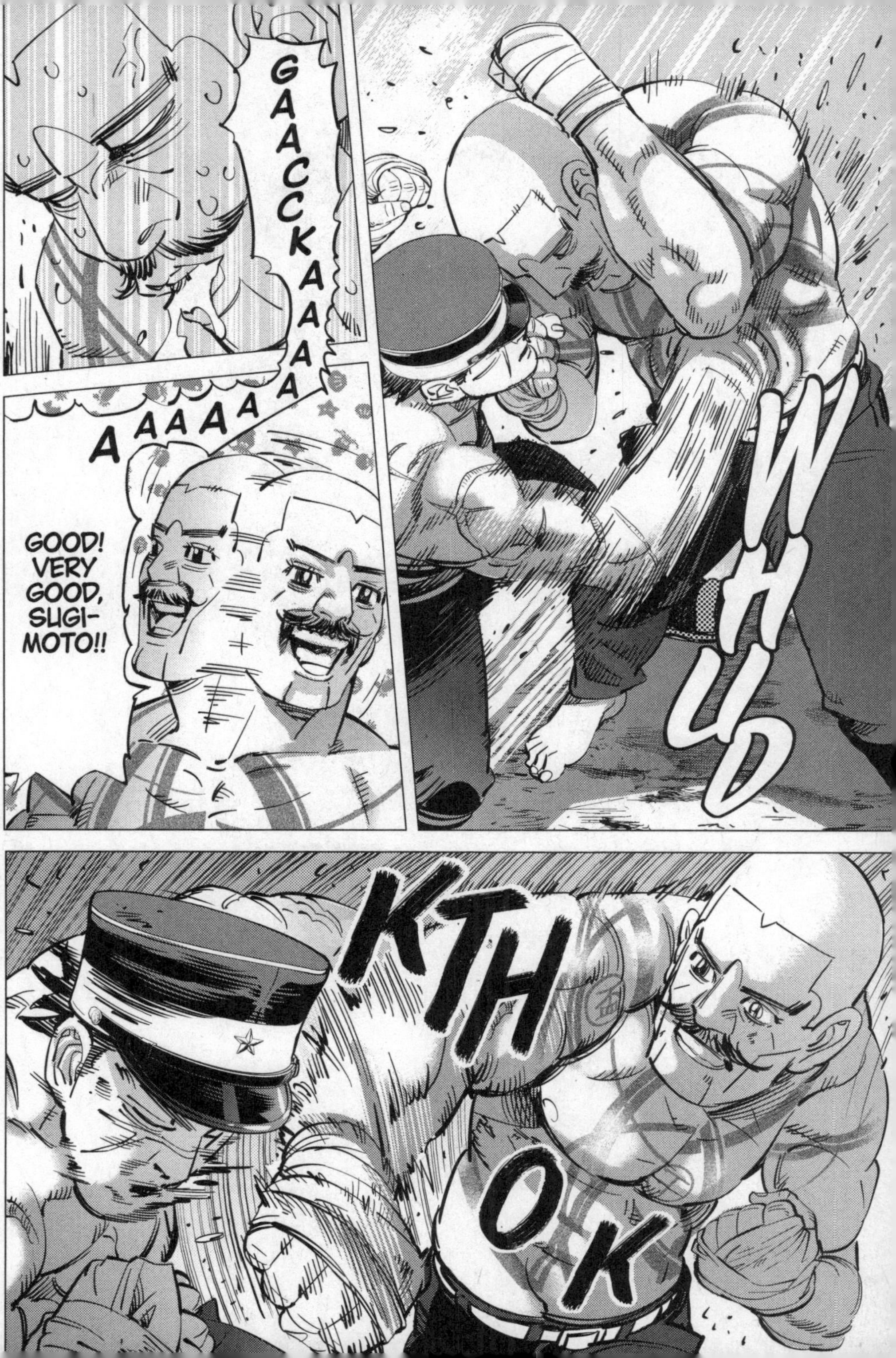
WHUD
GAACCKAAAAAAAAAAA
GOOD! VERY GOOD, SUGIMOTO!!
KTHOOK

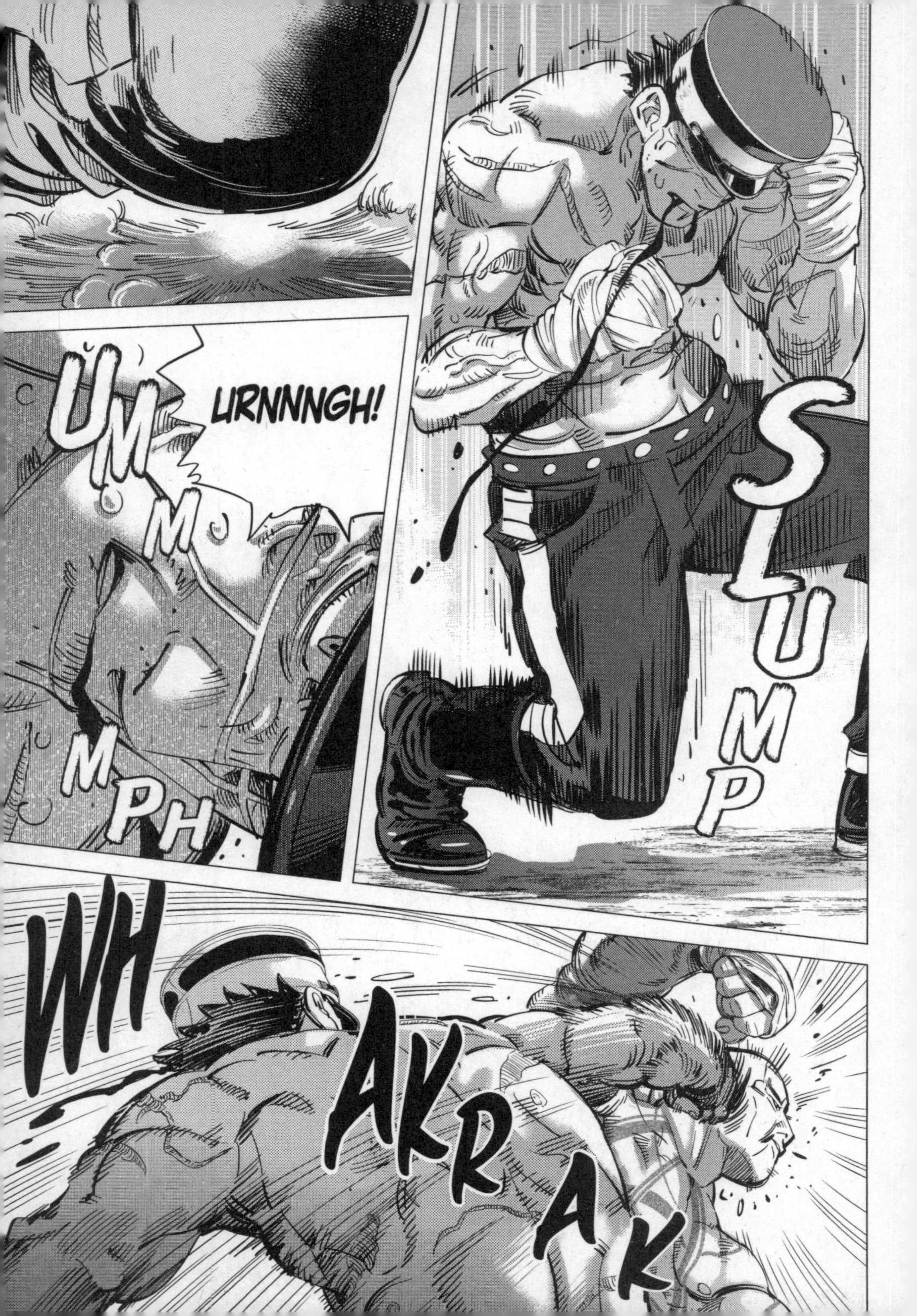
SLUMP
UMMMPH
URNNNGH!
WHAKRAK

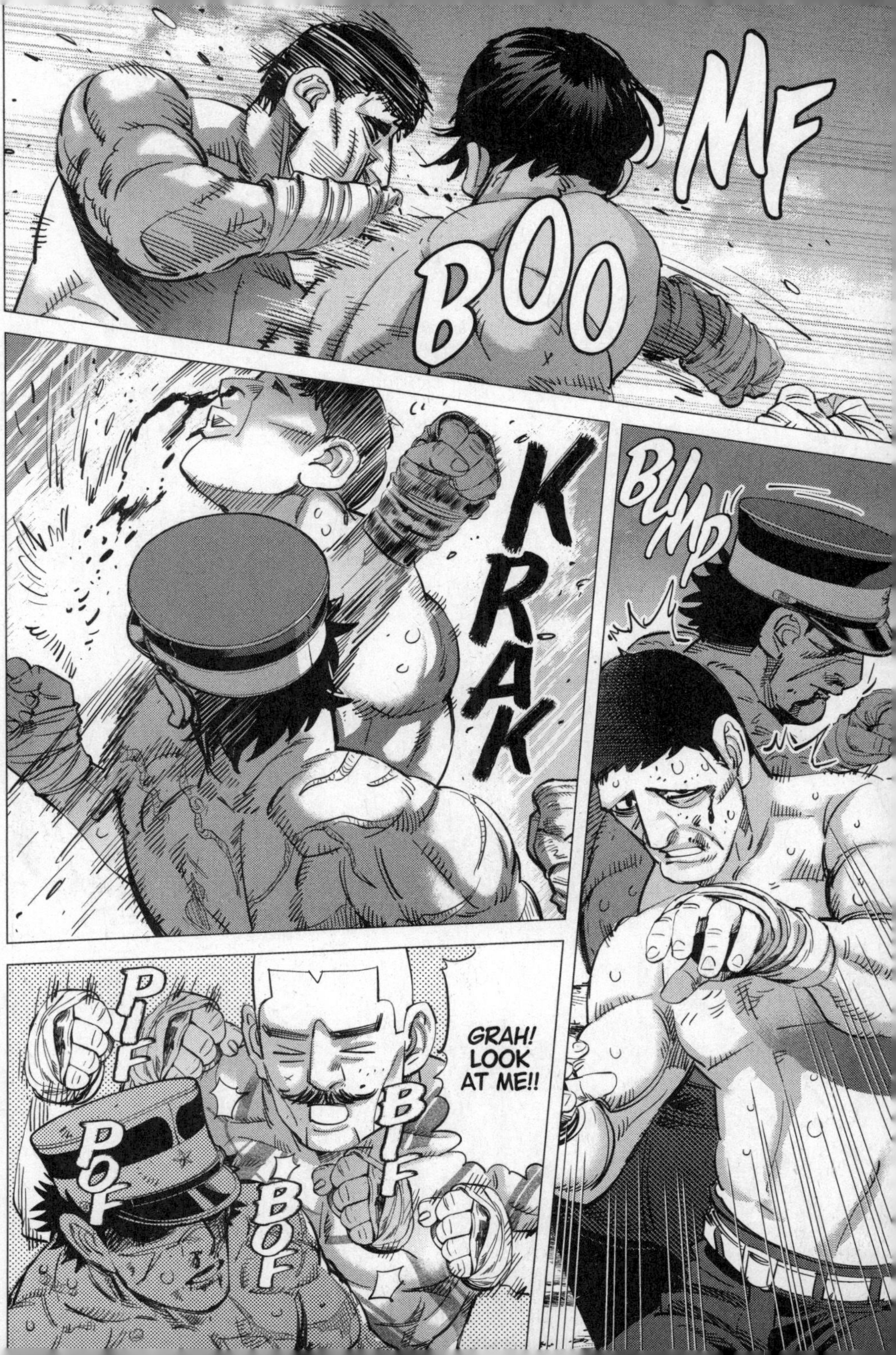
BOO
MF
BUMP
KRAK
GRAH! LOOK AT ME!!
PIF
BIF
POF
BOF

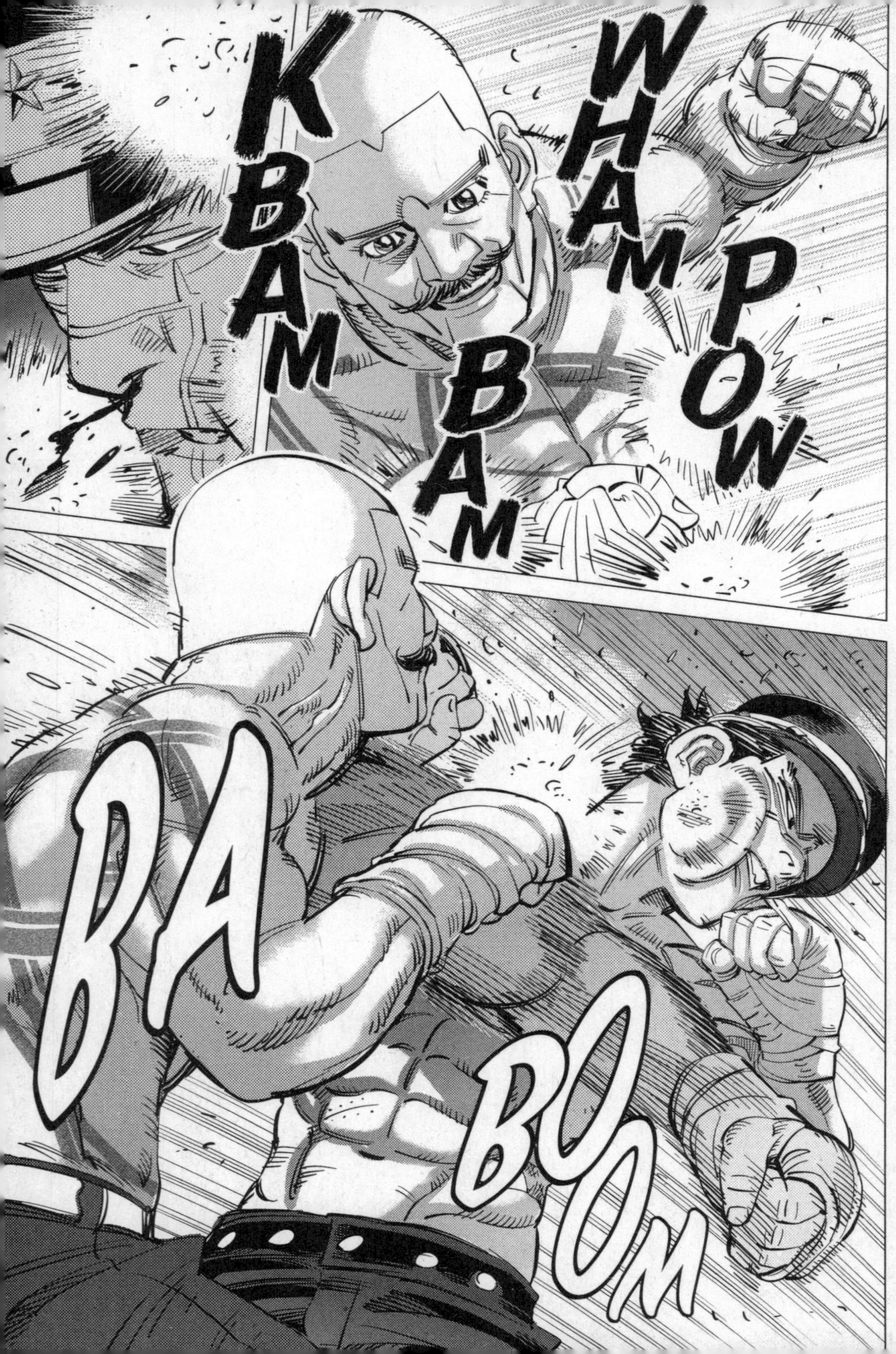
WHAM
POW
BAM
KBAM
BA
BOOM

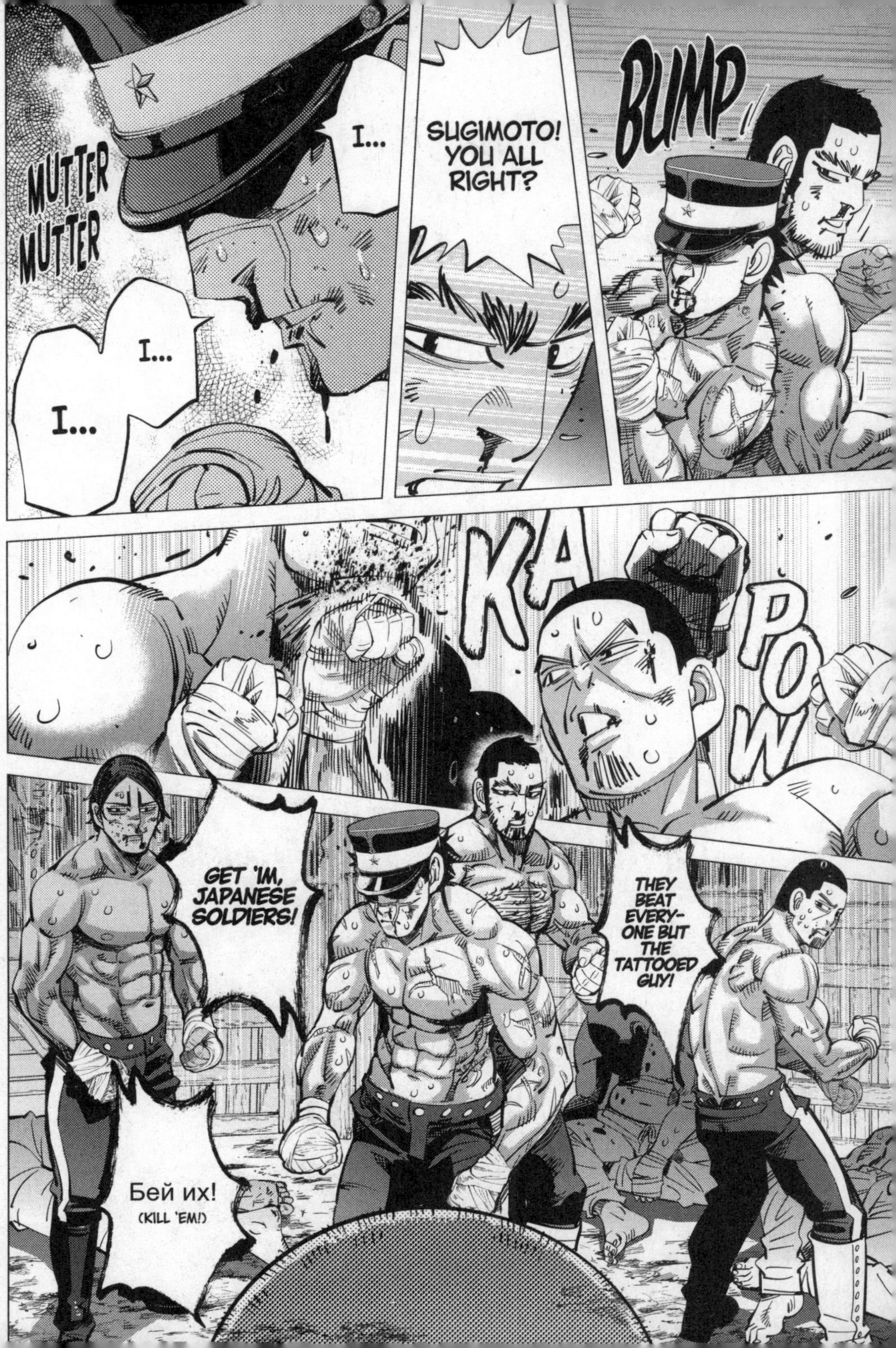
BUMP
SUGIMOTO! YOU ALL RIGHT?
I...
MUTTER MUTTER
I...
I...
KA POW
THEY BEAT EVERY-ONE BUT THE TATTOOED GUY!
GET 'IM, JAPANESE SOLDIERS!
Бей их!
(KILL 'EM!)

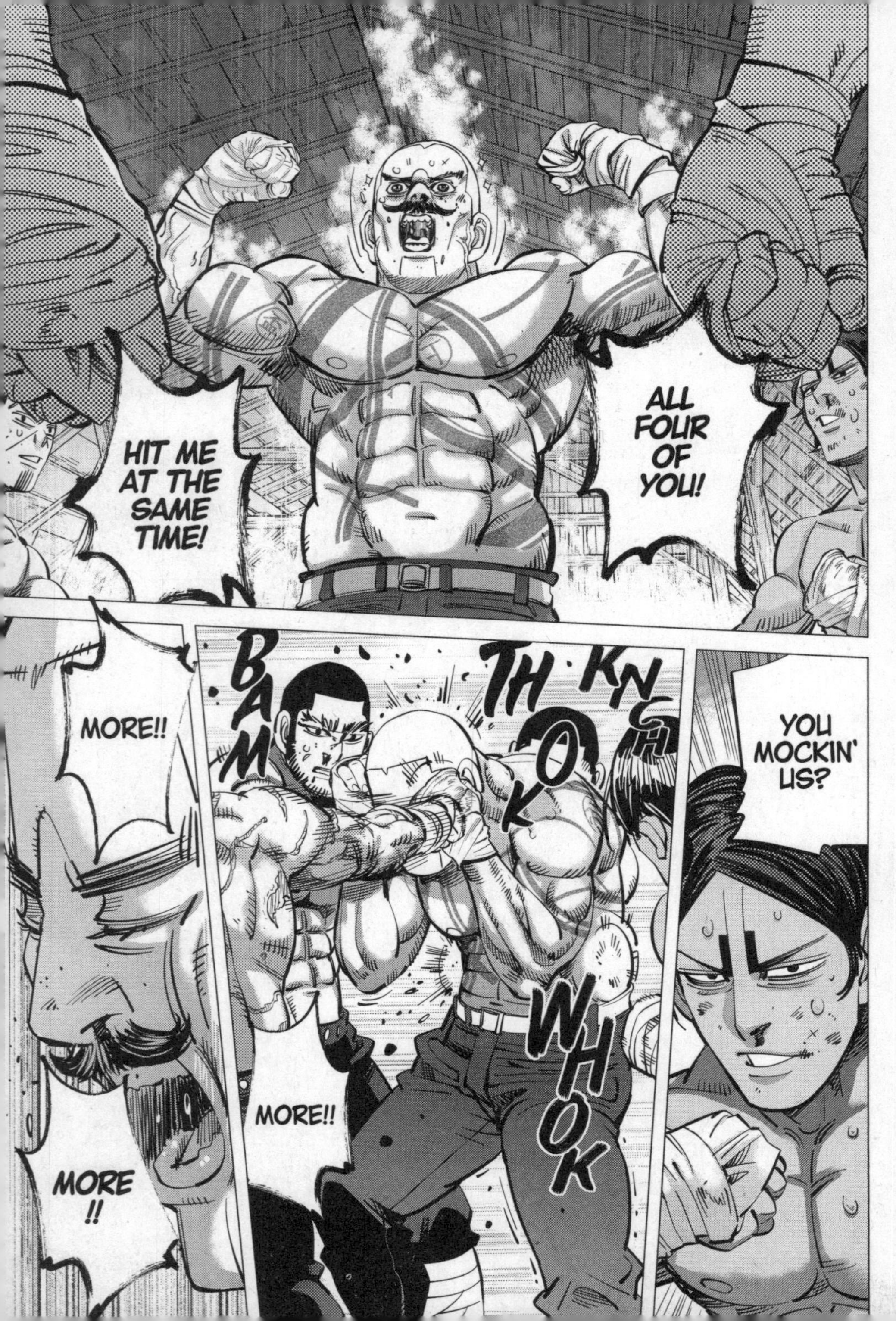
ALL FOUR OF YOU!
HIT ME AT THE SAME TIME!
YOU MOCKIN' US?
KNCH
THOK
BAM
WHOK
MORE!!
MORE!!
MORE !!

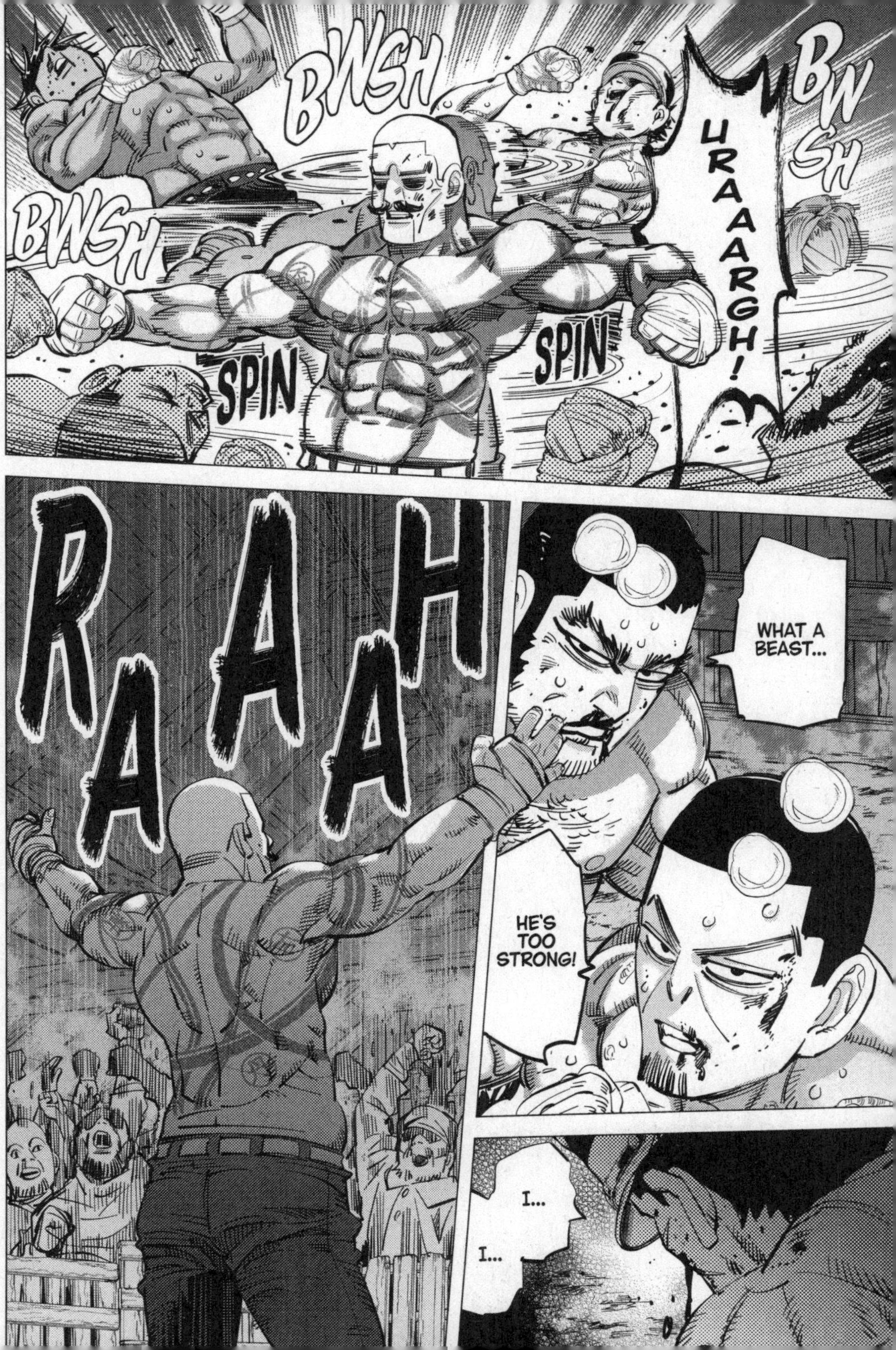
BWSH
URAAAARGH!
BWSH
SPIN
SPIN
BWSH
WHAT A BEAST...
HE'S TOO STRONG!
I...
I...
RAAAAH

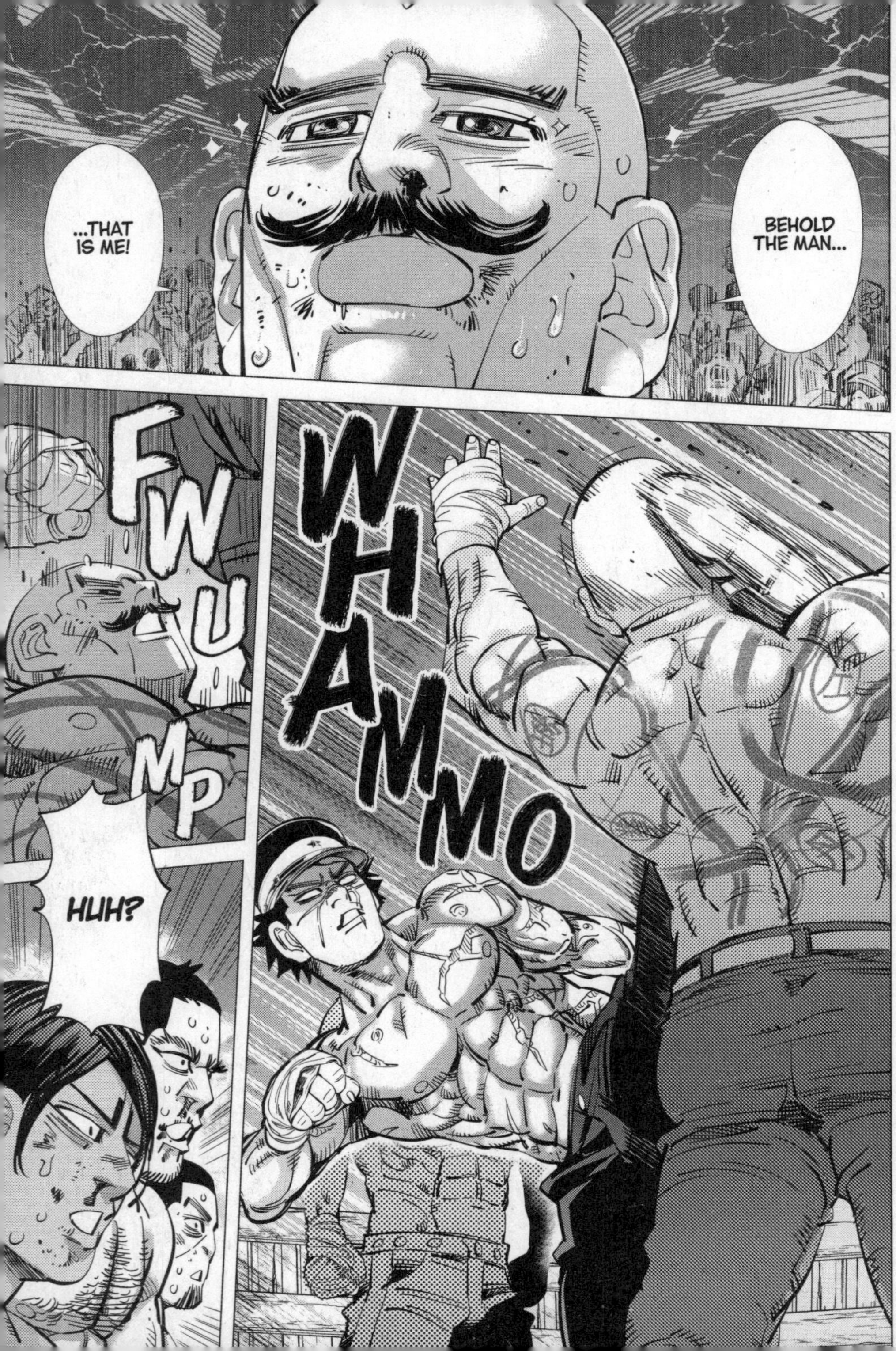
BEHOLD THE MAN...
...THAT IS ME!
WHAMMO
FWUMP
HUH?

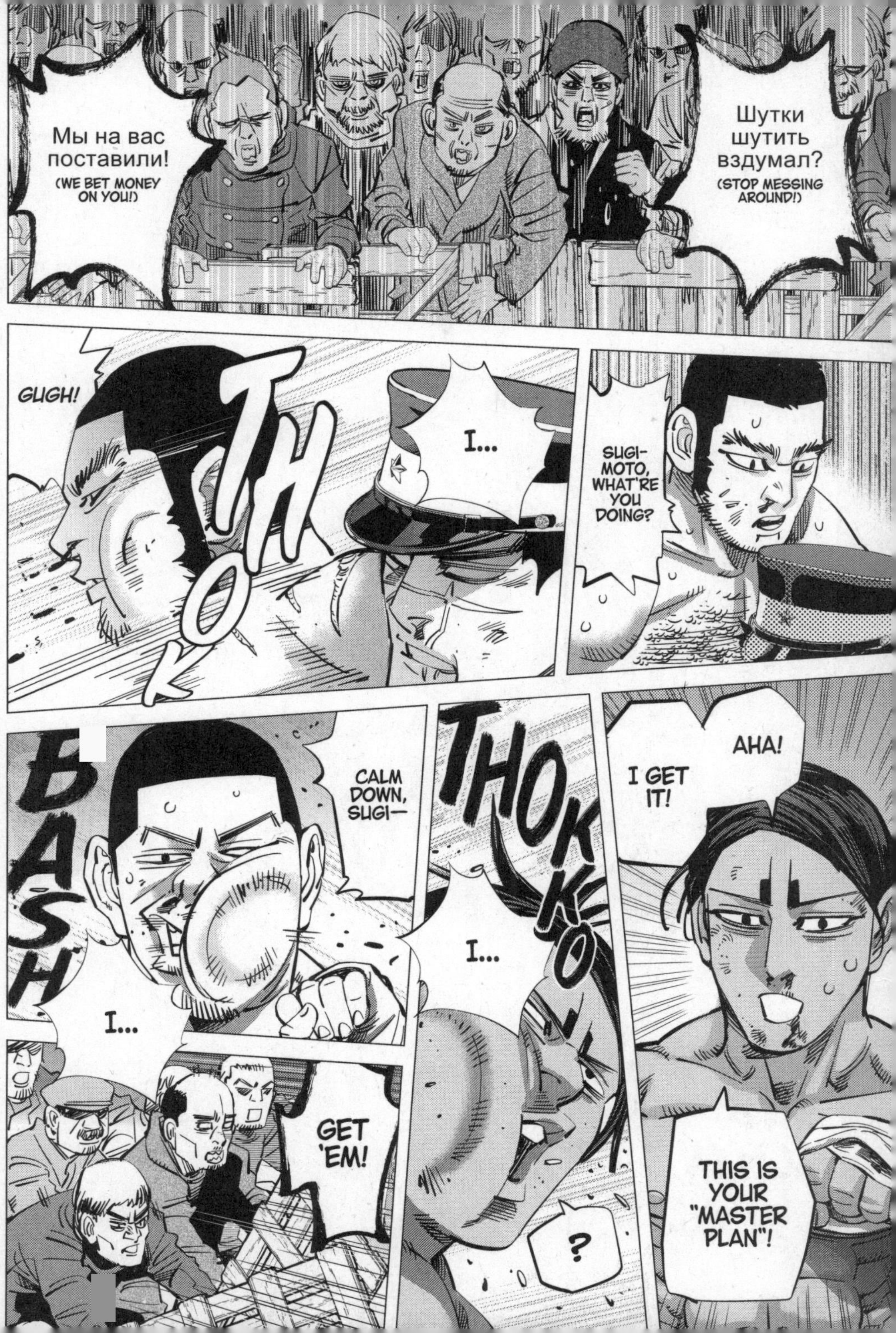

Шутки шутить вздумал?
(STOP MESSING AROUND!)
Мы на вас поставили!
(WE BET MONEY ON YOU!)
SUGI-MOTO, WHAT'RE YOU DOING?
I...
GUGH!
THOK
AHA!
I GET IT!
THOK
I...
?
CALM DOWN, SUGI—
BASH
I...
GET 'EM!
THIS IS YOUR "MASTER PLAN"!

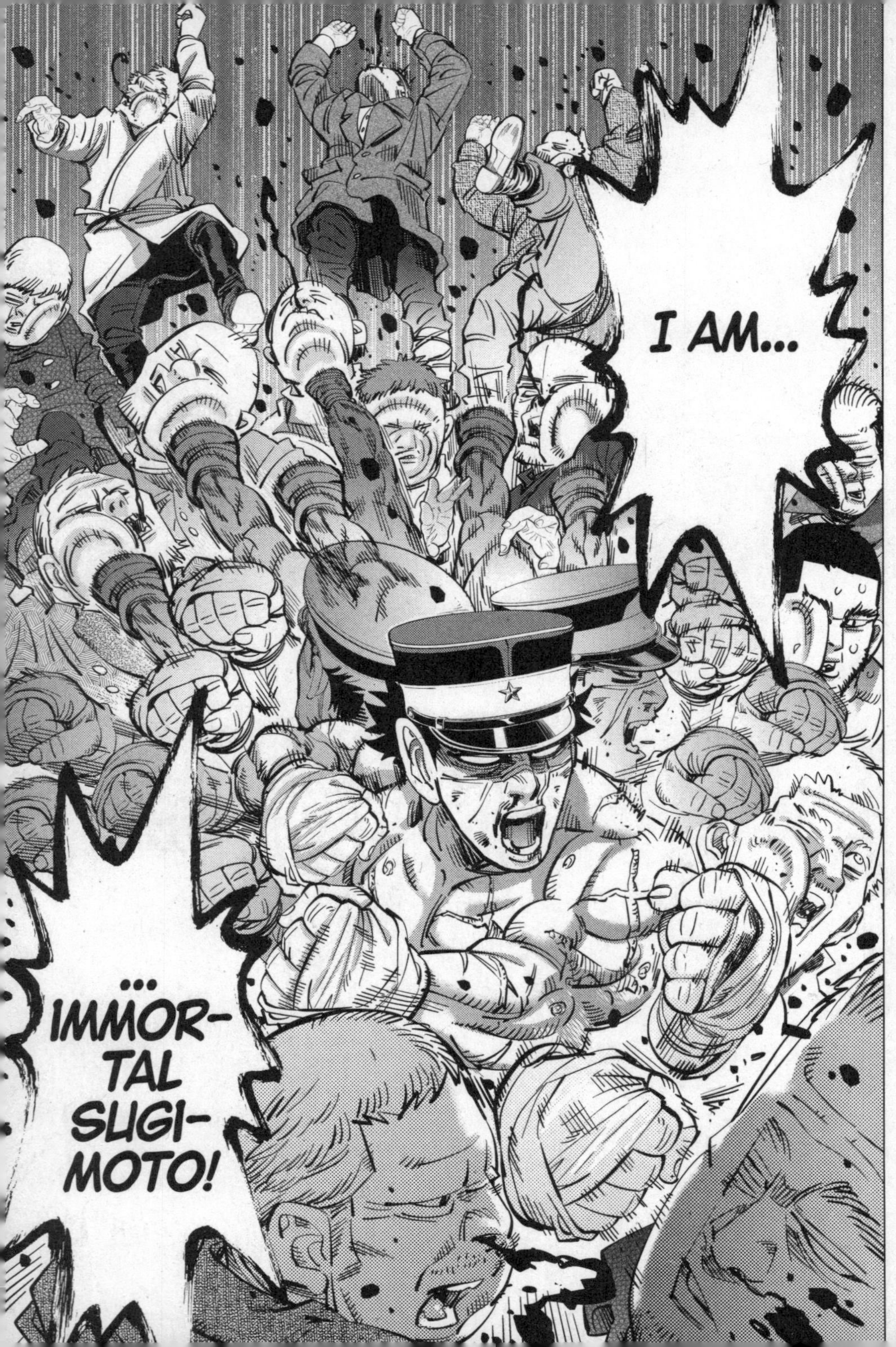
I AM...
...IMMOR-
TAL
SUGI-
MOTO!

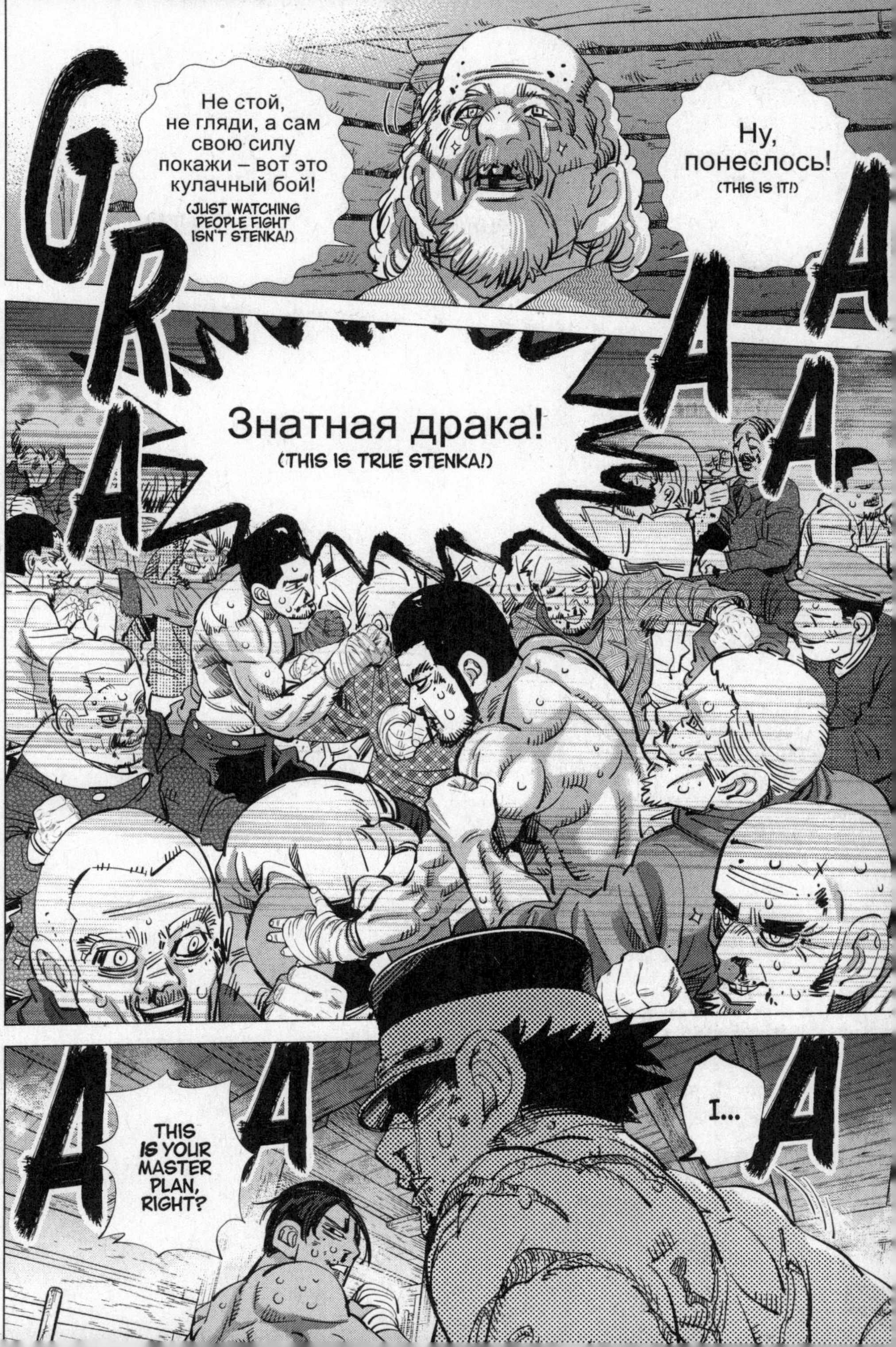
Ну, понеслось!
(THIS IS IT!)
Не стой, не гляди, а сам свою силу покажи – вот это кулачный бой!
(JUST WATCHING PEOPLE FIGHT ISN'T STENKA!)
GRAAAAAAAAA
Знатная драка!
(THIS IS TRUE STENKA!)
I...
THIS IS YOUR MASTER PLAN, RIGHT?

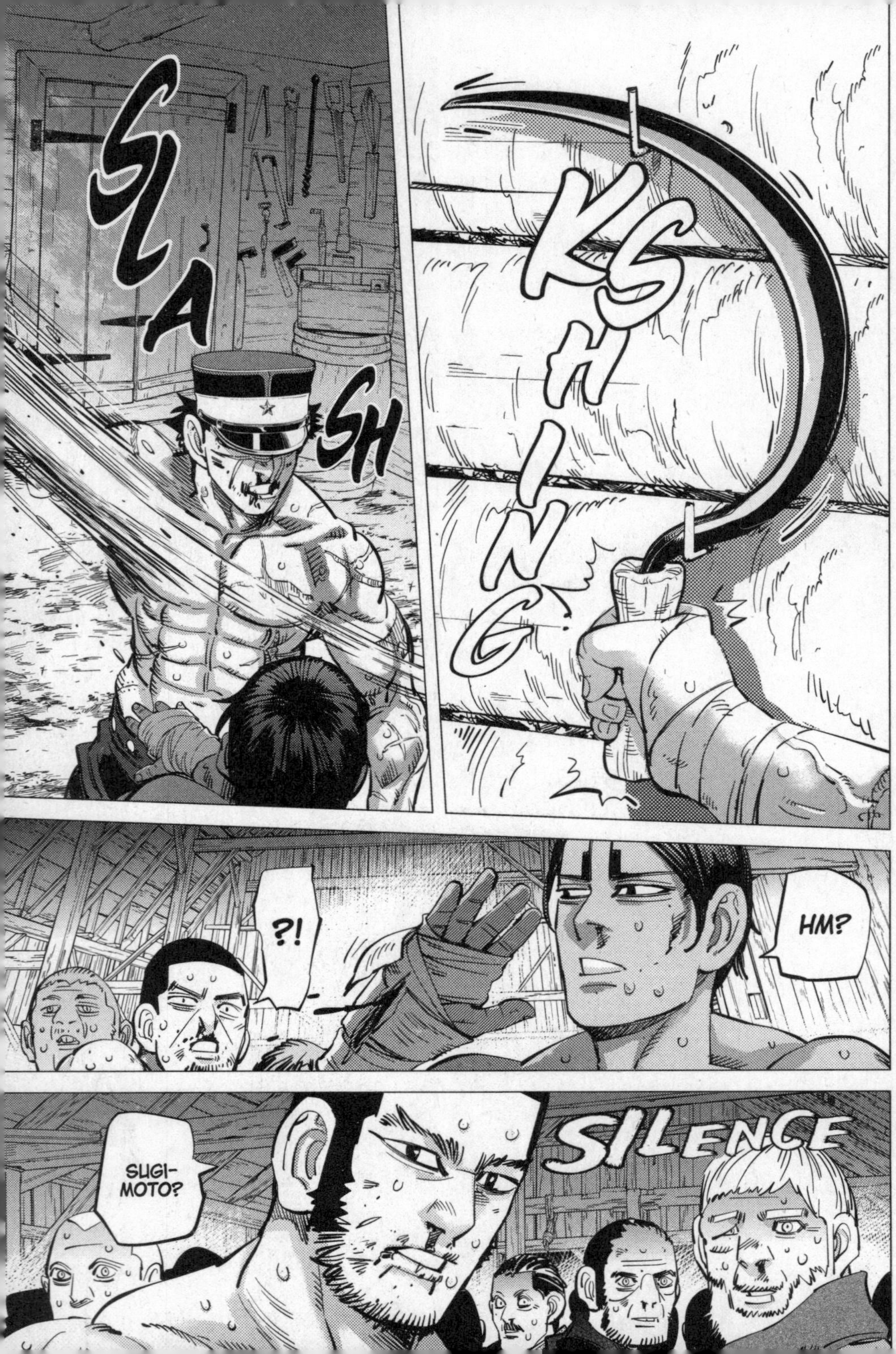
KSHING
SLASH
HM?
?!
SILENCE
SUGI-
MOTO?

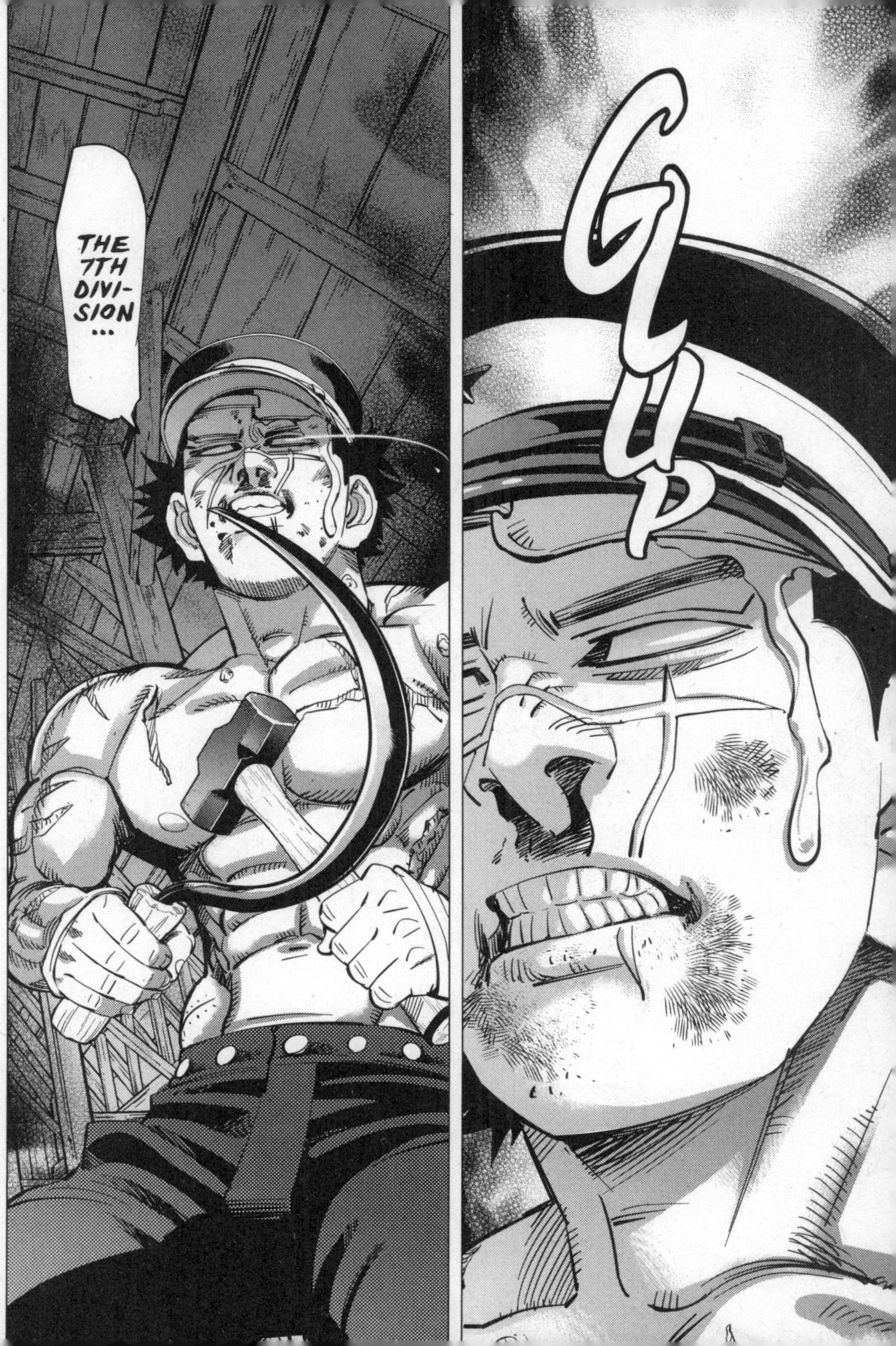
GULP
THE 7TH DIVISION...

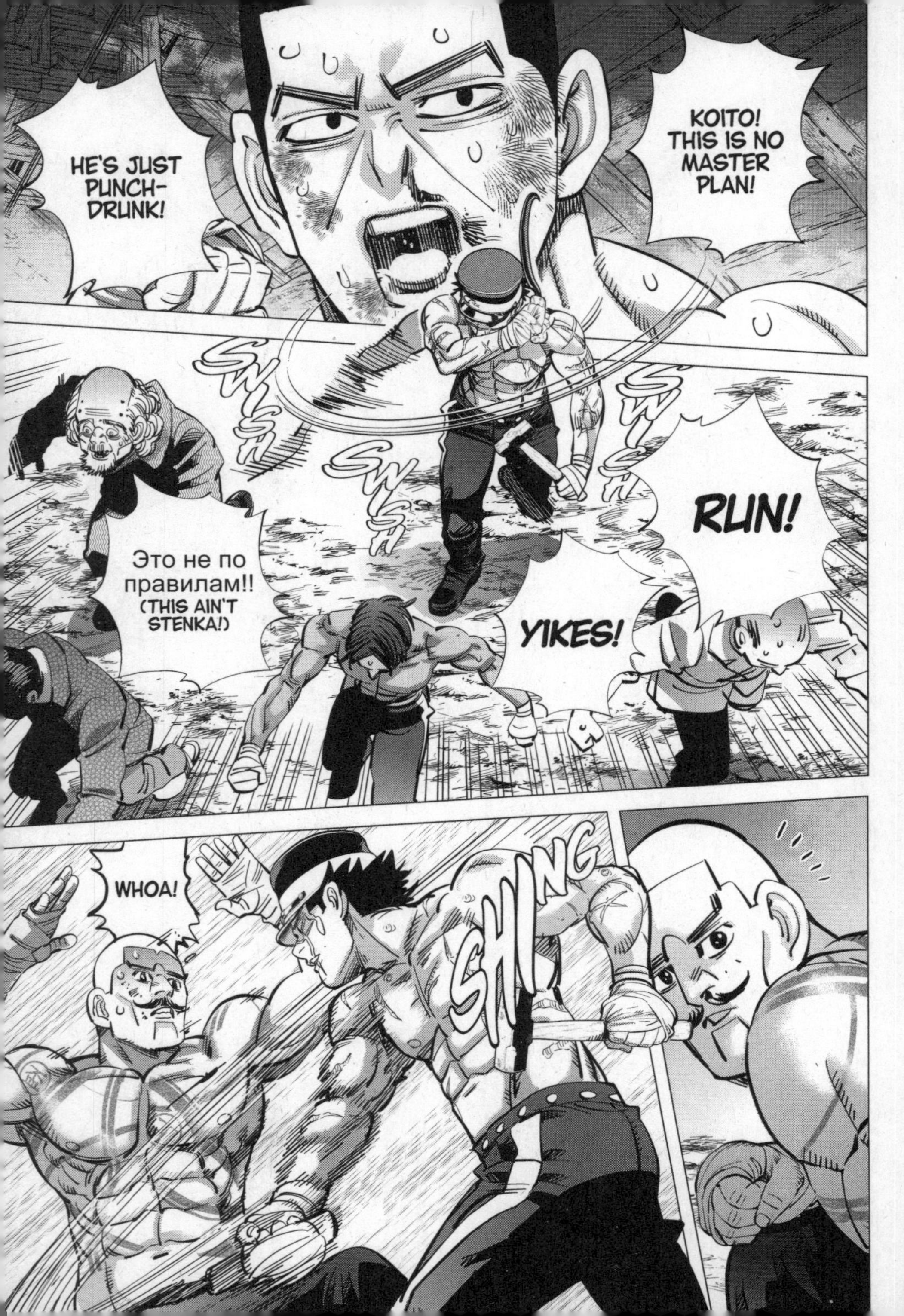
KOITO! THIS IS NO MASTER PLAN!
HE'S JUST PUNCH-DRUNK!
SWISH
RUN!
SWISH
SWISH
YIKES!
Это не по правилам!! (THIS AIN'T STENKA!)
SHING
WHOA!

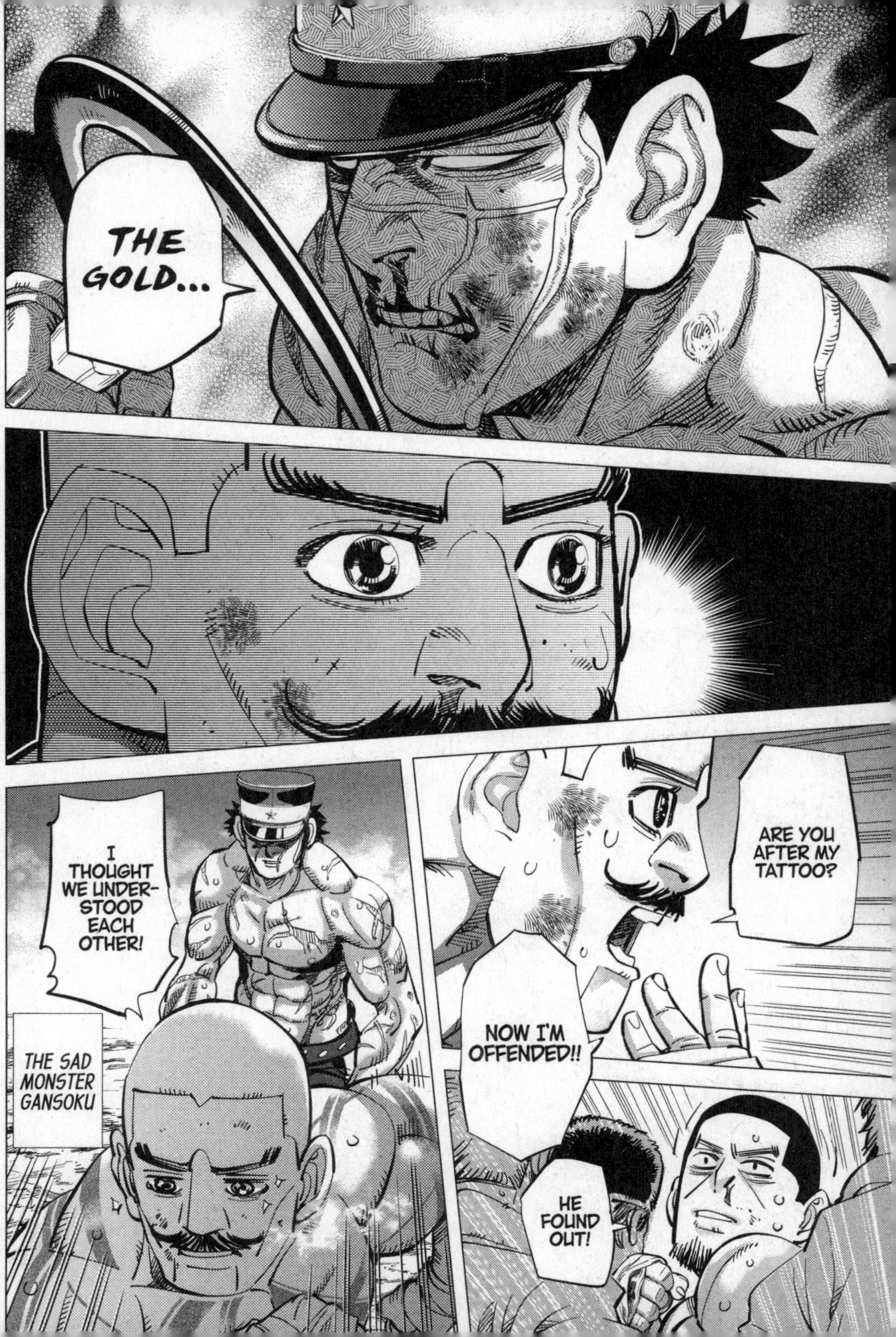
THE GOLD...
ARE YOU AFTER MY TATTOO?
NOW I'M OFFENDED!!
HE FOUND OUT!
I THOUGHT WE UNDER-STOOD EACH OTHER!
THE SAD MONSTER GANSOKU

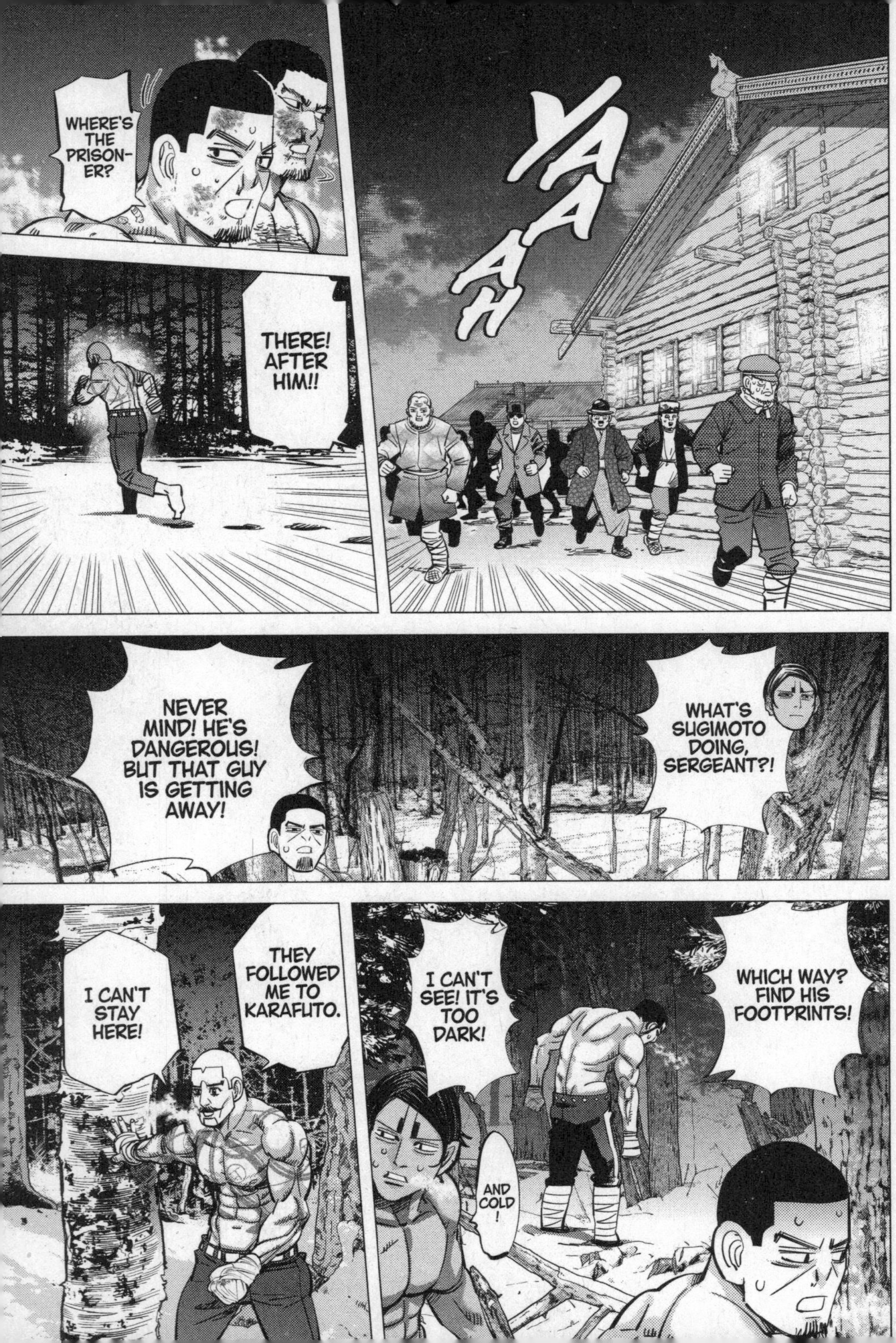
YAAAAH
WHERE'S THE PRISONER?
THERE! AFTER HIM!!
WHAT'S SUGIMOTO DOING, SERGEANT?!
NEVER MIND! HE'S DANGEROUS! BUT THAT GUY IS GETTING AWAY!
WHICH WAY? FIND HIS FOOTPRINTS!
I CAN'T SEE! IT'S TOO DARK!
AND COLD!
THEY FOLLOWED ME TO KARAFUTO.
I CAN'T STAY HERE!

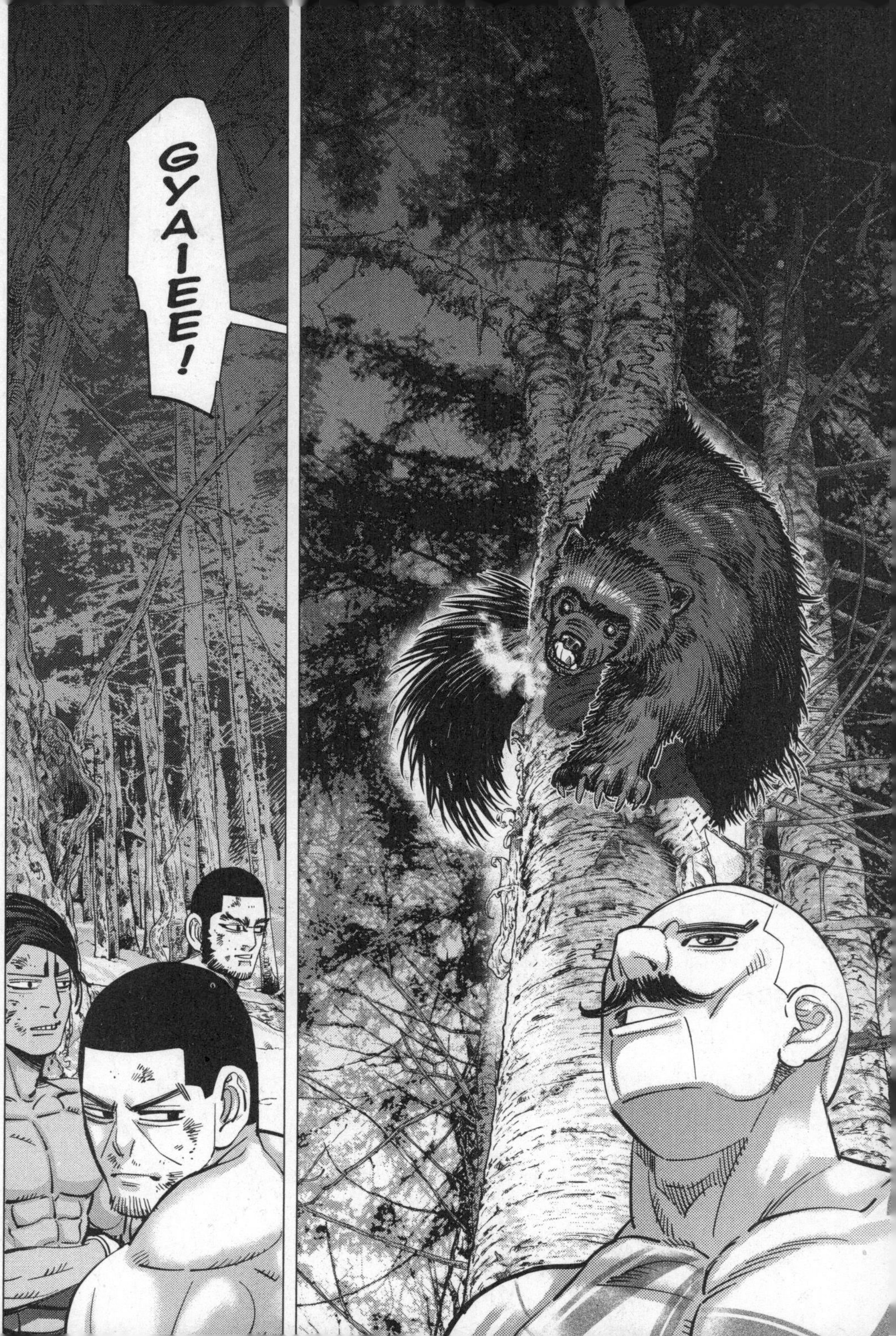
GYAIEE!

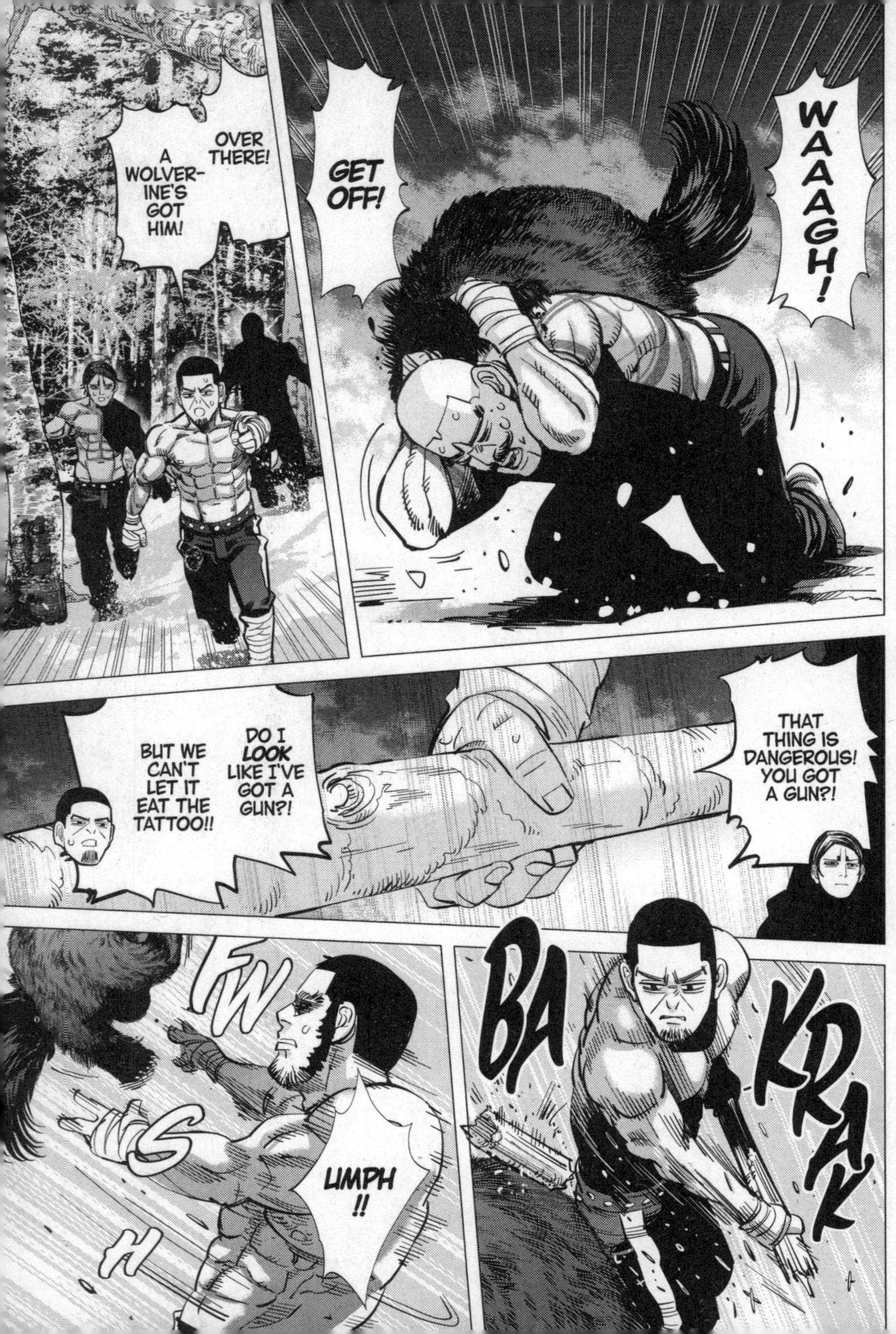
WAAAGH!
GET OFF!
OVER THERE!
A WOLVERINE'S GOT HIM!
THAT THING IS DANGEROUS! YOU GOT A GUN?!
DO I **LOOK** LIKE I'VE GOT A GUN?!
BUT WE CAN'T LET IT EAT THE TATTOO!!
BA
KRAK
FW
S
H
UMPH !!

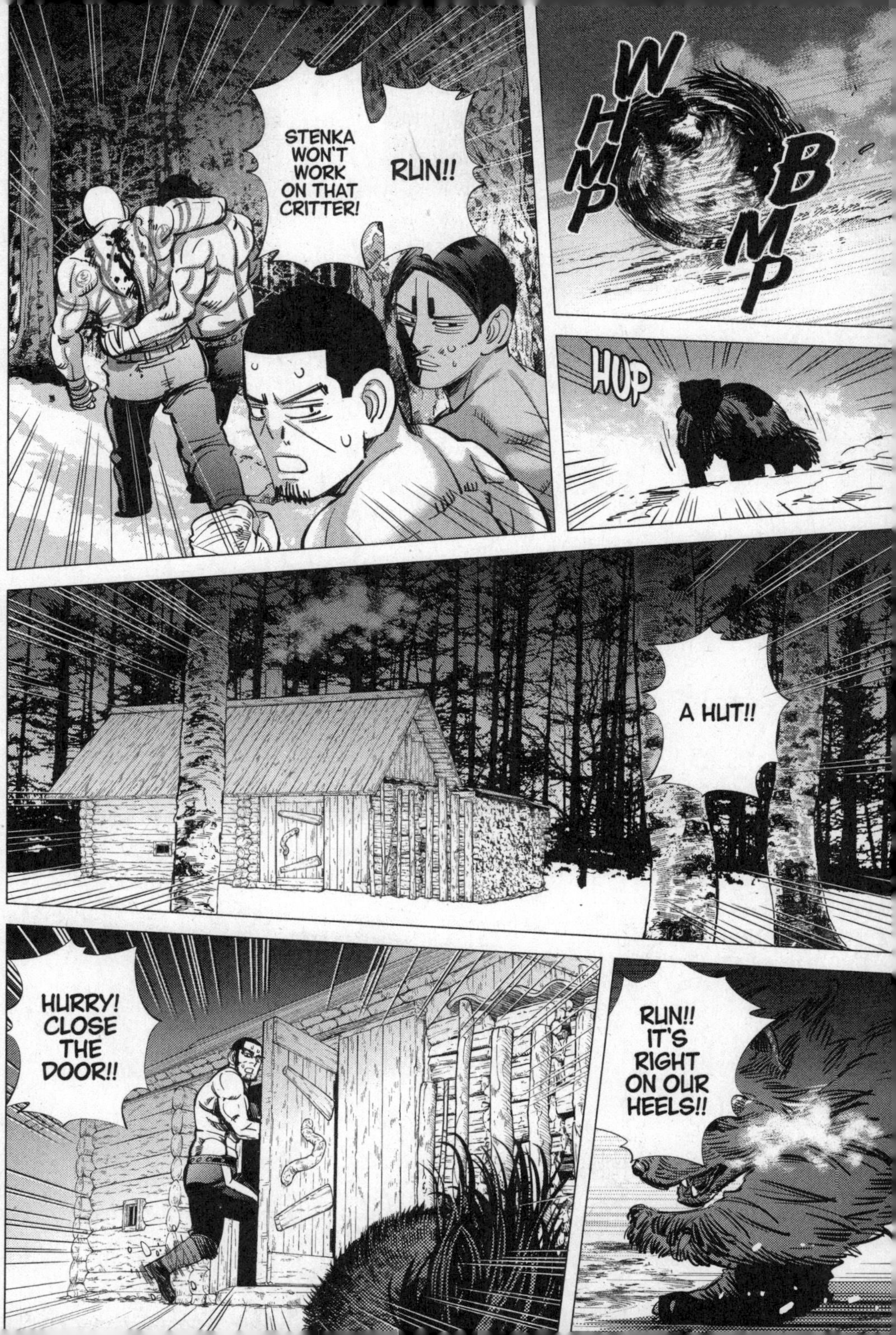
WHMP
BMP
HUP
RUN!!
STENKA WON'T WORK ON THAT CRITTER!
A HUT!!
RUN!! IT'S RIGHT ON OUR HEELS!!
HURRY! CLOSE THE DOOR!!

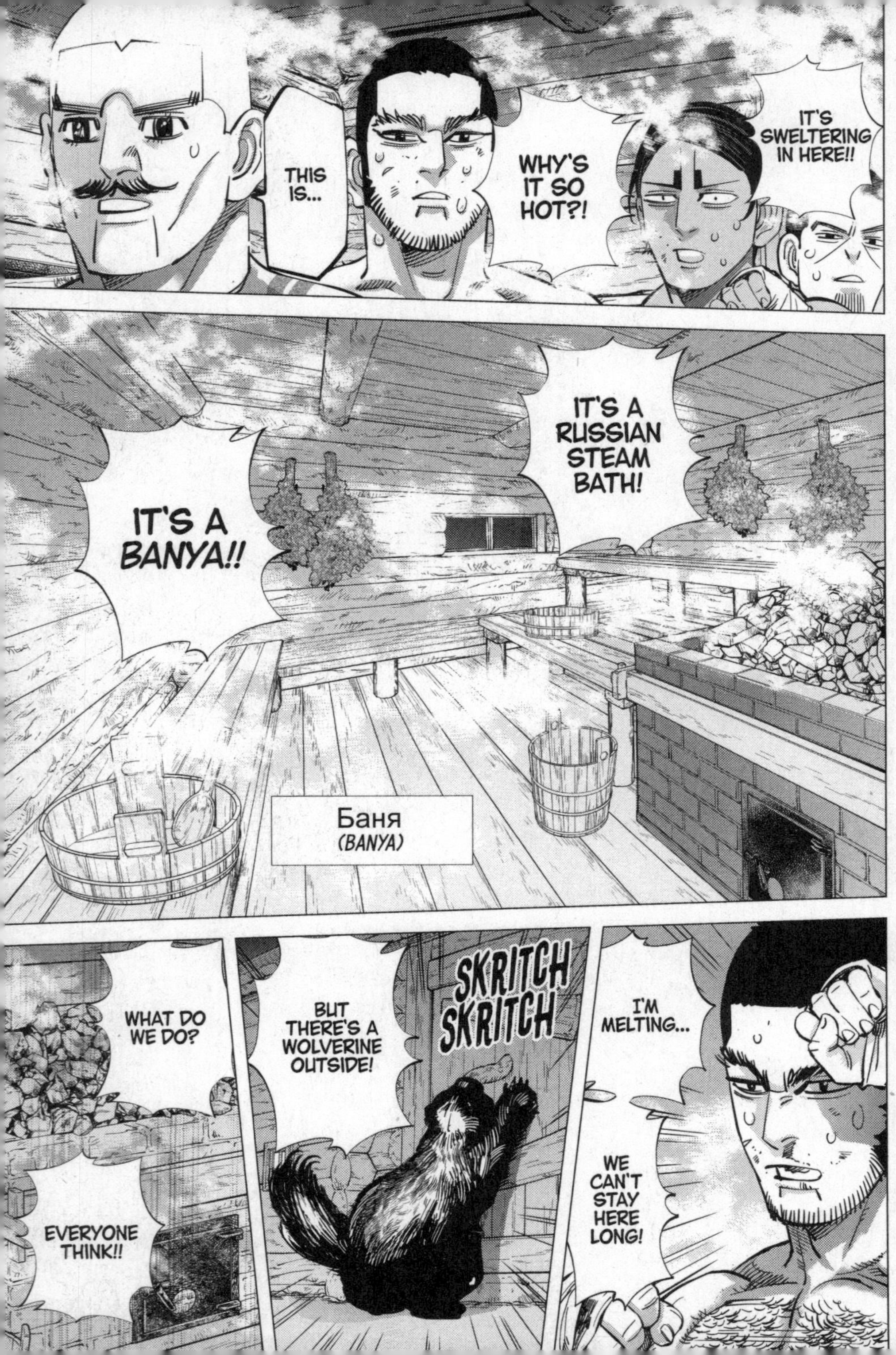
IT'S SWELTERING IN HERE!!
WHY'S IT SO HOT?!
THIS IS...
IT'S A RUSSIAN STEAM BATH!
IT'S A BANYA!!
Баня
(BANYA)
I'M MELTING...
WE CAN'T STAY HERE LONG!
SKRITCH SKRITCH
BUT THERE'S A WOLVERINE OUTSIDE!
WHAT DO WE DO?
EVERYONE THINK!!

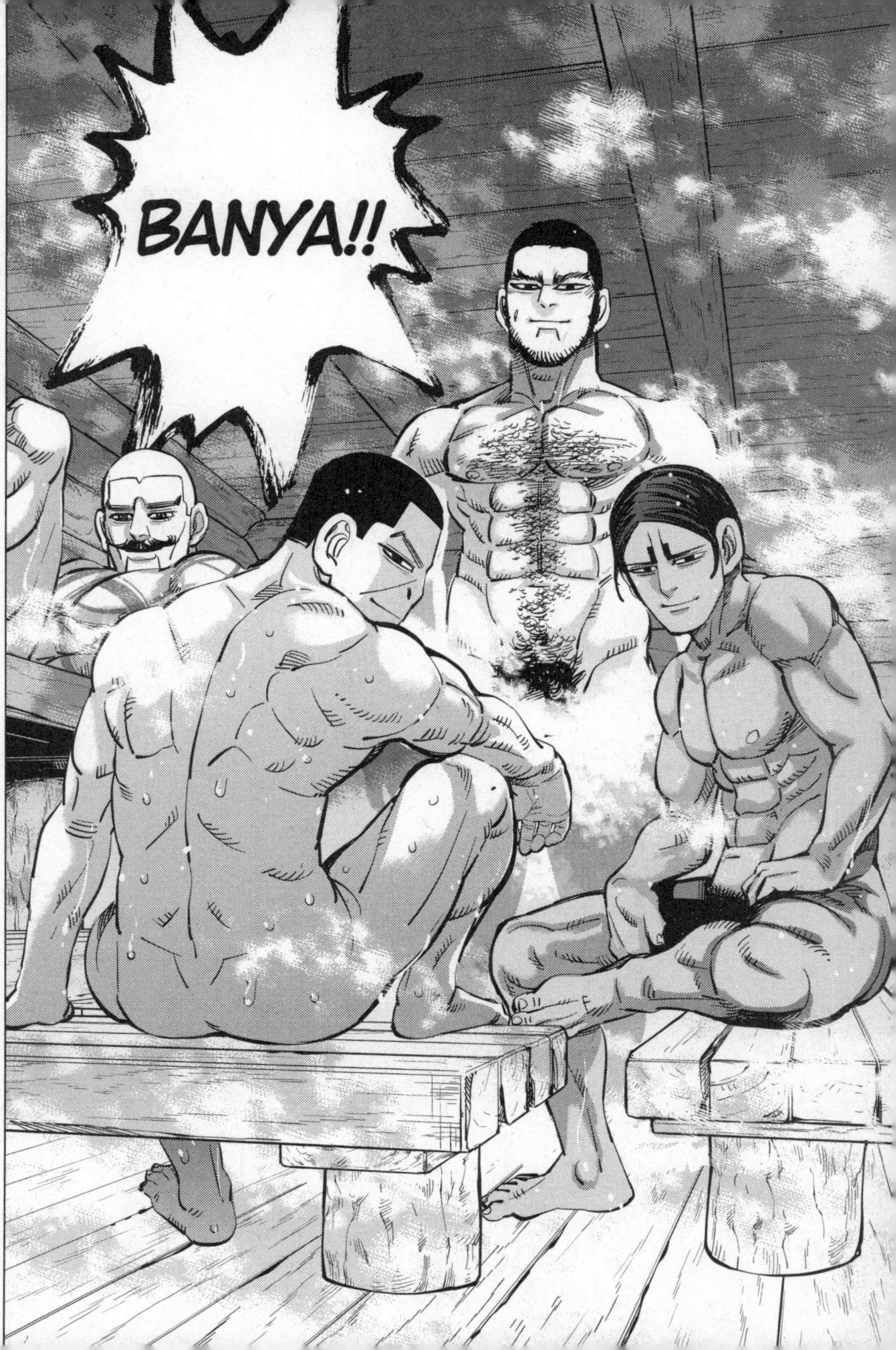
BANYA!!

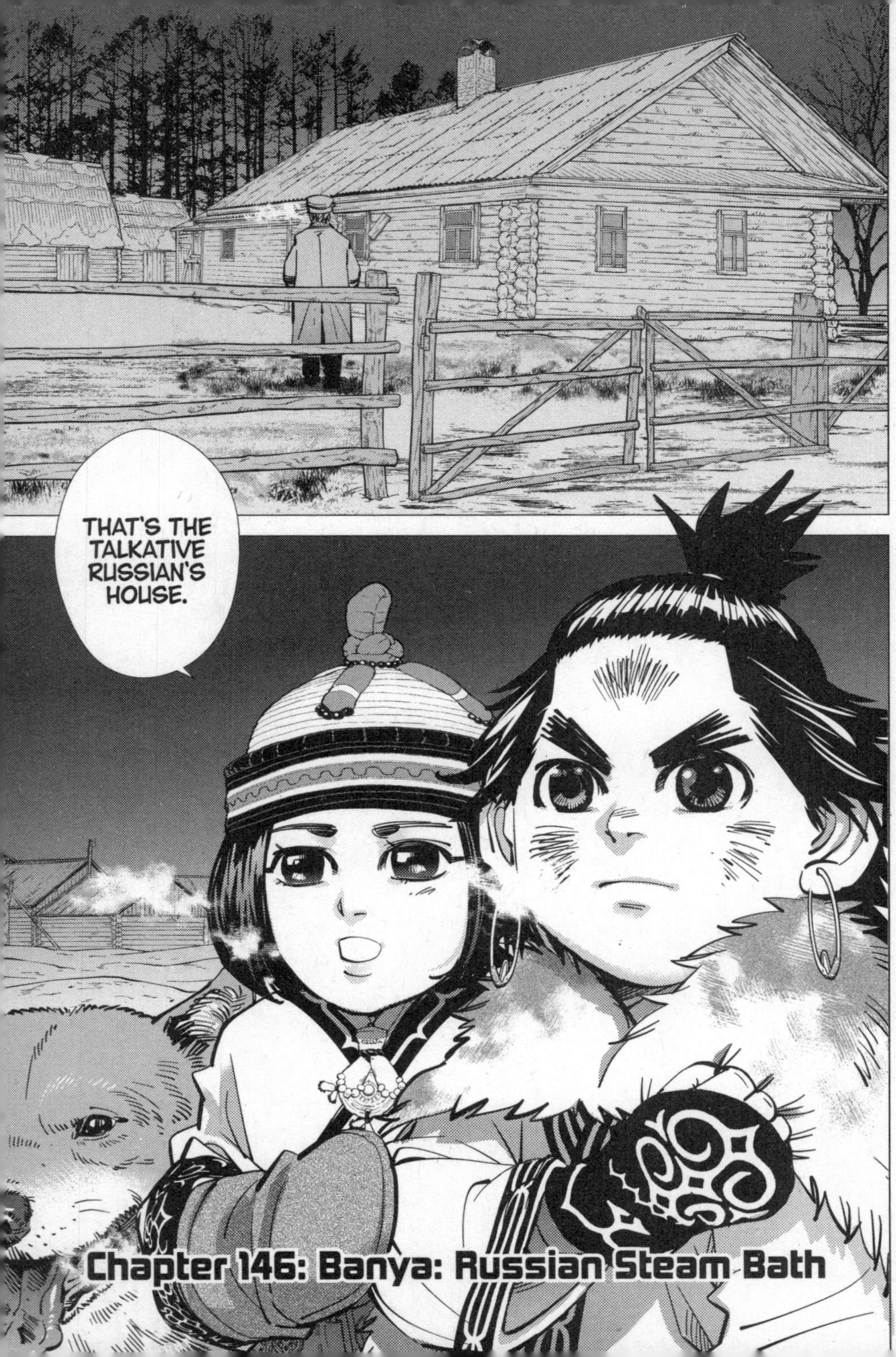
THAT'S THE TALKATIVE RUSSIAN'S HOUSE.
Chapter 146: Banya: Russian Steam Bath

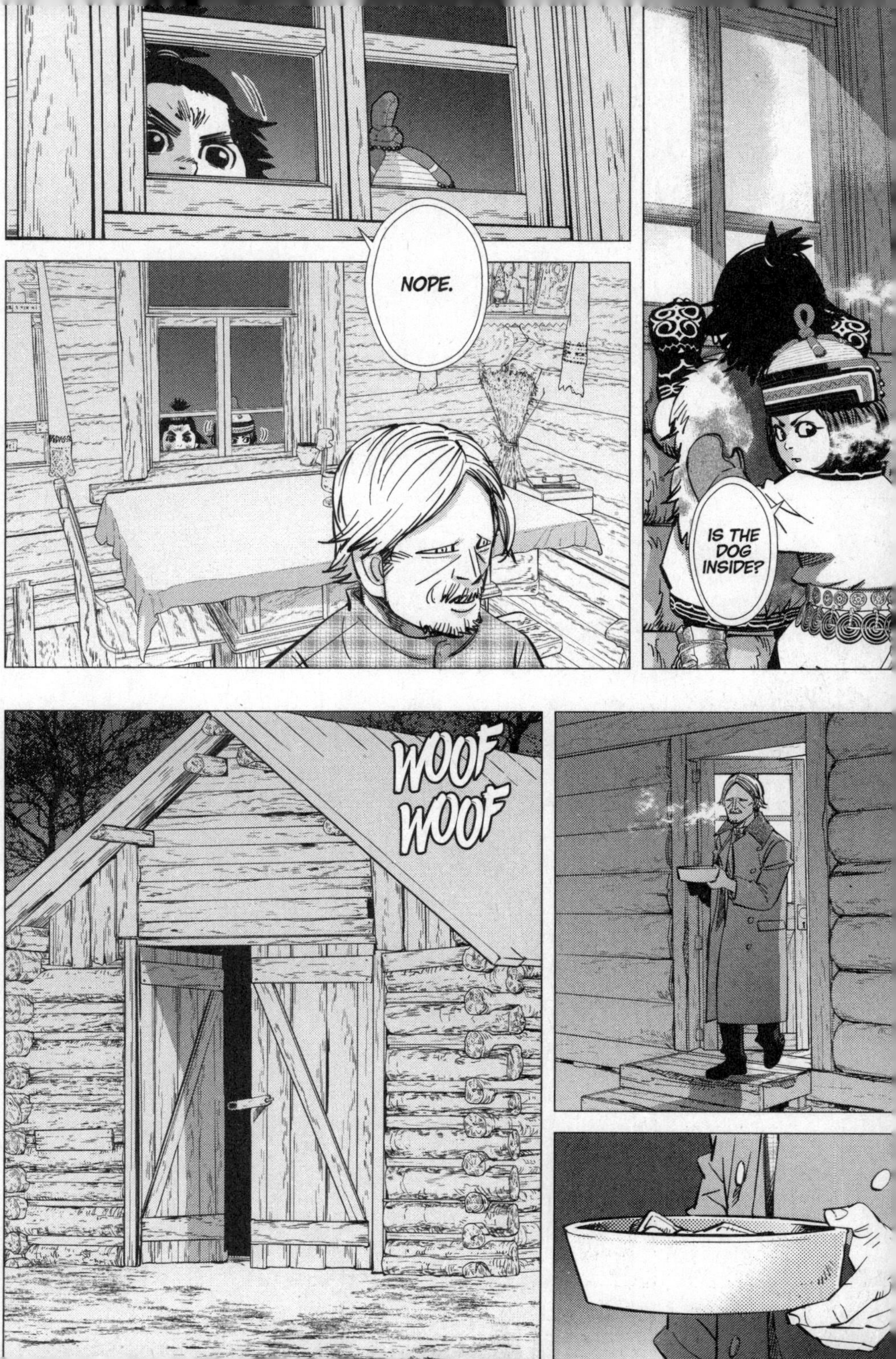
IS THE DOG INSIDE?
NOPE.
WOOF WOOF

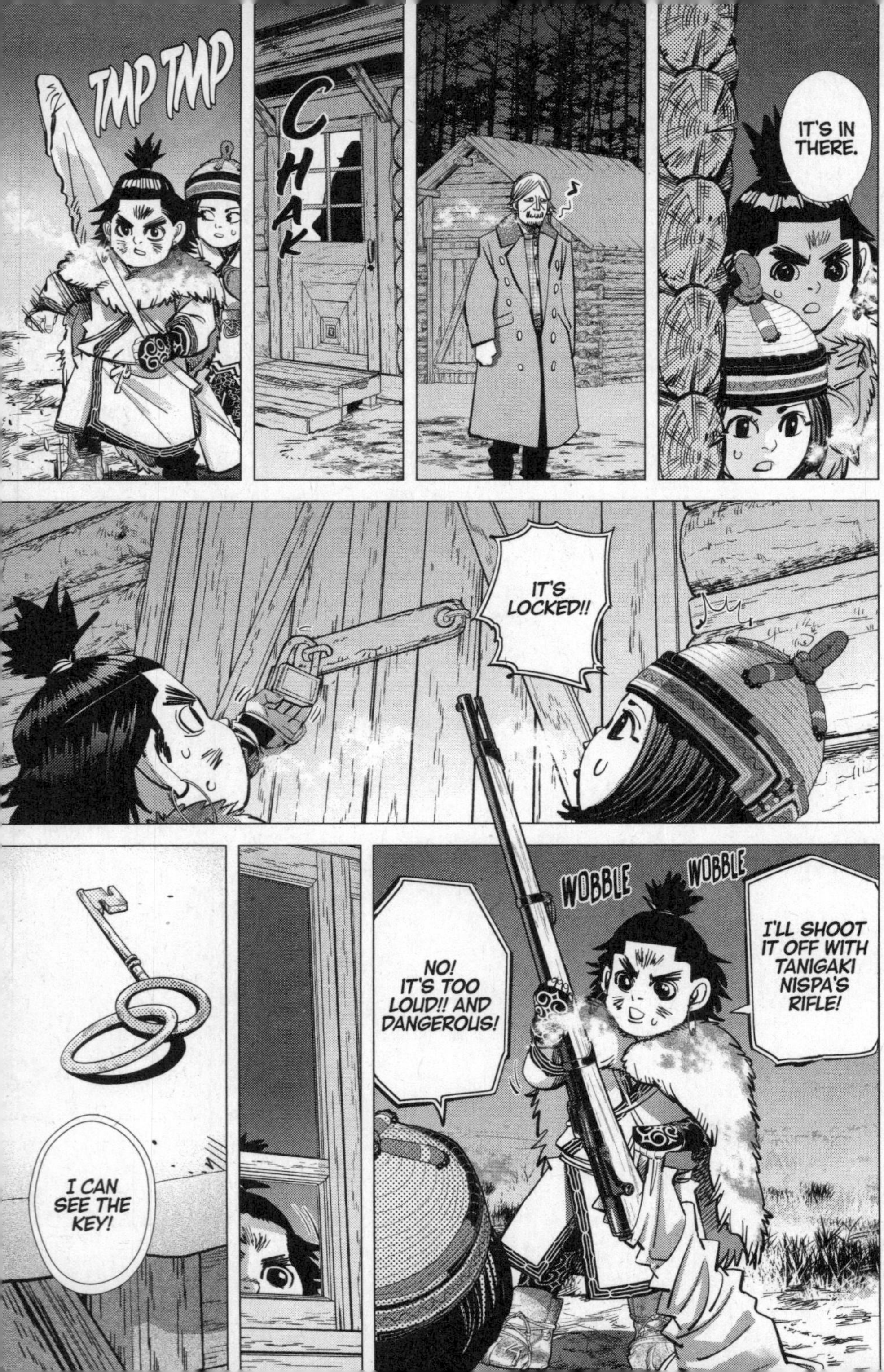
IT'S IN THERE.
CHAK
TMP TMP
IT'S LOCKED!!
WOBBLE WOBBLE
I'LL SHOOT IT OFF WITH TANIGAKI NISPA'S RIFLE!
NO! IT'S TOO LOUD!! AND DANGEROUS!
I CAN SEE THE KEY!

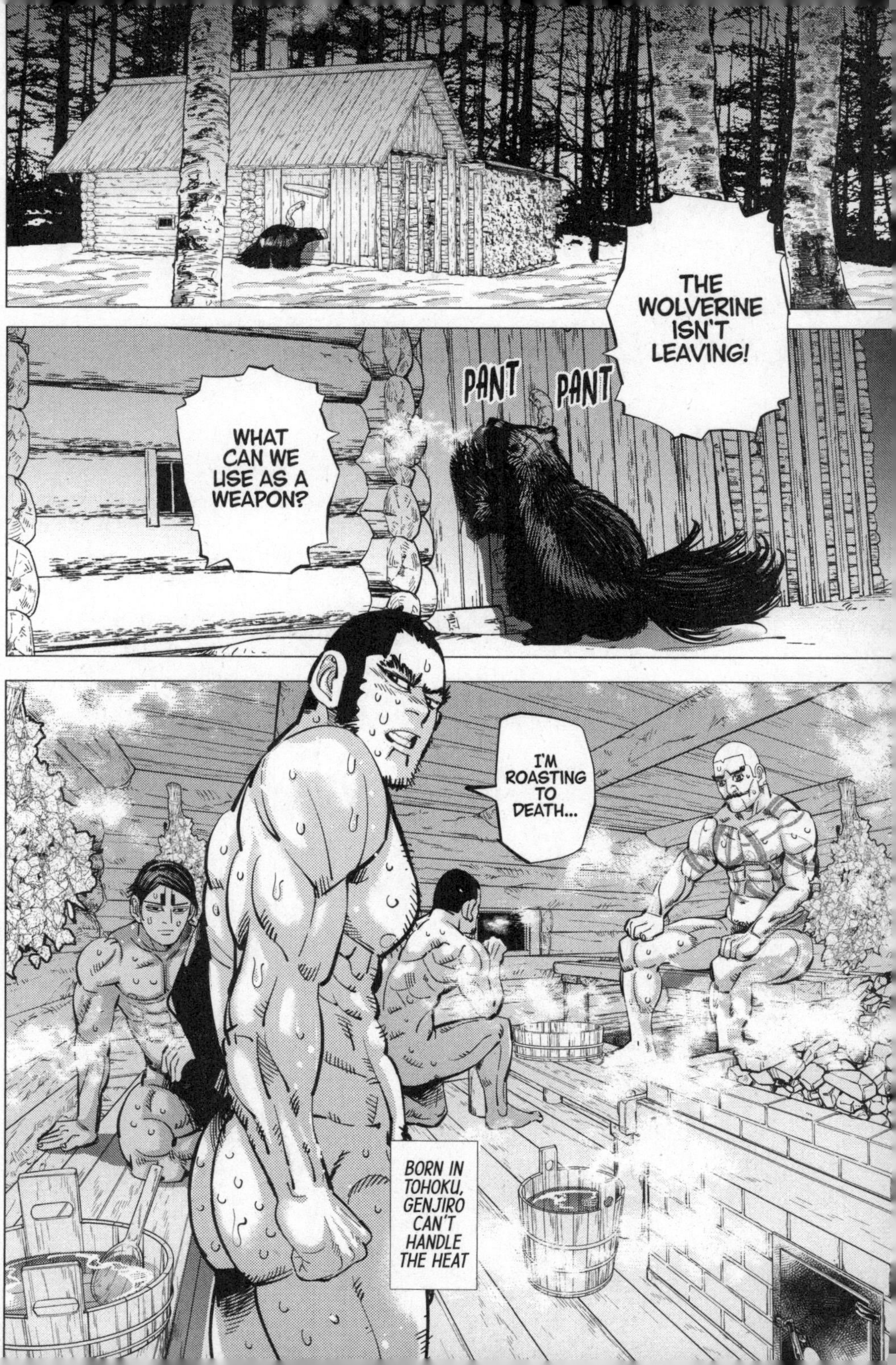
THE WOLVERINE ISN'T LEAVING!
PANT PANT
WHAT CAN WE USE AS A WEAPON?
I'M ROASTING TO DEATH...
BORN IN TOHOKU, GENJIRO CAN'T HANDLE THE HEAT

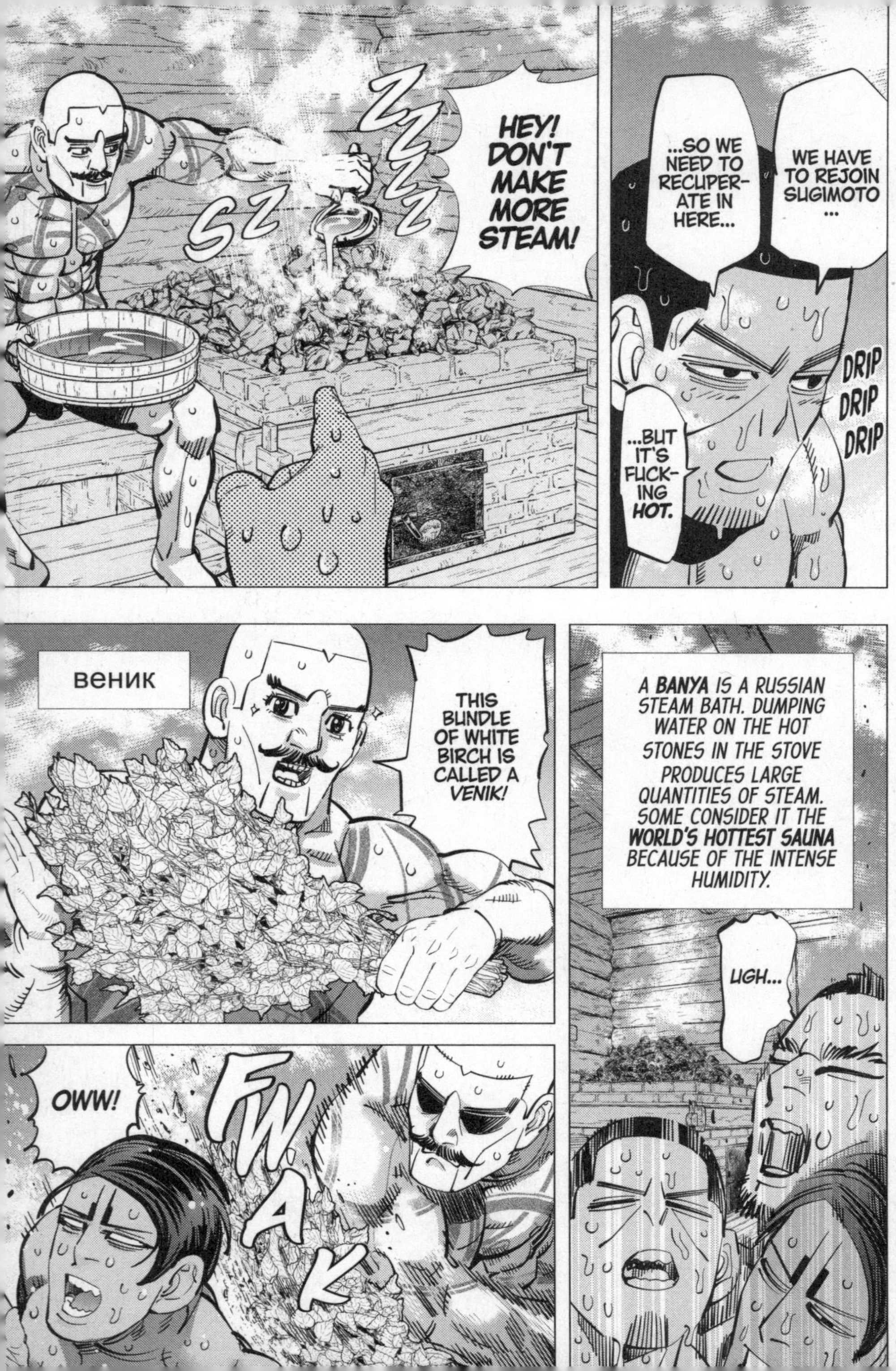
WE HAVE TO REJOIN SUGIMOTO ...
...SO WE NEED TO RECUPER-ATE IN HERE...
...BUT IT'S FUCKING HOT.
DRIP DRIP DRIP
HEY! DON'T MAKE MORE STEAM!
SZZ
ZZZZ
A BANYA IS A RUSSIAN STEAM BATH. DUMPING WATER ON THE HOT STONES IN THE STOVE PRODUCES LARGE QUANTITIES OF STEAM. SOME CONSIDER IT THE WORLD'S HOTTEST SAUNA BECAUSE OF THE INTENSE HUMIDITY.
UGH...
веник
THIS BUNDLE OF WHITE BIRCH IS CALLED A VENIK!
FWAK
OWW!

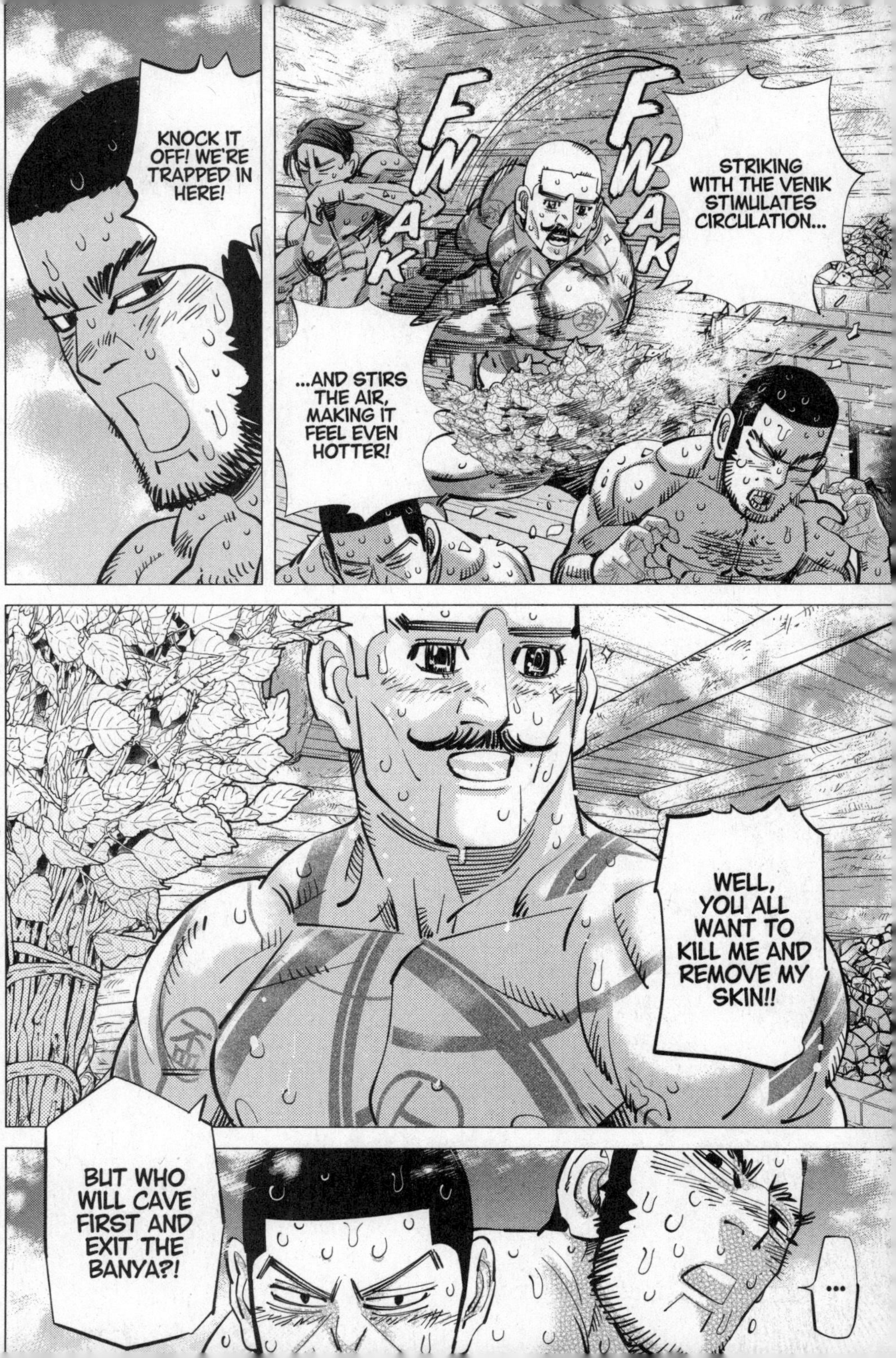
FWAK
STRIKING WITH THE VENIK STIMULATES CIRCULATION...
FWAK
...AND STIRS THE AIR, MAKING IT FEEL EVEN HOTTER!
KNOCK IT OFF! WE'RE TRAPPED IN HERE!
WELL, YOU ALL WANT TO KILL ME AND REMOVE MY SKIN!!
...
BUT WHO WILL CAVE FIRST AND EXIT THE BANYA?!

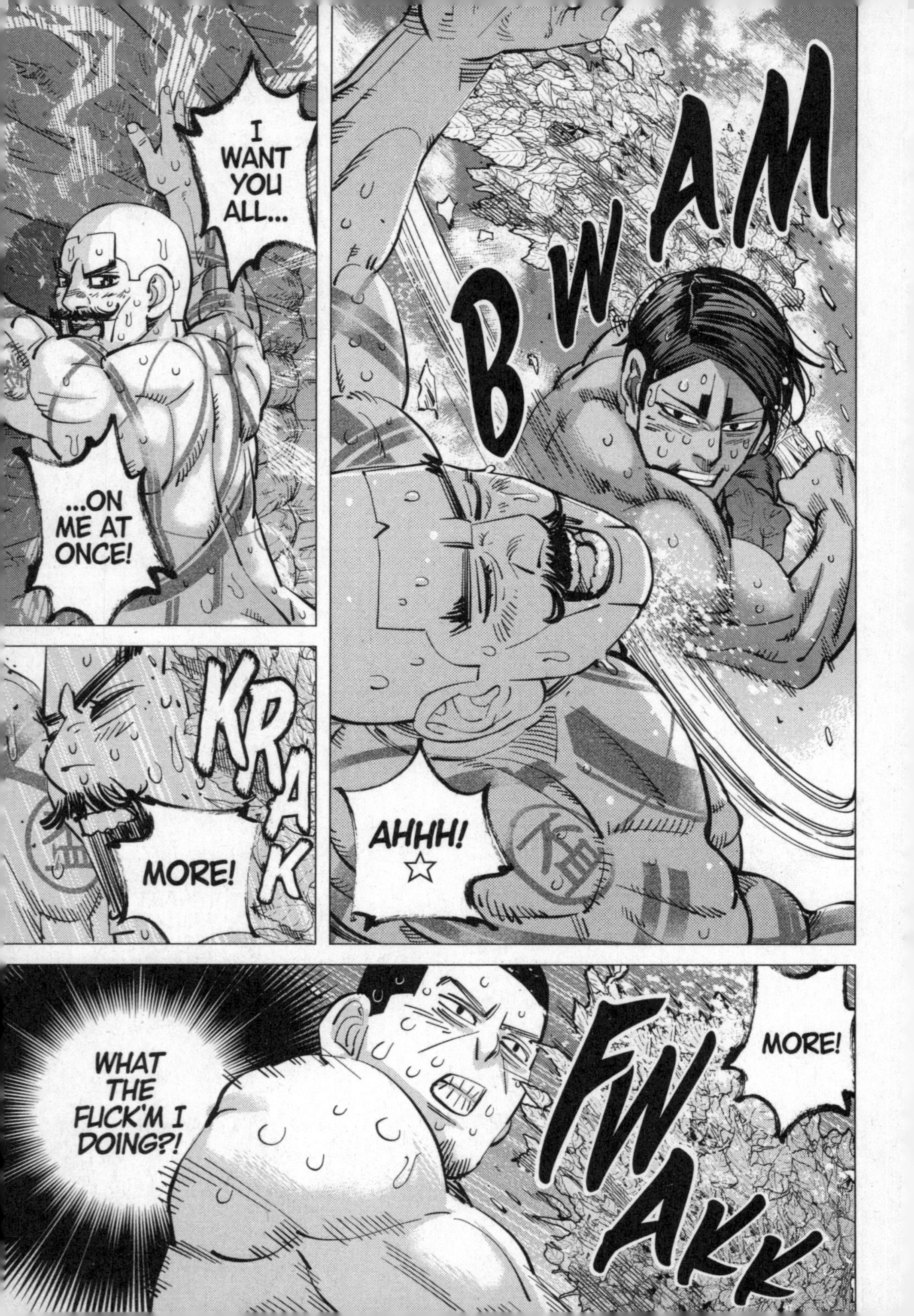
BWAM
AHHH! ☆
I WANT YOU ALL...
...ON ME AT ONCE!
KRAK
MORE!
MORE!
FWAKK
WHAT THE FUCK'M I DOING?!

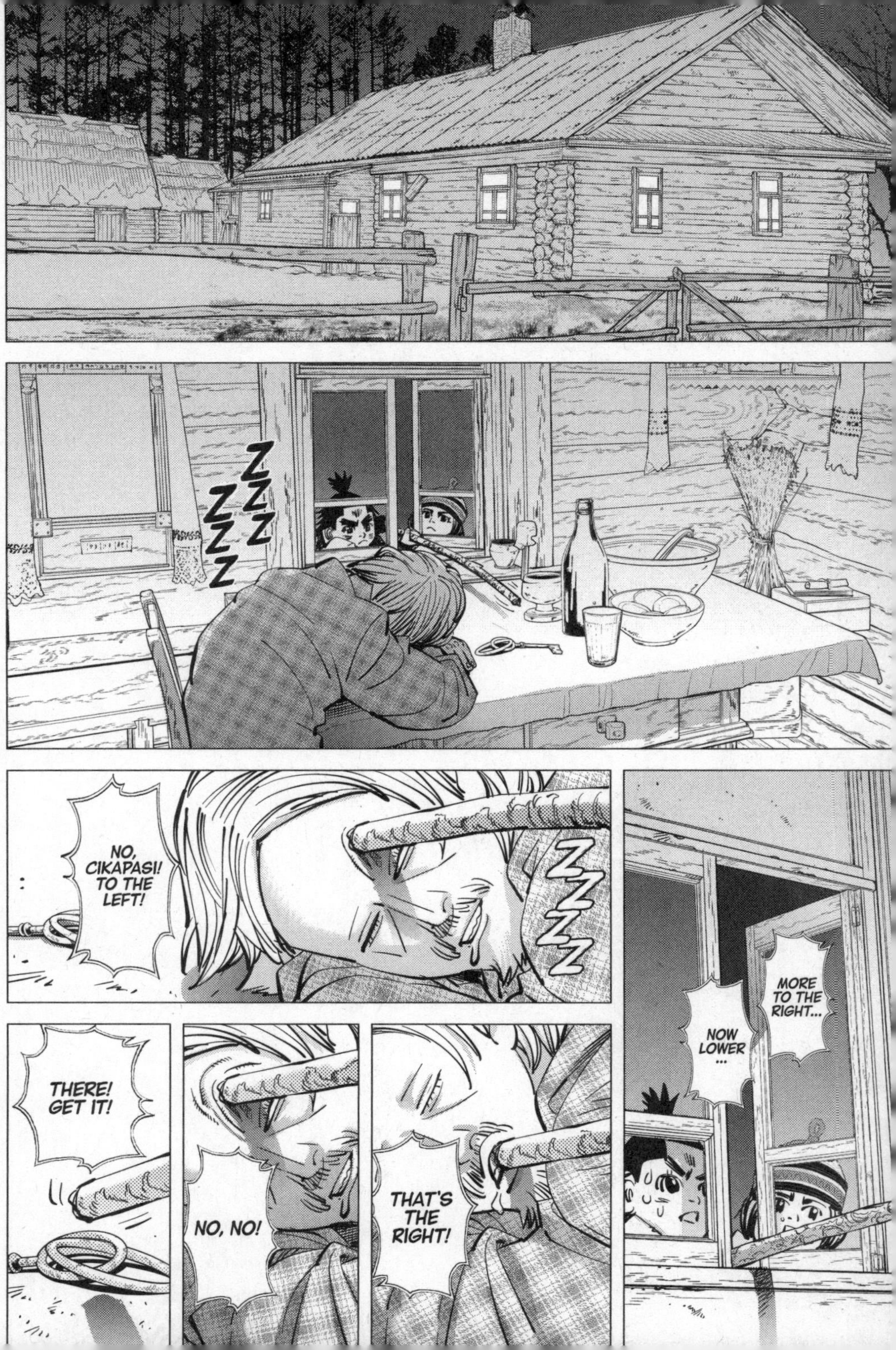
ZZZZZZ
MORE TO THE RIGHT...
NOW LOWER...
NO, CIKAPASI! TO THE LEFT!
ZZZZZ
THAT'S THE RIGHT!
NO, NO!
THERE! GET IT!

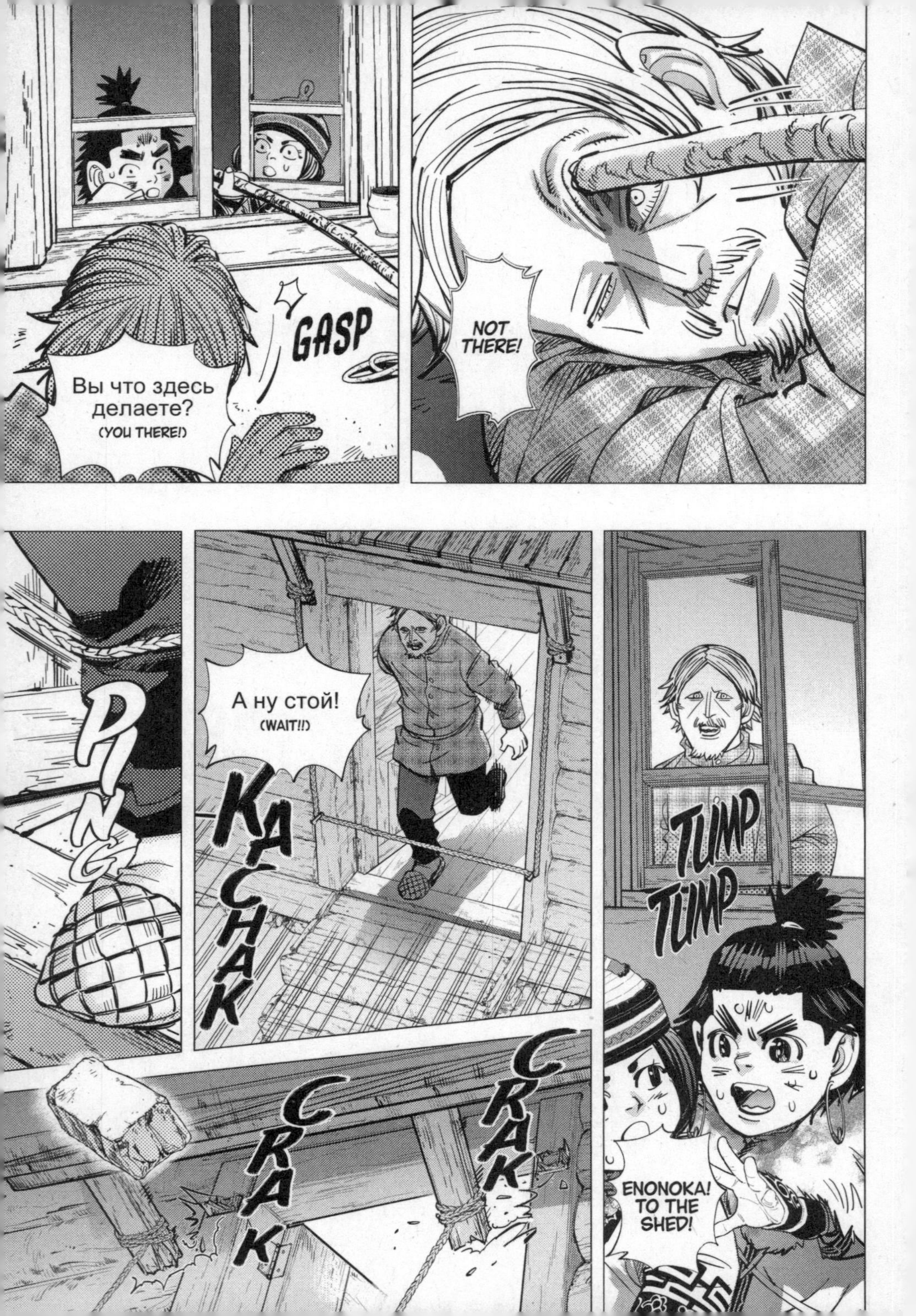
NOT THERE!
GASP
Вы что здесь делаете?
(YOU THERE!)
TUMP TUMP
ENONOKA! TO THE SHED!
А ну стой!
(WAIT!!)
KACHAK
PING
CRAK CRAK CRAK

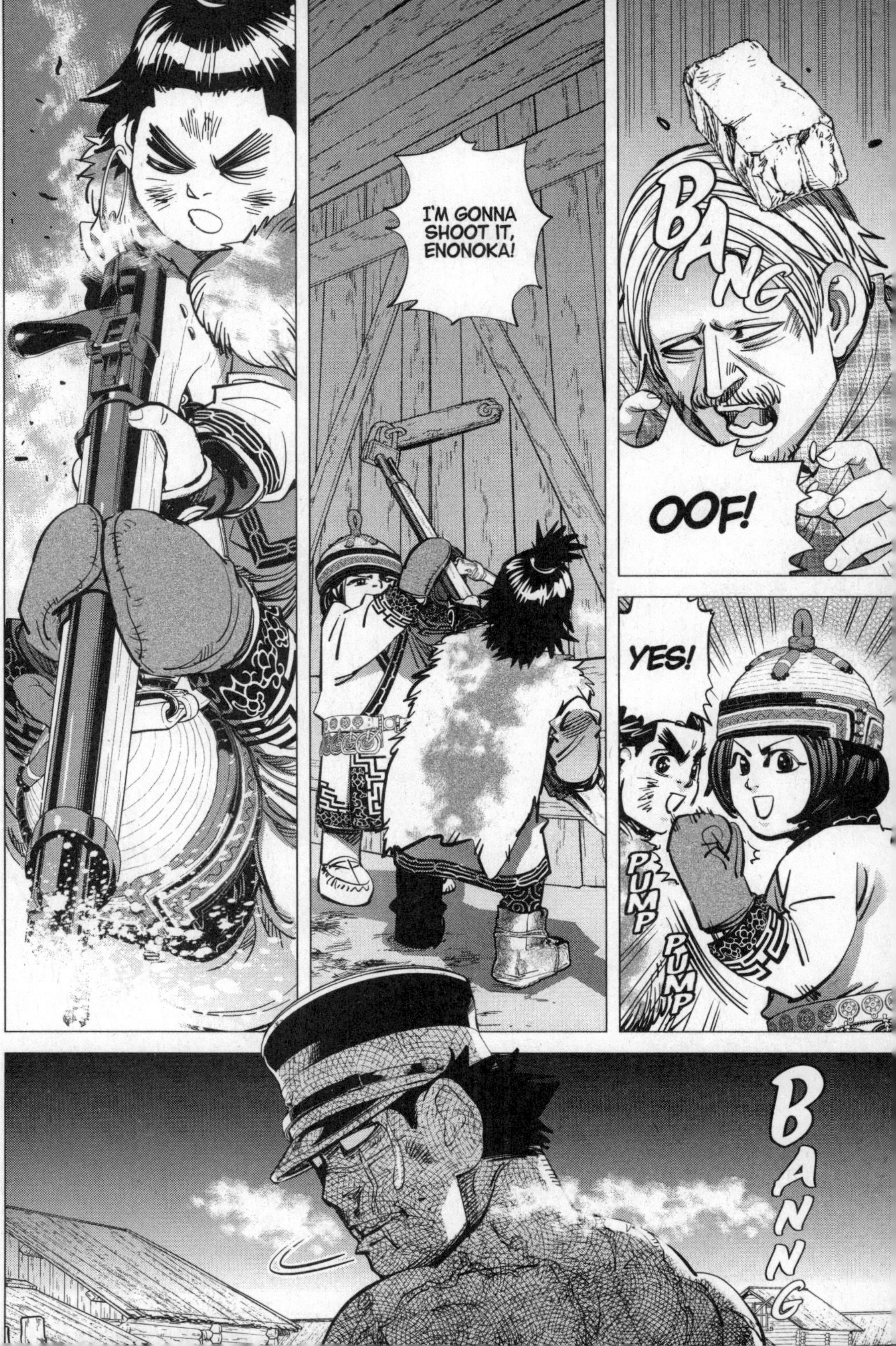
BANG
OOF!
YES!
PUMP PUMP
I'M GONNA SHOOT IT, ENONOKA!
BANNG

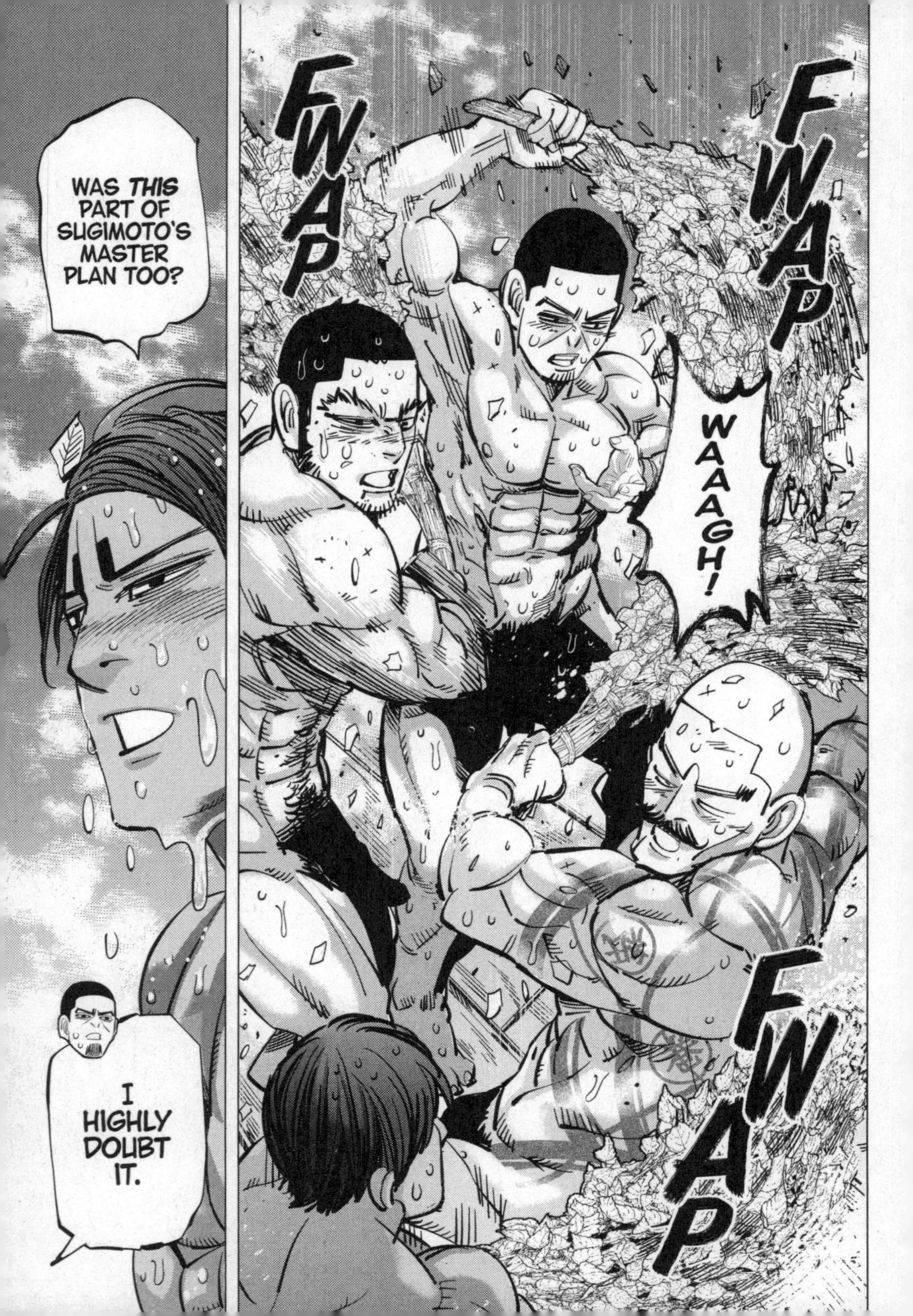
FWAP
FWAP
WAAAGH!
FWAP
WAS THIS PART OF SUGIMOTO'S MASTER PLAN TOO?
I HIGHLY DOUBT IT.

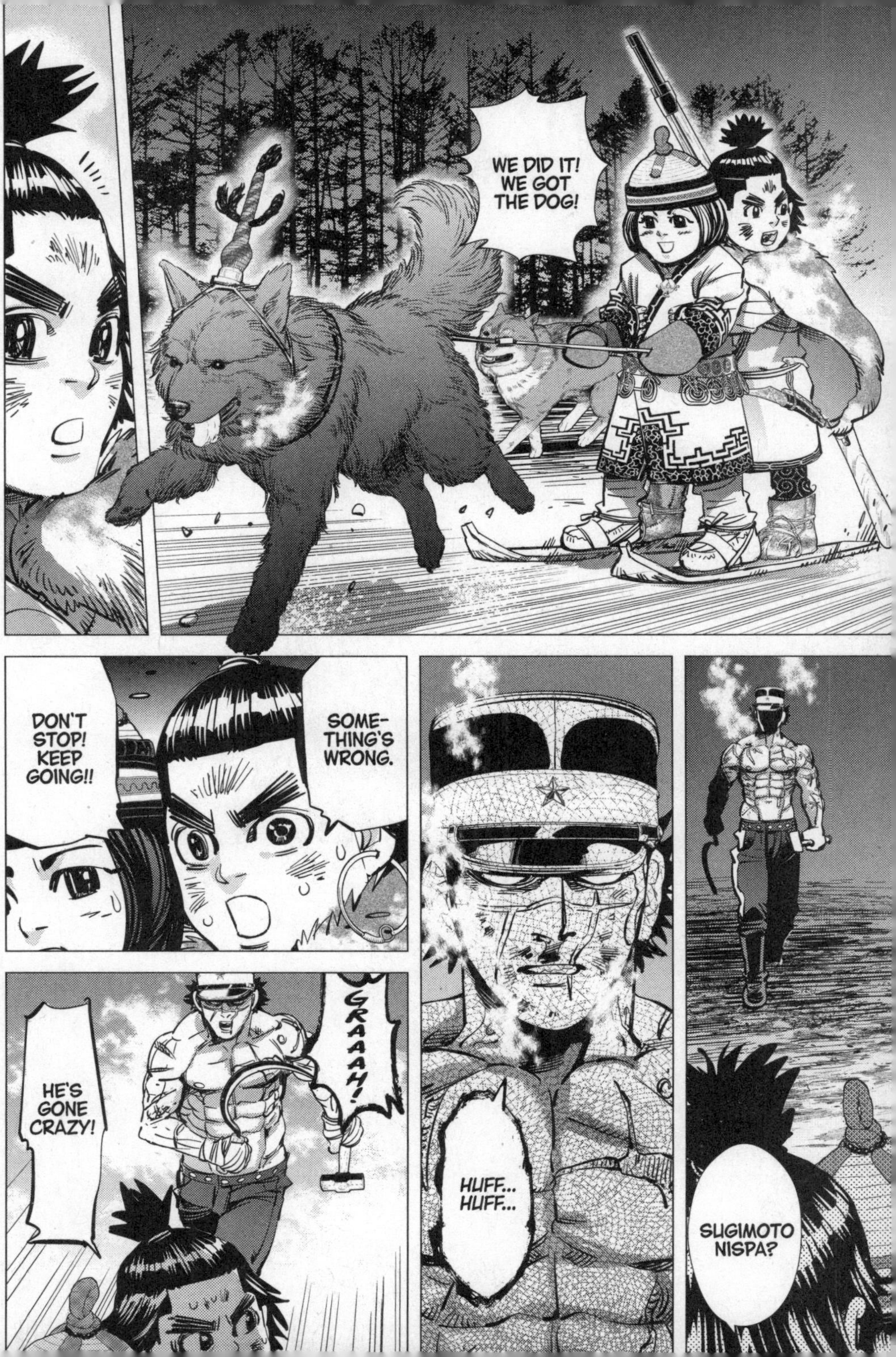
WE DID IT! WE GOT THE DOG!
SUGIMOTO NISPA?
HUFF... HUFF...
SOME-THING'S WRONG.
DON'T STOP! KEEP GOING!!
GRAAAAH!
HE'S GONE CRAZY!

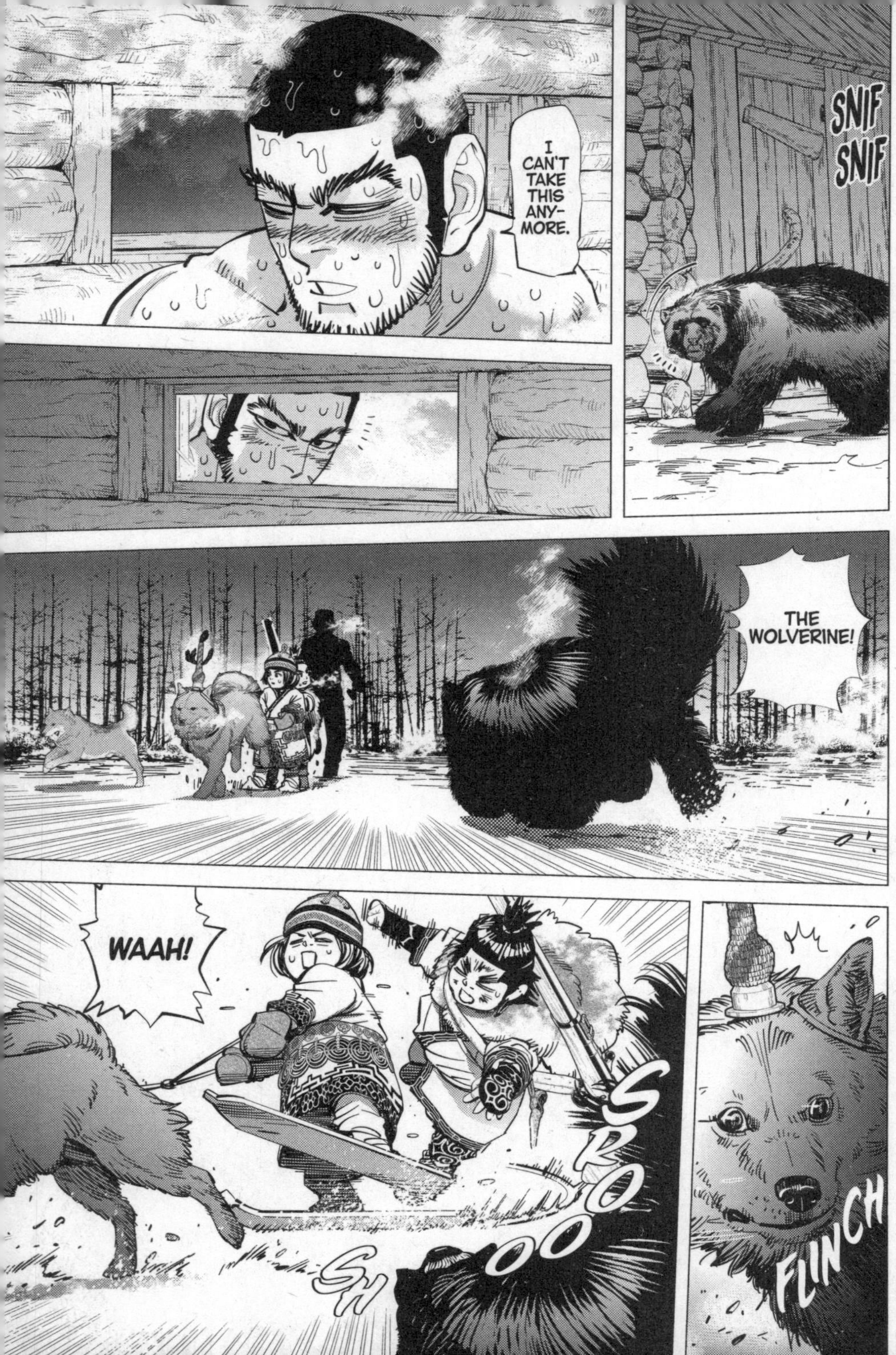
SNIF SNIF
I CAN'T TAKE THIS ANYMORE.
THE WOLVERINE!
FLINCH
WAAH!
SROOOOSH

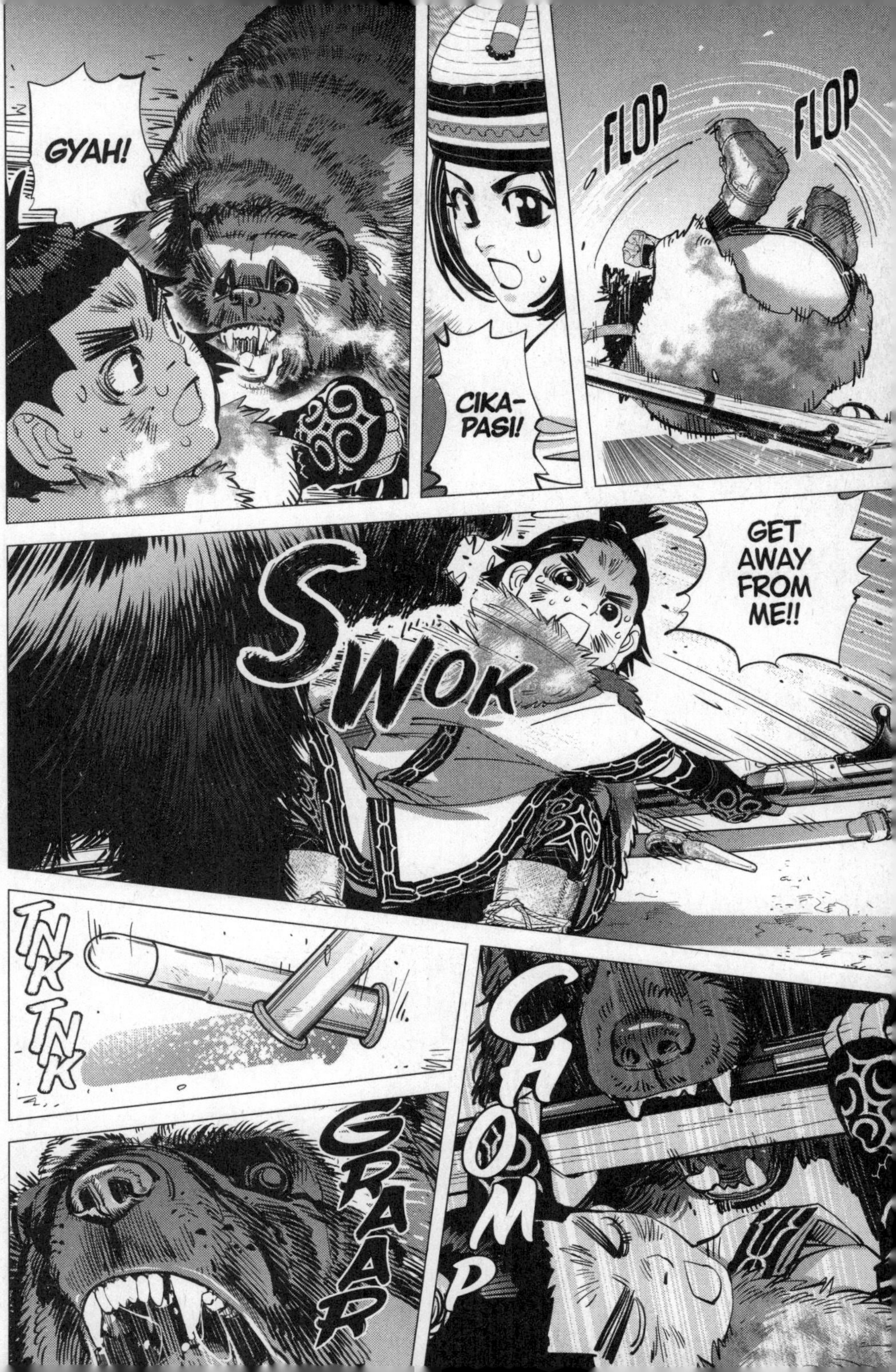
FLOP
FLOP
CIKA-PASI!
GYAH!
GET AWAY FROM ME!!
SWOK
CHOMP
TNK TNK
GRAAR

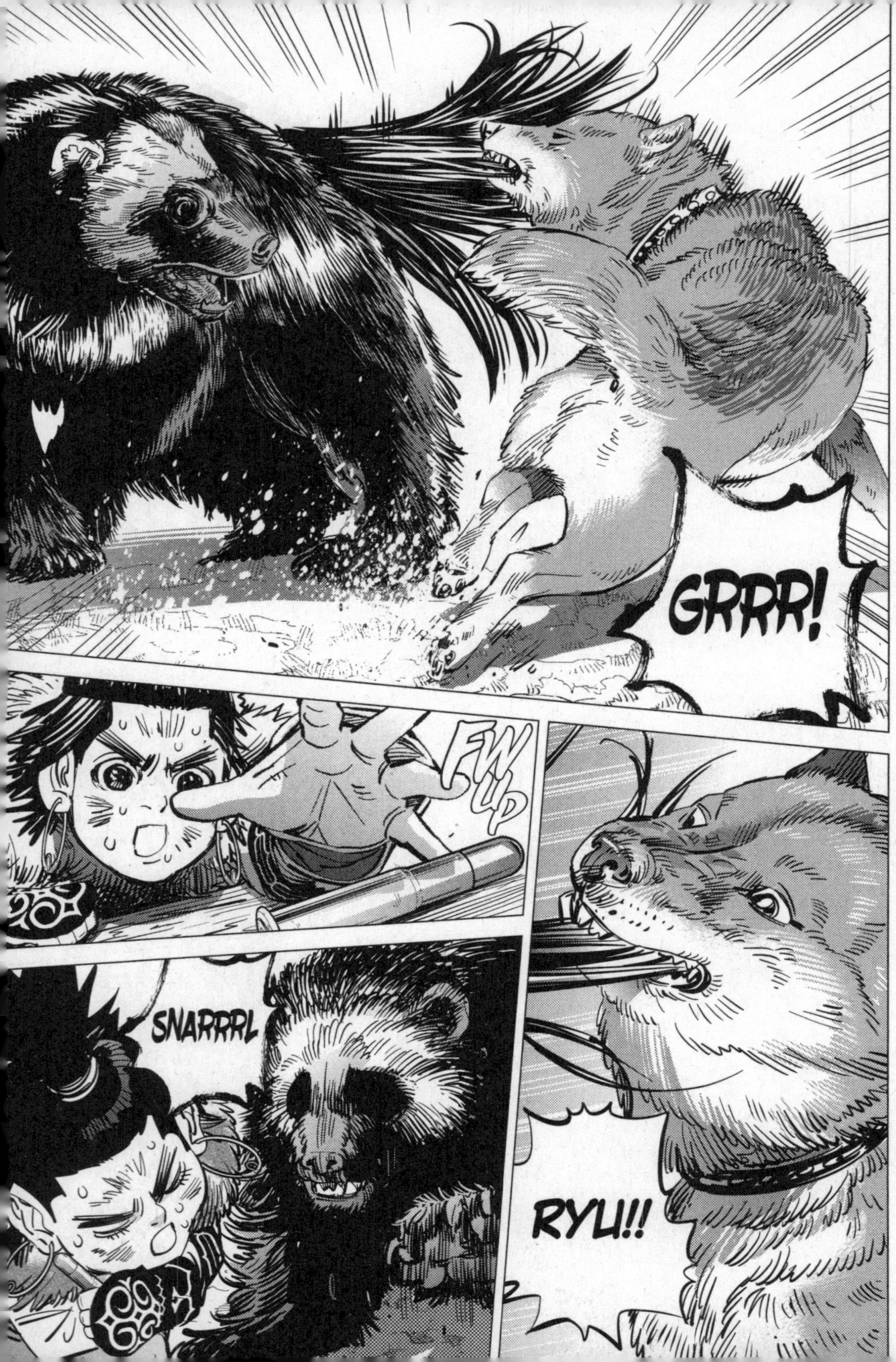
GRRR!
RYU!!
FWUP
SNARRRL

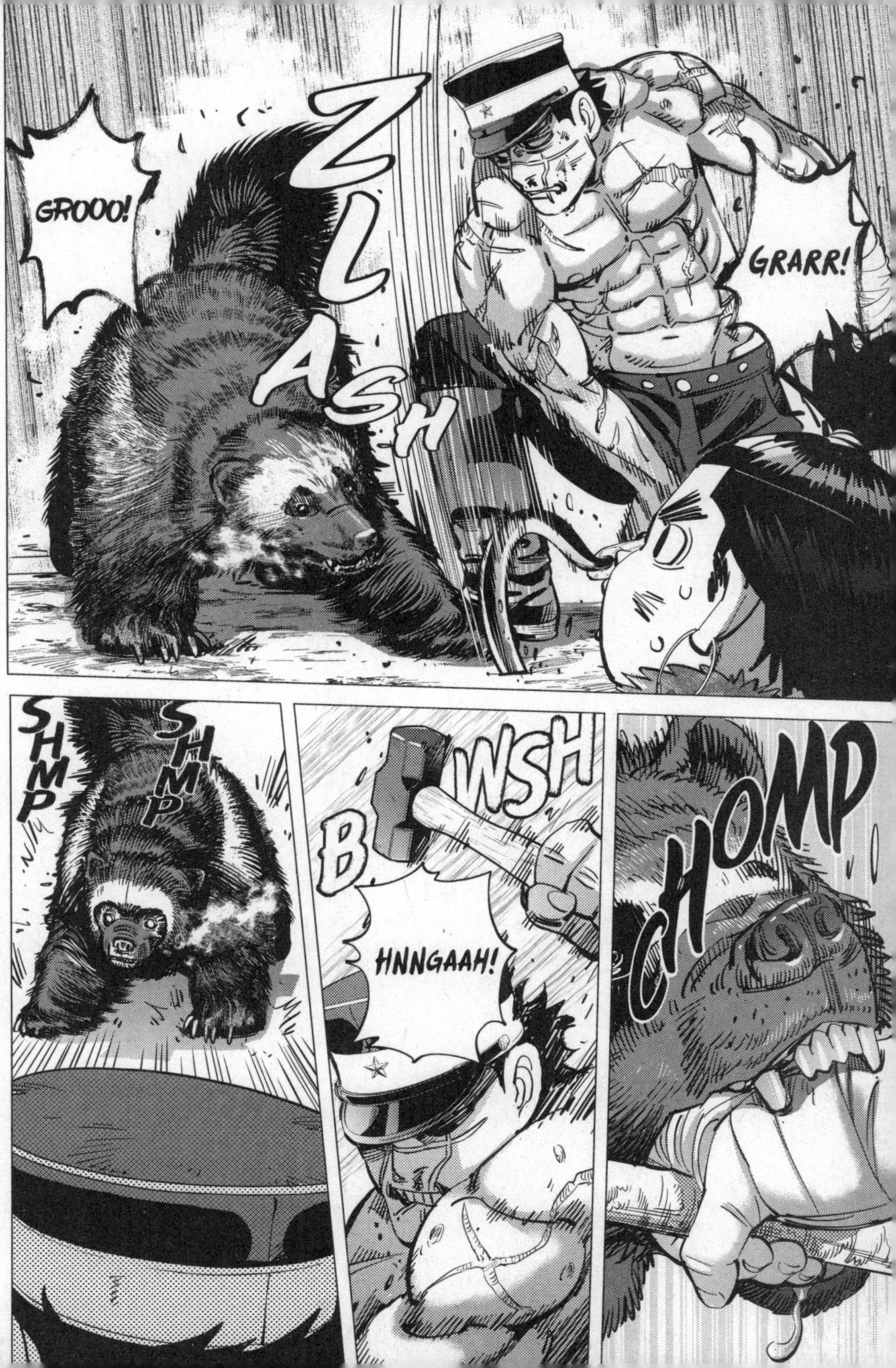
GRARR!
ZLASH
GROOO!
CHOMP
BWSH
HNNGAAH!
SHMP
SHMP

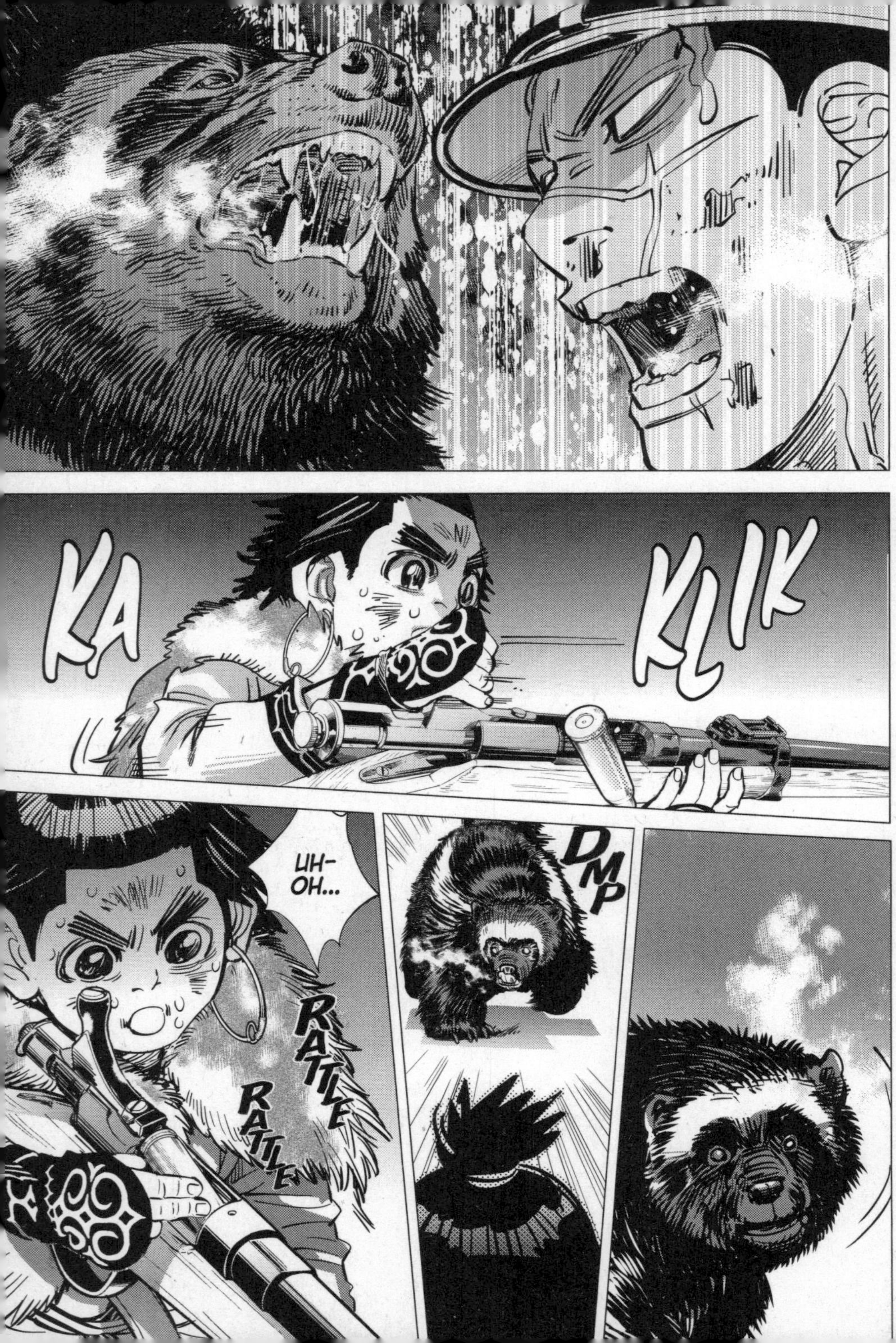
KA
KLIK
DMP
UH-OH...
RATTLE
RATTLE

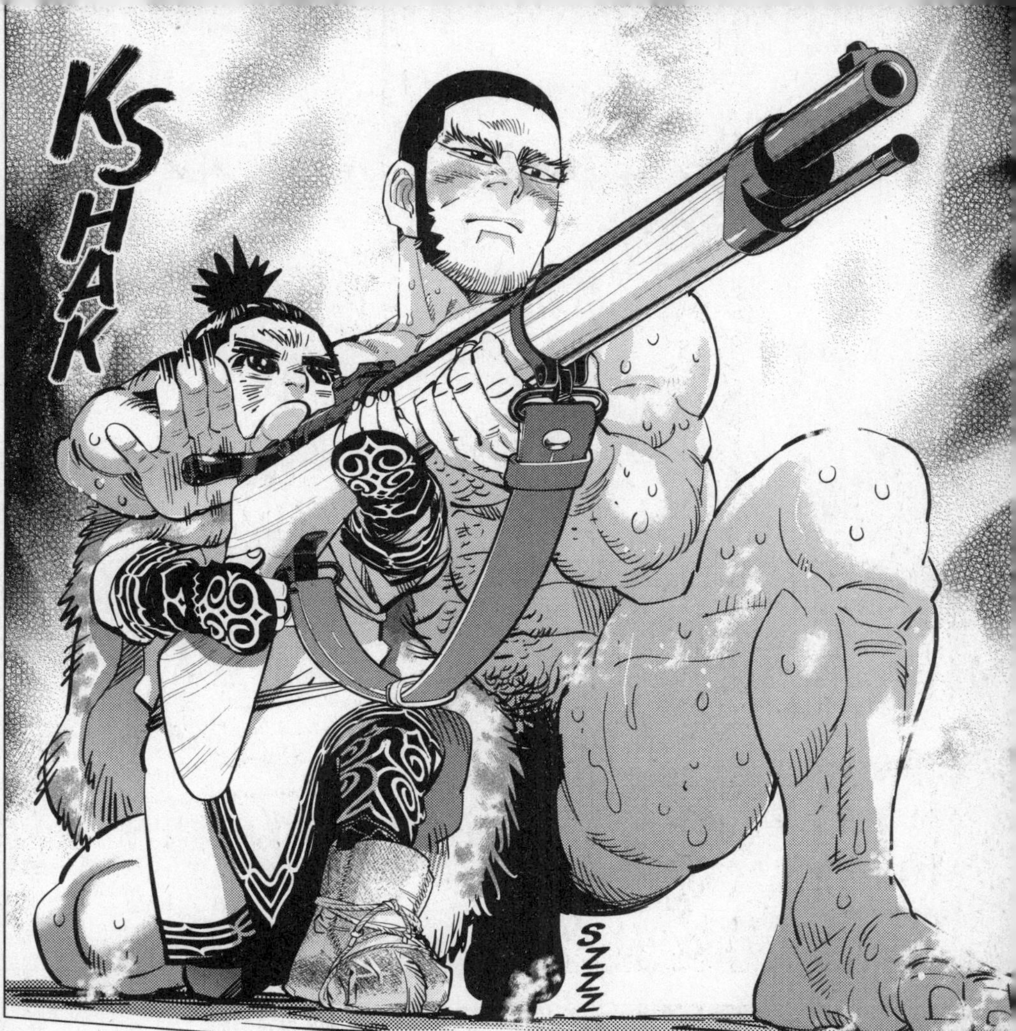
KSHAK
SZZZ
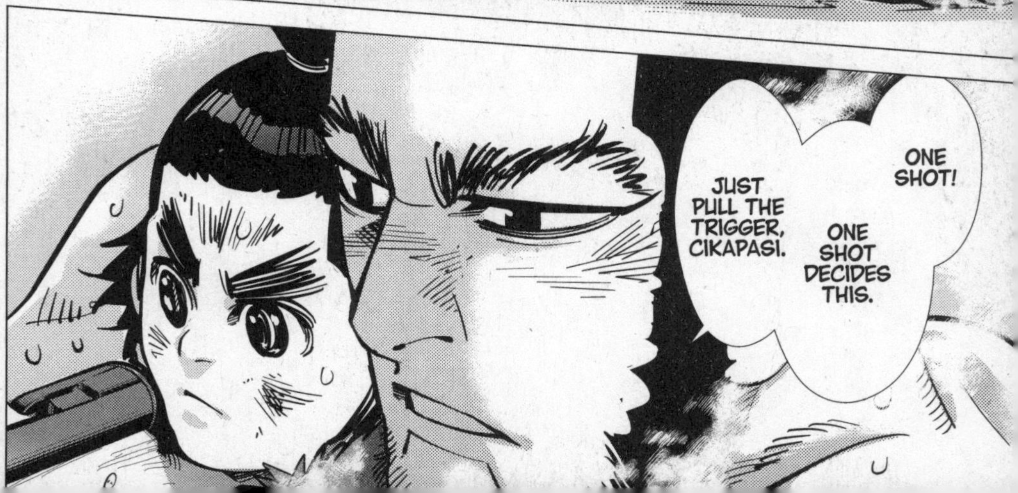
ONE SHOT!
ONE SHOT DECIDES THIS.
JUST PULL THE TRIGGER, CIKAPASI.

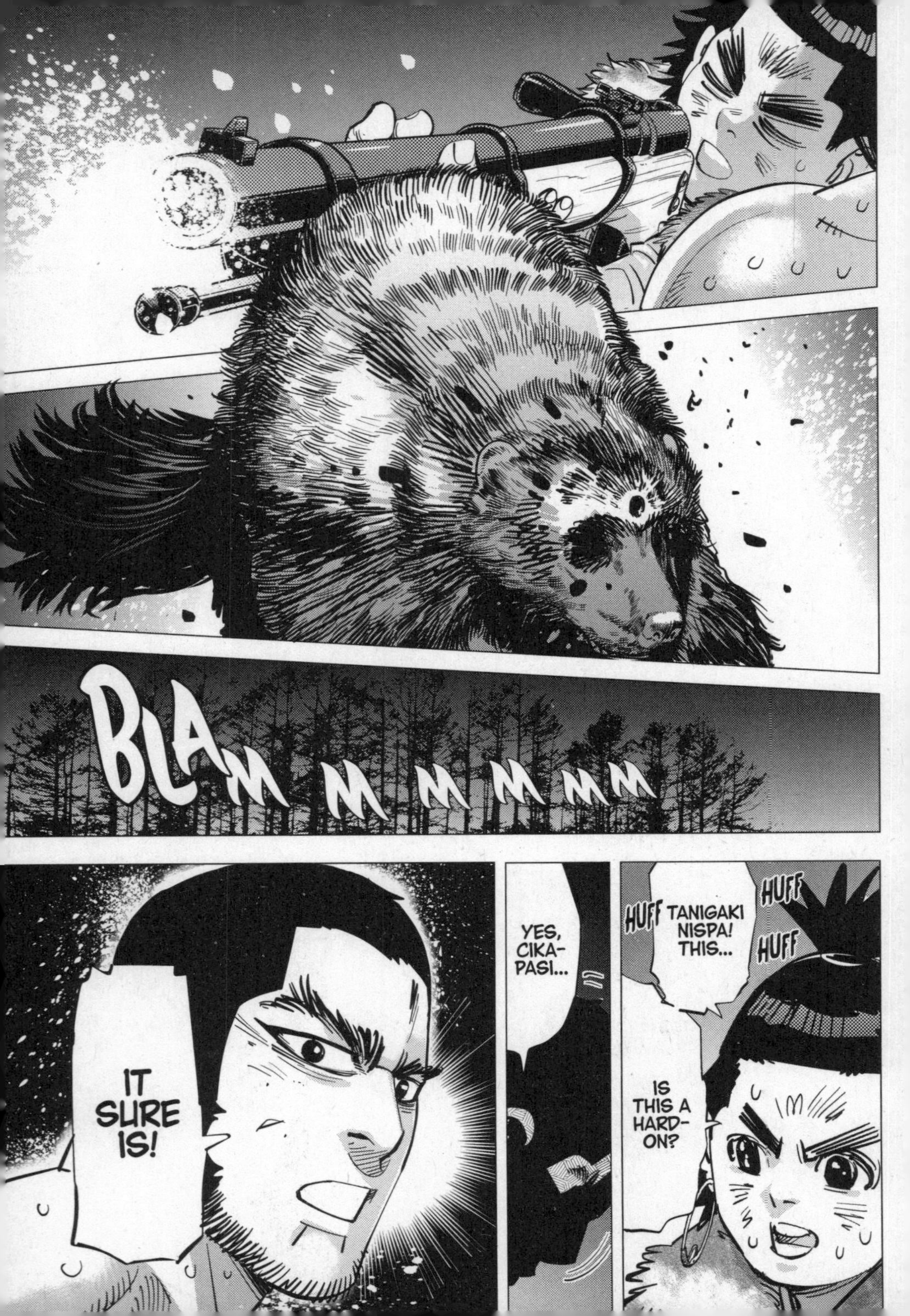

BLAMMMMMMM
HUFF
HUFF
TANIGAKI NISPA! THIS...
HUFF
IS THIS A HARD-ON?
YES, CIKAPASI...
IT SURE IS!

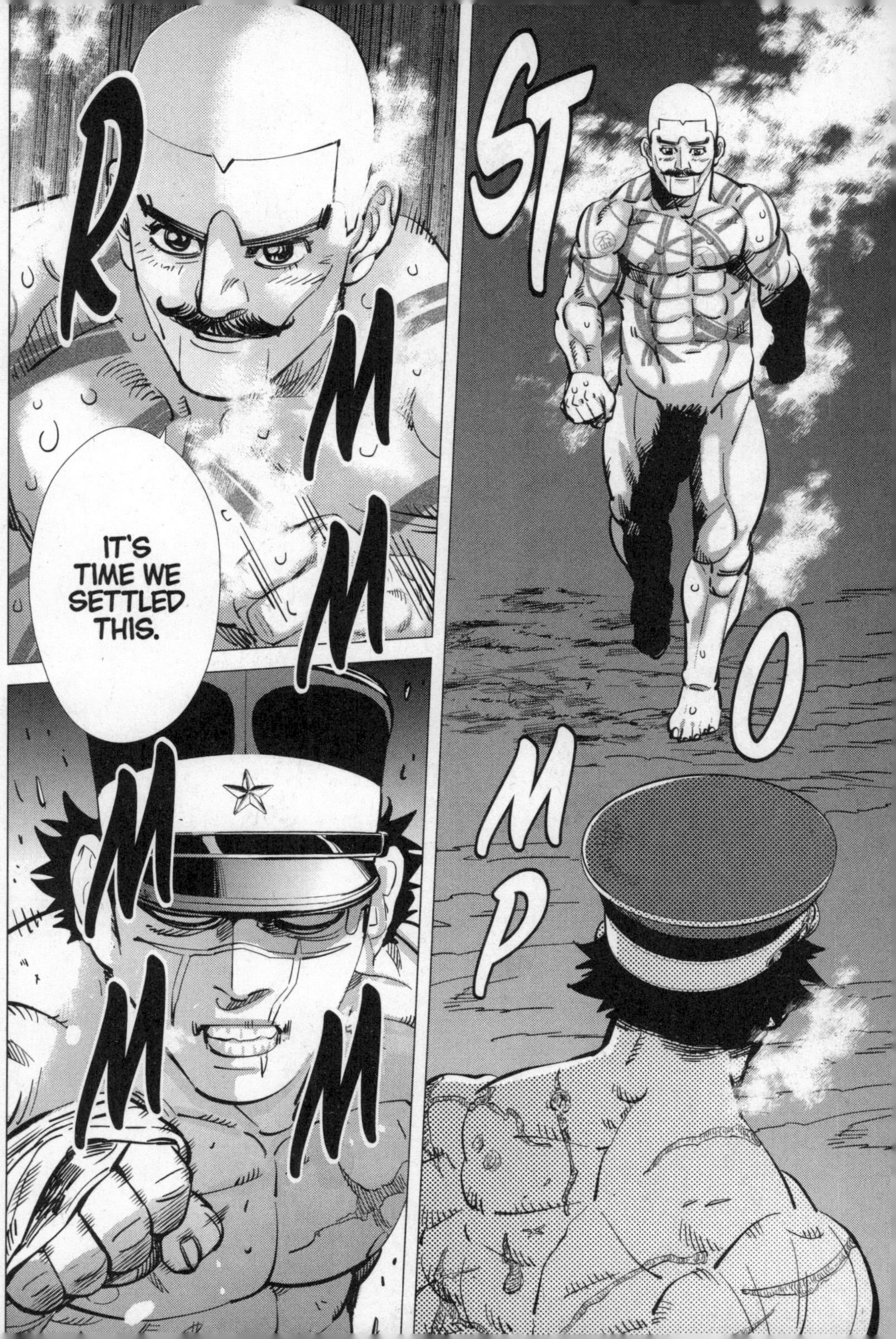
STOMP
RMMM
IT'S TIME WE SETTLED THIS.
MMMM

Chapter 147: Don't Kill the Sea Lions

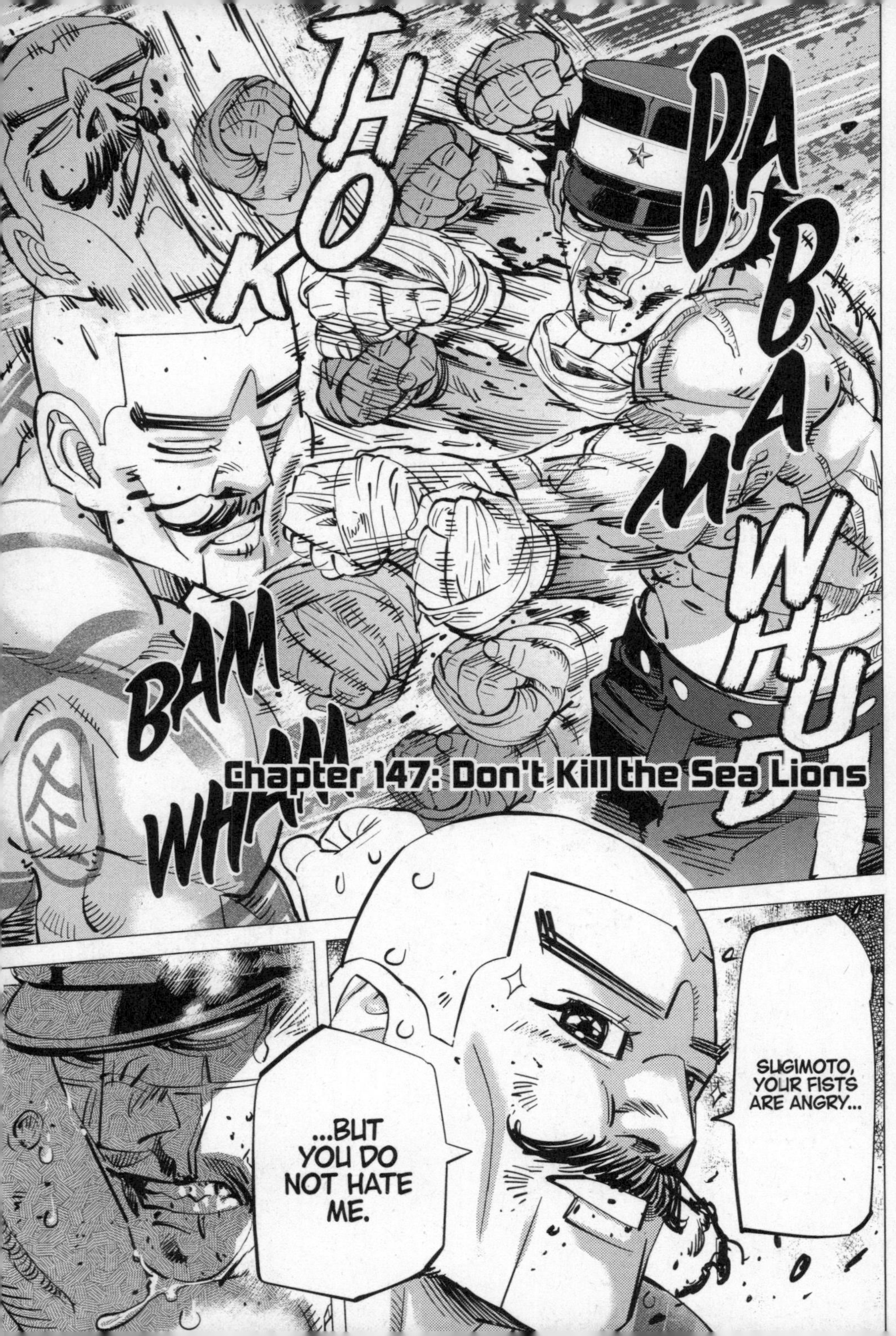
BABAM
WHUD
THOK
BAM
WHAM
SUGIMOTO, YOUR FISTS ARE ANGRY...
...BUT YOU DO NOT HATE ME.

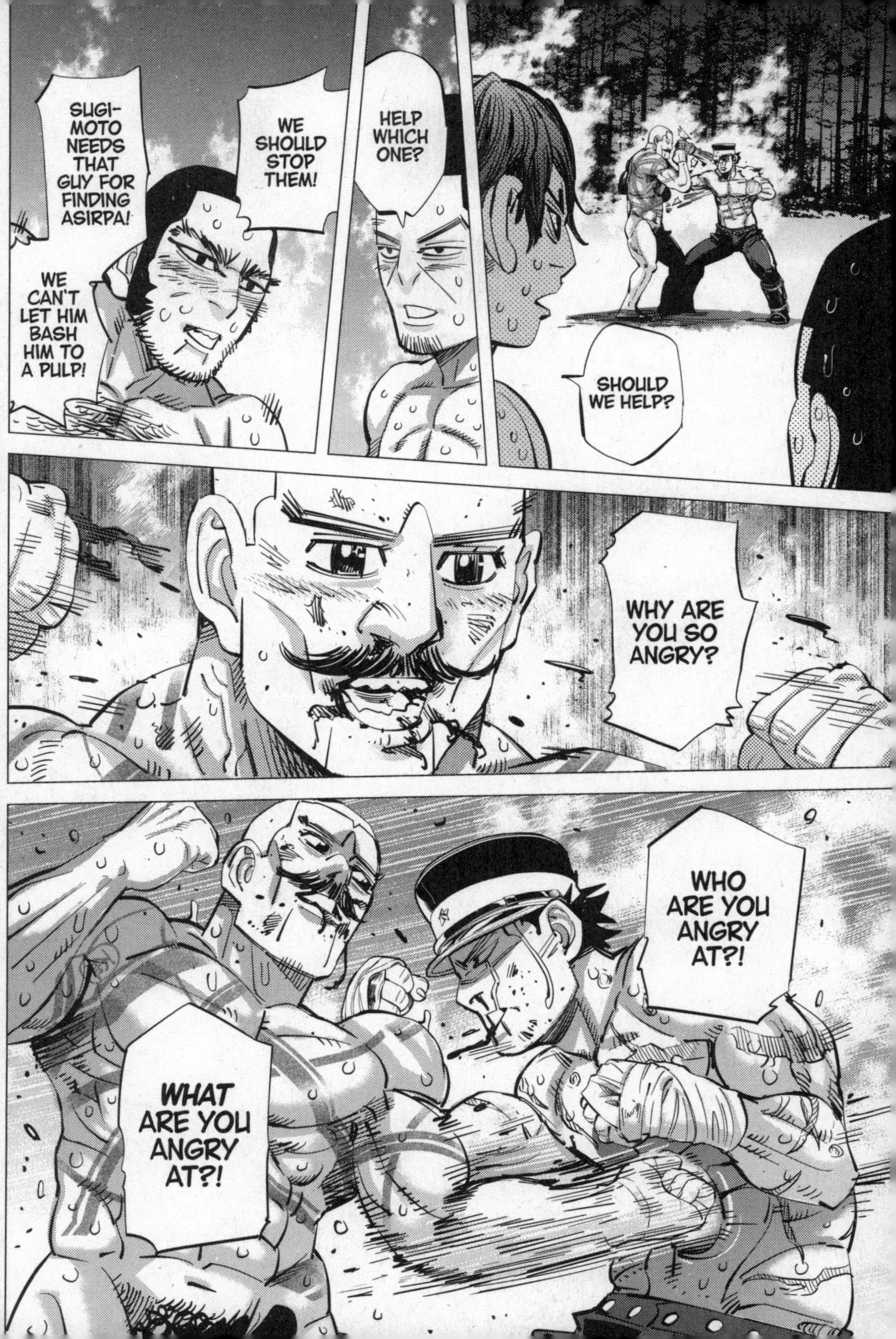
SHOULD WE HELP?
HELP WHICH ONE?
WE SHOULD STOP THEM!
SUGI-MOTO NEEDS THAT GUY FOR FINDING ASIRPA!
WE CAN'T LET HIM BASH HIM TO A PULP!
WHY ARE YOU SO ANGRY?
WHO ARE YOU ANGRY AT?!
WHAT ARE YOU ANGRY AT?!

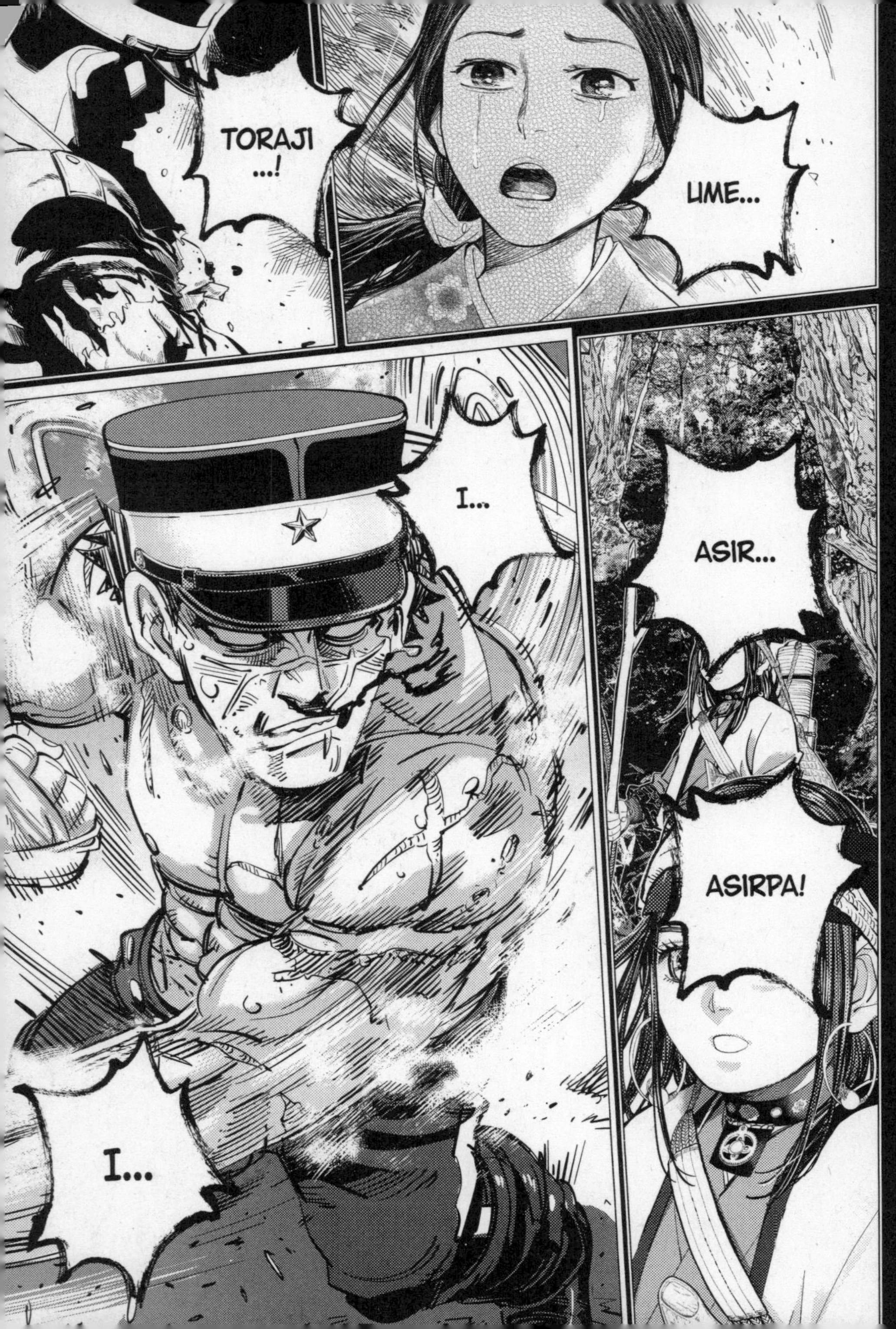
UME...
TORAJI ...!
ASIR...
ASIRPA!
I...
I...

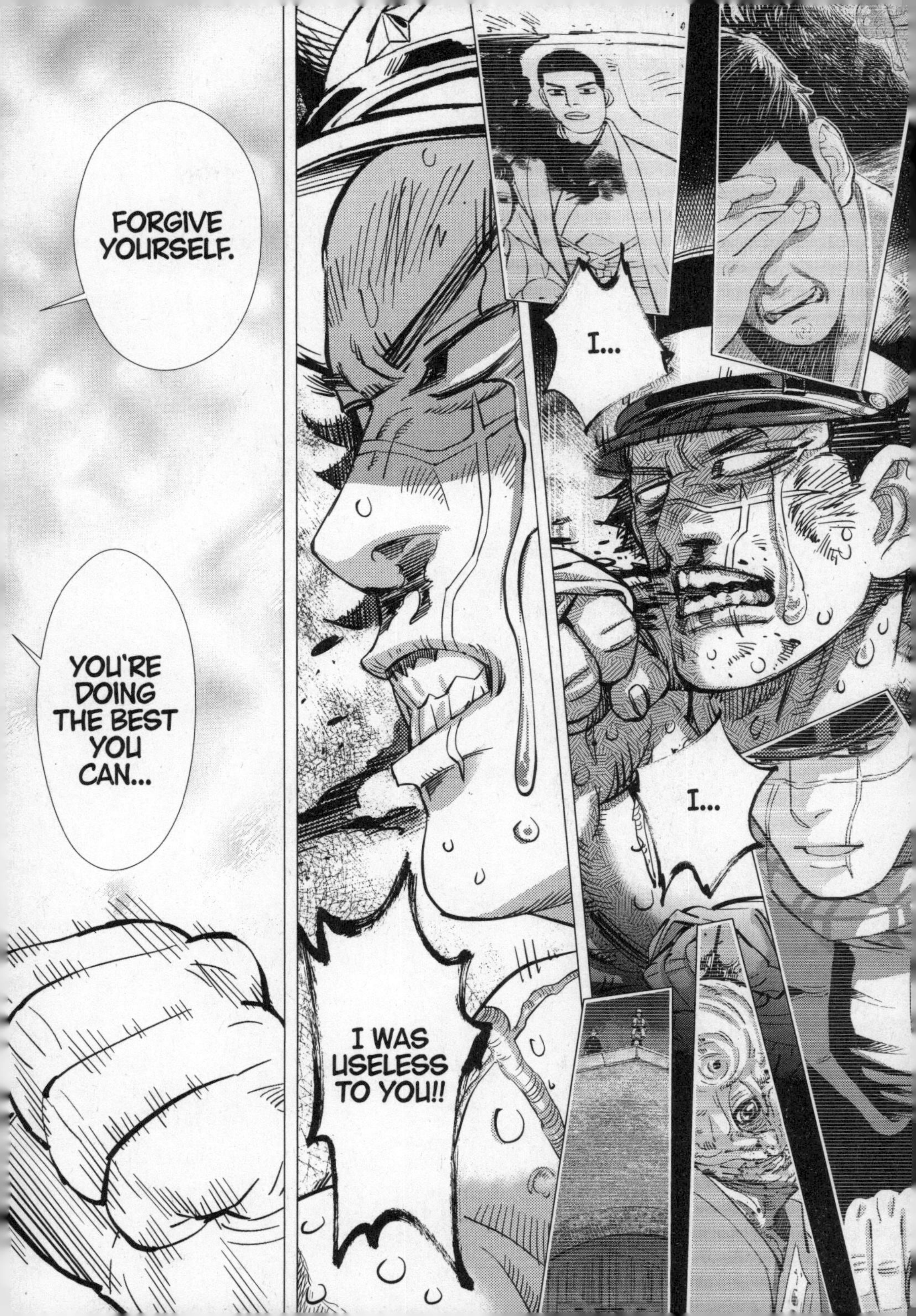
I...
I...
I WAS USELESS TO YOU!!
FORGIVE YOURSELF.
YOU'RE DOING THE BEST YOU CAN...

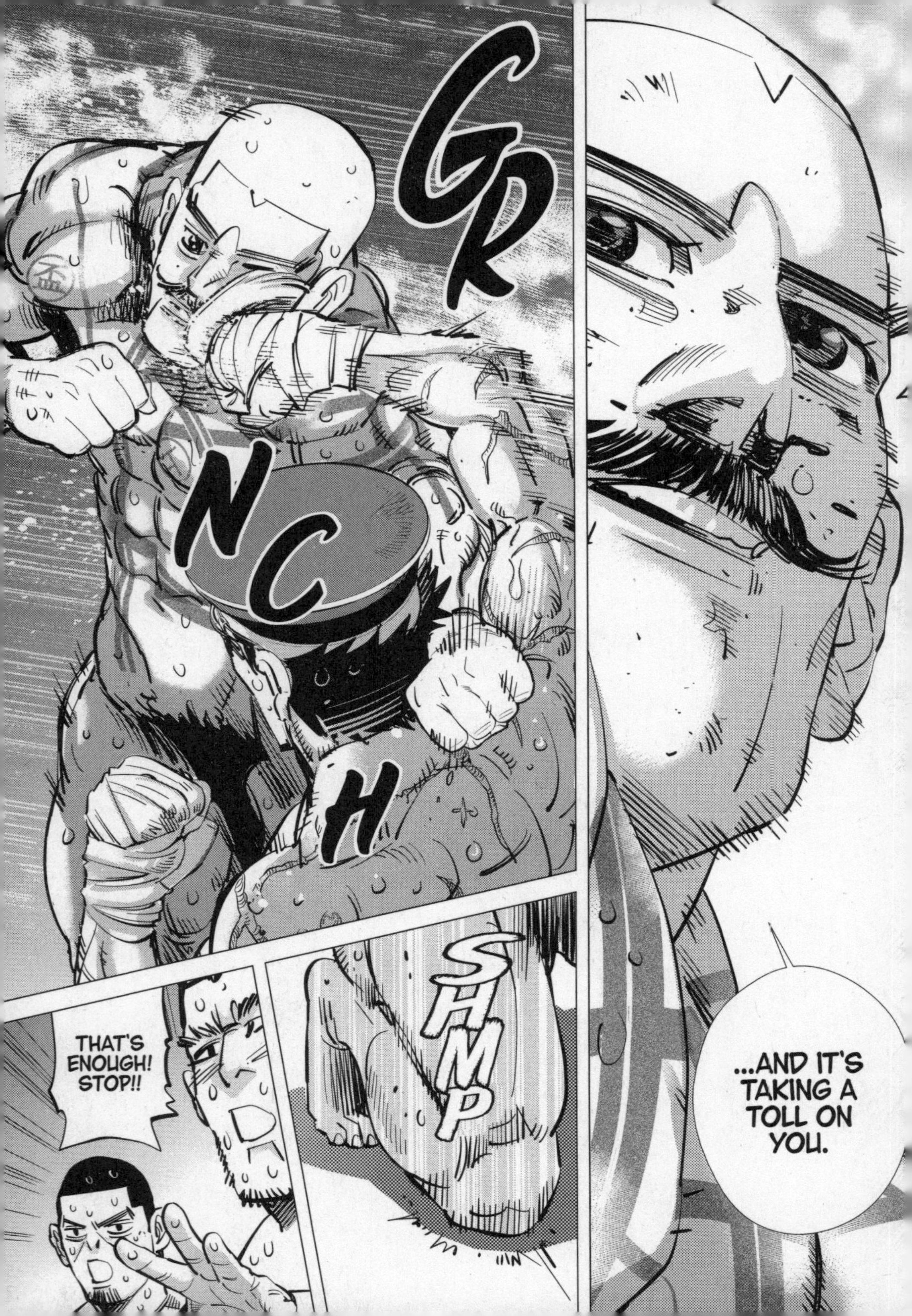
...AND IT'S TAKING A TOLL ON YOU.
GRNCH
SHMP
THAT'S ENOUGH! STOP!!

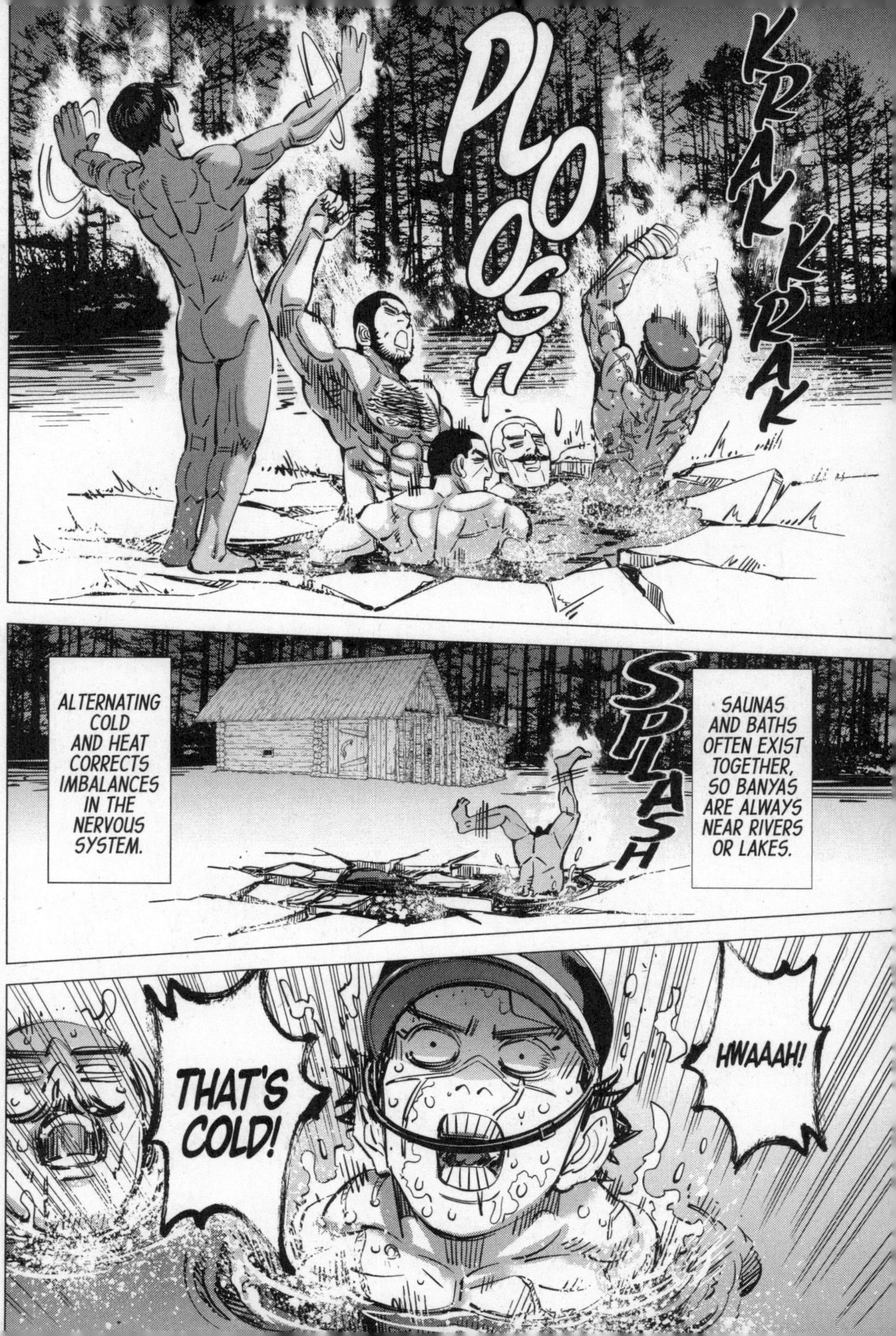
KRAKKRAK
PLOOSH
SAUNAS AND BATHS OFTEN EXIST TOGETHER, SO BANYAS ARE ALWAYS NEAR RIVERS OR LAKES.
SPLASH
ALTERNATING COLD AND HEAT CORRECTS IMBALANCES IN THE NERVOUS SYSTEM.
HWAAAH!
THAT'S COLD!

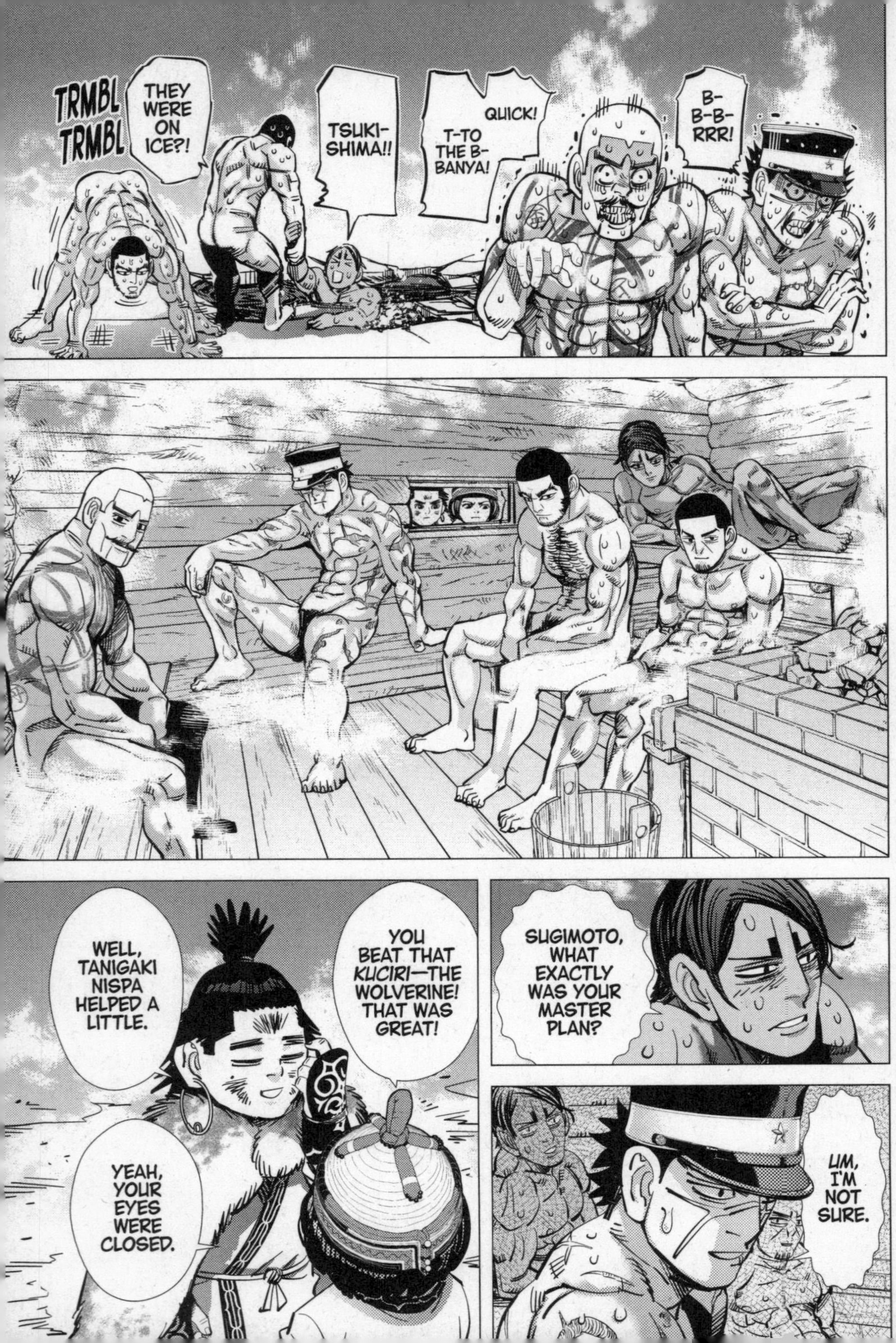
B-
B-B-RRR!
QUICK!
T-TO THE B-BANYA!
TSUKI-SHIMA!!
THEY WERE ON ICE?!
TRMBL TRMBL
SUGIMOTO, WHAT EXACTLY WAS YOUR MASTER PLAN?
UM, I'M NOT SURE.
YOU BEAT THAT KUCIRI—THE WOLVERINE! THAT WAS GREAT!
WELL, TANIGAKI NISPA HELPED A LITTLE.
YEAH, YOUR EYES WERE CLOSED.

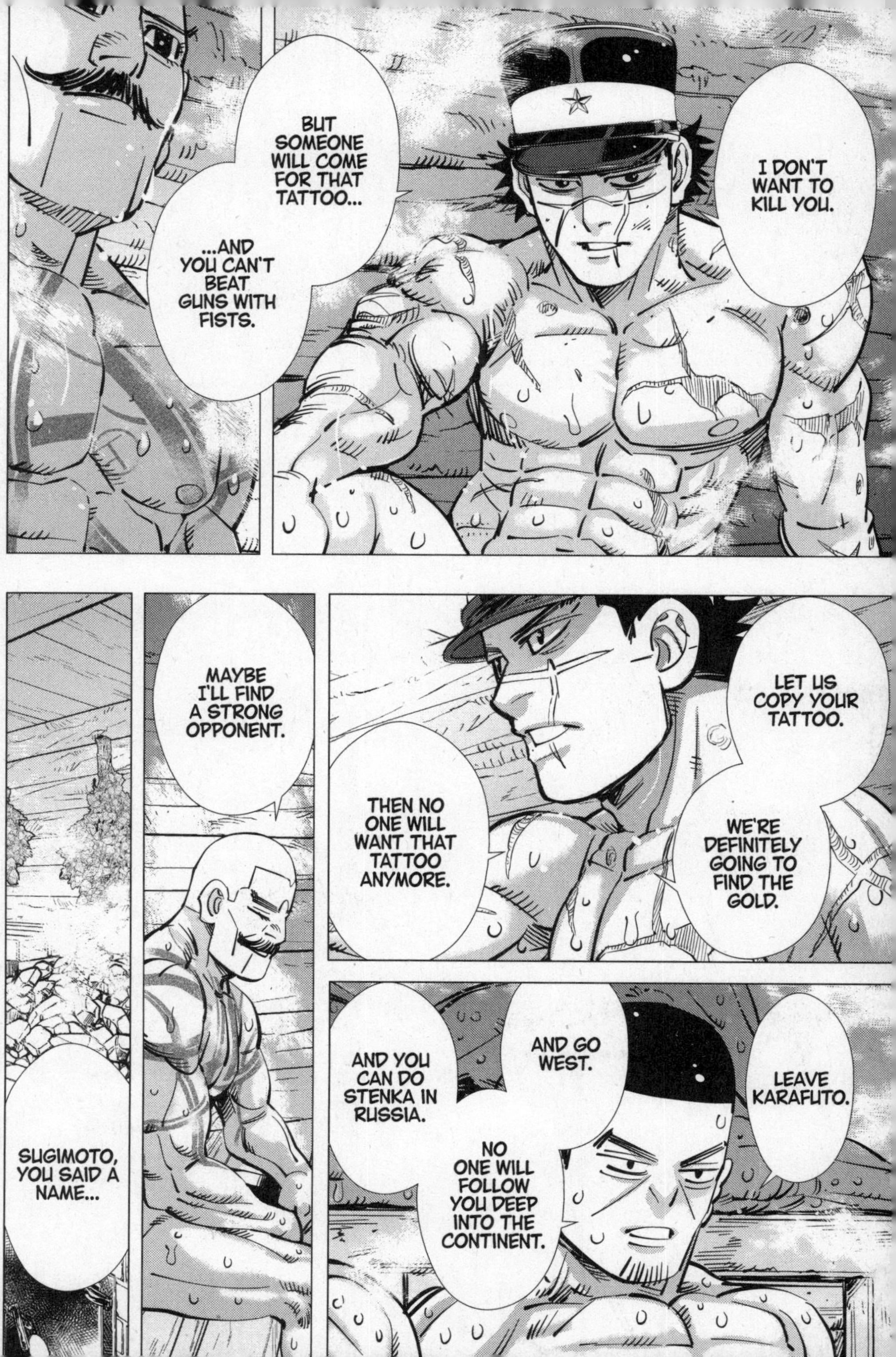
I DON'T WANT TO KILL YOU.
BUT SOMEONE WILL COME FOR THAT TATTOO...
...AND YOU CAN'T BEAT GUNS WITH FISTS.
LET US COPY YOUR TATTOO.
WE'RE DEFINITELY GOING TO FIND THE GOLD.
THEN NO ONE WILL WANT THAT TATTOO ANYMORE.
LEAVE KARAFUTO.
AND GO WEST.
AND YOU CAN DO STENKA IN RUSSIA.
NO ONE WILL FOLLOW YOU DEEP INTO THE CONTINENT.
MAYBE I'LL FIND A STRONG OPPONENT.
SUGIMOTO, YOU SAID A NAME...

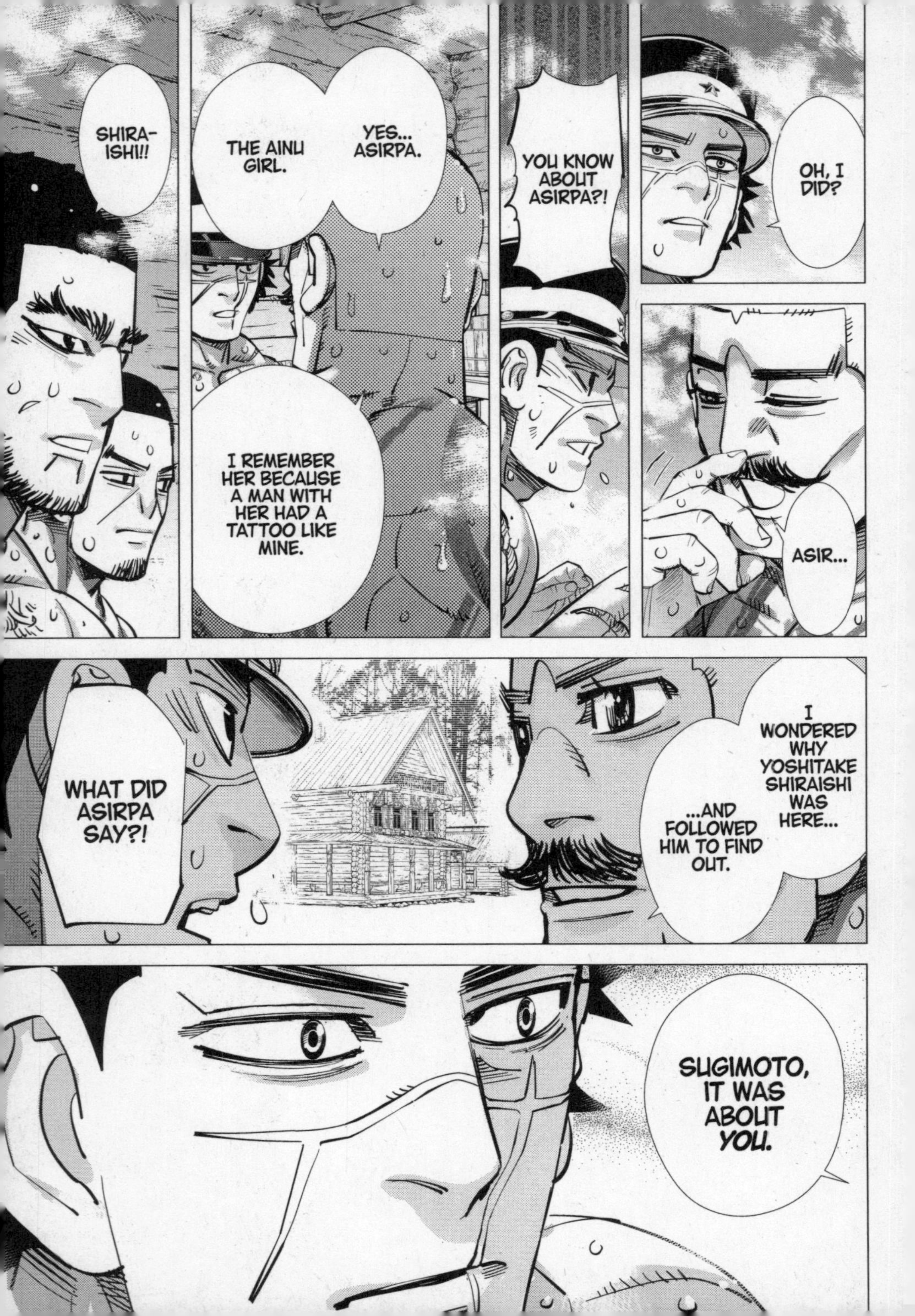
OH, I DID?
ASIR...
YOU KNOW ABOUT ASIRPA?!
YES... ASIRPA.
THE AINU GIRL.
I REMEMBER HER BECAUSE A MAN WITH HER HAD A TATTOO LIKE MINE.
SHIRA-ISHI!!
I WONDERED WHY YOSHITAKE SHIRAISHI WAS HERE...
...AND FOLLOWED HIM TO FIND OUT.
WHAT DID ASIRPA SAY?!
SUGIMOTO, IT WAS ABOUT YOU.

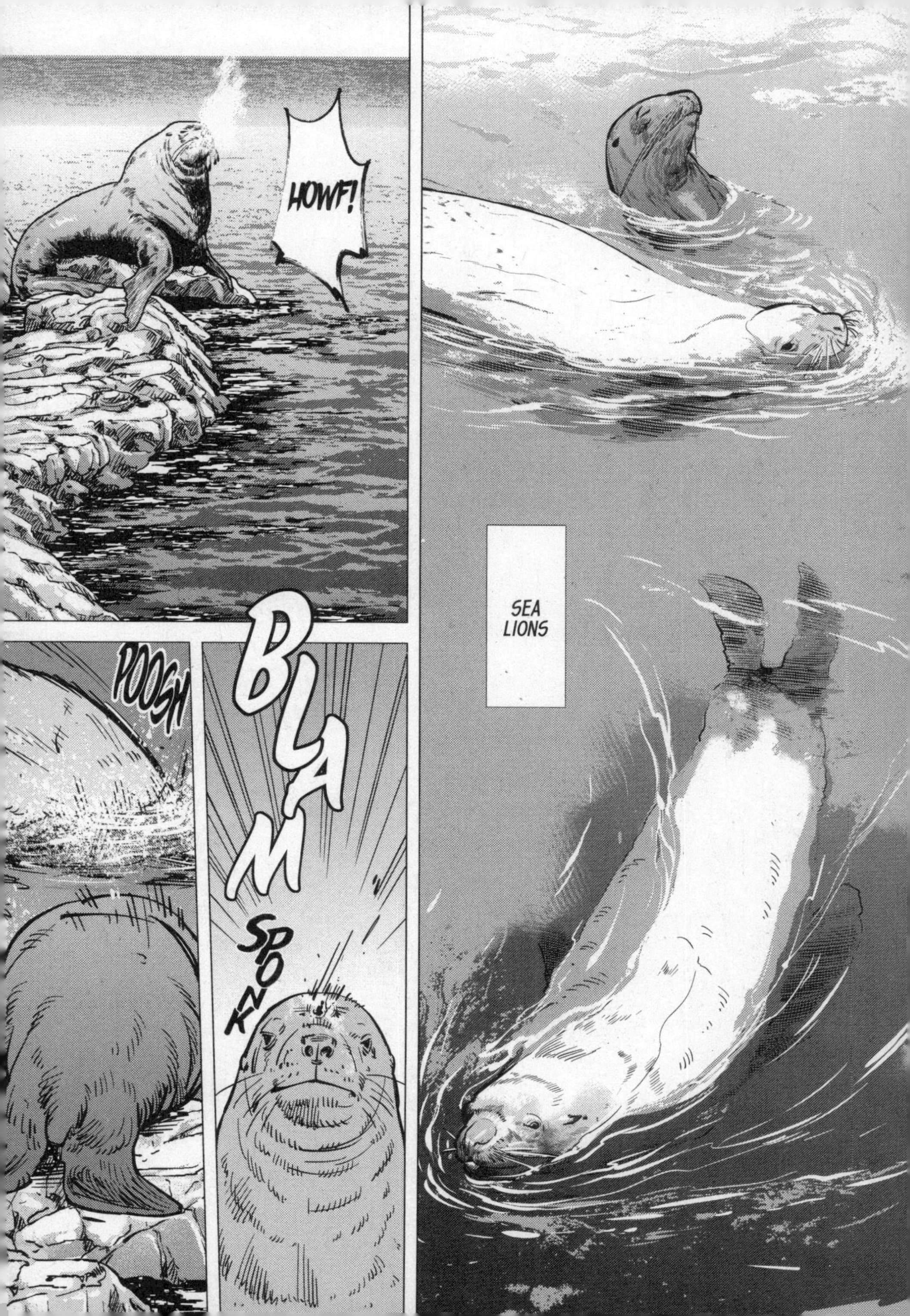
SEA LIONS
HOWF!
BLAM
SPONK
POOSH

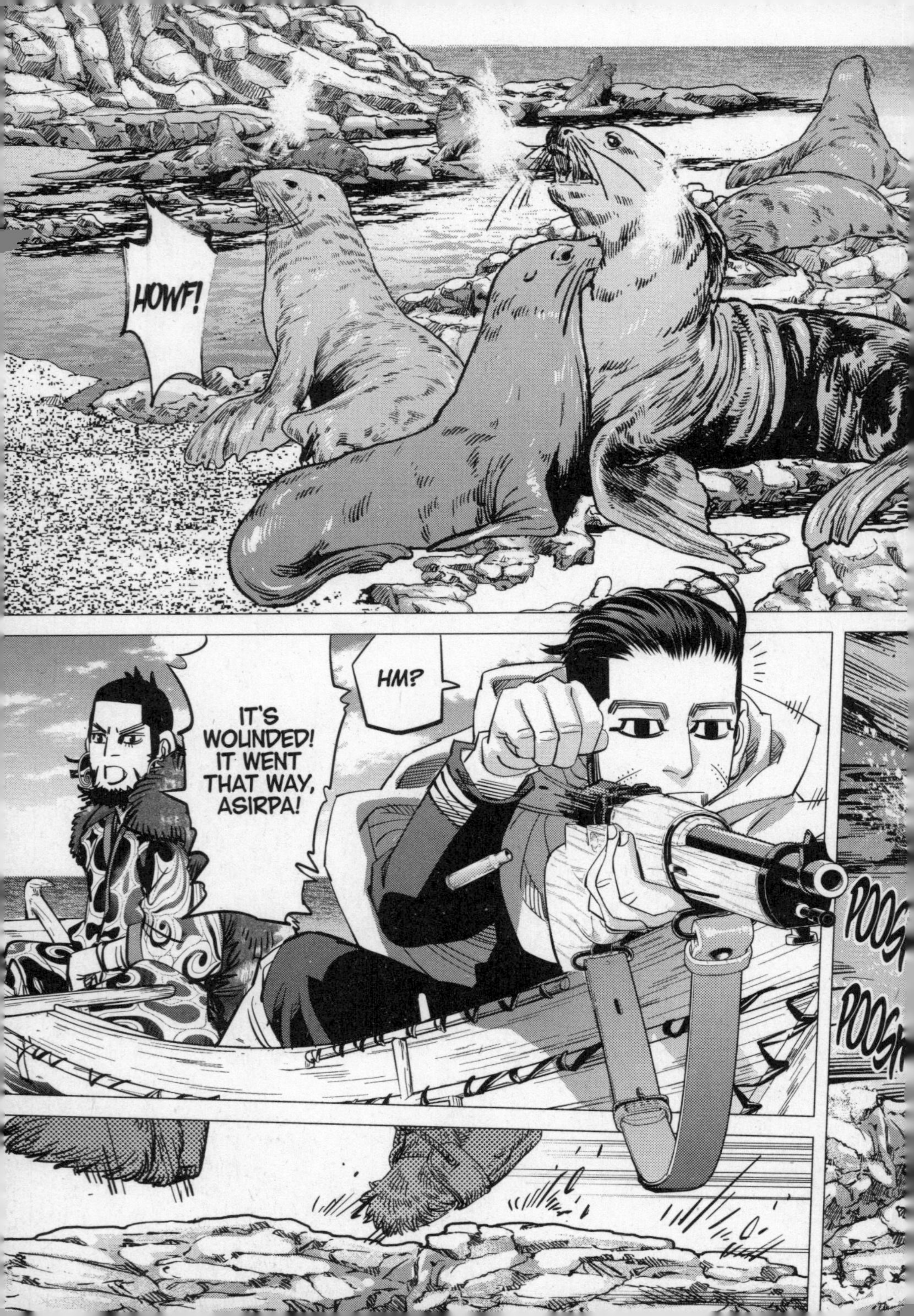
HOWF!
POOSH
POOSH
HM?
IT'S WOUNDED! IT WENT THAT WAY, ASIRPA!

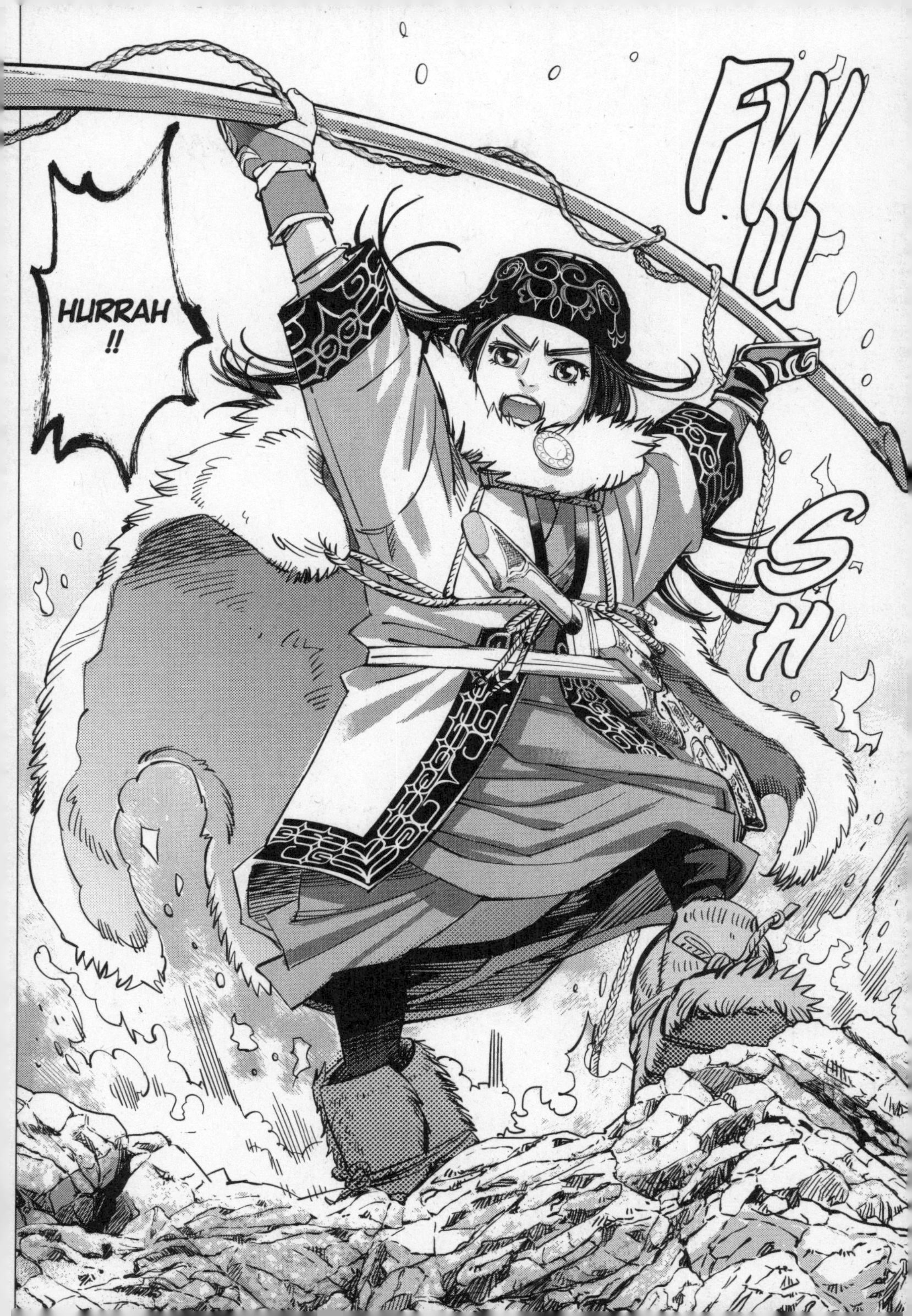
FWI
SSH
HURRAH !!

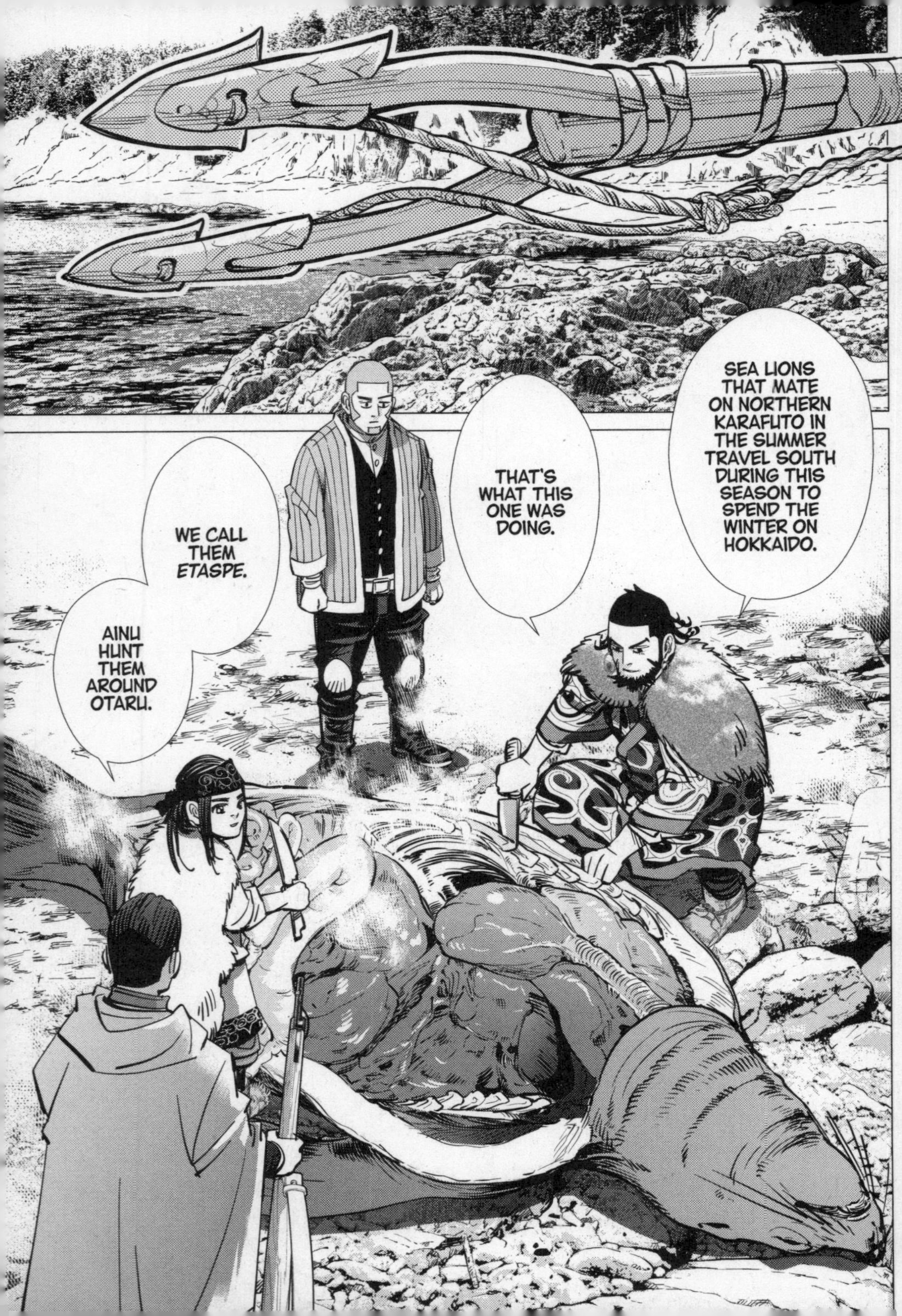
SEA LIONS THAT MATE ON NORTHERN KARAFUTO IN THE SUMMER TRAVEL SOUTH DURING THIS SEASON TO SPEND THE WINTER ON HOKKAIDO.
THAT'S WHAT THIS ONE WAS DOING.
WE CALL THEM ETASPE.
AINU HUNT THEM AROUND OTARU.

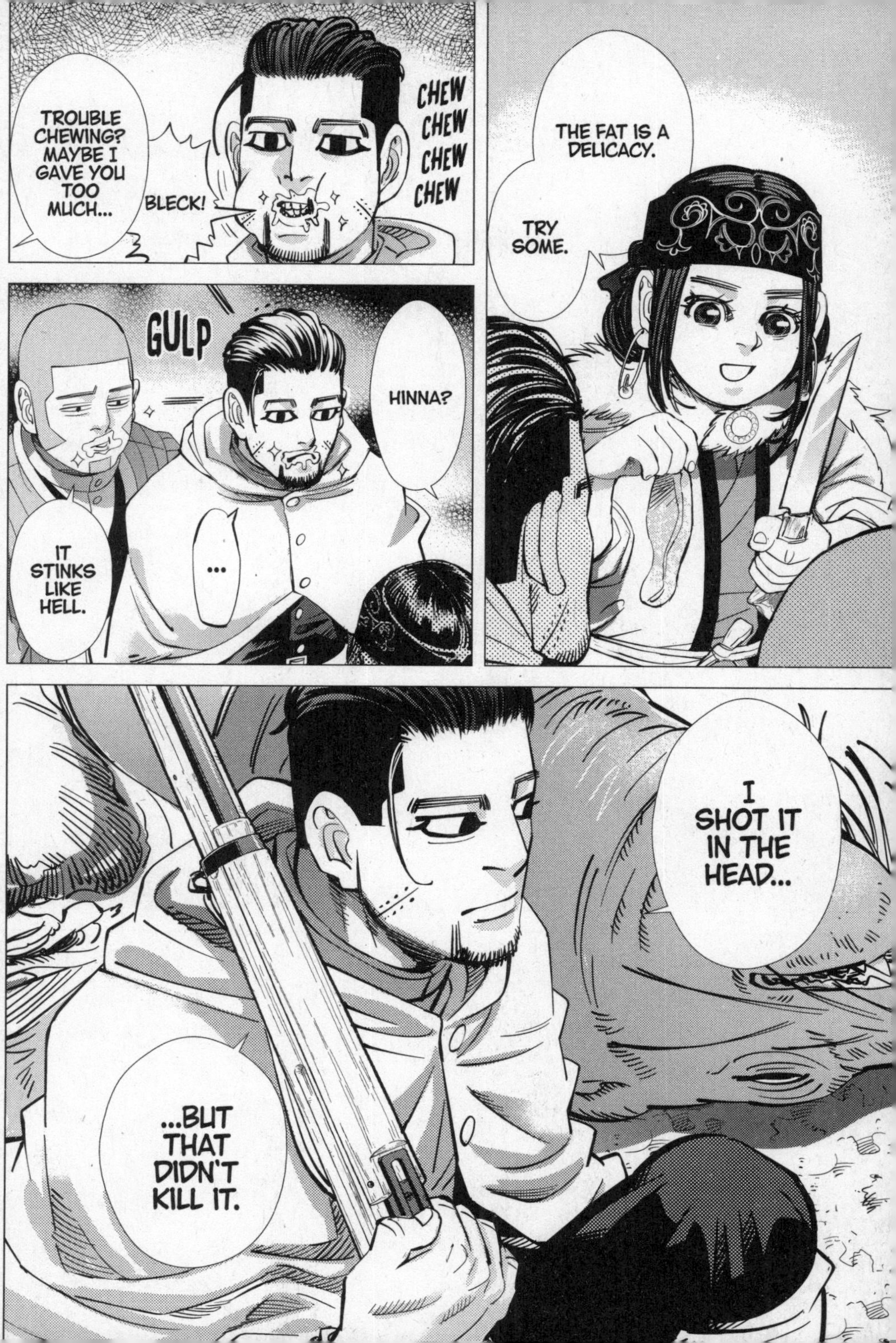
THE FAT IS A DELICACY.
TRY SOME.
CHEW CHEW CHEW CHEW
BLECK!
TROUBLE CHEWING? MAYBE I GAVE YOU TOO MUCH...
HINNA?
GULP
...
IT STINKS LIKE HELL.
I SHOT IT IN THE HEAD...
...BUT THAT DIDN'T KILL IT.

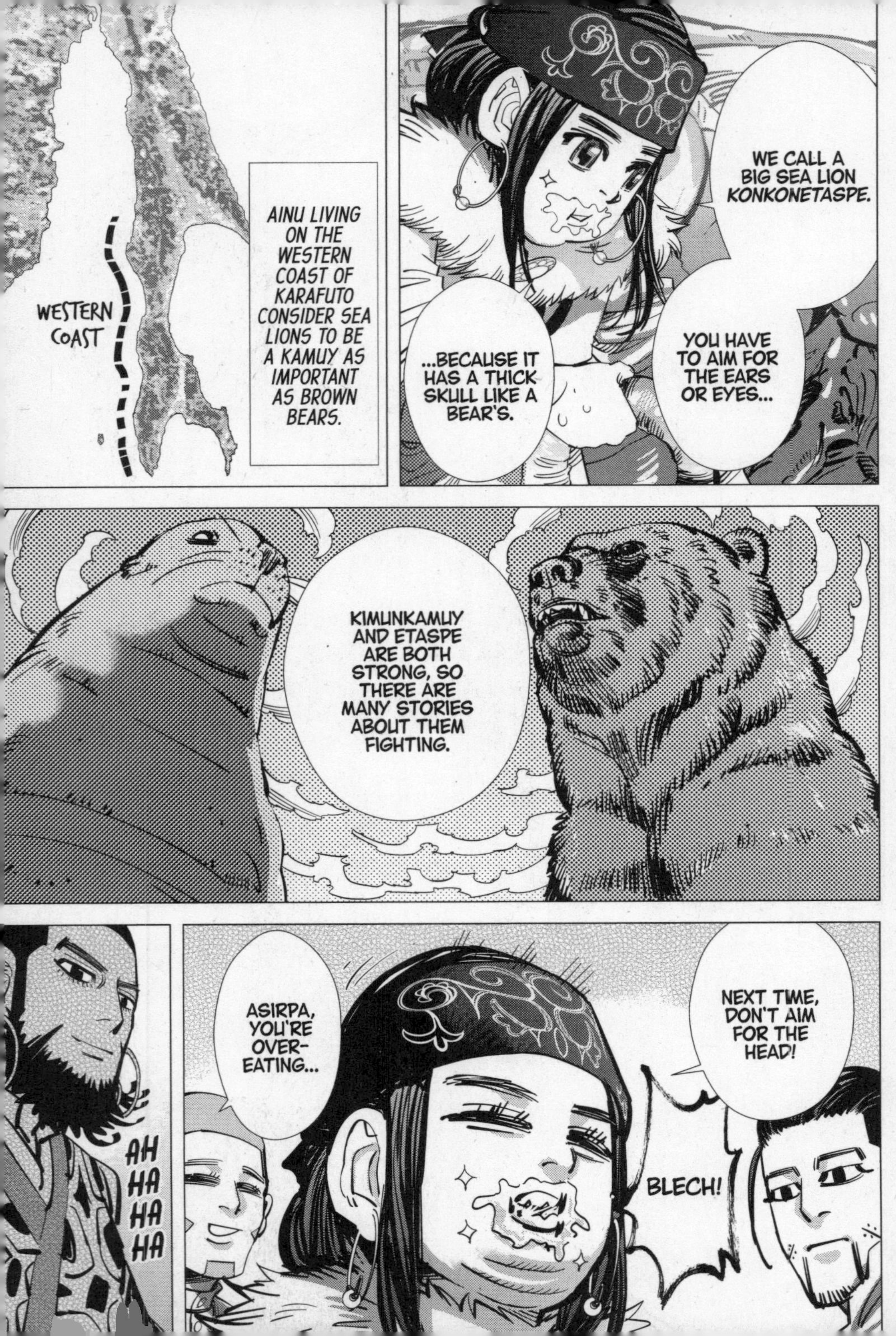
WE CALL A BIG SEA LION KONKONETASPE.
YOU HAVE TO AIM FOR THE EARS OR EYES...
...BECAUSE IT HAS A THICK SKULL LIKE A BEAR'S.
AINU LIVING ON THE WESTERN COAST OF KARAFUTO CONSIDER SEA LIONS TO BE A KAMUY AS IMPORTANT AS BROWN BEARS.
WESTERN COAST
KIMUNKAMUY AND ETASPE ARE BOTH STRONG, SO THERE ARE MANY STORIES ABOUT THEM FIGHTING.
NEXT TIME, DON'T AIM FOR THE HEAD!
BLECH!
ASIRPA, YOU'RE OVER-EATING...
AH HA HA HA HA

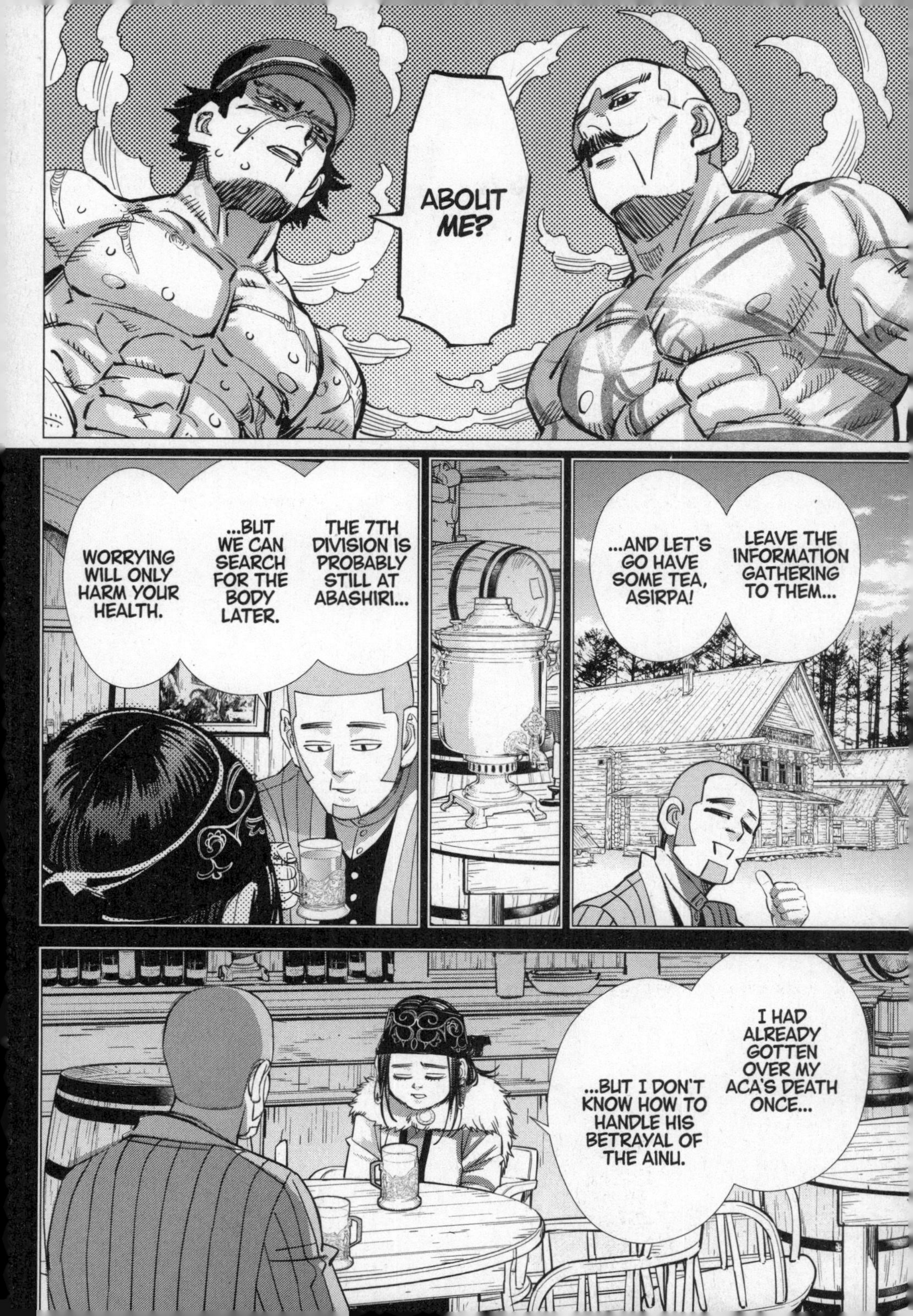
ABOUT ME?
LEAVE THE INFORMATION GATHERING TO THEM...
...AND LET'S GO HAVE SOME TEA, ASIRPA!
THE 7TH DIVISION IS PROBABLY STILL AT ABASHIRI...
...BUT WE CAN SEARCH FOR THE BODY LATER.
WORRYING WILL ONLY HARM YOUR HEALTH.
I HAD ALREADY GOTTEN OVER MY ACA'S DEATH ONCE...
...BUT I DON'T KNOW HOW TO HANDLE HIS BETRAYAL OF THE AINU.

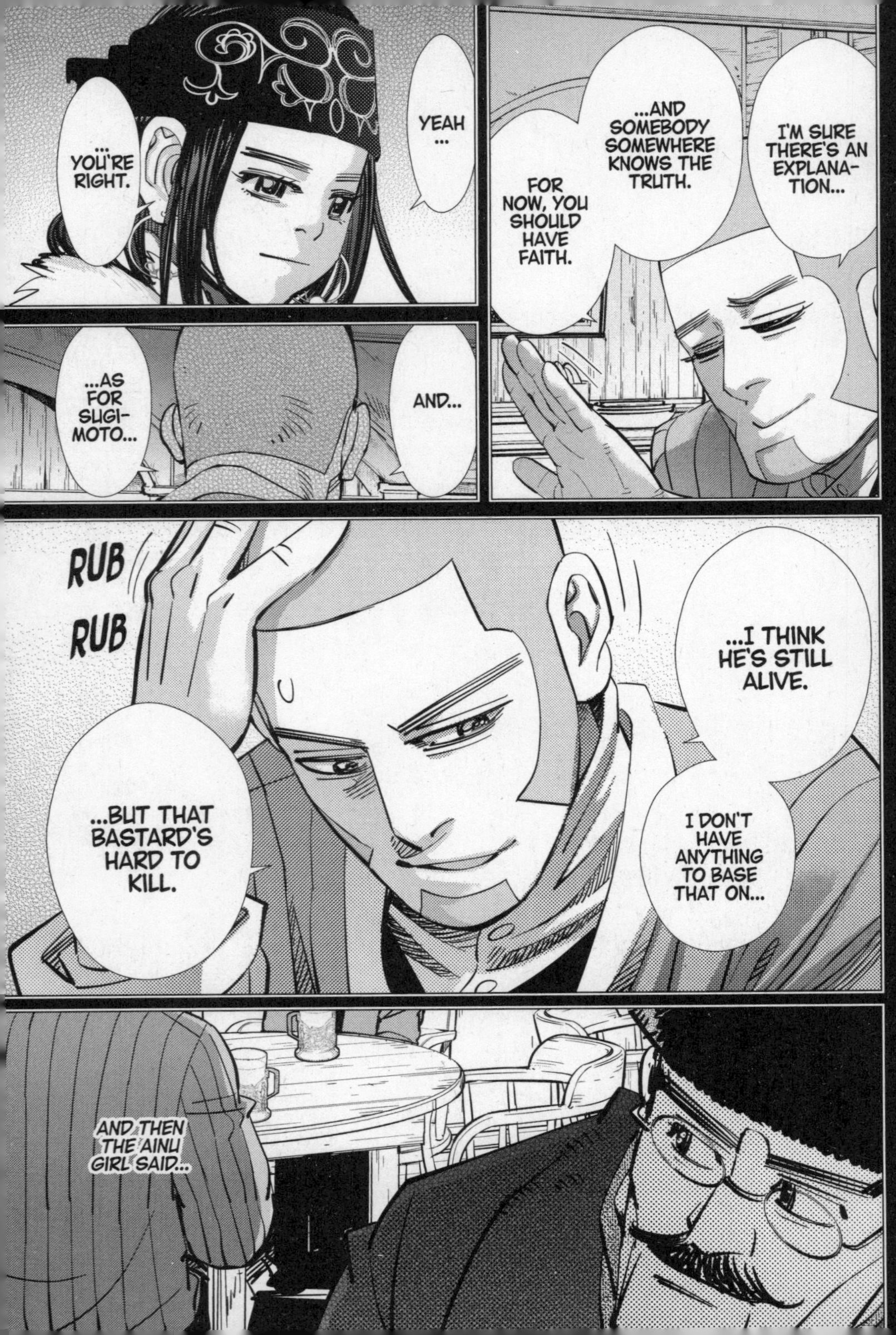
I'M SURE THERE'S AN EXPLANATION...
...AND SOMEBODY SOMEWHERE KNOWS THE TRUTH.
FOR NOW, YOU SHOULD HAVE FAITH.
YEAH...
...YOU'RE RIGHT.
AND...
...AS FOR SUGIMOTO...
...I THINK HE'S STILL ALIVE.
I DON'T HAVE ANYTHING TO BASE THAT ON...
RUB
RUB
...BUT THAT BASTARD'S HARD TO KILL.
AND THEN THE AINU GIRL SAID...

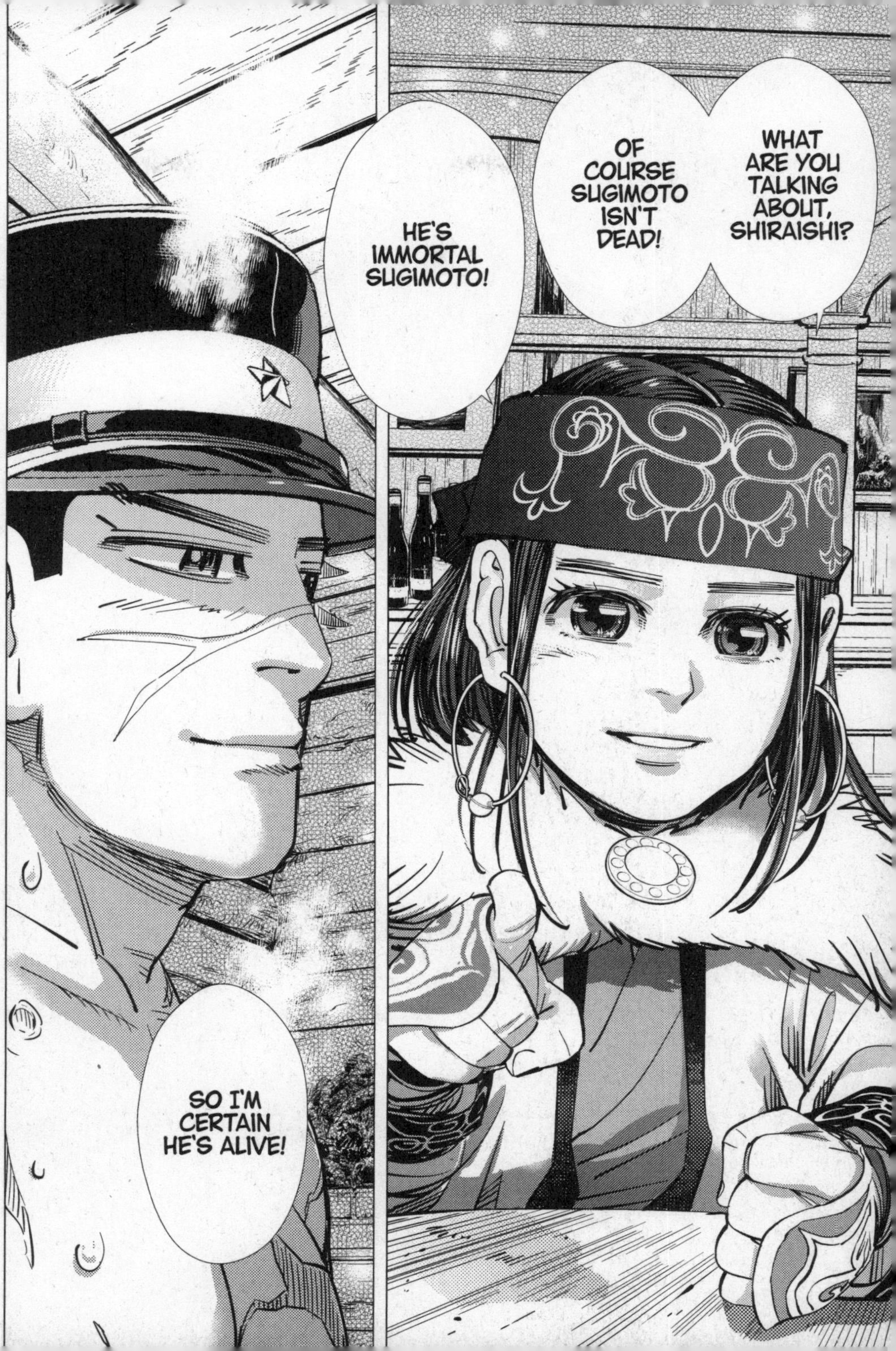
WHAT ARE YOU TALKING ABOUT, SHIRAISHI?
OF COURSE SUGIMOTO ISN'T DEAD!
HE'S IMMORTAL SUGIMOTO!
SO I'M CERTAIN HE'S ALIVE!

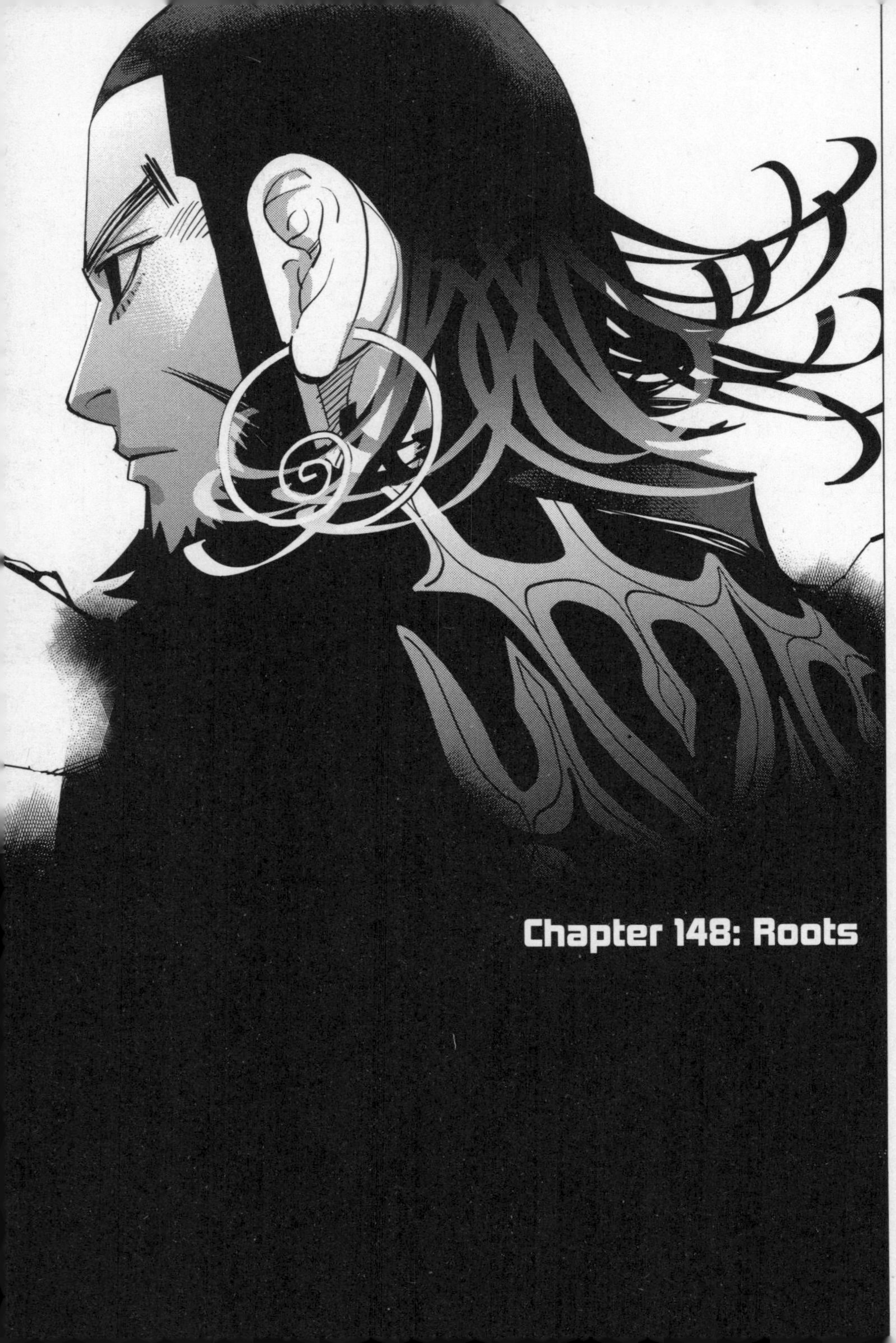
Chapter 148: Roots

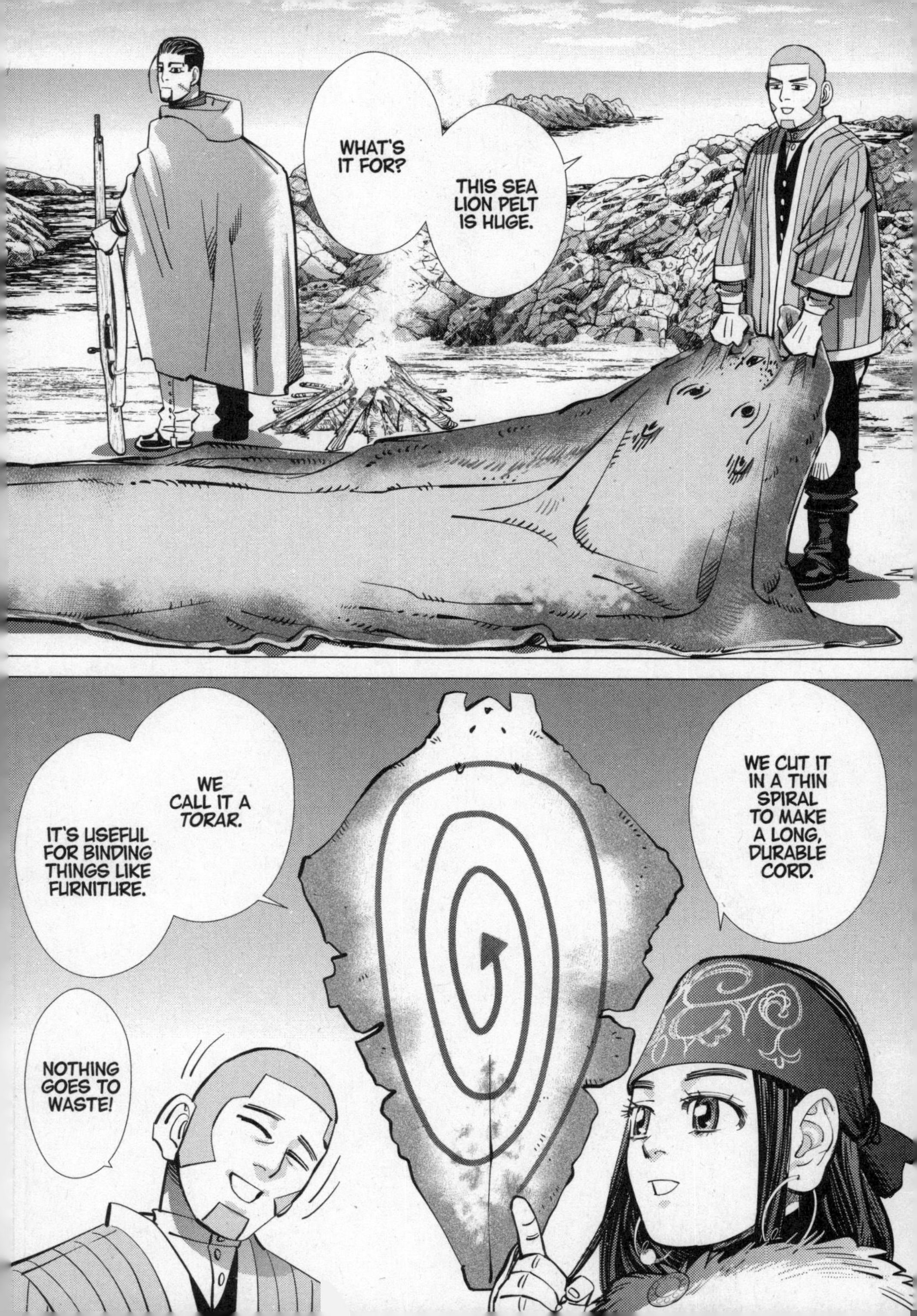
THIS SEA LION PELT IS HUGE.
WHAT'S IT FOR?
WE CUT IT IN A THIN SPIRAL TO MAKE A LONG, DURABLE CORD.
WE CALL IT A *TORAR.*
IT'S USEFUL FOR BINDING THINGS LIKE FURNITURE.
NOTHING GOES TO WASTE!

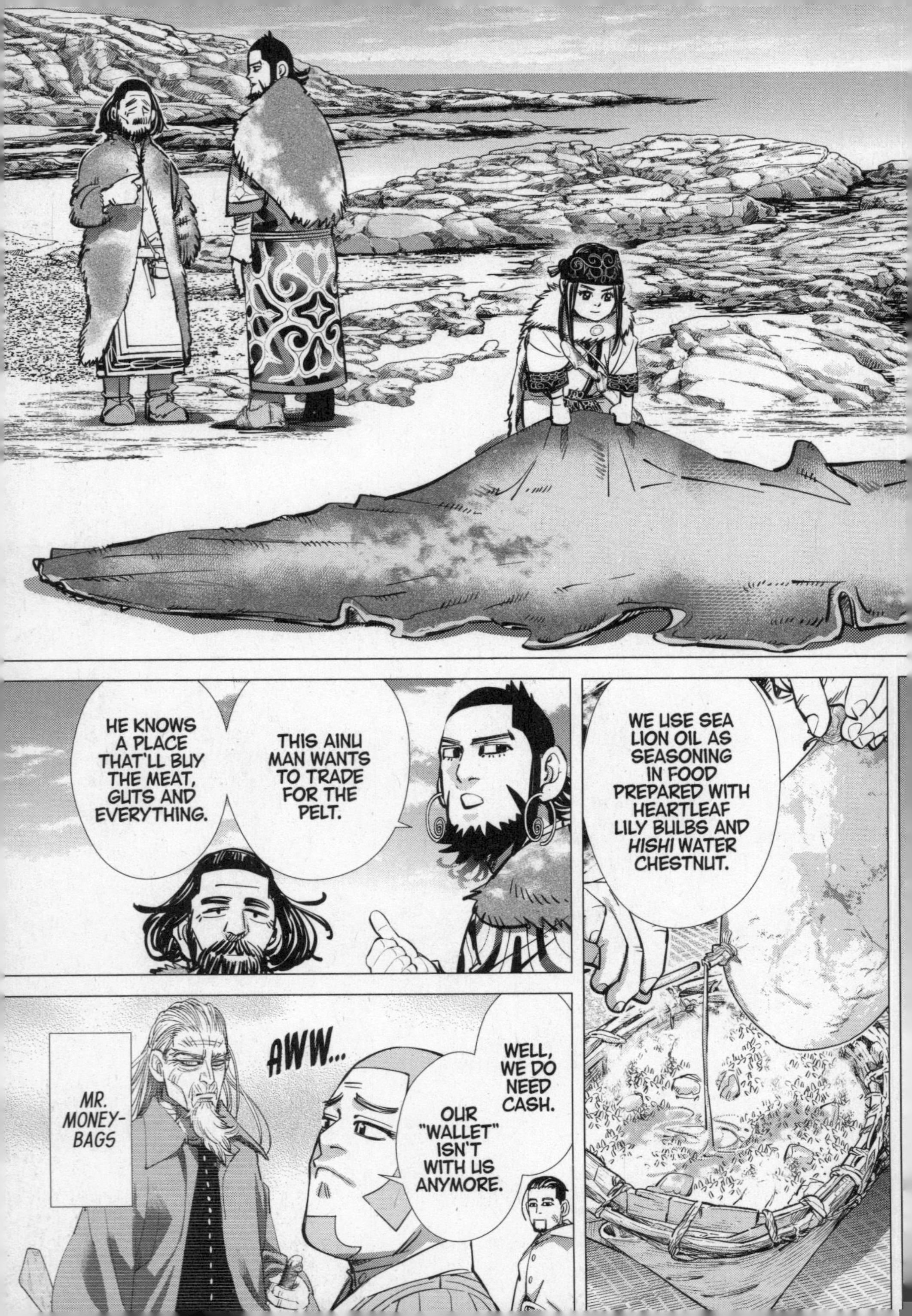
WE USE SEA LION OIL AS SEASONING IN FOOD PREPARED WITH HEARTLEAF LILY BULBS AND HISHI WATER CHESTNUT.
THIS AINU MAN WANTS TO TRADE FOR THE PELT.
HE KNOWS A PLACE THAT'LL BUY THE MEAT, GUTS AND EVERYTHING.
WELL, WE DO NEED CASH.
OUR "WALLET" ISN'T WITH US ANYMORE.
AWW...
MR. MONEY-BAGS

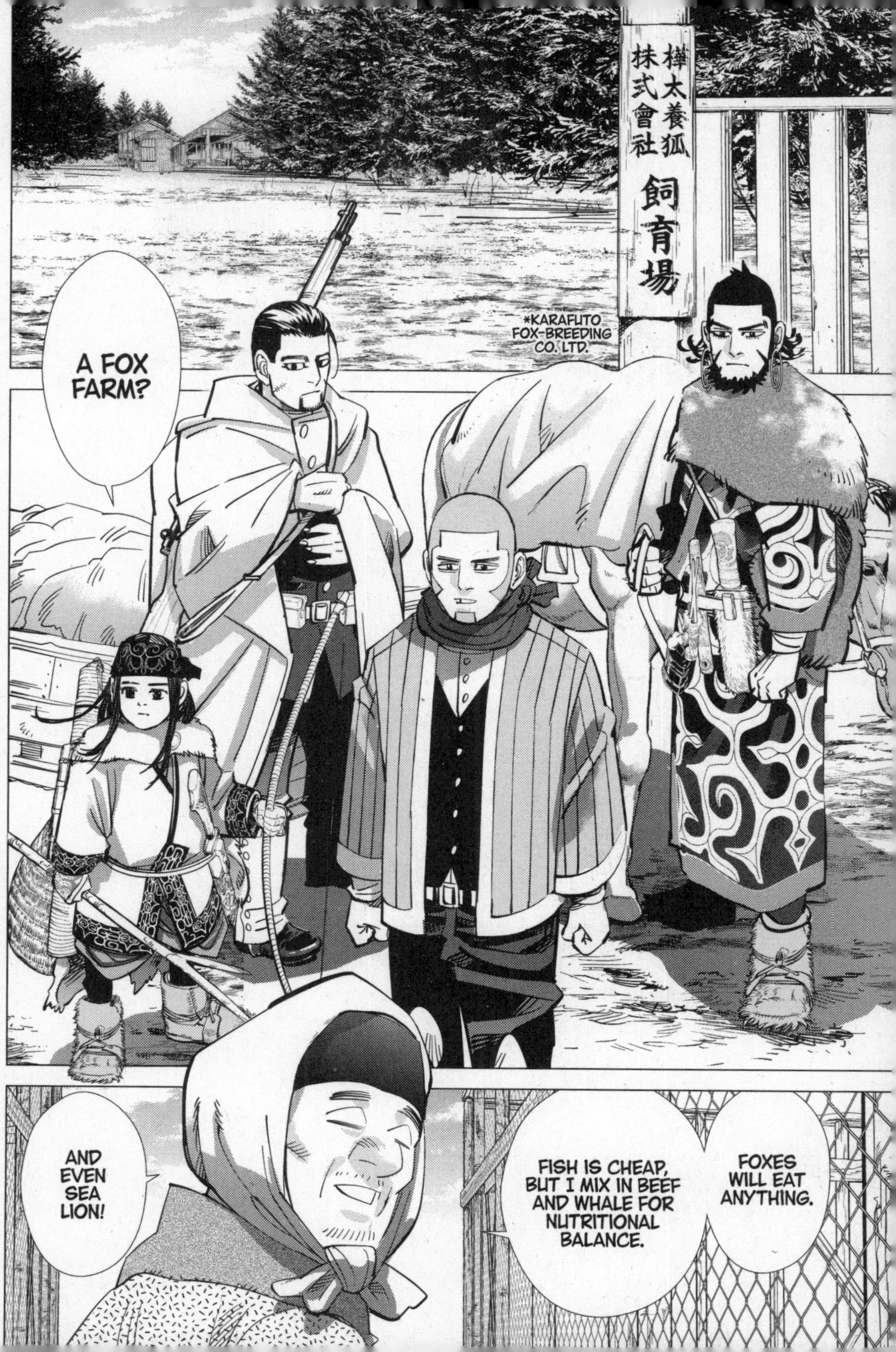
樺太養狐株式會社 飼育場
*KARAFUTO FOX-BREEDING CO. LTD.
A FOX FARM?
FOXES WILL EAT ANYTHING.
FISH IS CHEAP, BUT I MIX IN BEEF AND WHALE FOR NUTRITIONAL BALANCE.
AND EVEN SEA LION!

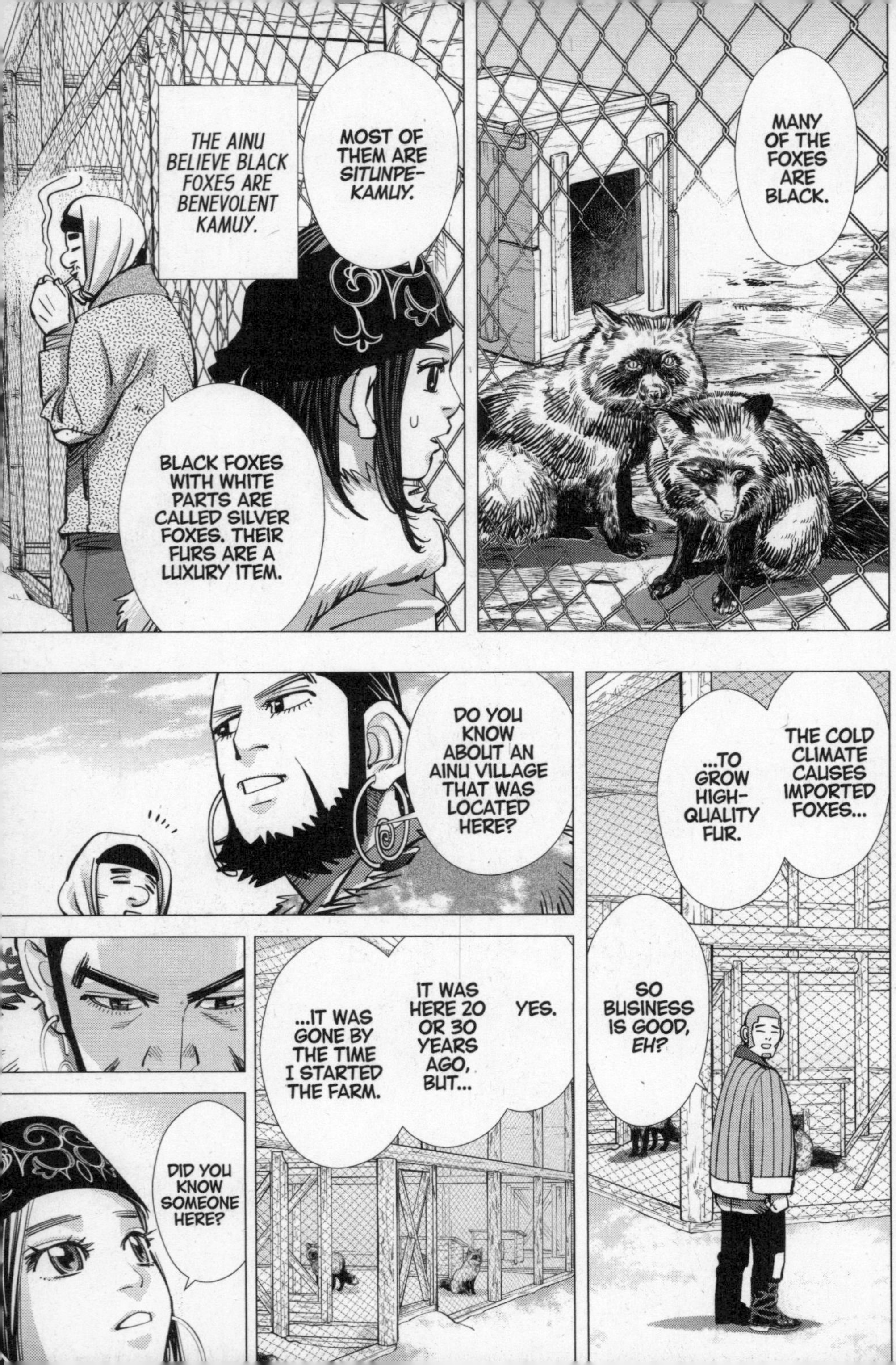
MANY OF THE FOXES ARE BLACK.
MOST OF THEM ARE SITUNPE-KAMUY.
THE AINU BELIEVE BLACK FOXES ARE BENEVOLENT KAMUY.
BLACK FOXES WITH WHITE PARTS ARE CALLED SILVER FOXES. THEIR FURS ARE A LUXURY ITEM.
THE COLD CLIMATE CAUSES IMPORTED FOXES...
...TO GROW HIGH-QUALITY FUR.
SO BUSINESS IS GOOD, EH?
DO YOU KNOW ABOUT AN AINU VILLAGE THAT WAS LOCATED HERE?
YES.
IT WAS HERE 20 OR 30 YEARS AGO, BUT...
...IT WAS GONE BY THE TIME I STARTED THE FARM.
DID YOU KNOW SOMEONE HERE?

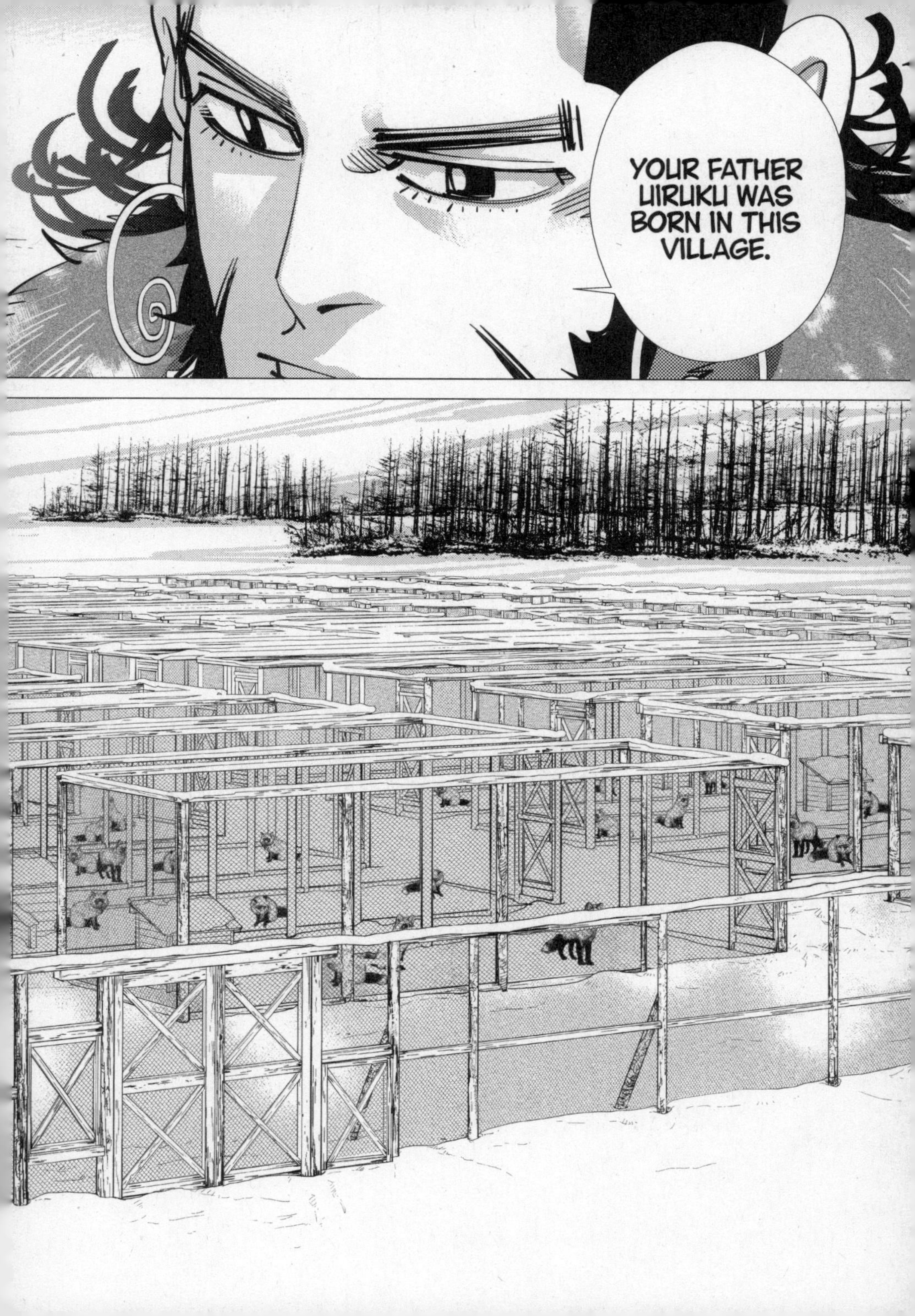
YOUR FATHER UIRUKU WAS BORN IN THIS VILLAGE.

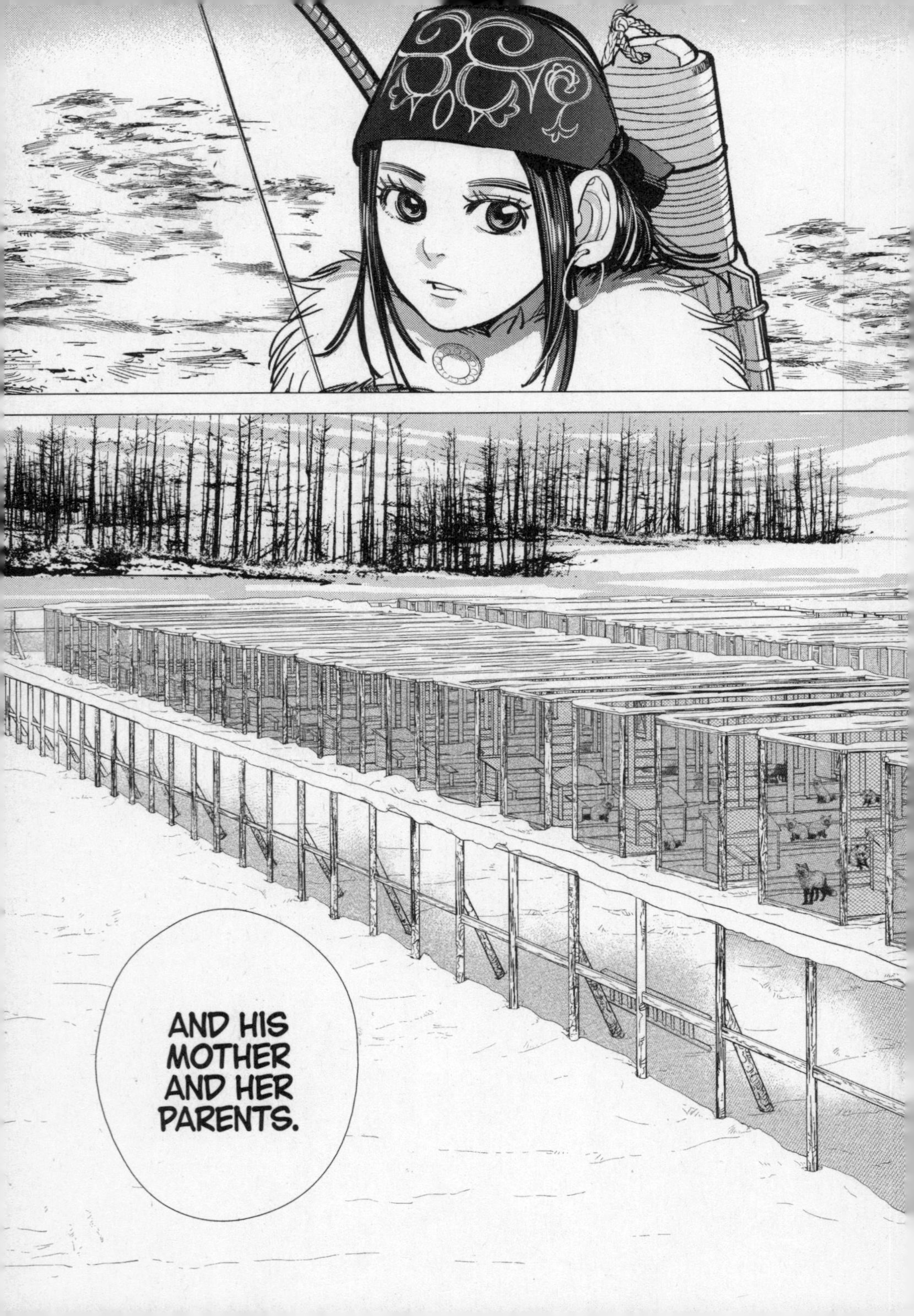
AND HIS MOTHER AND HER PARENTS.

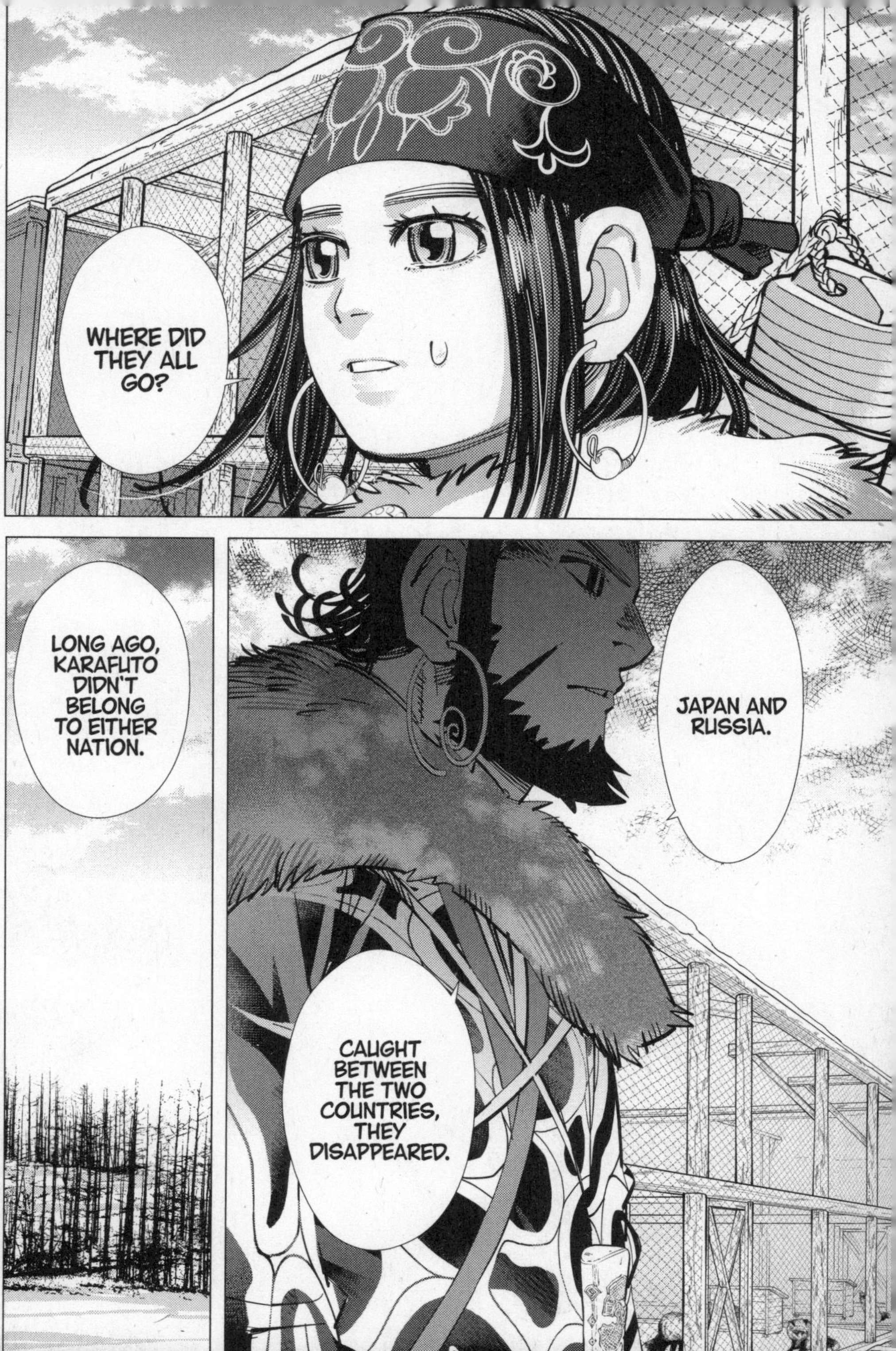
WHERE DID THEY ALL GO?
JAPAN AND RUSSIA.
CAUGHT BETWEEN THE TWO COUNTRIES, THEY DISAPPEARED.
LONG AGO, KARAFUTO DIDN'T BELONG TO EITHER NATION.

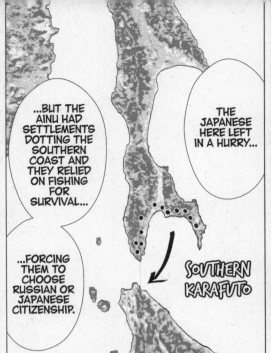

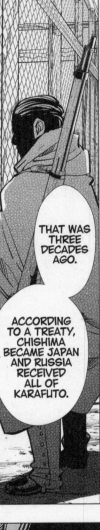

THAT WAS THREE DECADES AGO.
ACCORDING TO A TREATY, CHISHIMA BECAME JAPAN AND RUSSIA RECEIVED ALL OF KARAFUTO.
THE JAPANESE HERE LEFT IN A HURRY...
...BUT THE AINU HAD SETTLEMENTS DOTTING THE SOUTHERN COAST AND THEY RELIED ON FISHING FOR SURVIVAL...
SOUTHERN KARAFUTO
...FORCING THEM TO CHOOSE RUSSIAN OR JAPANESE CITIZENSHIP.
EIGHT HUNDRED FORTY-ONE CHOSE TO BE JAPANESE.
AT THE TIME, APPROXI-MATELY 2,000 AINU LIVED ON SOUTHERN KARAFUTO.
MOST OF THE AINU IN UIRUKU'S VILLAGE LEFT FOR HOKKAIDO ON JAPANESE BOATS.
HIS MOTHER WAS KARAFUTO AINU AND HIS FATHER WAS POLISH, SO THEY REMAINED BEHIND.

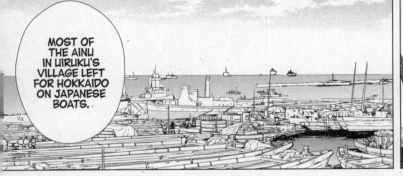

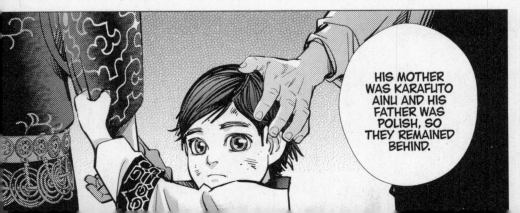

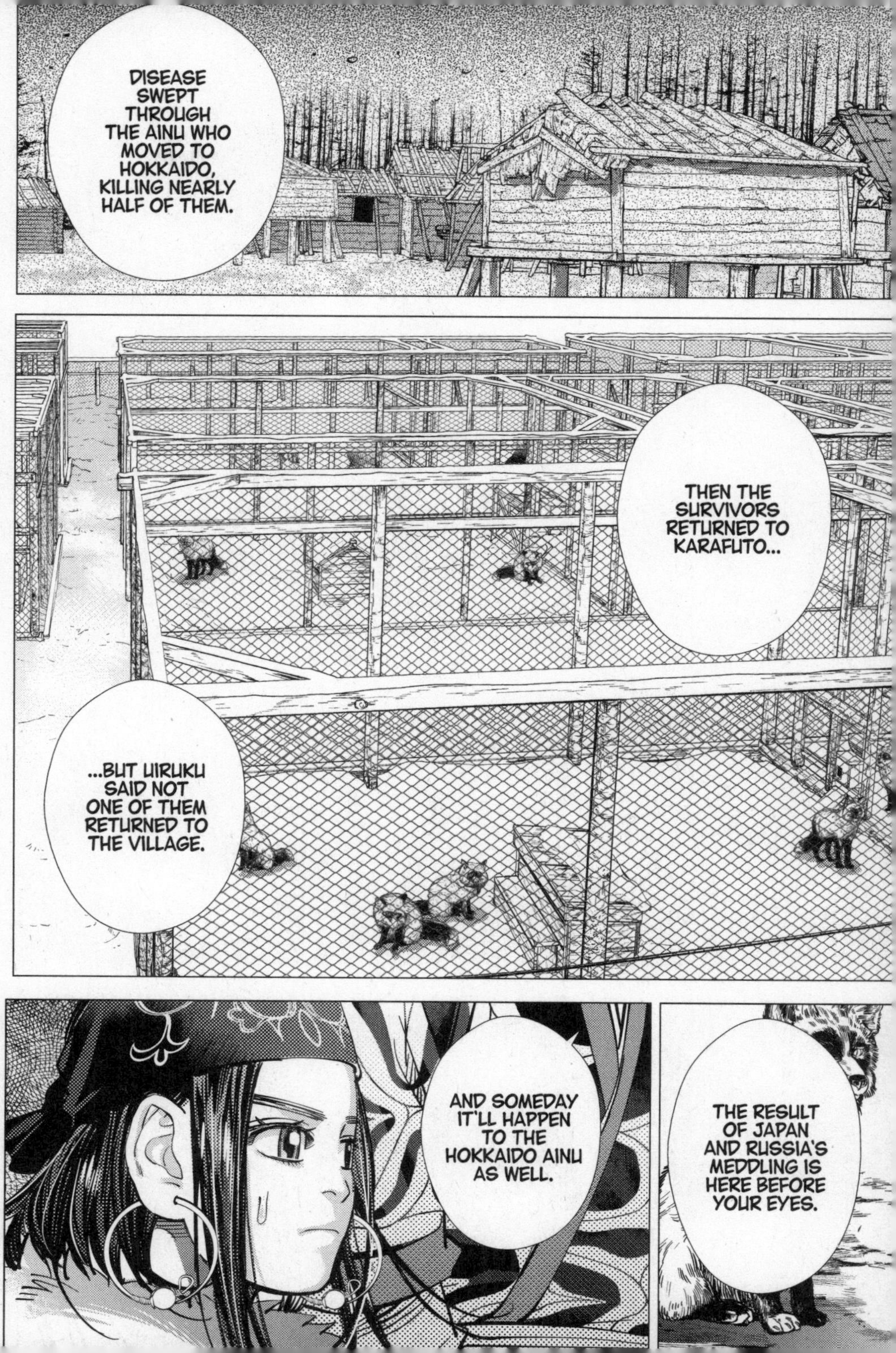
DISEASE SWEPT THROUGH THE AINU WHO MOVED TO HOKKAIDO, KILLING NEARLY HALF OF THEM.
THEN THE SURVIVORS RETURNED TO KARAFUTO...
...BUT WIRUKU SAID NOT ONE OF THEM RETURNED TO THE VILLAGE.
THE RESULT OF JAPAN AND RUSSIA'S MEDDLING IS HERE BEFORE YOUR EYES.
AND SOMEDAY IT'LL HAPPEN TO THE HOKKAIDO AINU AS WELL.

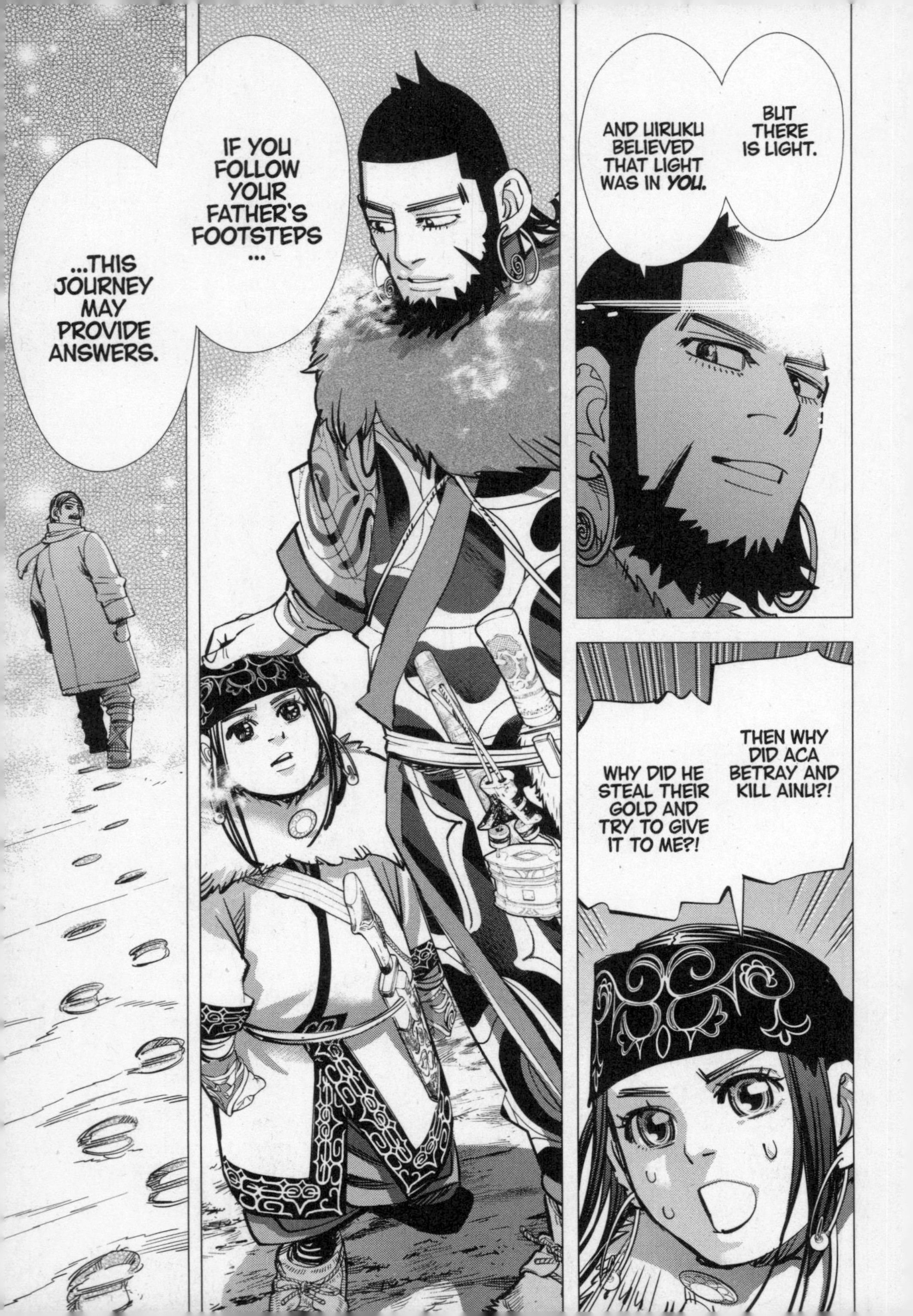
BUT THERE IS LIGHT.
AND UIRUKU BELIEVED THAT LIGHT WAS IN *YOU*.
THEN WHY DID ACA BETRAY AND KILL AINU?!
WHY DID HE STEAL THEIR GOLD AND TRY TO GIVE IT TO ME?!
IF YOU FOLLOW YOUR FATHER'S FOOTSTEPS ...
...THIS JOURNEY MAY PROVIDE ANSWERS.

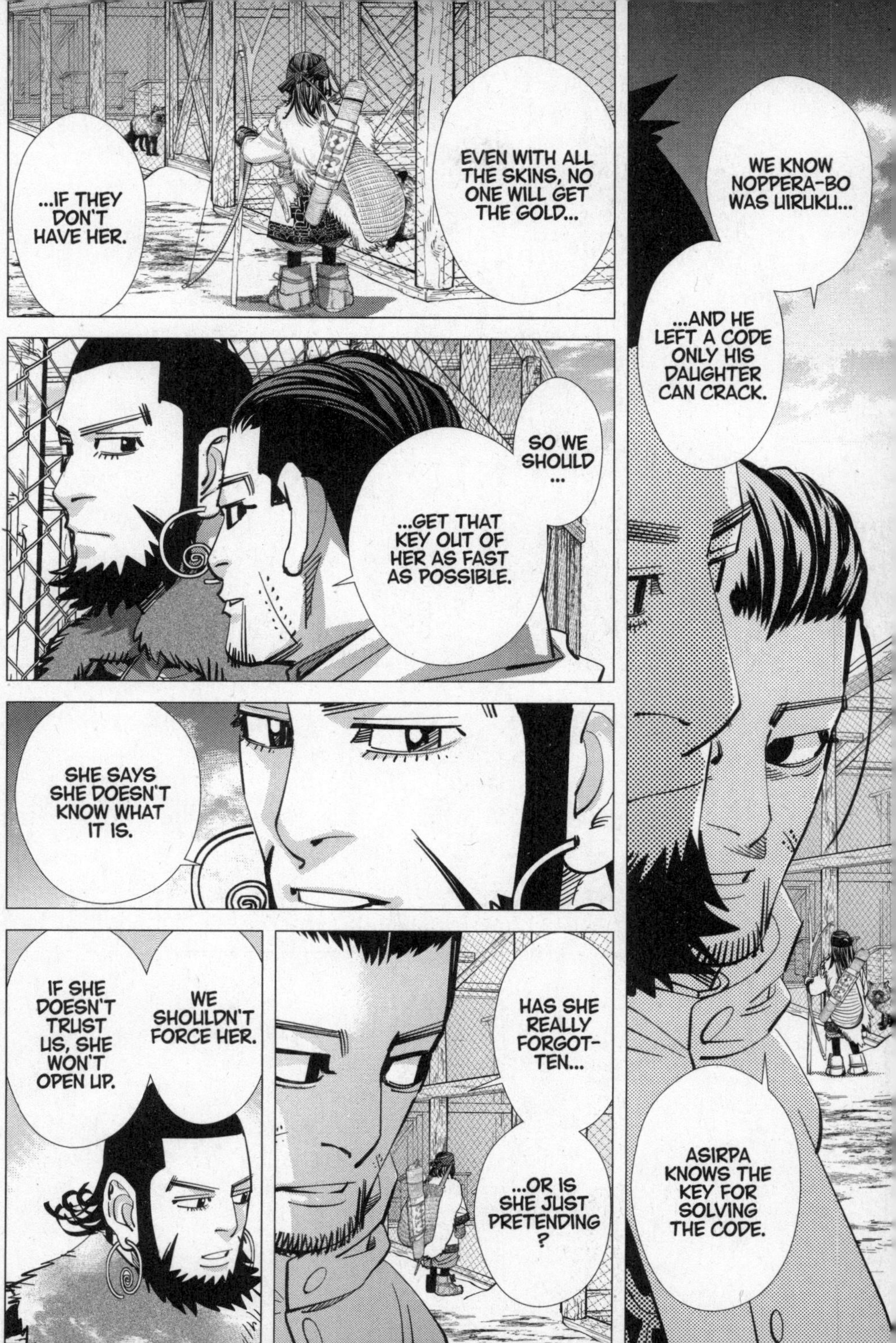
WE KNOW NOPPERA-BO WAS UIRUKU...
...AND HE LEFT A CODE ONLY HIS DAUGHTER CAN CRACK.
ASIRPA KNOWS THE KEY FOR SOLVING THE CODE.
EVEN WITH ALL THE SKINS, NO ONE WILL GET THE GOLD...
...IF THEY DON'T HAVE HER.
SO WE SHOULD...
...GET THAT KEY OUT OF HER AS FAST AS POSSIBLE.
SHE SAYS SHE DOESN'T KNOW WHAT IT IS.
HAS SHE REALLY FORGOT-TEN...
...OR IS SHE JUST PRETENDING?
WE SHOULDN'T FORCE HER.
IF SHE DOESN'T TRUST US, SHE WON'T OPEN UP.

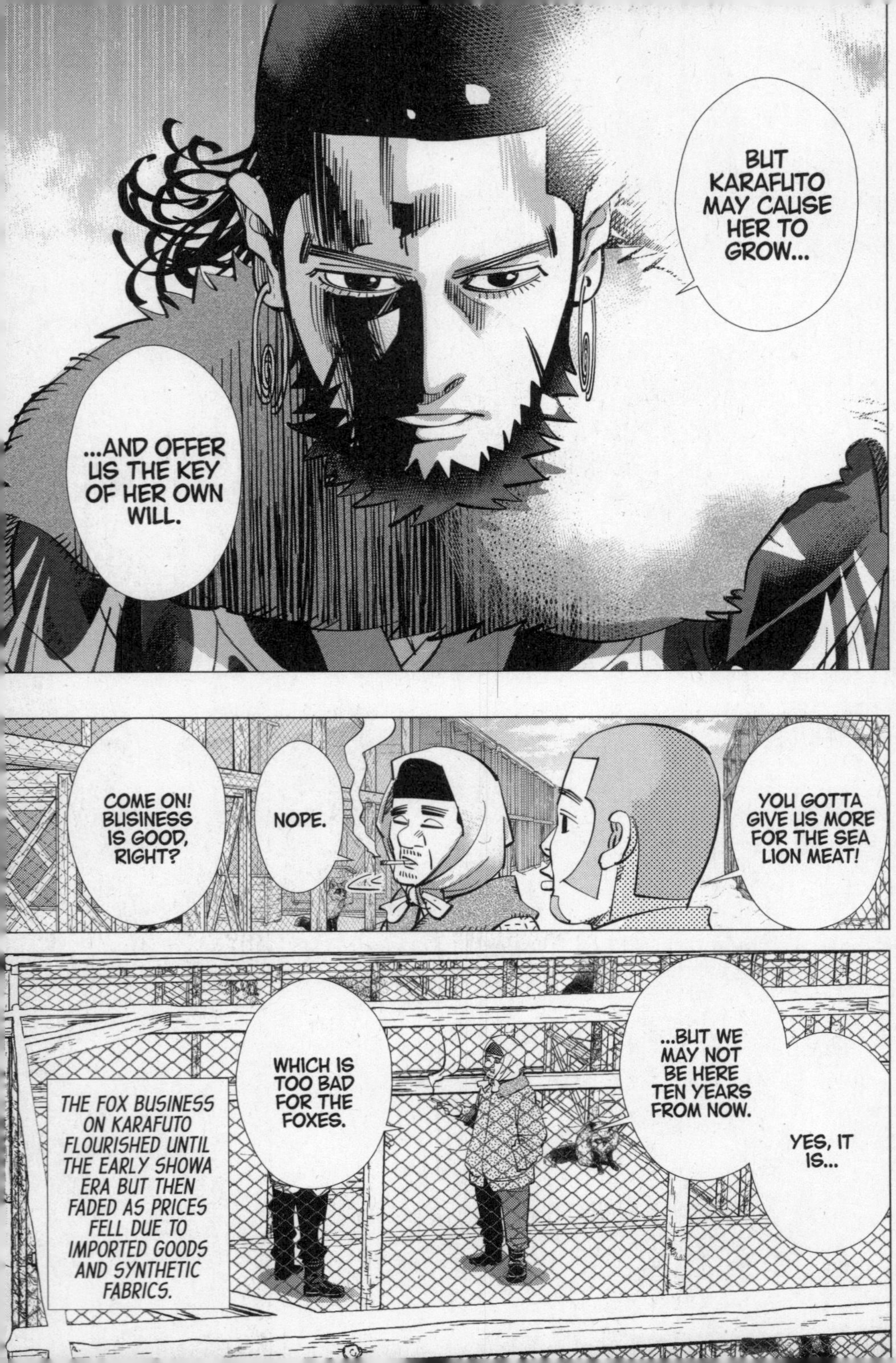
BUT KARAFUTO MAY CAUSE HER TO GROW...
...AND OFFER US THE KEY OF HER OWN WILL.
YOU GOTTA GIVE US MORE FOR THE SEA LION MEAT!
NOPE.
COME ON! BUSINESS IS GOOD, RIGHT?
YES, IT IS...
...BUT WE MAY NOT BE HERE TEN YEARS FROM NOW.
WHICH IS TOO BAD FOR THE FOXES.
THE FOX BUSINESS ON KARAFUTO FLOURISHED UNTIL THE EARLY SHOWA ERA BUT THEN FADED AS PRICES FELL DUE TO IMPORTED GOODS AND SYNTHETIC FABRICS.

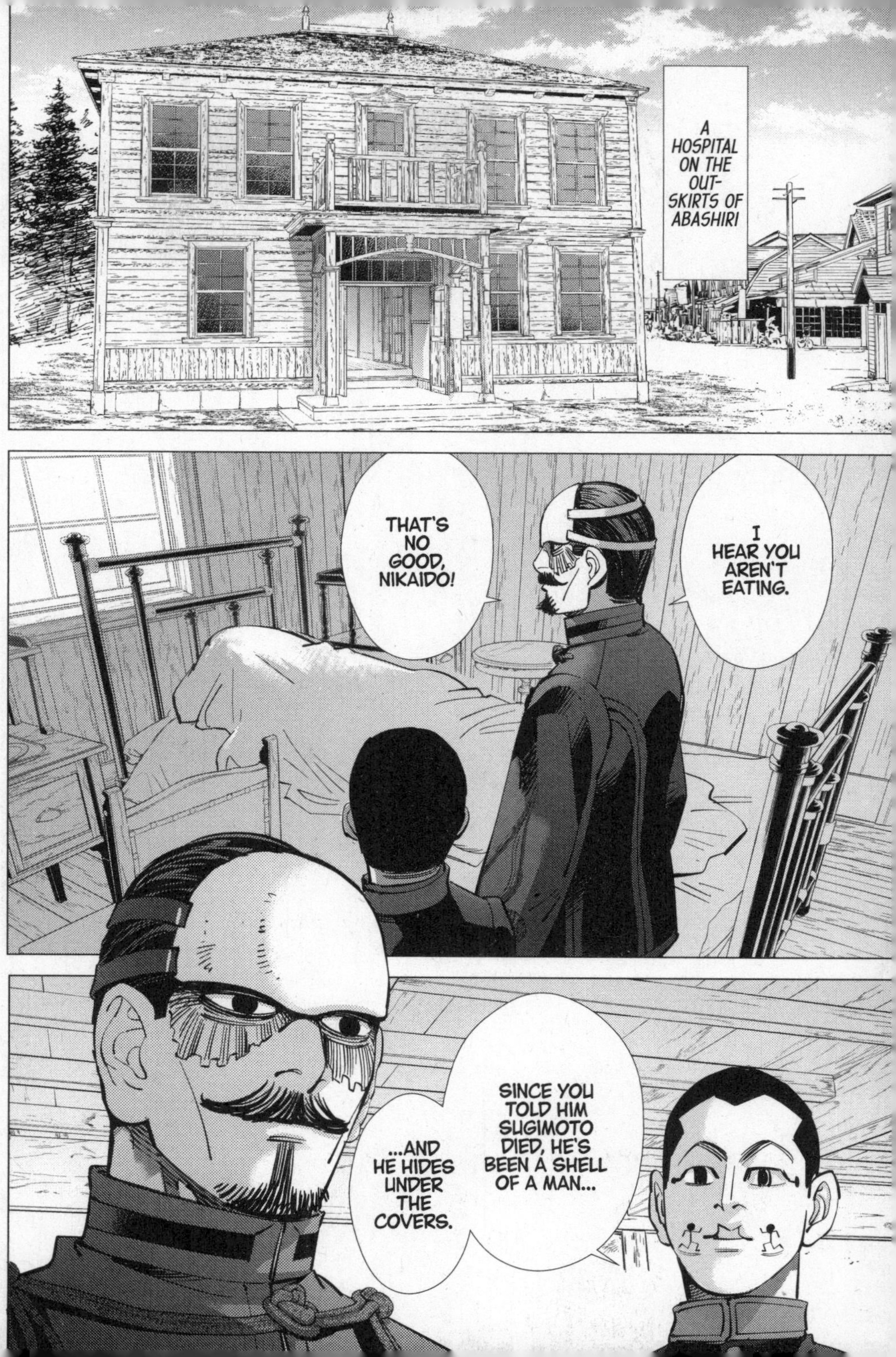
A HOSPITAL ON THE OUT-SKIRTS OF ABASHIRI
I HEAR YOU AREN'T EATING.
THAT'S NO GOOD, NIKAIDO!
SINCE YOU TOLD HIM SUGIMOTO DIED, HE'S BEEN A SHELL OF A MAN...
...AND HE HIDES UNDER THE COVERS.

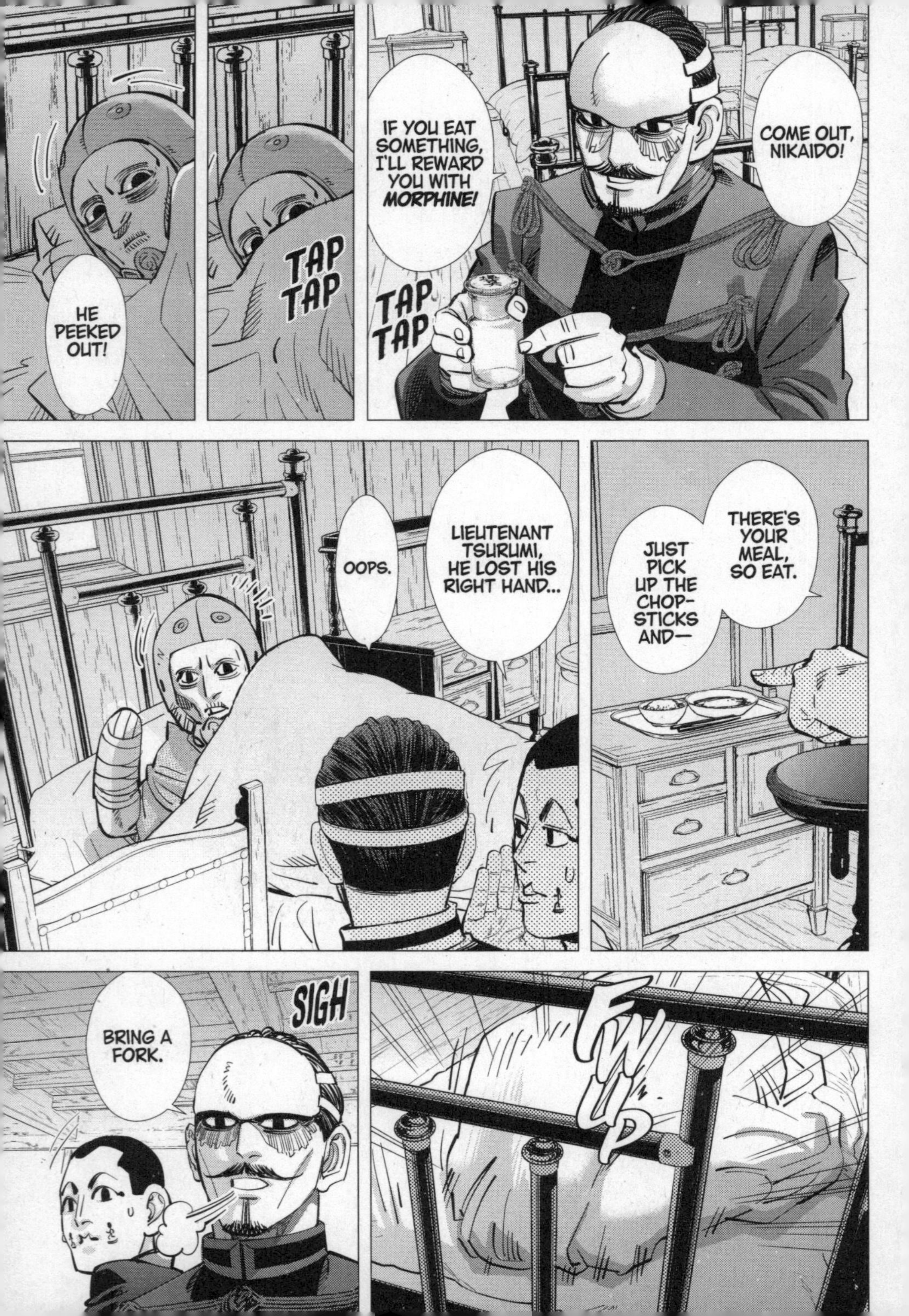
COME OUT, NIKAIDO!
IF YOU EAT SOMETHING, I'LL REWARD YOU WITH MORPHINE!
TAP TAP
TAP TAP
HE PEEKED OUT!
THERE'S YOUR MEAL, SO EAT.
JUST PICK UP THE CHOP-STICKS AND—
LIEUTENANT TSURUMI, HE LOST HIS RIGHT HAND...
OOPS.
FWUP
SIGH
BRING A FORK.

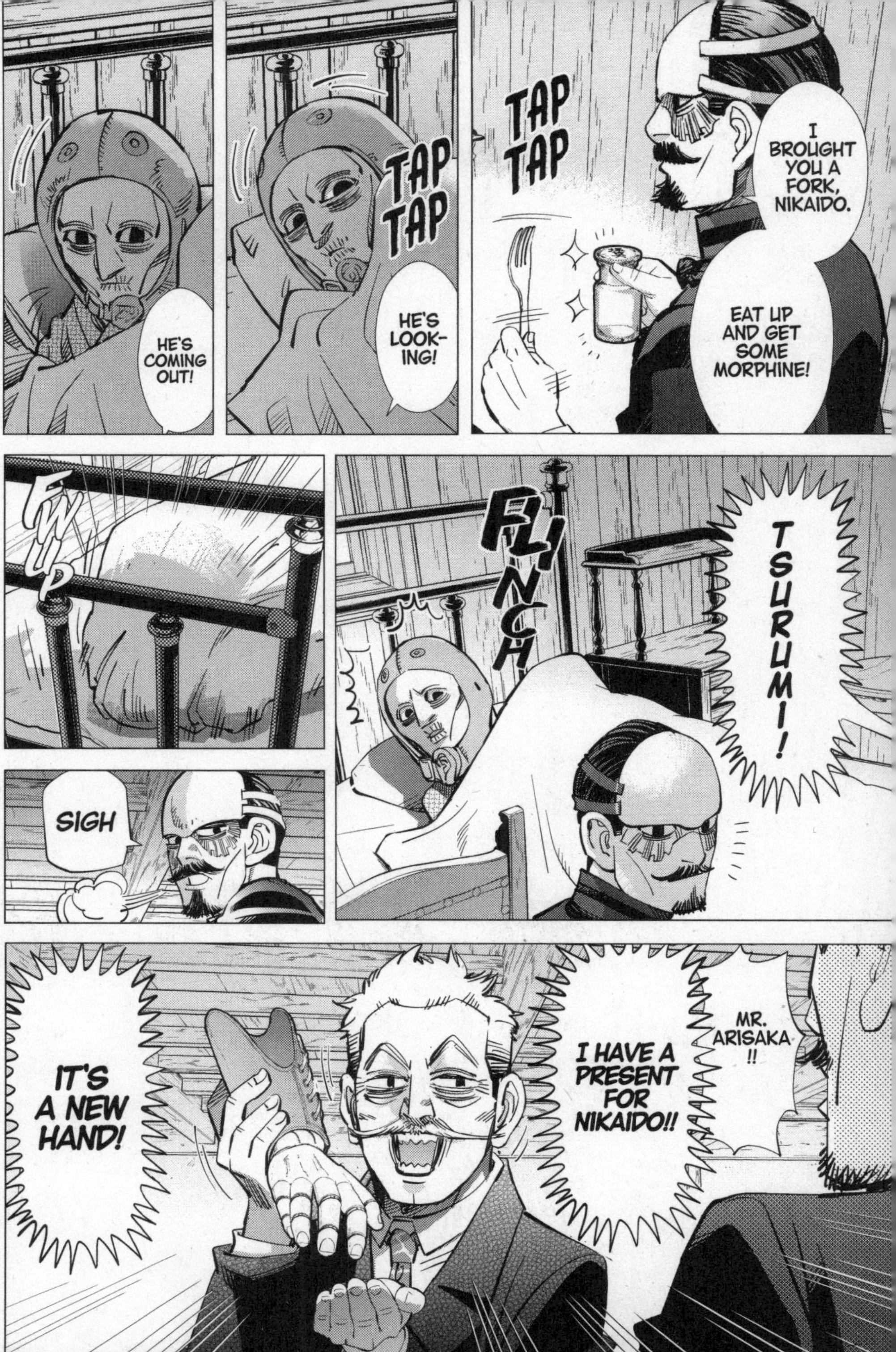
TAP TAP
I BROUGHT YOU A FORK, NIKAIDO.
EAT UP AND GET SOME MORPHINE!
TAP TAP
HE'S LOOKING!
HE'S COMING OUT!
FLINCH
TSURUMI!
FWUP
SIGH
MR. ARISAKA!!
I HAVE A PRESENT FOR NIKAIDO!!
IT'S A NEW HAND!

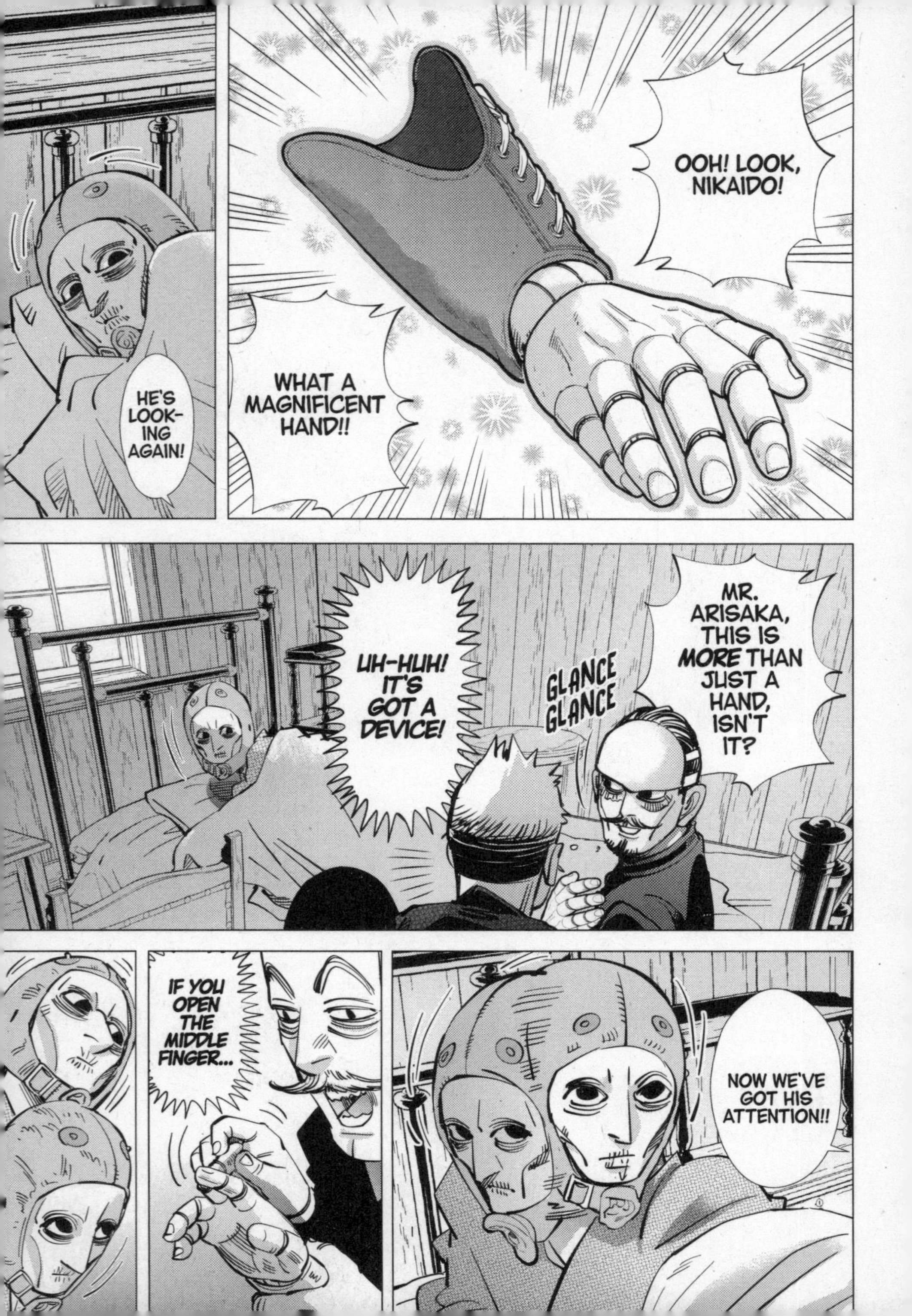
OOH! LOOK, NIKAIDO!
WHAT A MAGNIFICENT HAND!!
HE'S LOOKING AGAIN!
MR. ARISAKA, THIS IS MORE THAN JUST A HAND, ISN'T IT?
GLANCE GLANCE
UH-HUH! IT'S GOT A DEVICE!
NOW WE'VE GOT HIS ATTENTION!!
IF YOU OPEN THE MIDDLE FINGER...

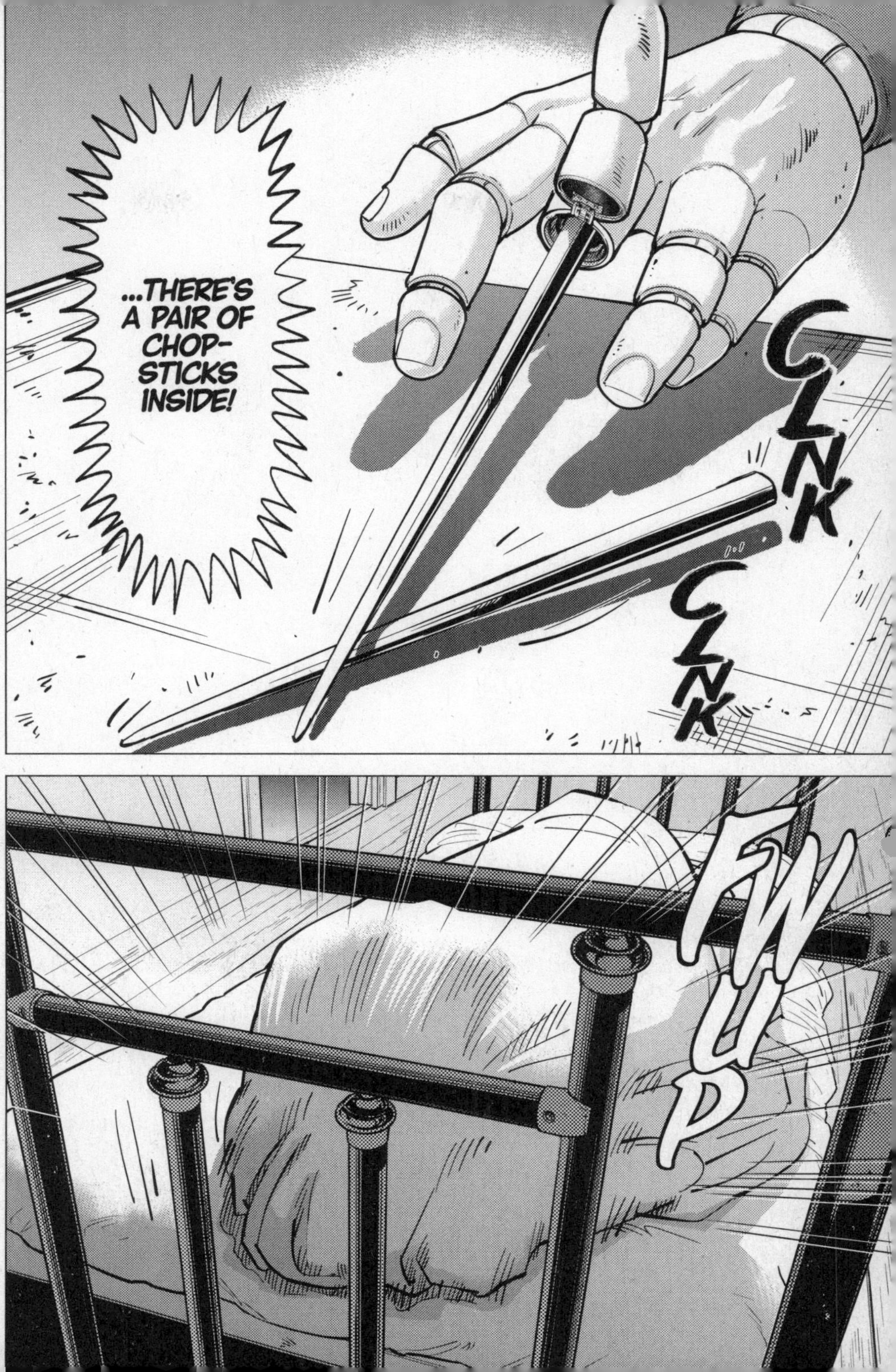
...THERE'S A PAIR OF CHOP-STICKS INSIDE!
CLNK
CLNK
FWUP

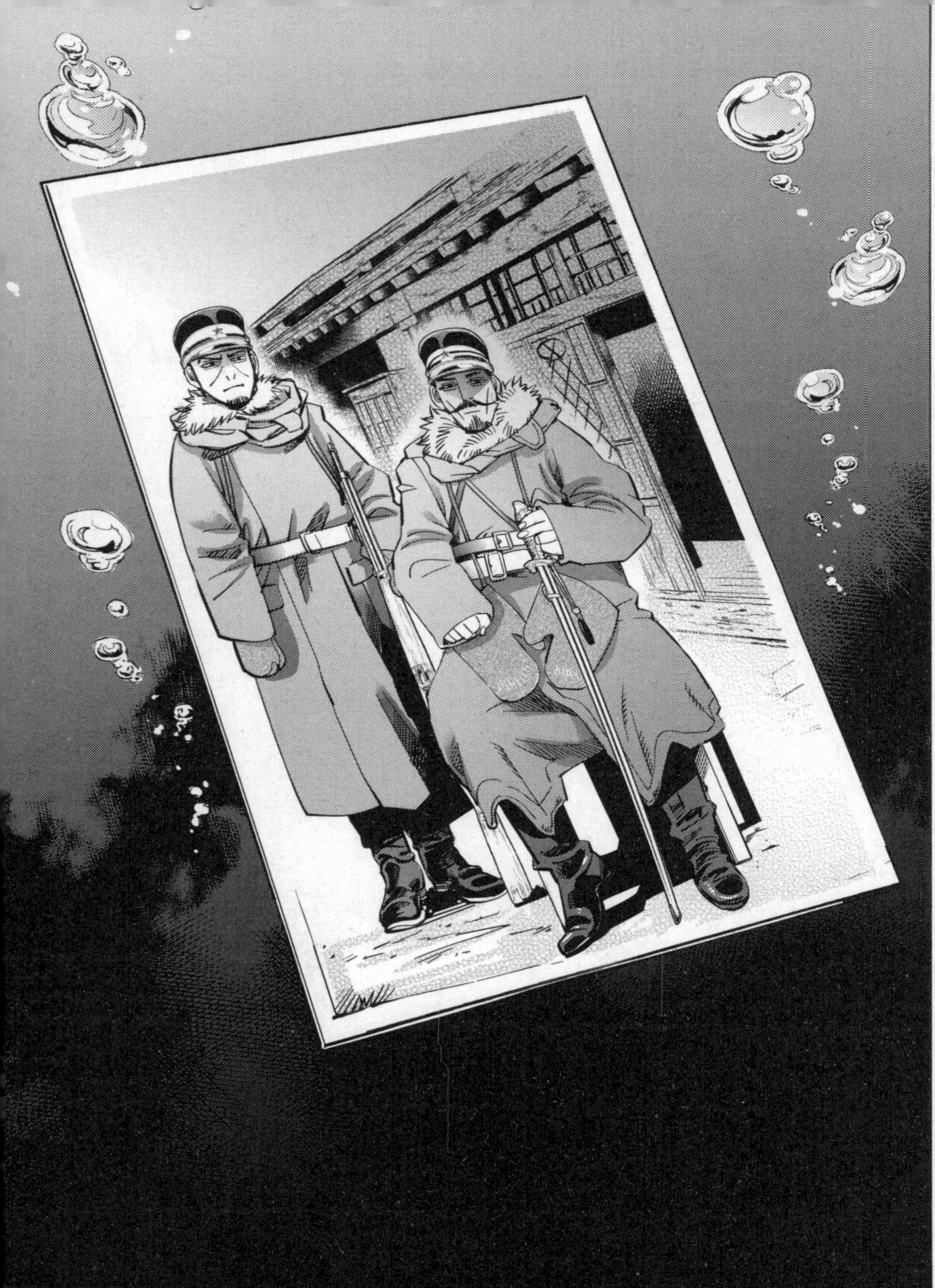

Chapter 149: Igogusa

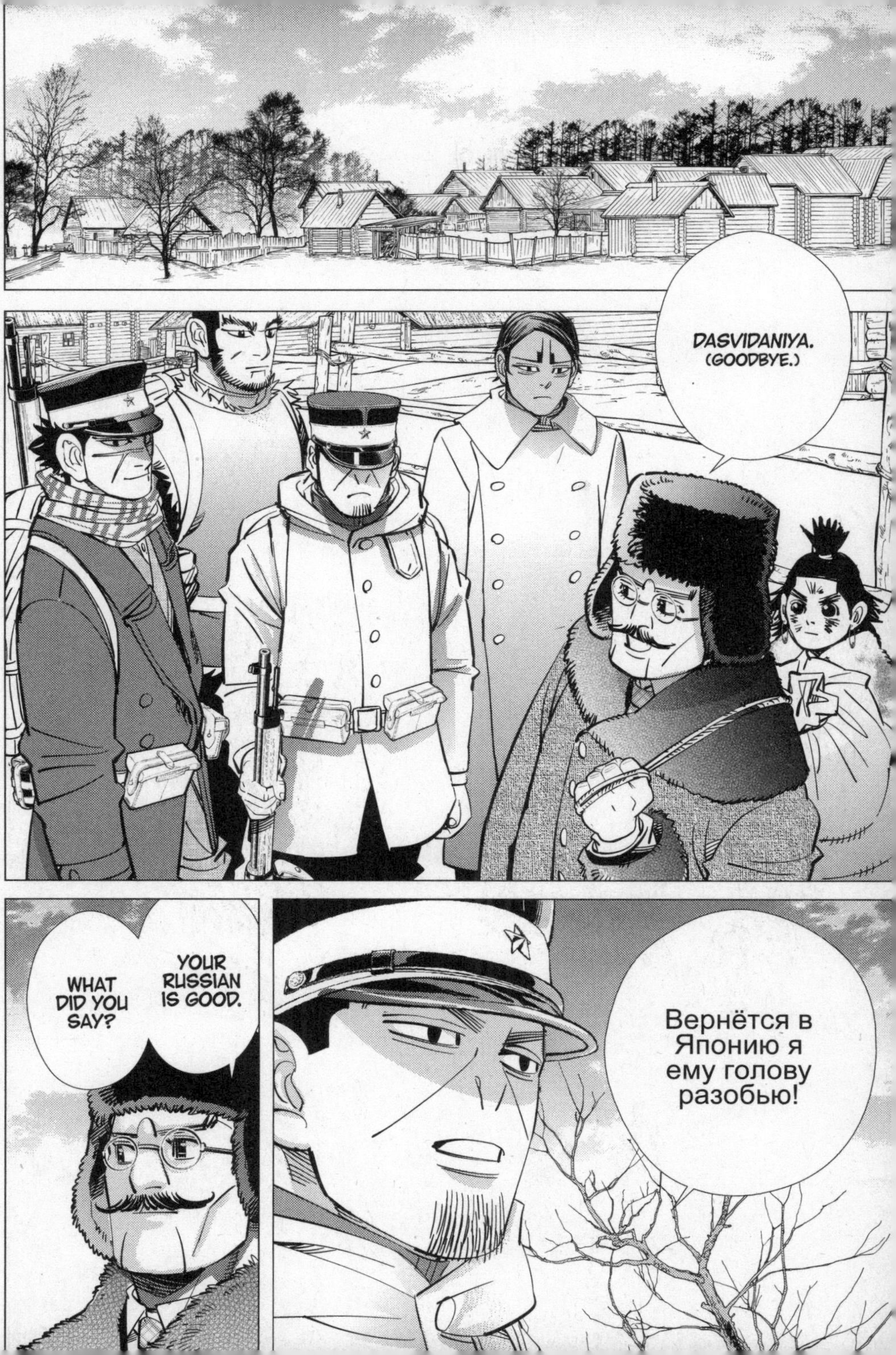
DASVIDANIYA.
(GOODBYE.)
Вернётся в Японию я ему голову разобью!
YOUR RUSSIAN IS GOOD.
WHAT DID YOU SAY?

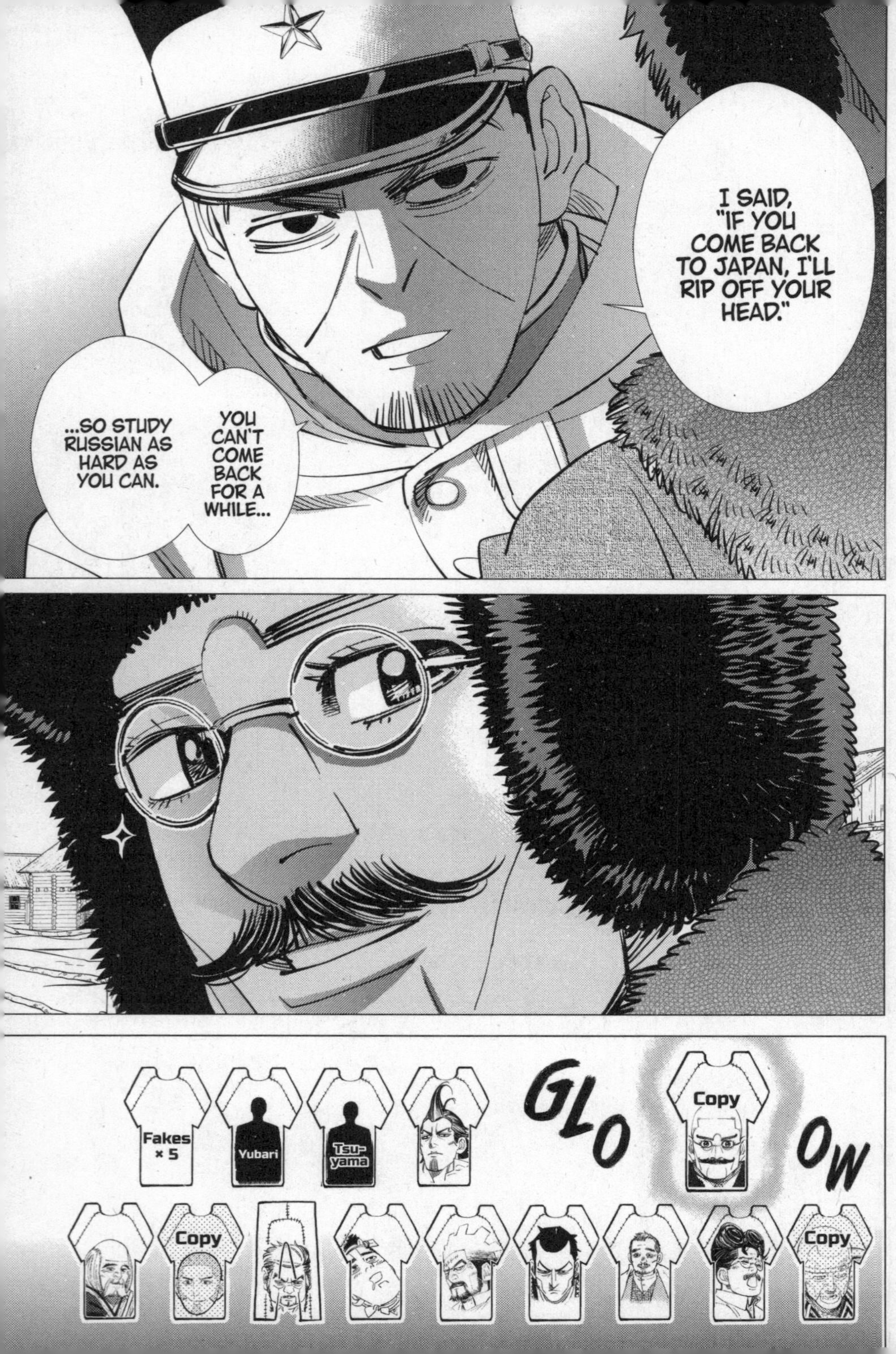
I SAID, "IF YOU COME BACK TO JAPAN, I'LL RIP OFF YOUR HEAD."
YOU CAN'T COME BACK FOR A WHILE...
...SO STUDY RUSSIAN AS HARD AS YOU CAN.
GLOOW
Copy
Tsu-yama
Yubari
Fakes × 5
Copy
Copy

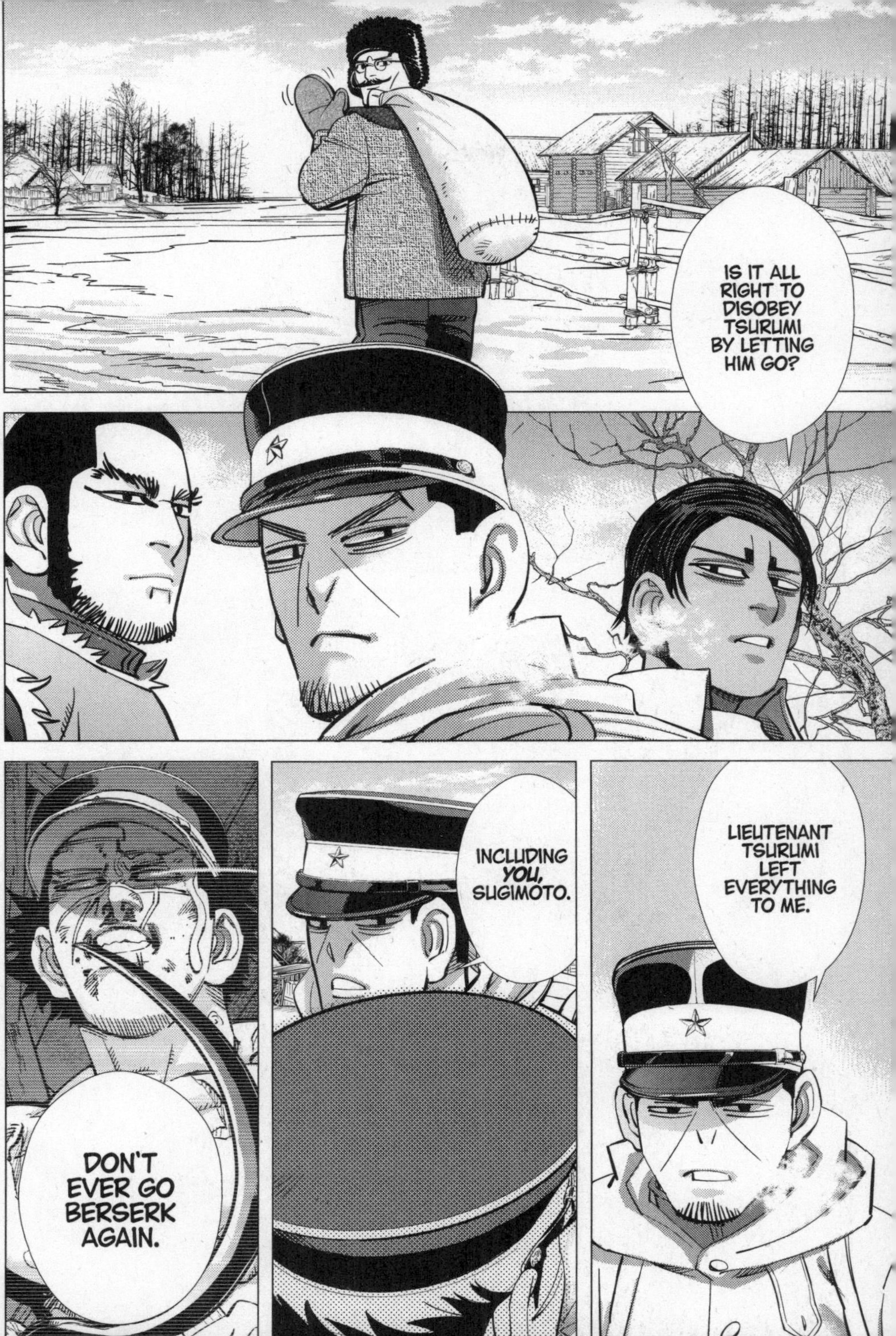
IS IT ALL RIGHT TO DISOBEY TSURUMI BY LETTING HIM GO?
LIEUTENANT TSURUMI LEFT EVERYTHING TO ME.
INCLUDING *YOU*, SUGIMOTO.
DON'T EVER GO BERSERK AGAIN.

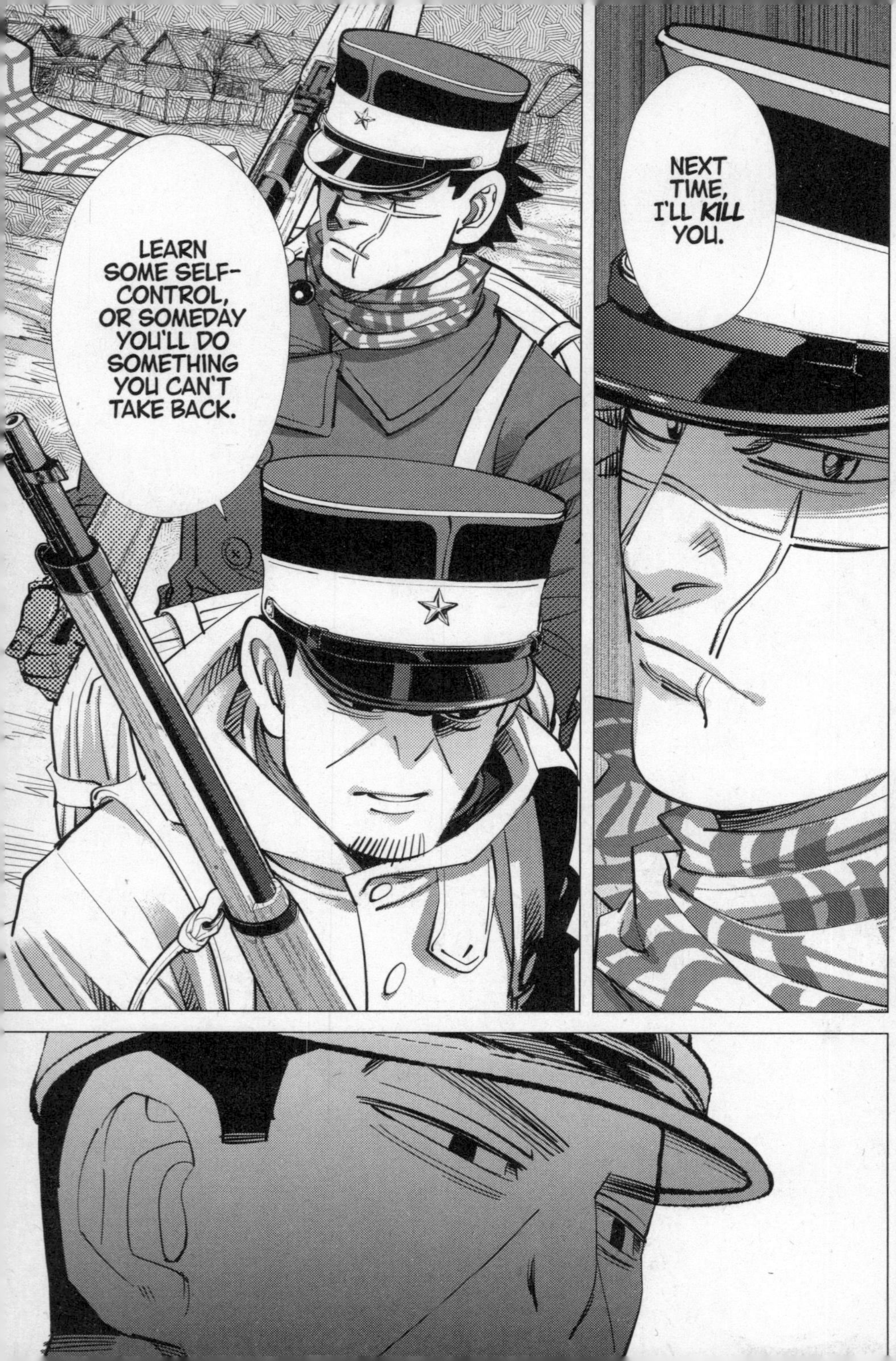
NEXT TIME, I'LL KILL YOU.
LEARN SOME SELF-CONTROL, OR SOMEDAY YOU'LL DO SOMETHING YOU CAN'T TAKE BACK.

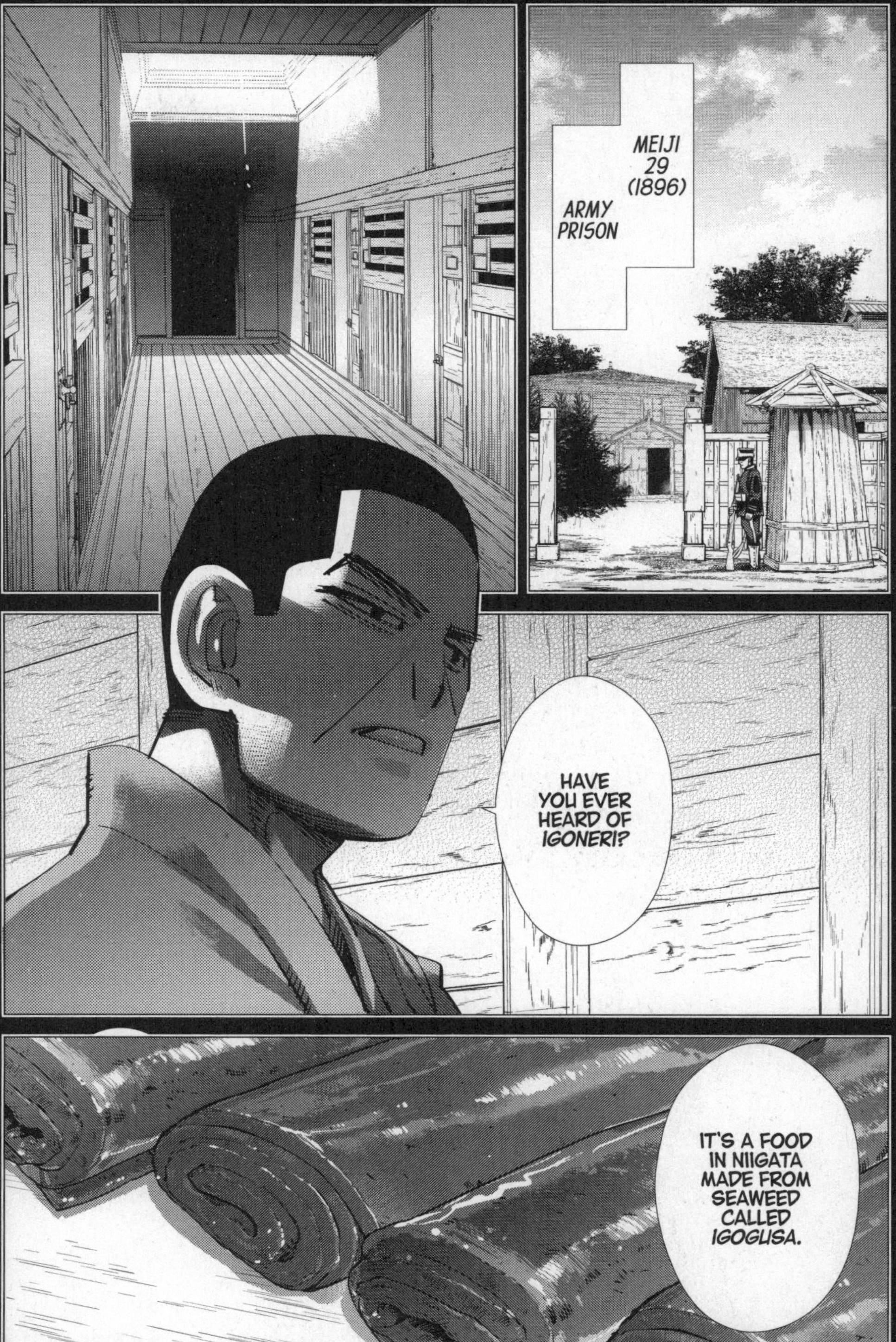
MEIJI 29 (1896)
ARMY PRISON
HAVE YOU EVER HEARD OF IGONERI?
IT'S A FOOD IN NIIGATA MADE FROM SEAWEED CALLED IGOGUSA.

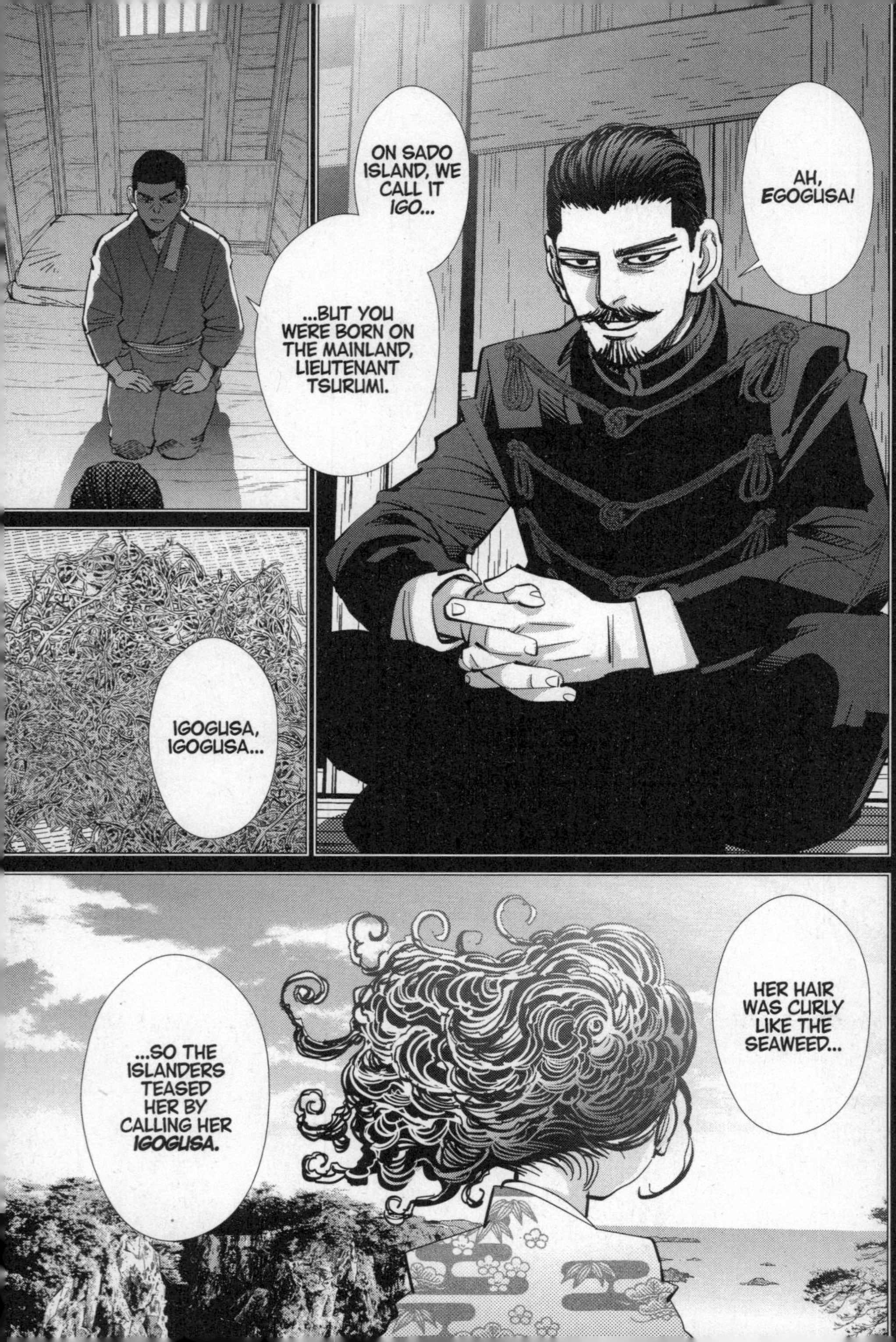
AH, EGOGUSA!
ON SADO ISLAND, WE CALL IT IGO...
...BUT YOU WERE BORN ON THE MAINLAND, LIEUTENANT TSURUMI.
IGOGUSA, IGOGUSA...
HER HAIR WAS CURLY LIKE THE SEAWEED...
...SO THE ISLANDERS TEASED HER BY CALLING HER IGOGUSA.

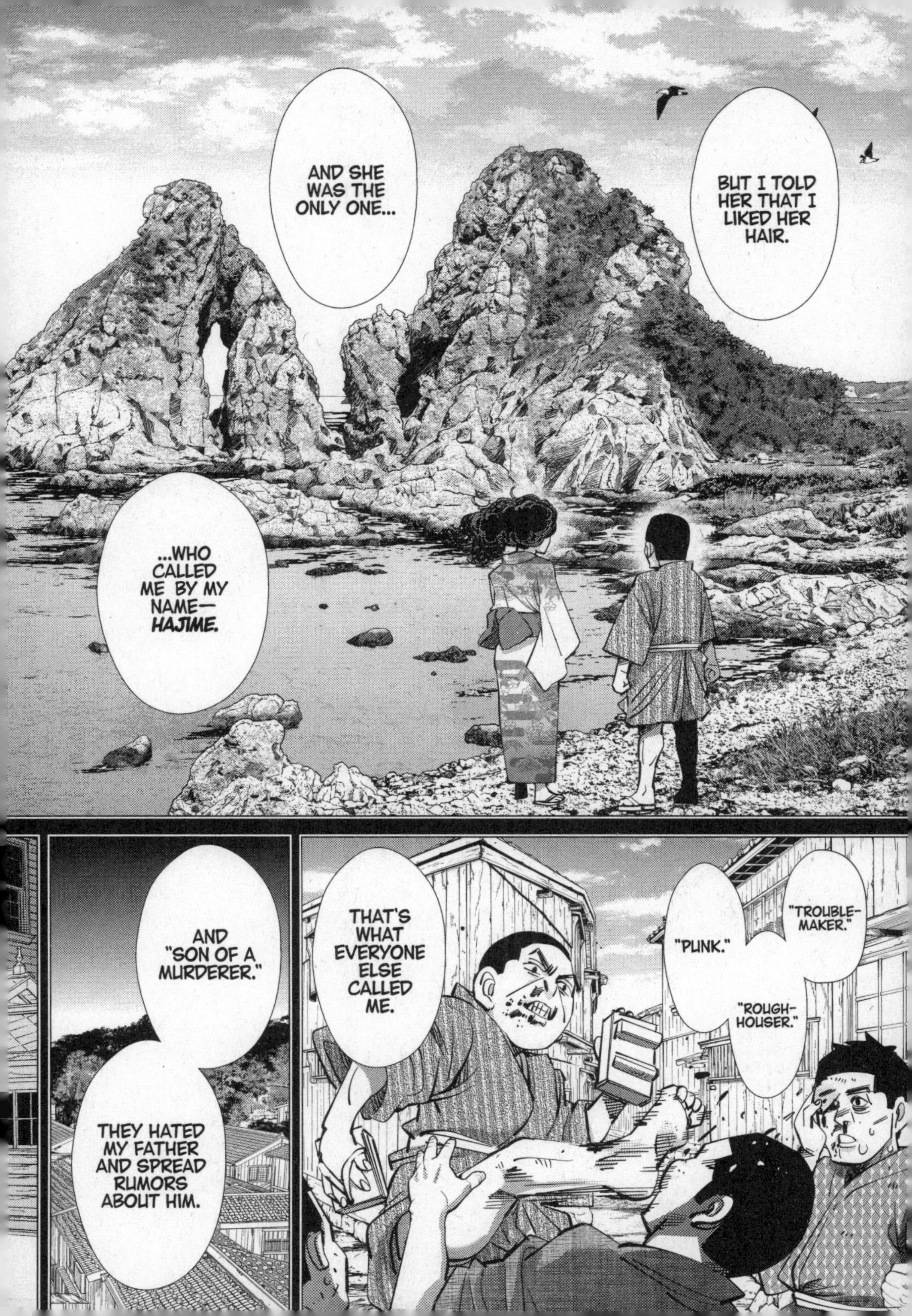
BUT I TOLD HER THAT I LIKED HER HAIR.
AND SHE WAS THE ONLY ONE...
...WHO CALLED ME BY MY NAME—HAJIME.
"TROUBLE-MAKER."
"PUNK."
"ROUGH-HOUSER."
THAT'S WHAT EVERYONE ELSE CALLED ME.
AND "SON OF A MURDERER."
THEY HATED MY FATHER AND SPREAD RUMORS ABOUT HIM.

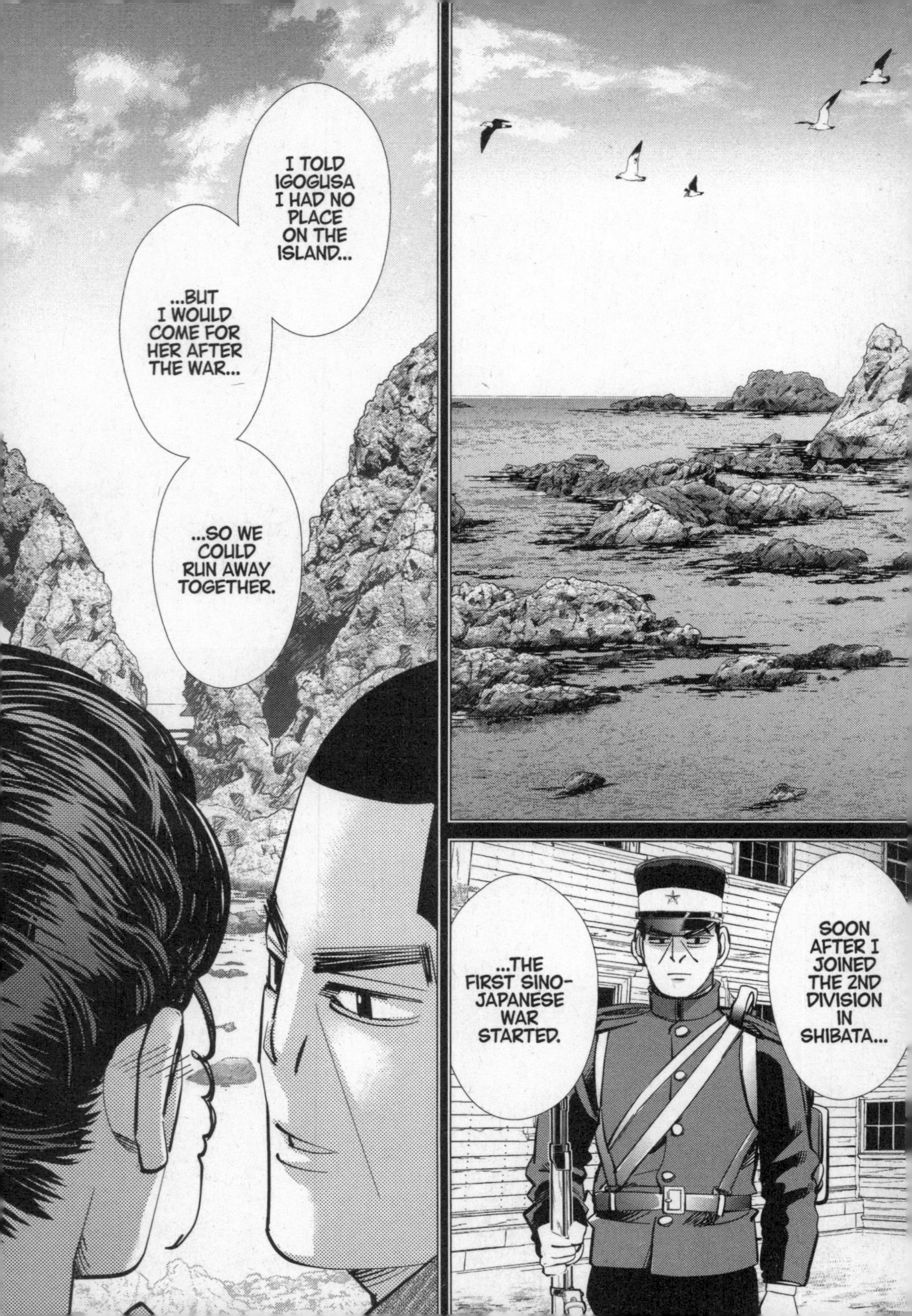
SOON AFTER I JOINED THE 2ND DIVISION IN SHIBATA...
...THE FIRST SINO-JAPANESE WAR STARTED.
I TOLD IGOGUSA I HAD NO PLACE ON THE ISLAND...
...BUT I WOULD COME FOR HER AFTER THE WAR...
...SO WE COULD RUN AWAY TOGETHER.

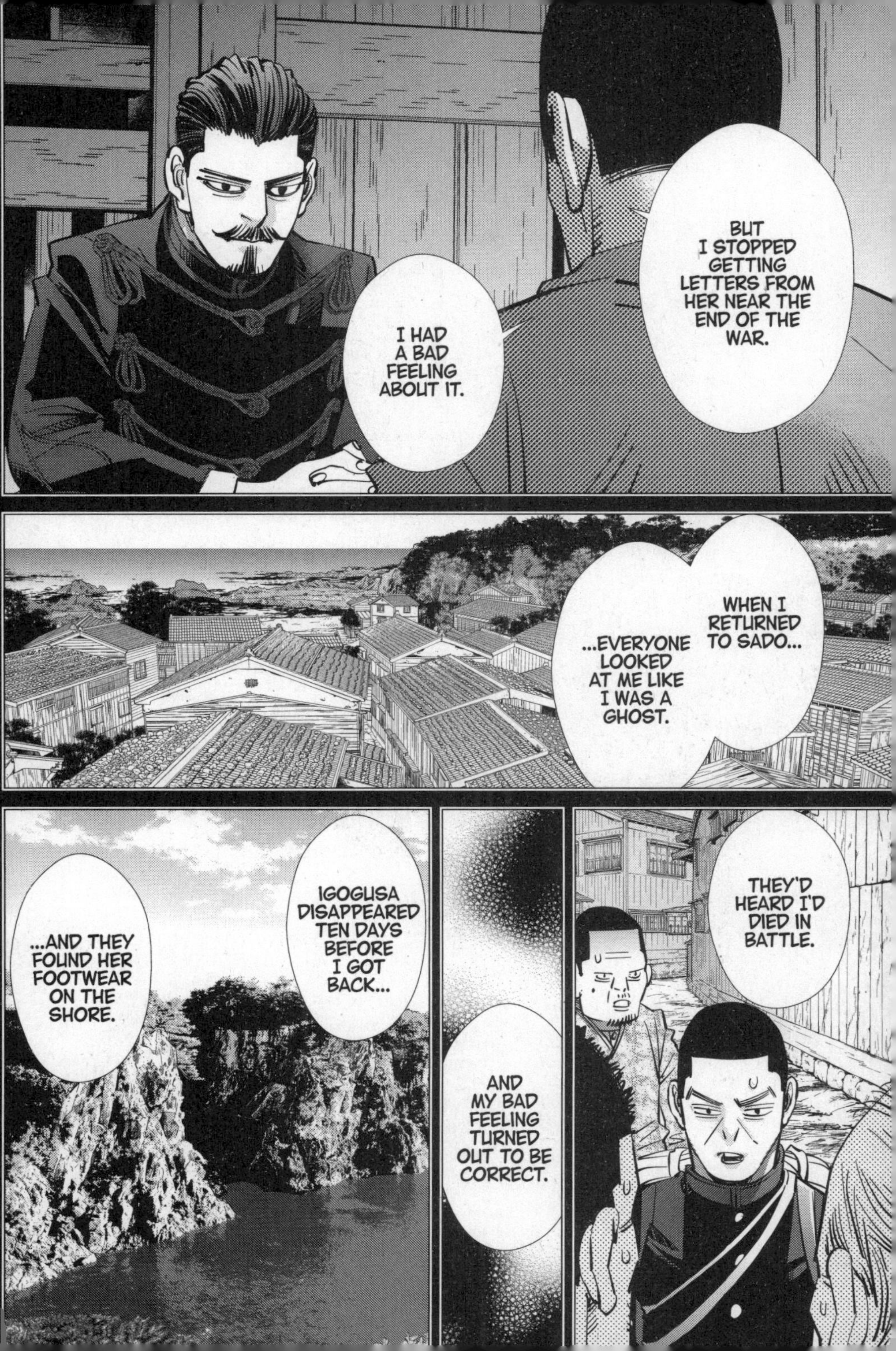
BUT I STOPPED GETTING LETTERS FROM HER NEAR THE END OF THE WAR.
I HAD A BAD FEELING ABOUT IT.
WHEN I RETURNED TO SADO...
...EVERYONE LOOKED AT ME LIKE I WAS A GHOST.
THEY'D HEARD I'D DIED IN BATTLE.
AND MY BAD FEELING TURNED OUT TO BE CORRECT.
IGOGUSA DISAPPEARED TEN DAYS BEFORE I GOT BACK...
...AND THEY FOUND HER FOOTWEAR ON THE SHORE.

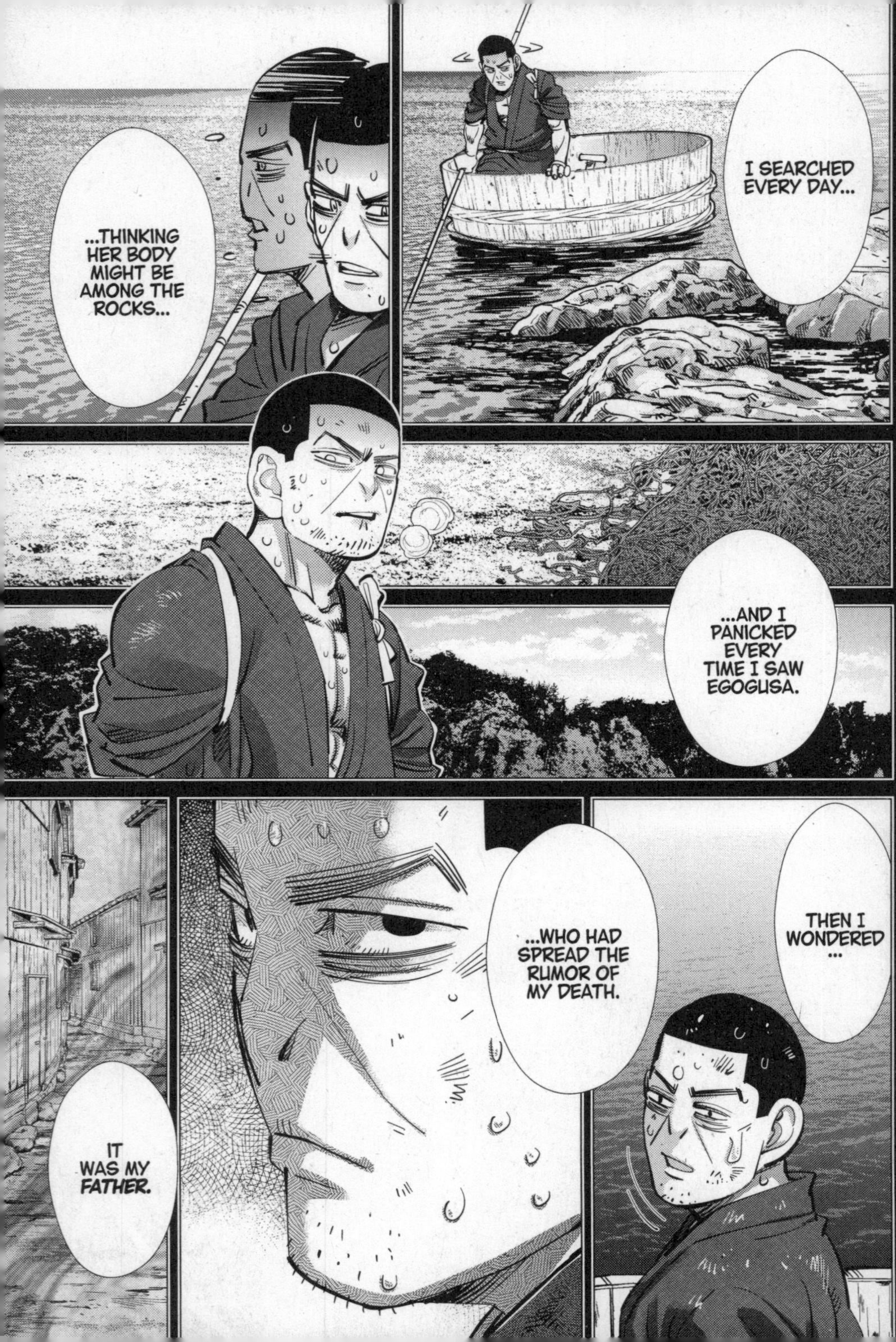
I SEARCHED EVERY DAY...
...THINKING HER BODY MIGHT BE AMONG THE ROCKS...
...AND I PANICKED EVERY TIME I SAW EGOGUSA.
THEN I WONDERED ...
...WHO HAD SPREAD THE RUMOR OF MY DEATH.
IT WAS MY FATHER.

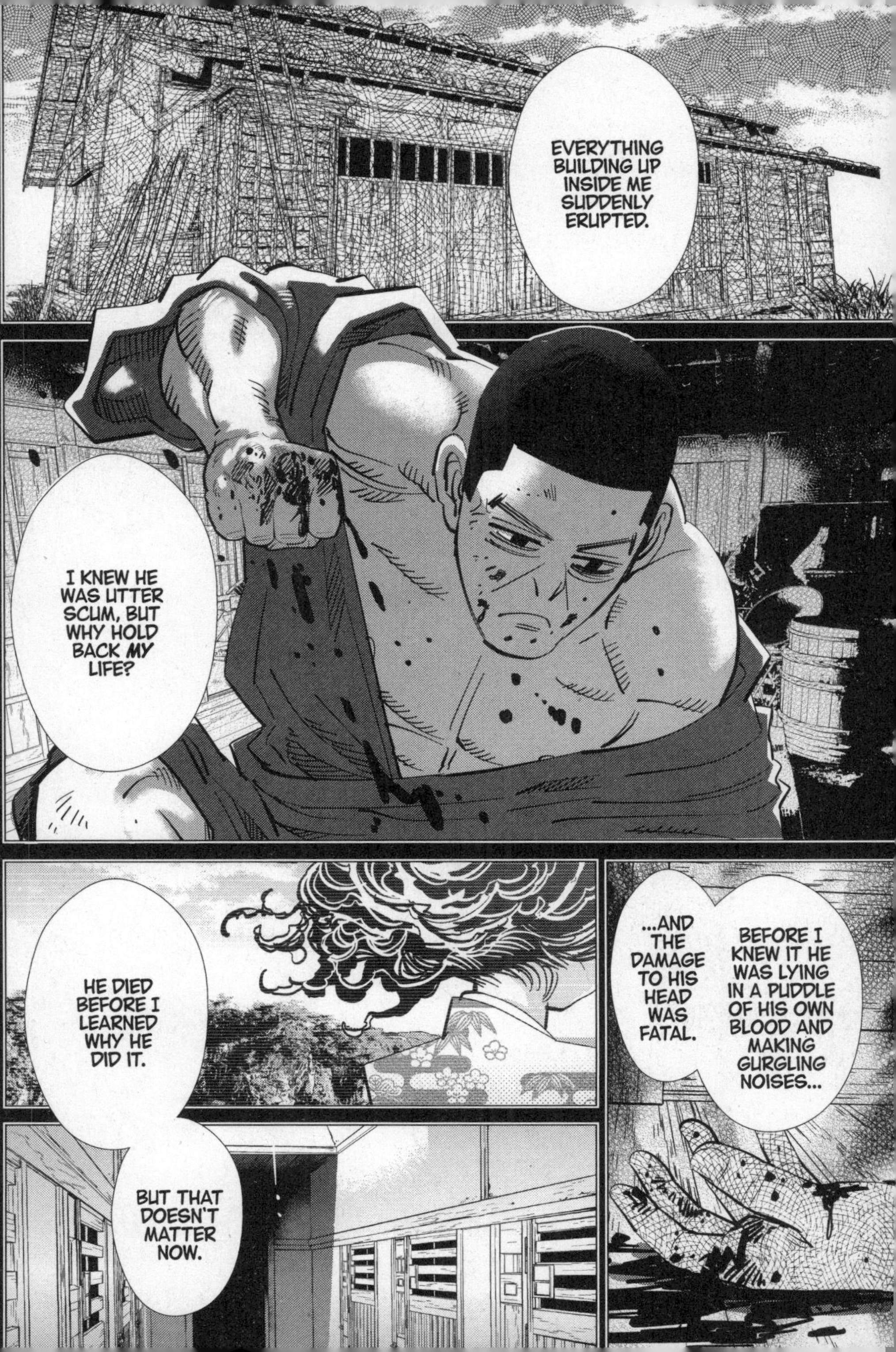
EVERYTHING BUILDING UP INSIDE ME SUDDENLY ERUPTED.
I KNEW HE WAS UTTER SCUM, BUT WHY HOLD BACK MY LIFE?
BEFORE I KNEW IT HE WAS LYING IN A PUDDLE OF HIS OWN BLOOD AND MAKING GURGLING NOISES...
...AND THE DAMAGE TO HIS HEAD WAS FATAL.
HE DIED BEFORE I LEARNED WHY HE DID IT.
BUT THAT DOESN'T MATTER NOW.

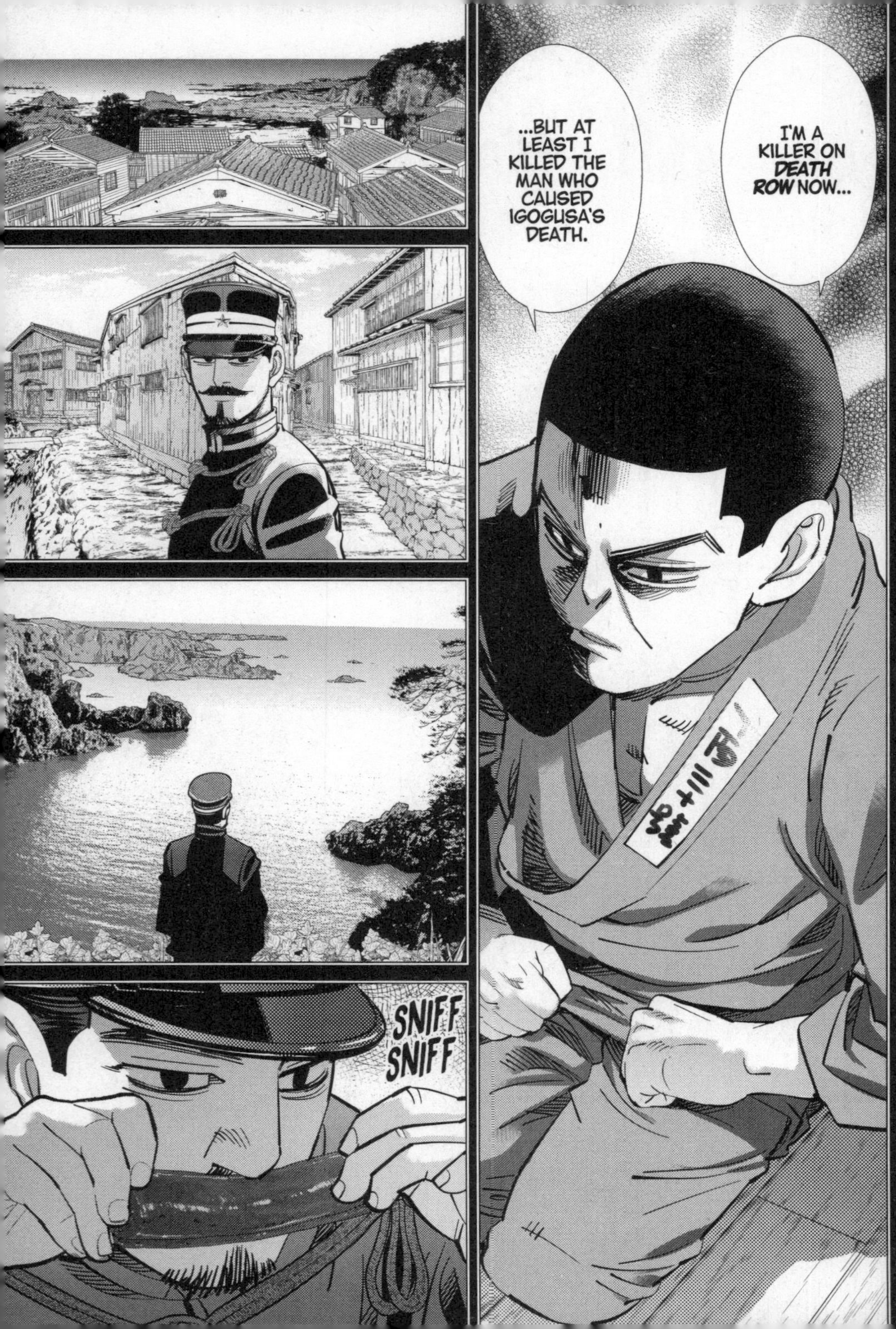
I'M A KILLER ON DEATH ROW NOW...
...BUT AT LEAST I KILLED THE MAN WHO CAUSED IGOGUSA'S DEATH.
SNIFF SNIFF

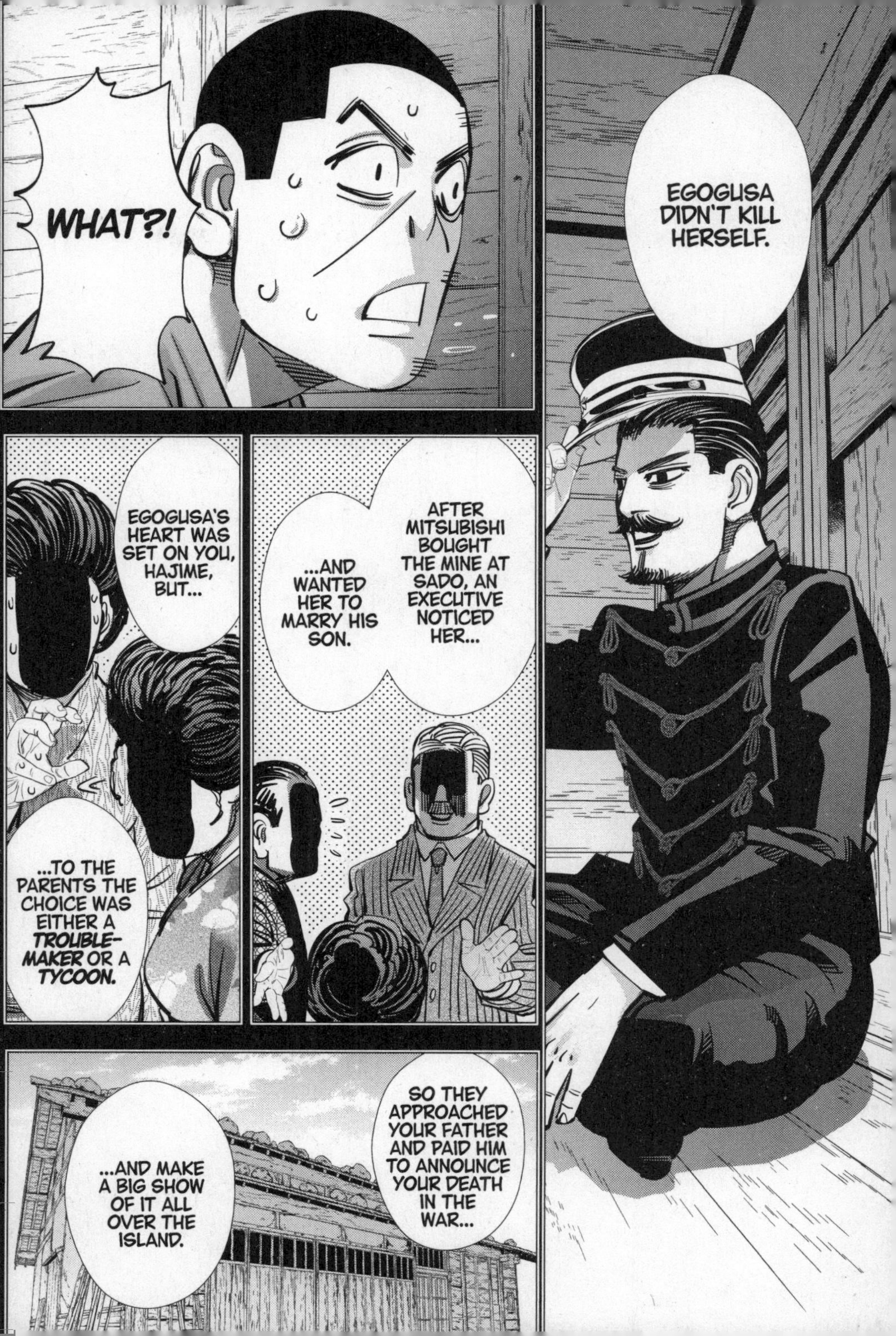
EGOGUSA DIDN'T KILL HERSELF.
WHAT?!
AFTER MITSUBISHI BOUGHT THE MINE AT SADO, AN EXECUTIVE NOTICED HER...
...AND WANTED HER TO MARRY HIS SON.
EGOGUSA'S HEART WAS SET ON YOU, HAJIME, BUT...
...TO THE PARENTS THE CHOICE WAS EITHER A *TROUBLE-MAKER* OR A *TYCOON*.
SO THEY APPROACHED YOUR FATHER AND PAID HIM TO ANNOUNCE YOUR DEATH IN THE WAR...
...AND MAKE A BIG SHOW OF IT ALL OVER THE ISLAND.

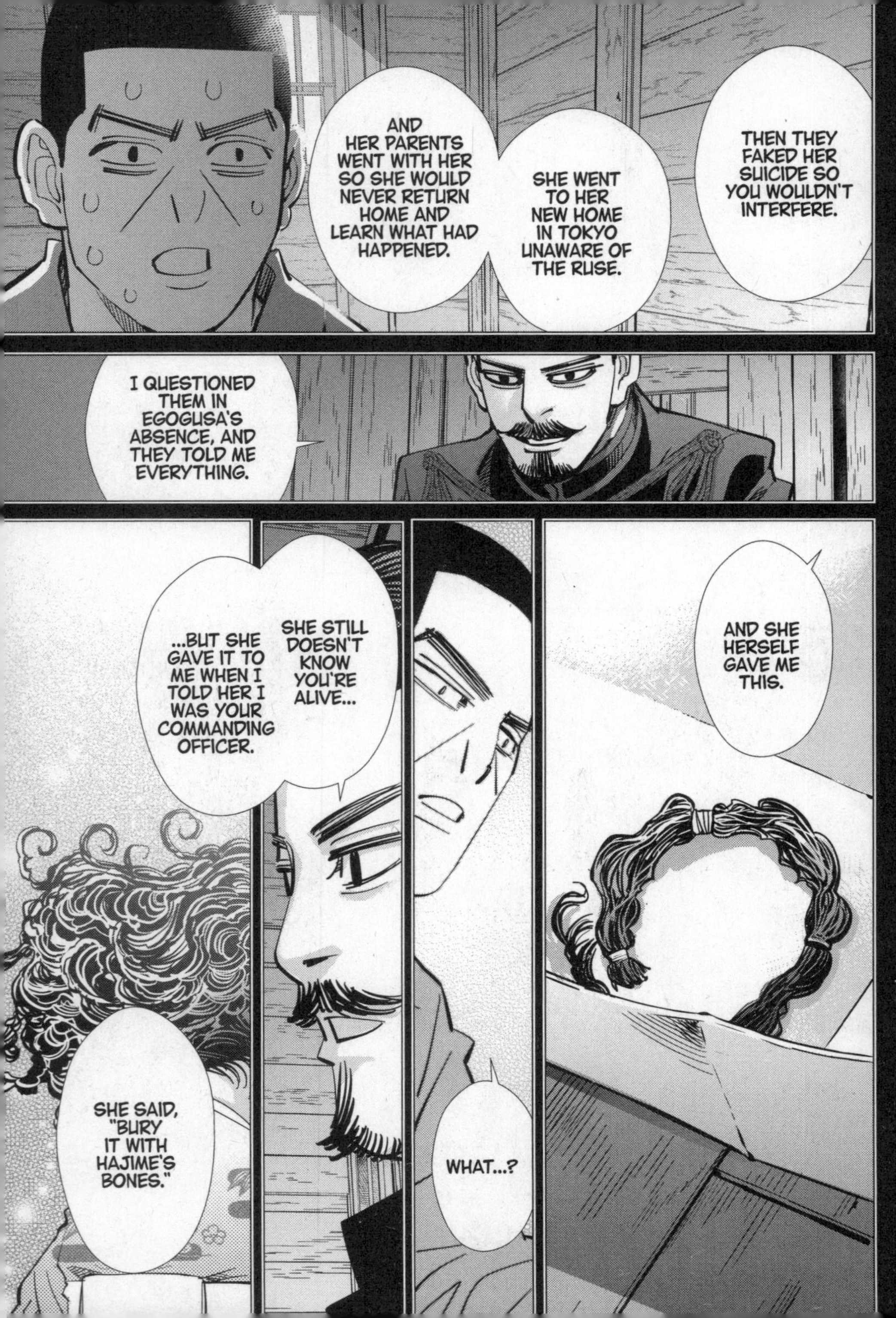
THEN THEY FAKED HER SUICIDE SO YOU WOULDN'T INTERFERE.
SHE WENT TO HER NEW HOME IN TOKYO UNAWARE OF THE RUSE.
AND HER PARENTS WENT WITH HER SO SHE WOULD NEVER RETURN HOME AND LEARN WHAT HAD HAPPENED.
I QUESTIONED THEM IN EGOGUSA'S ABSENCE, AND THEY TOLD ME EVERYTHING.
AND SHE HERSELF GAVE ME THIS.
WHAT...?
SHE STILL DOESN'T KNOW YOU'RE ALIVE...
...BUT SHE GAVE IT TO ME WHEN I TOLD HER I WAS YOUR COMMANDING OFFICER.
SHE SAID, "BURY IT WITH HAJIME'S BONES."

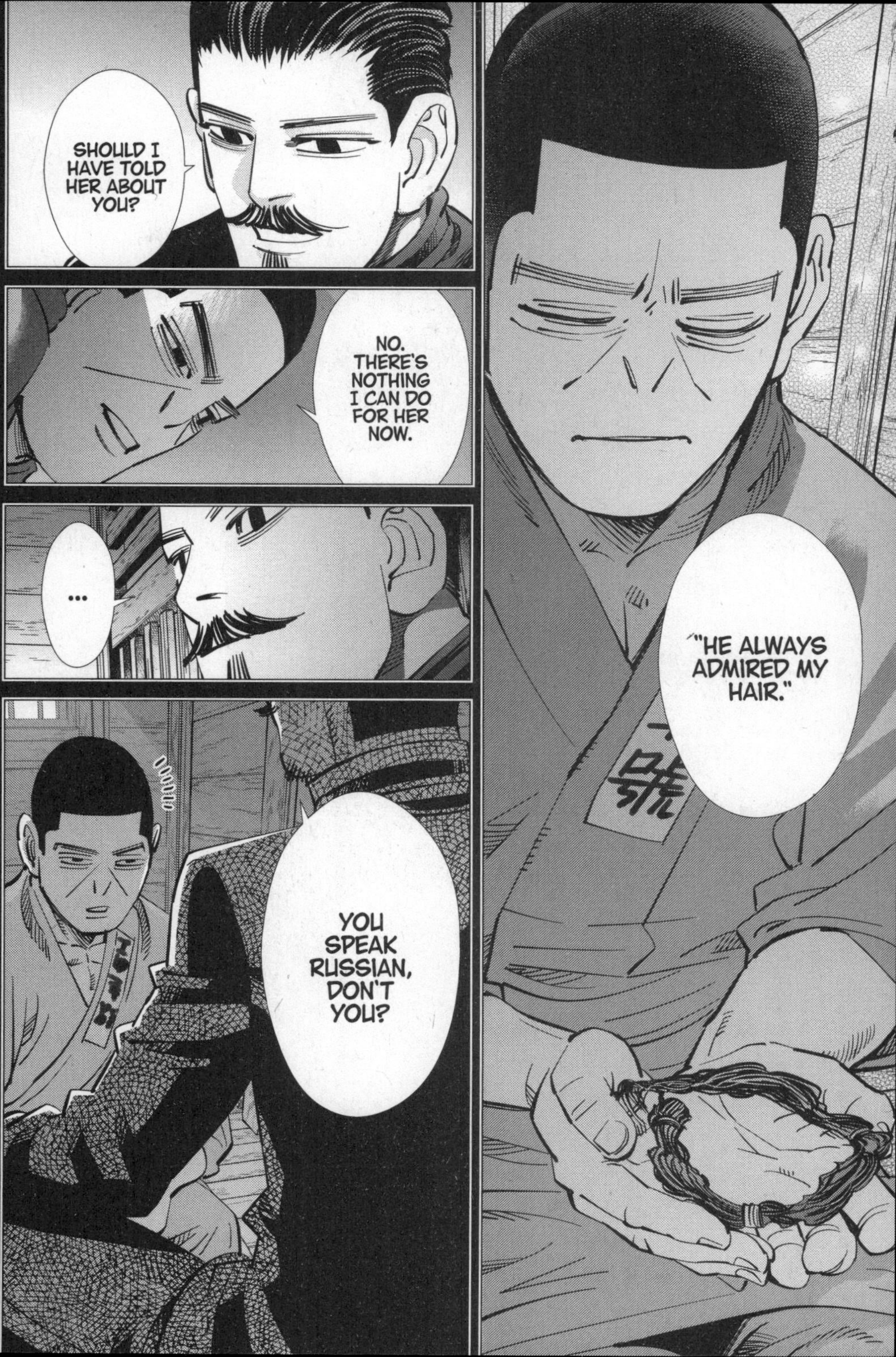
"HE ALWAYS ADMIRED MY HAIR."
SHOULD I HAVE TOLD HER ABOUT YOU?
NO. THERE'S NOTHING I CAN DO FOR HER NOW.
...
YOU SPEAK RUSSIAN, DON'T YOU?

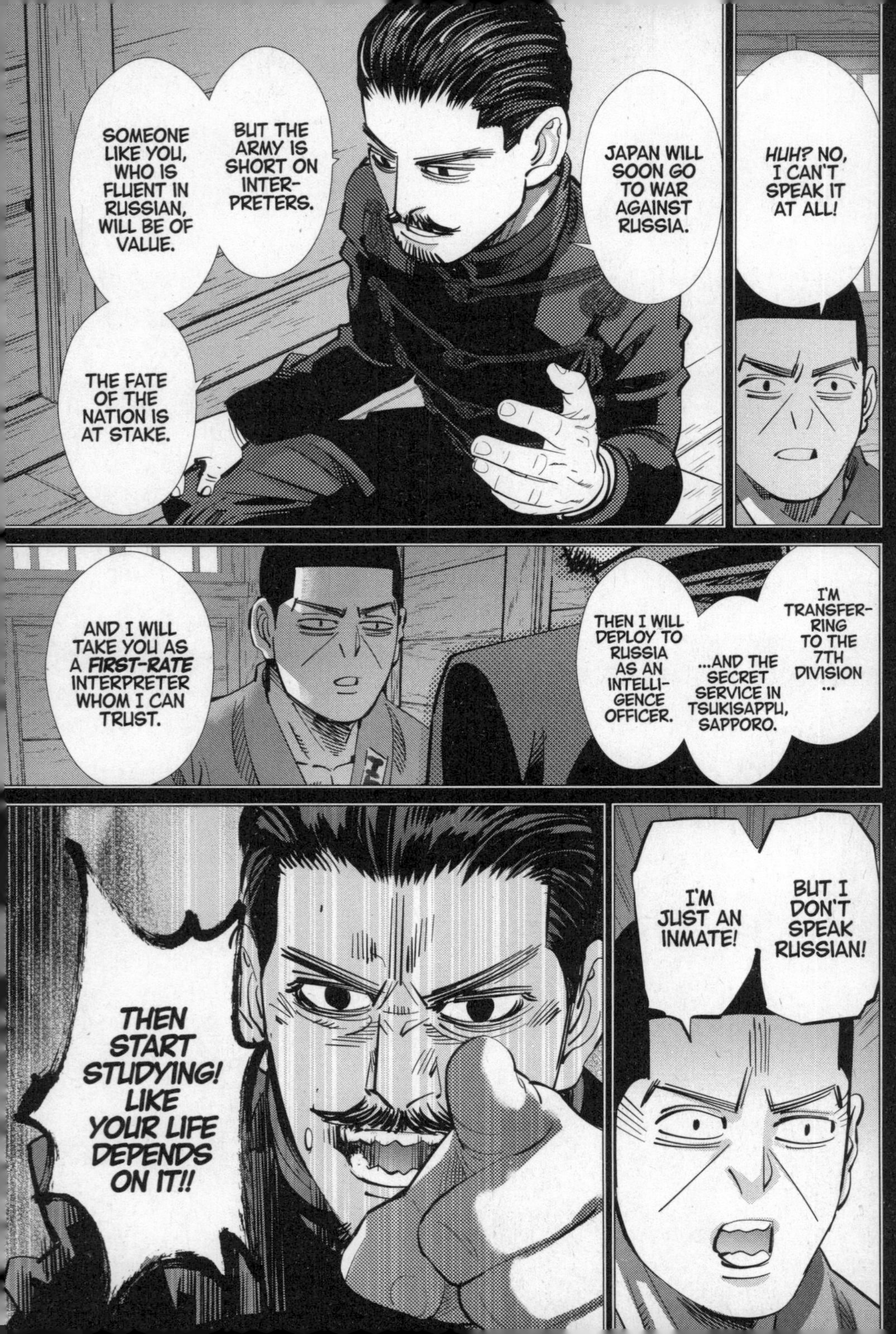
HUH? NO, I CAN'T SPEAK IT AT ALL!
JAPAN WILL SOON GO TO WAR AGAINST RUSSIA.
BUT THE ARMY IS SHORT ON INTER-PRETERS.
SOMEONE LIKE YOU, WHO IS FLUENT IN RUSSIAN, WILL BE OF VALUE.
THE FATE OF THE NATION IS AT STAKE.
I'M TRANSFER-RING TO THE 7TH DIVISION...
...AND THE SECRET SERVICE IN TSUKISAPPU, SAPPORO.
THEN I WILL DEPLOY TO RUSSIA AS AN INTELLI-GENCE OFFICER.
AND I WILL TAKE YOU AS A *FIRST-RATE* INTERPRETER WHOM I CAN TRUST.
BUT I DON'T SPEAK RUSSIAN!
I'M JUST AN INMATE!
THEN START STUDYING! LIKE YOUR LIFE DEPENDS ON IT!!

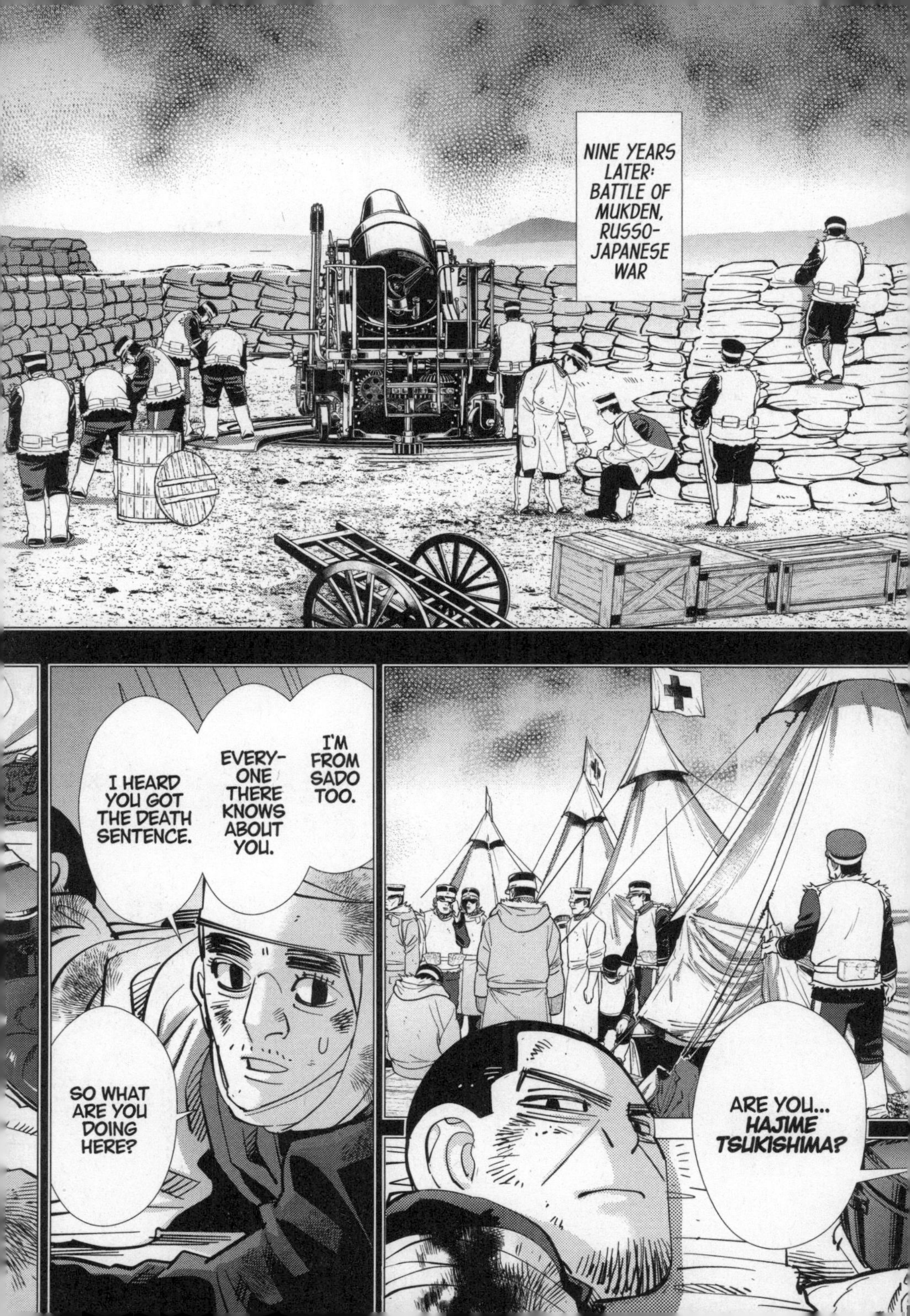
NINE YEARS LATER: BATTLE OF MUKDEN, RUSSO-JAPANESE WAR
ARE YOU... HAJIME TSUKISHIMA?
I'M FROM SADO TOO.
EVERYONE THERE KNOWS ABOUT YOU.
I HEARD YOU GOT THE DEATH SENTENCE.
SO WHAT ARE YOU DOING HERE?

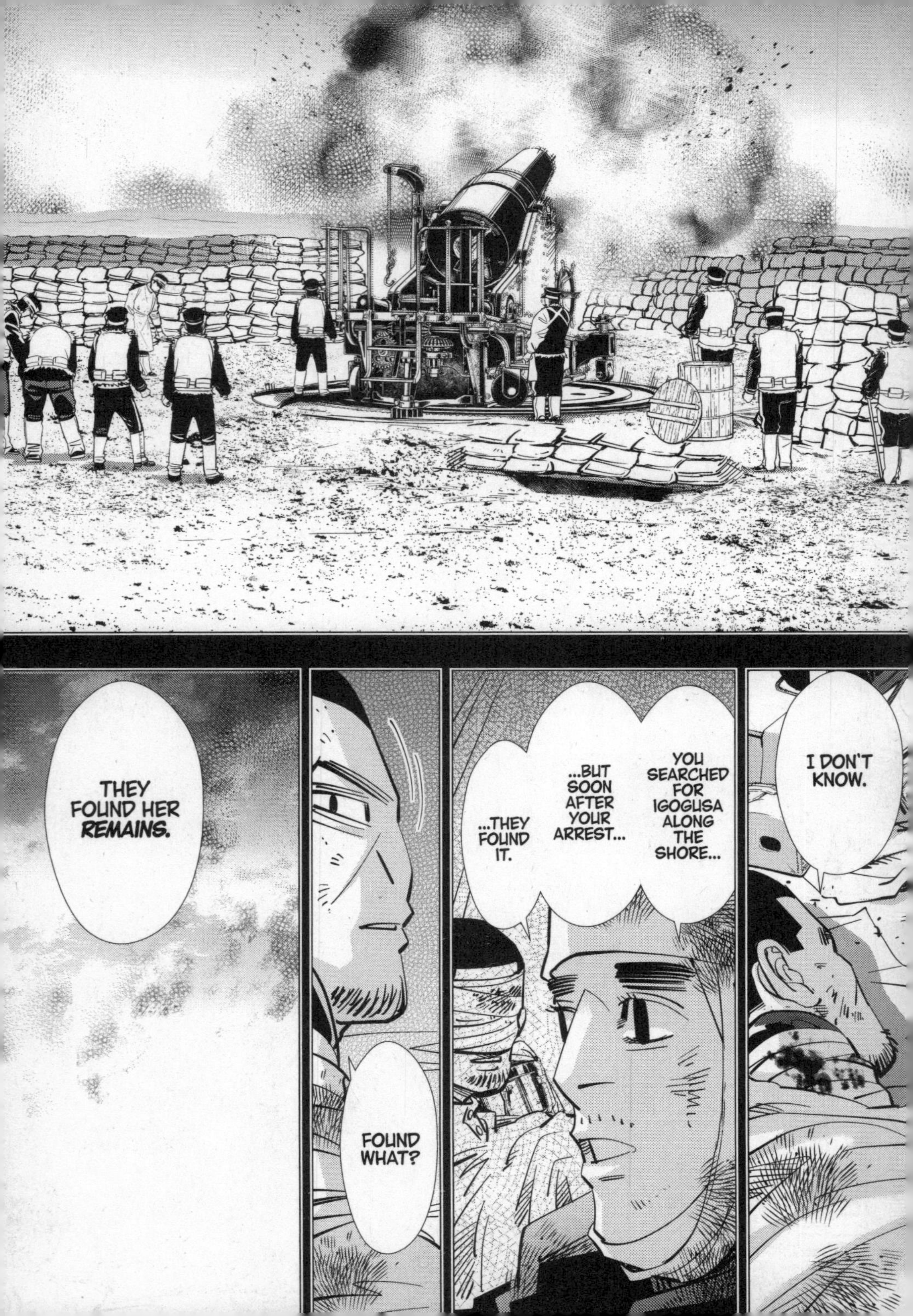
I DON'T KNOW.
YOU SEARCHED FOR IGOGUSA ALONG THE SHORE...
...BUT SOON AFTER YOUR ARREST...
...THEY FOUND IT.
FOUND WHAT?
THEY FOUND HER REMAINS.

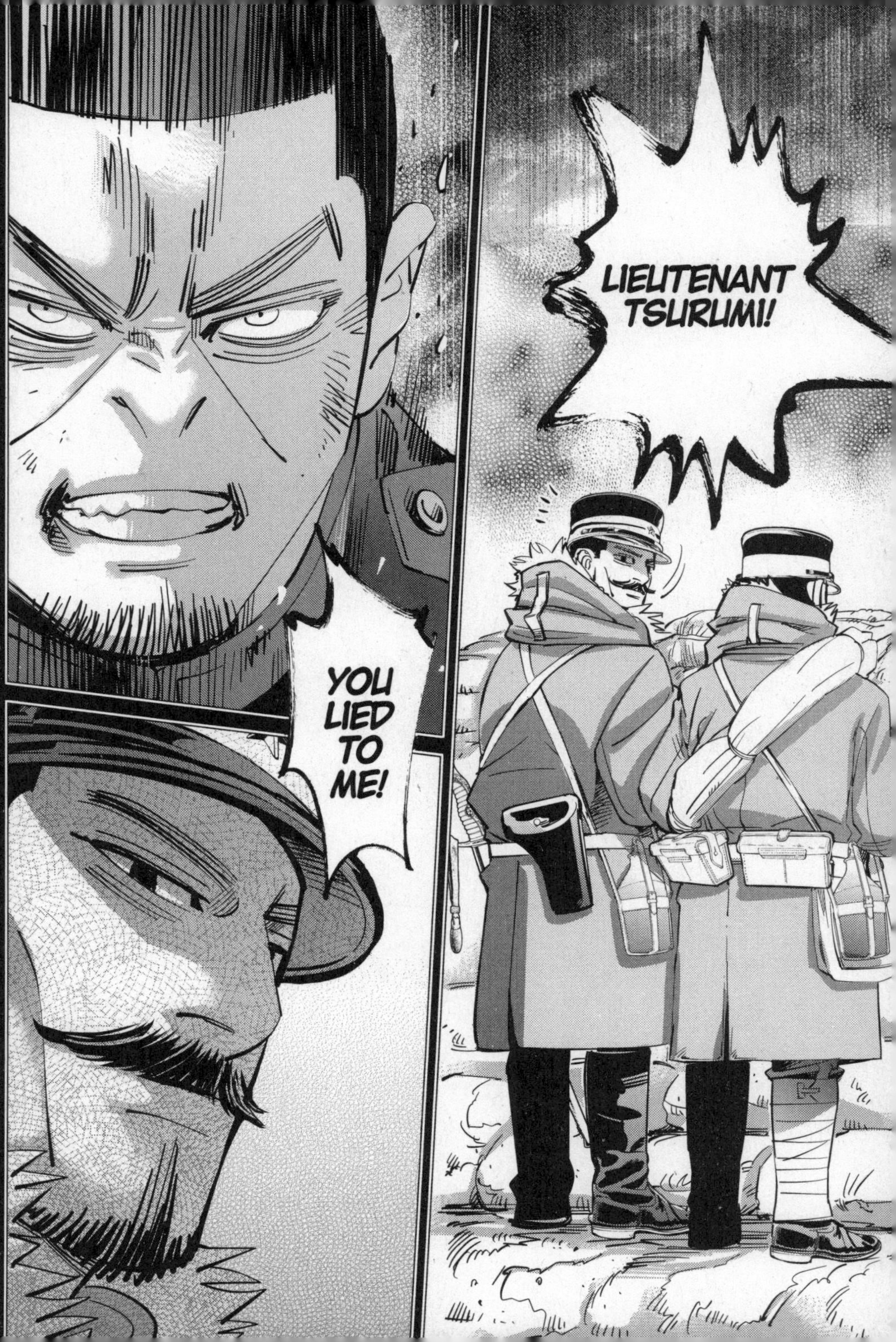
LIEUTENANT TSURUMI!
YOU LIED TO ME!

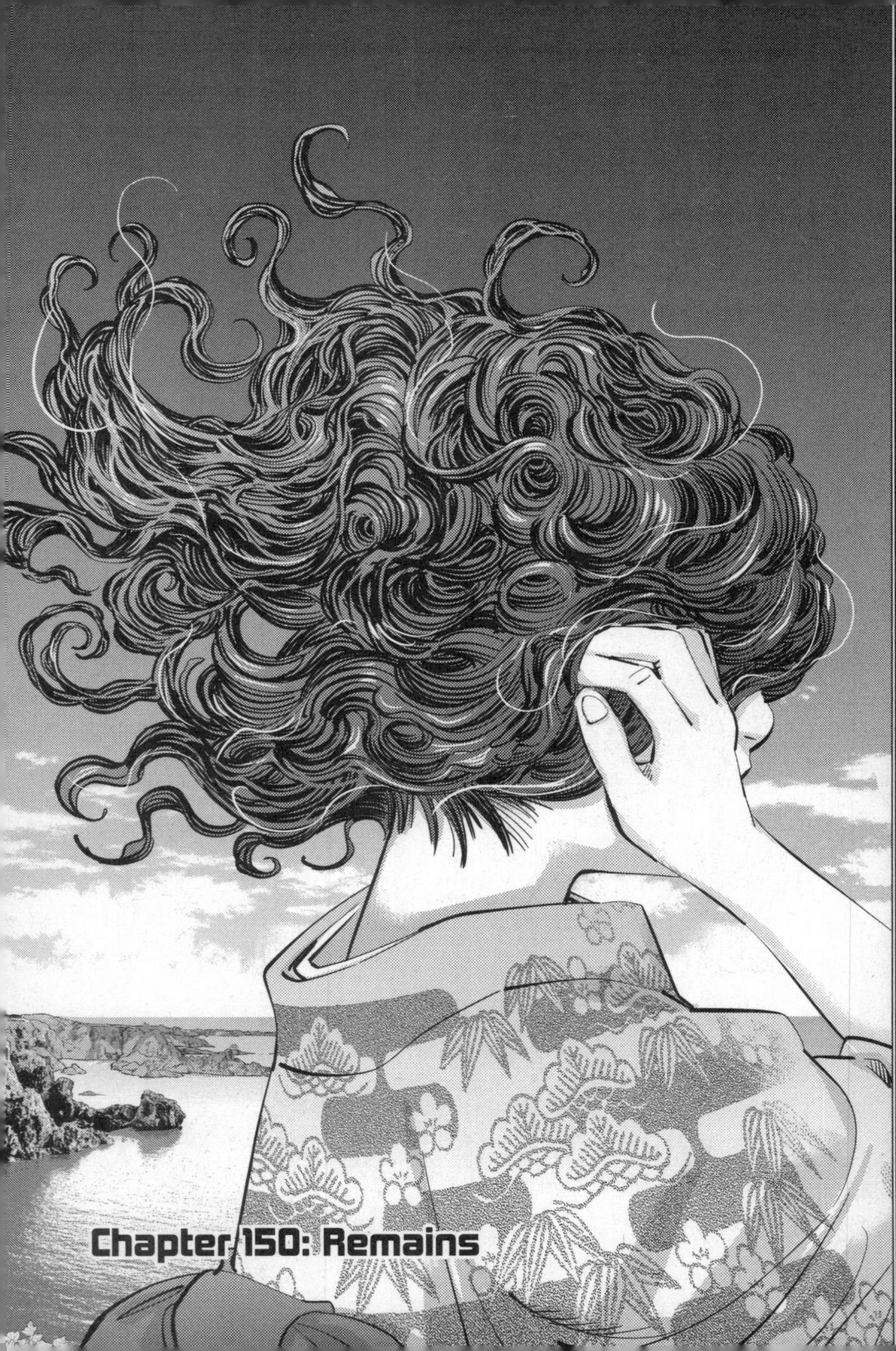

Chapter 150: Remains

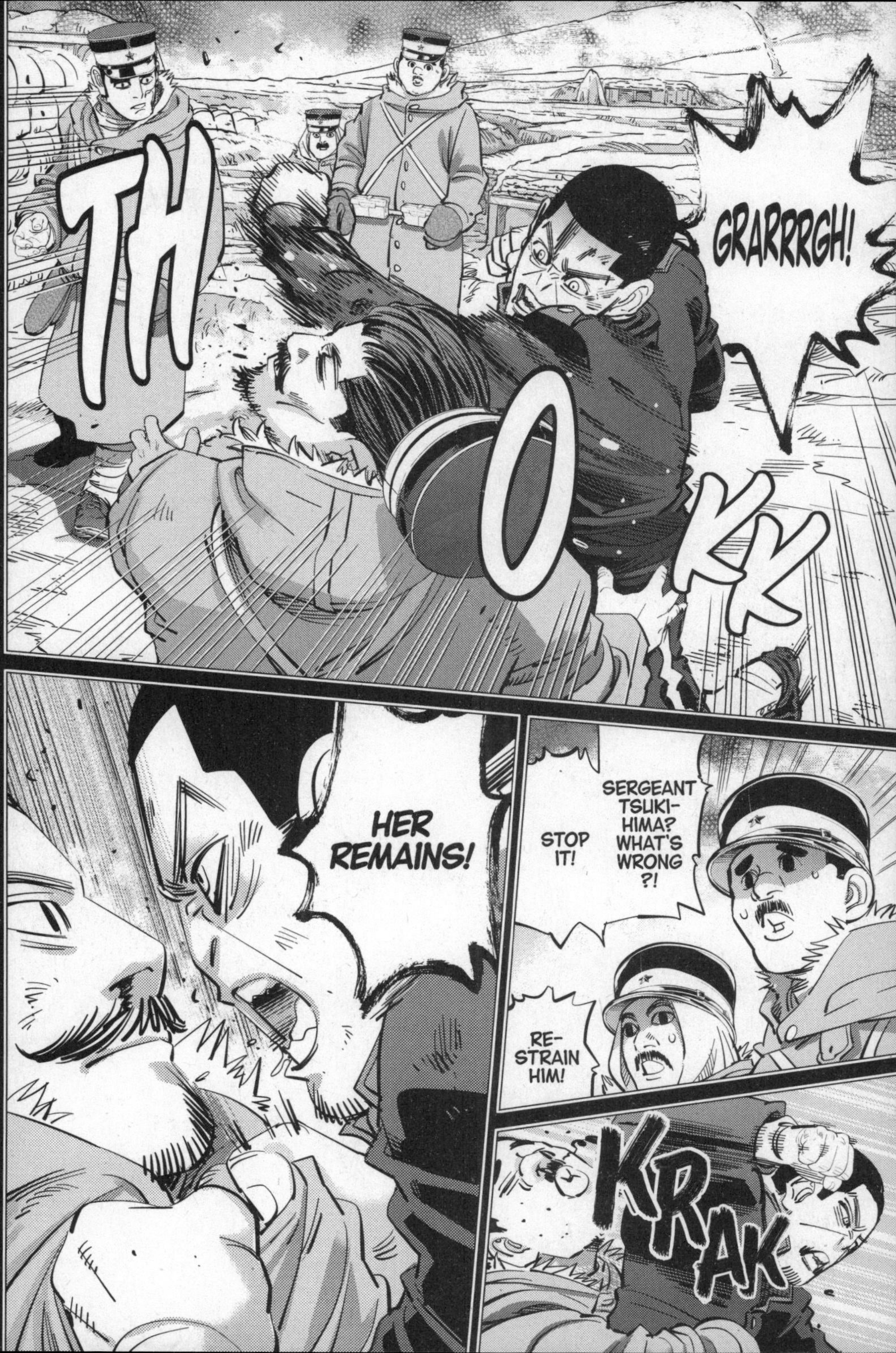
GRARRRGH!
THOKK
SERGEANT TSUKI-HIMA? WHAT'S WRONG?!
STOP IT!
RE-STRAIN HIM!
KRAK
HER REMAINS!

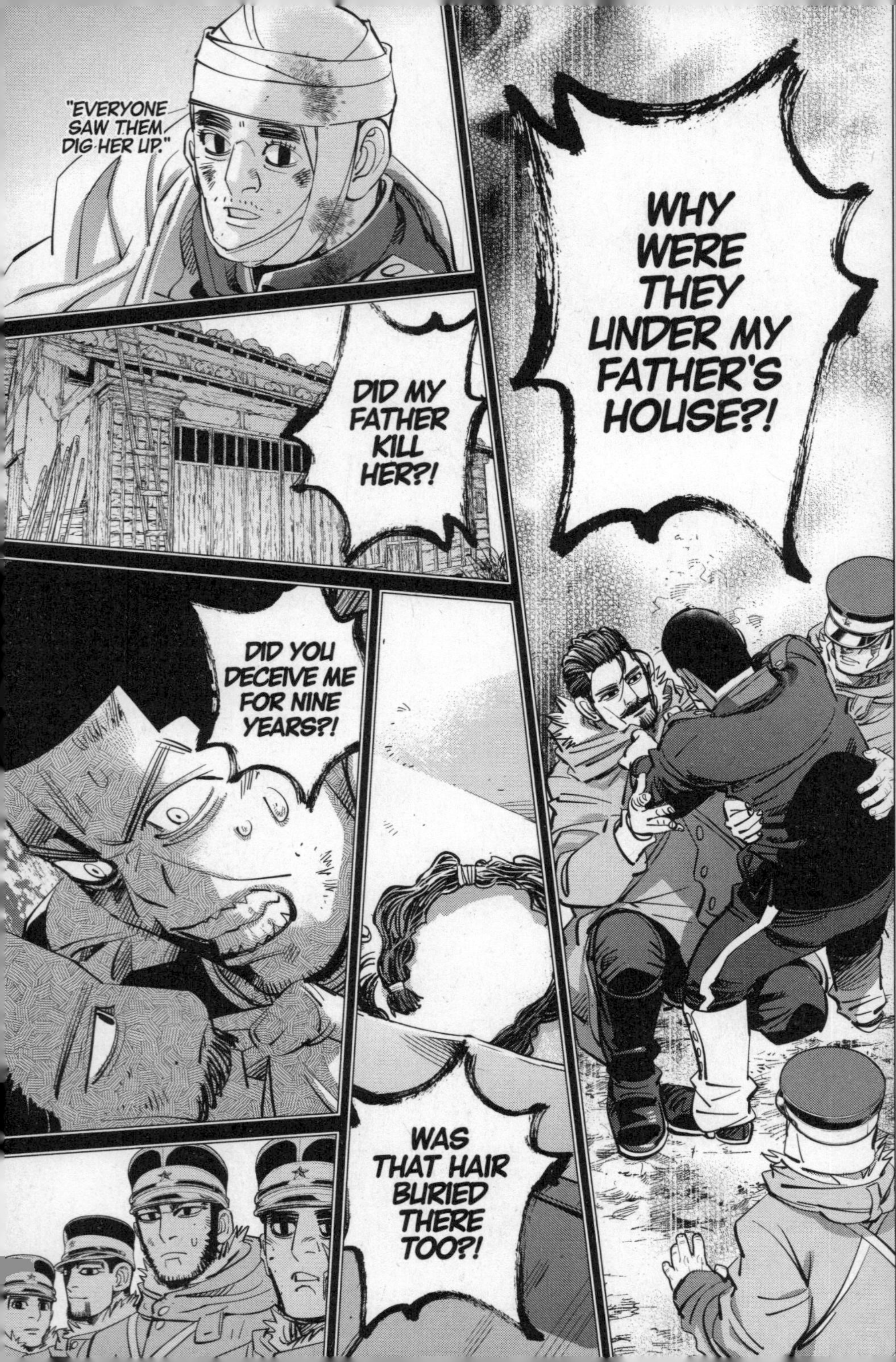
WHY WERE THEY UNDER MY FATHER'S HOUSE?!
"EVERYONE SAW THEM DIG HER UP."
DID MY FATHER KILL HER?!
DID YOU DECEIVE ME FOR NINE YEARS?!
WAS THAT HAIR BURIED THERE TOO?!

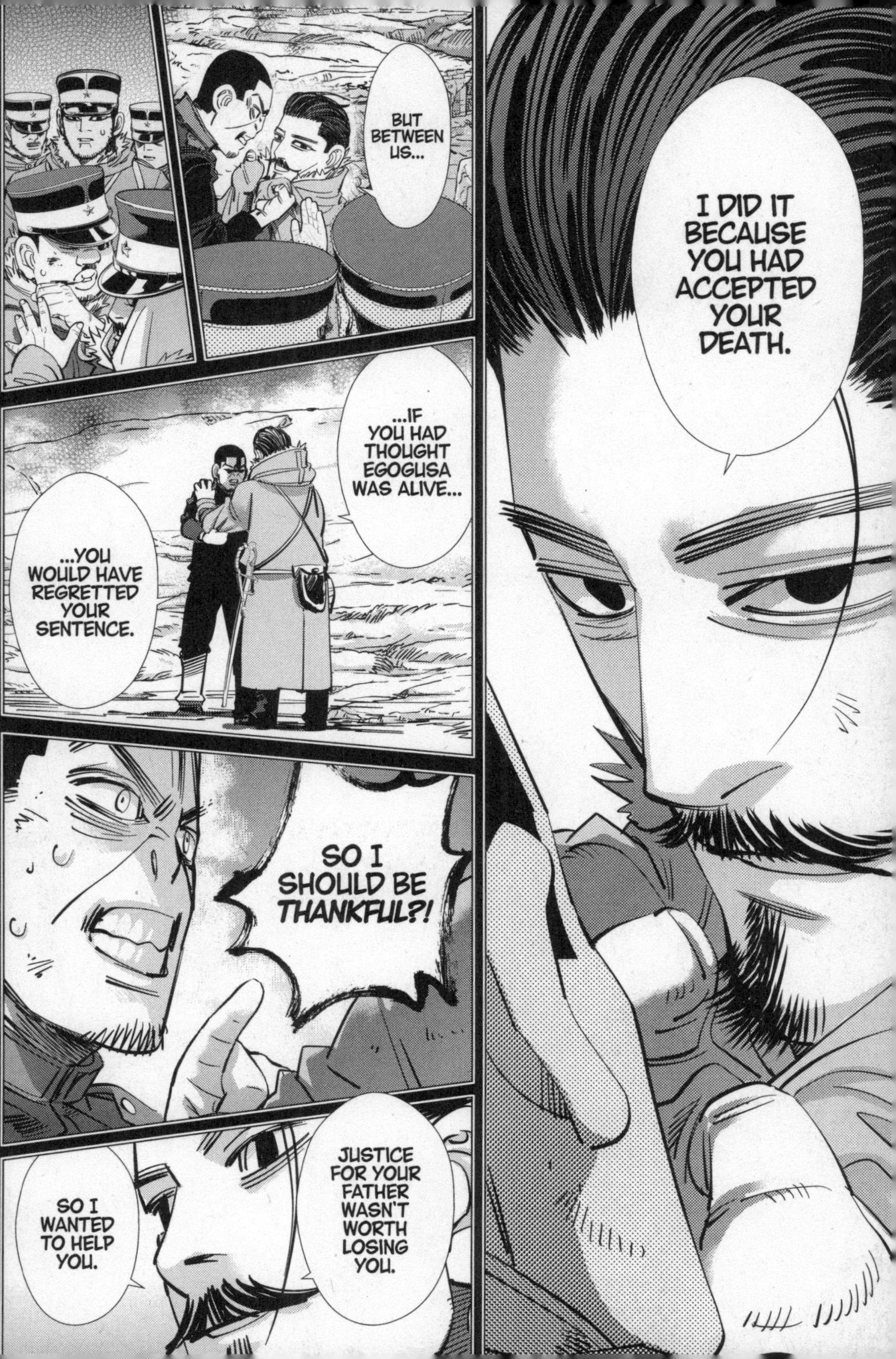
I DID IT BECAUSE YOU HAD ACCEPTED YOUR DEATH.
BUT BETWEEN US...
...IF YOU HAD THOUGHT EGOGUSA WAS ALIVE...
...YOU WOULD HAVE REGRETTED YOUR SENTENCE.
SO I SHOULD BE *THANKFUL?!*
JUSTICE FOR YOUR FATHER WASN'T WORTH LOSING YOU.
SO I WANTED TO HELP YOU.

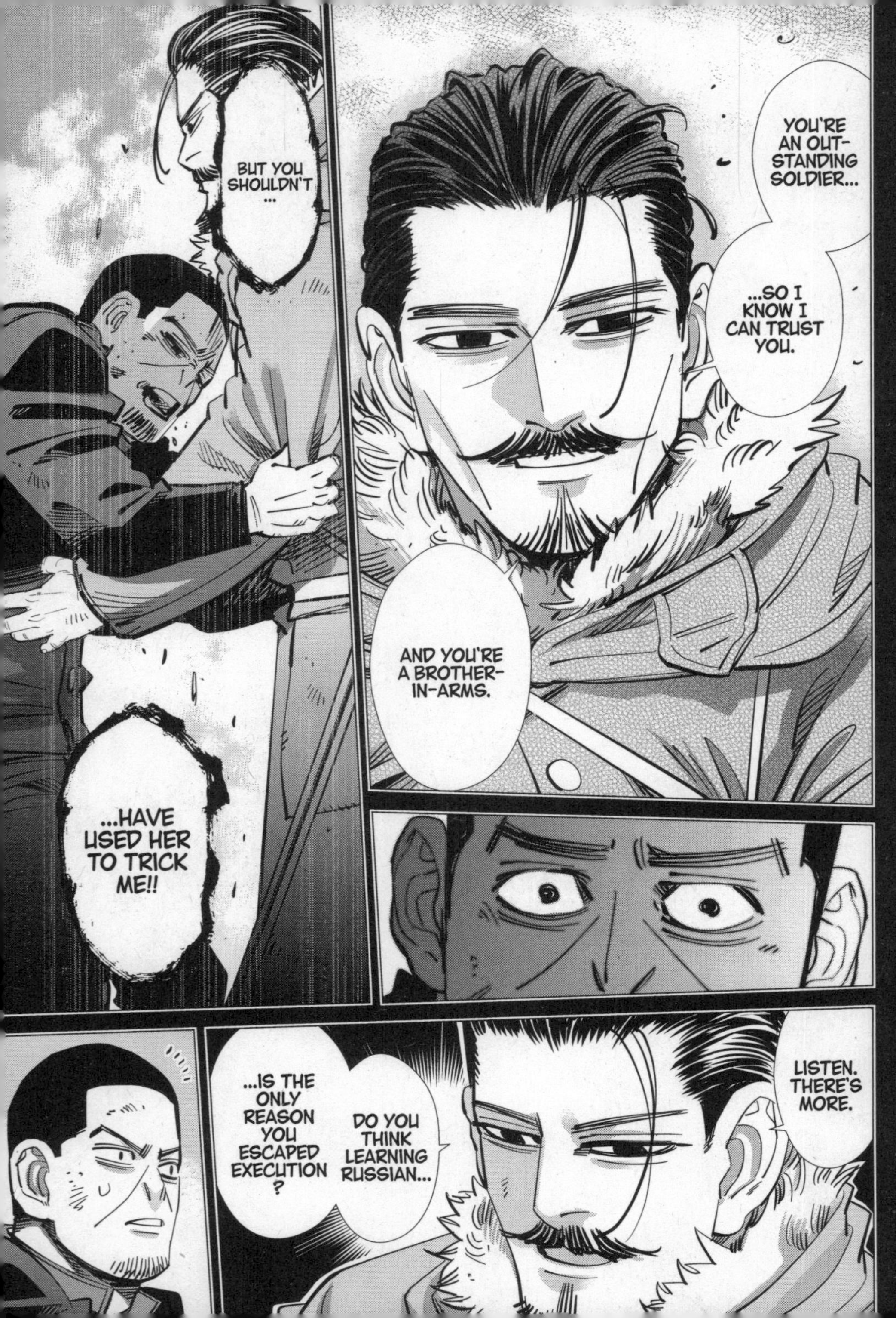
YOU'RE AN OUT-STANDING SOLDIER...
...SO I KNOW I CAN TRUST YOU.
AND YOU'RE A BROTHER-IN-ARMS.
BUT YOU SHOULDN'T ...
...HAVE USED HER TO TRICK ME!!
LISTEN. THERE'S MORE.
DO YOU THINK LEARNING RUSSIAN...
...IS THE ONLY REASON YOU ESCAPED EXECUTION ?

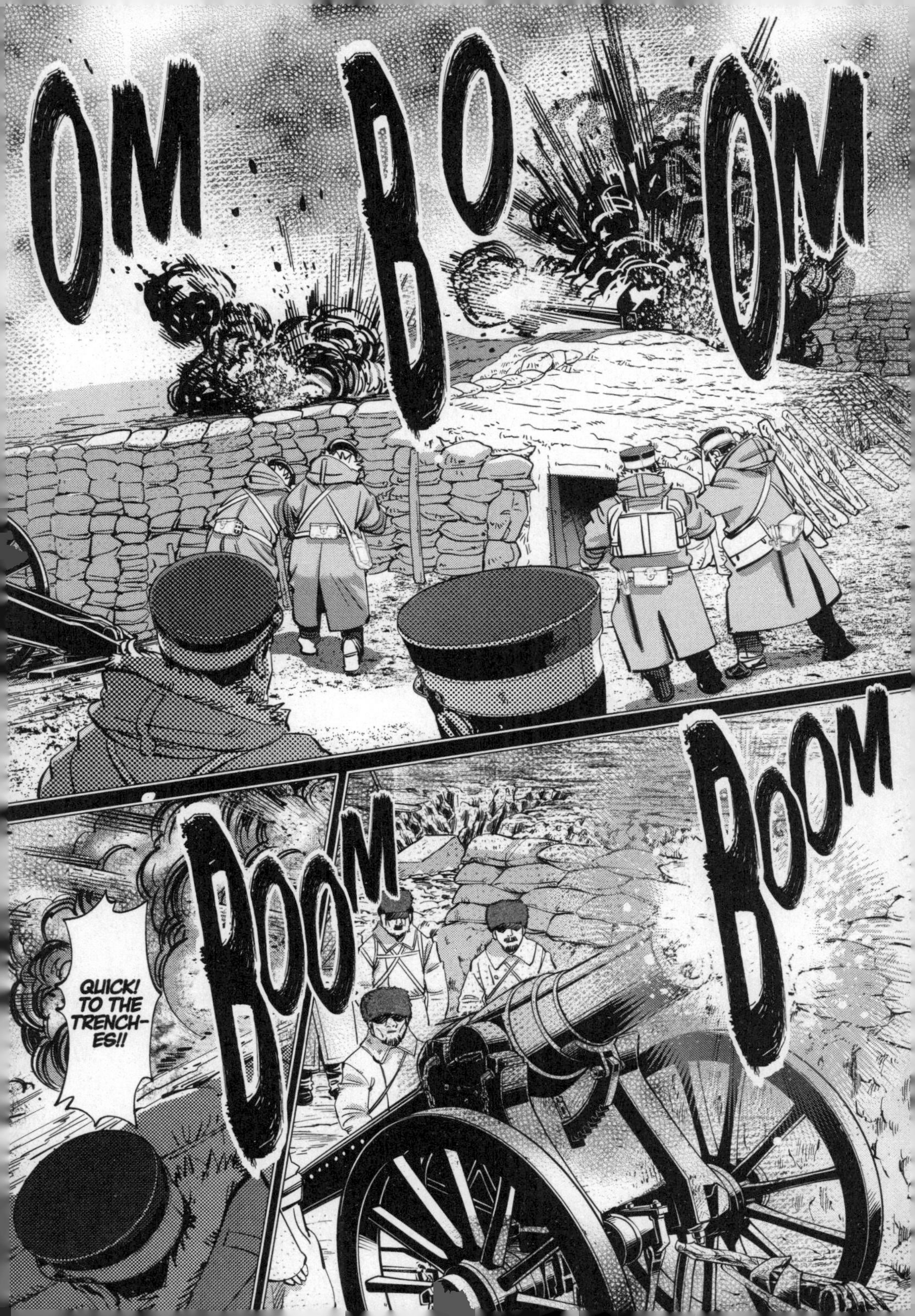
OM
BO
OM
BOOM
BOOM
QUICK! TO THE TRENCH-ES!!

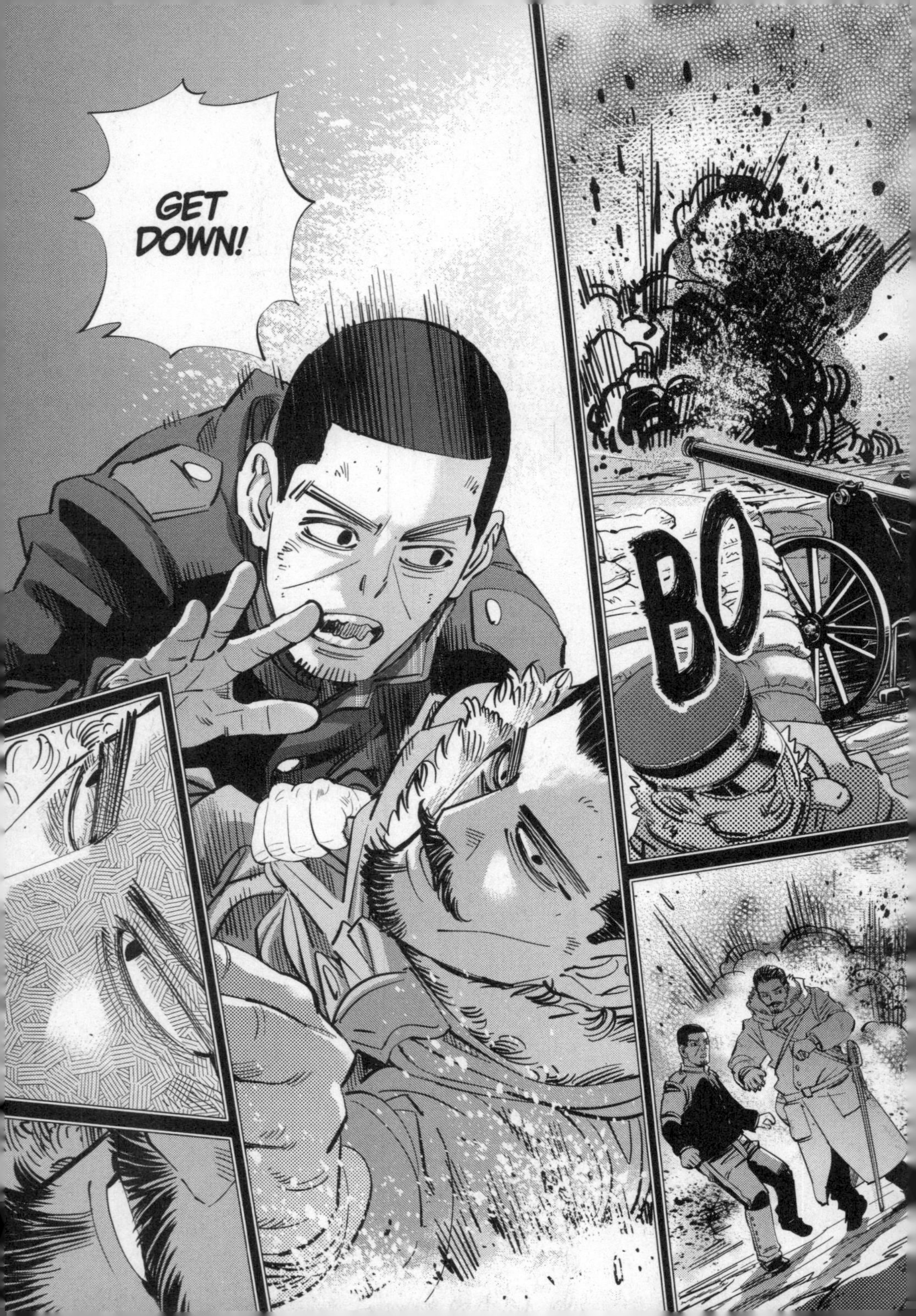
BO
GET DOWN!

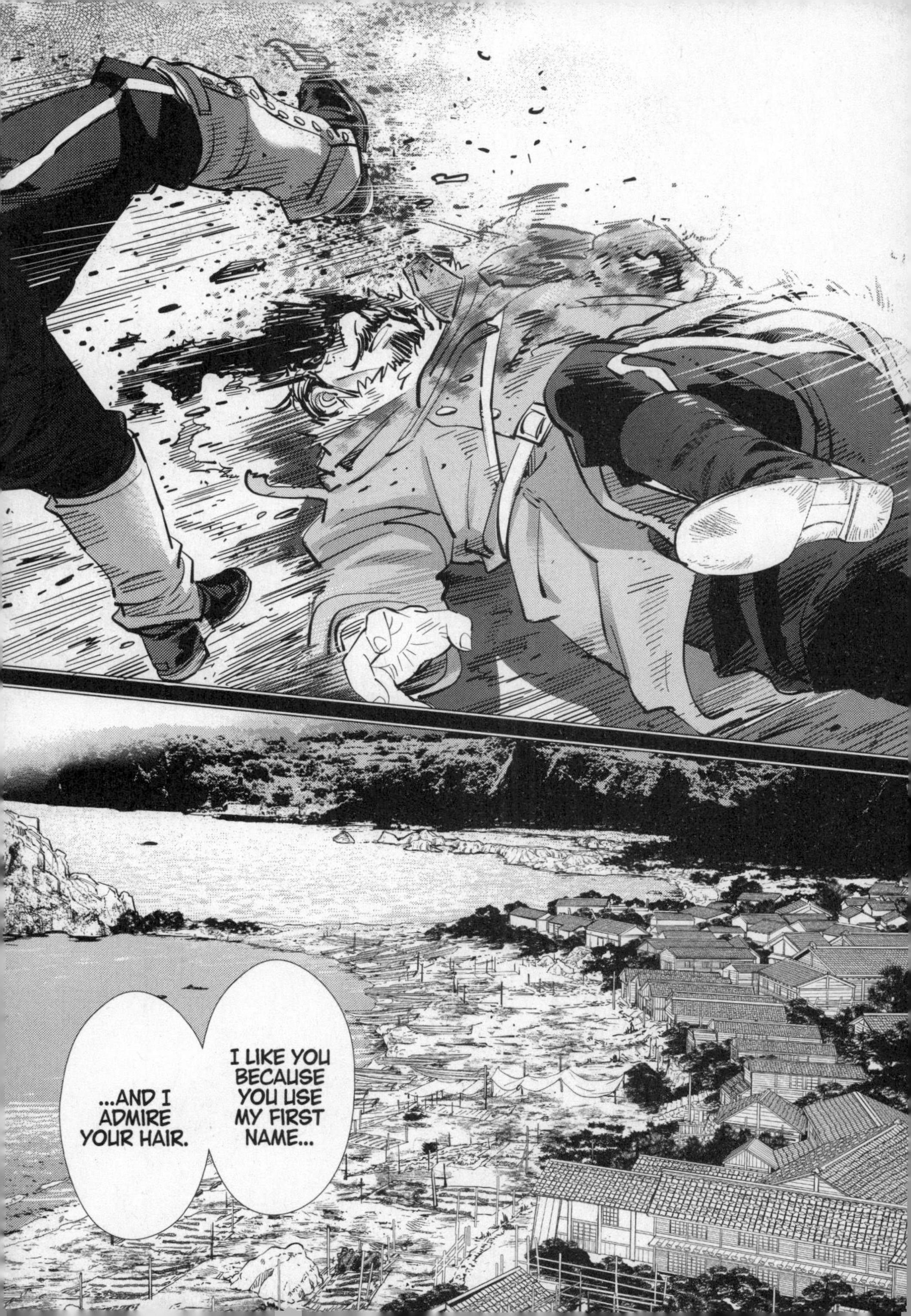
I LIKE YOU BECAUSE YOU USE MY FIRST NAME...
...AND I ADMIRE YOUR HAIR.

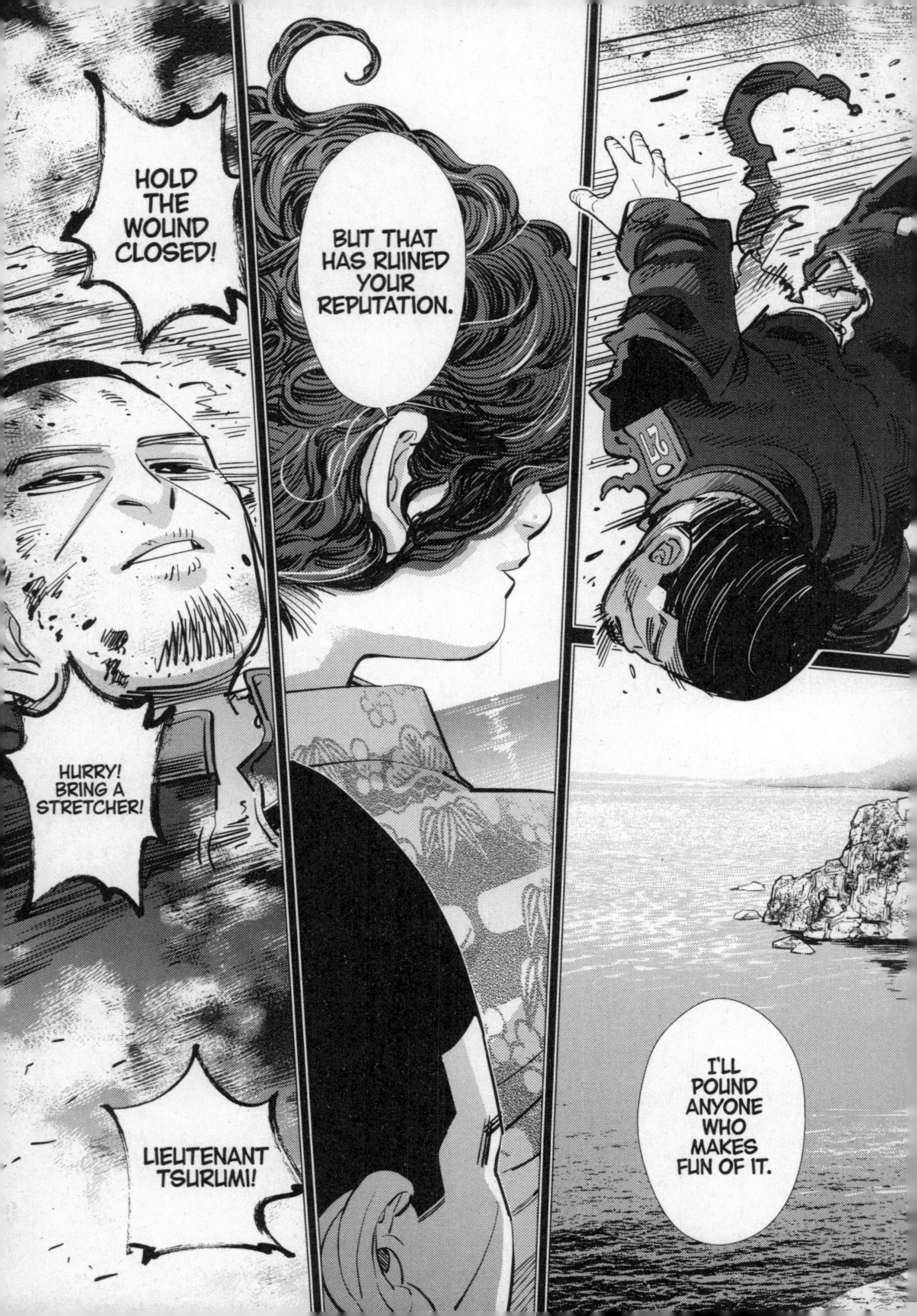
I'LL POUND ANYONE WHO MAKES FUN OF IT.
BUT THAT HAS RUINED YOUR REPUTATION.
HOLD THE WOUND CLOSED!
HURRY! BRING A STRETCHER!
LIEUTENANT TSURUMI!

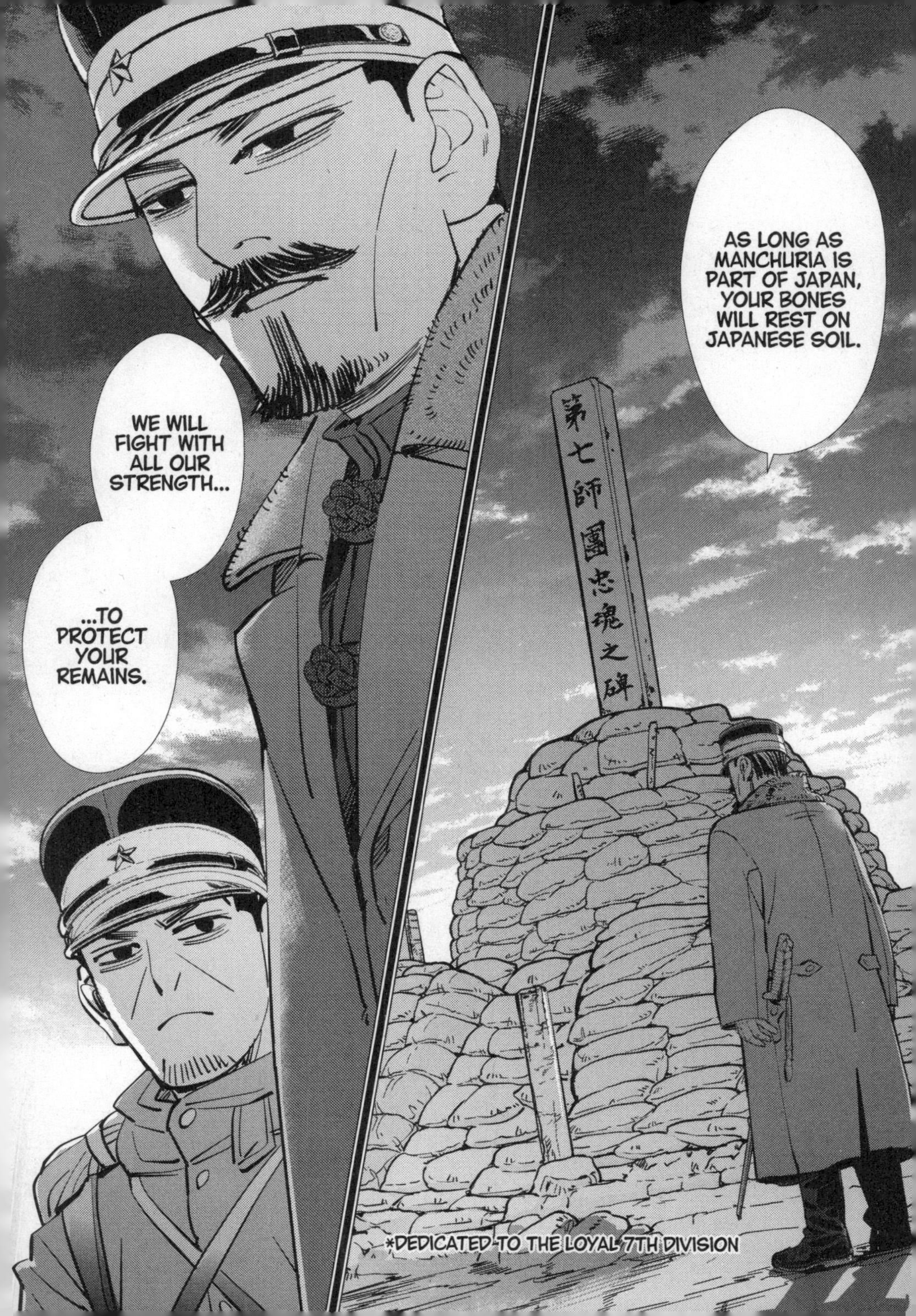
AS LONG AS MANCHURIA IS PART OF JAPAN, YOUR BONES WILL REST ON JAPANESE SOIL.
第七師團忠魂之碑
*DEDICATED TO THE LOYAL 7TH DIVISION
WE WILL FIGHT WITH ALL OUR STRENGTH...
...TO PROTECT YOUR REMAINS.

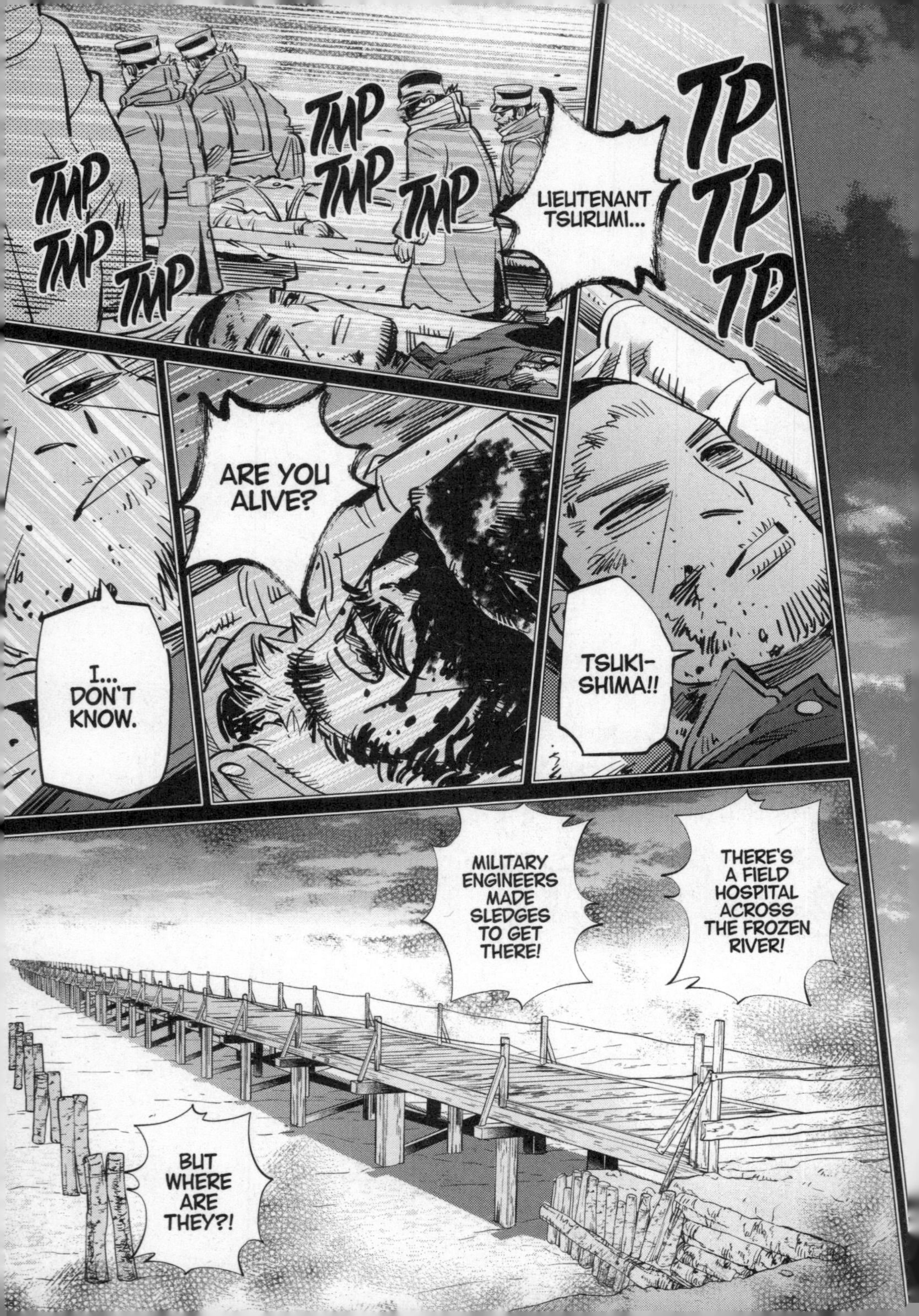
TP TP TP
LIEUTENANT TSURUMI...
TMP TMP TMP
TMP TMP TMP
TSUKI-SHIMA!!
ARE YOU ALIVE?
I... DON'T KNOW.
THERE'S A FIELD HOSPITAL ACROSS THE FROZEN RIVER!
MILITARY ENGINEERS MADE SLEDGES TO GET THERE!
BUT WHERE ARE THEY?!

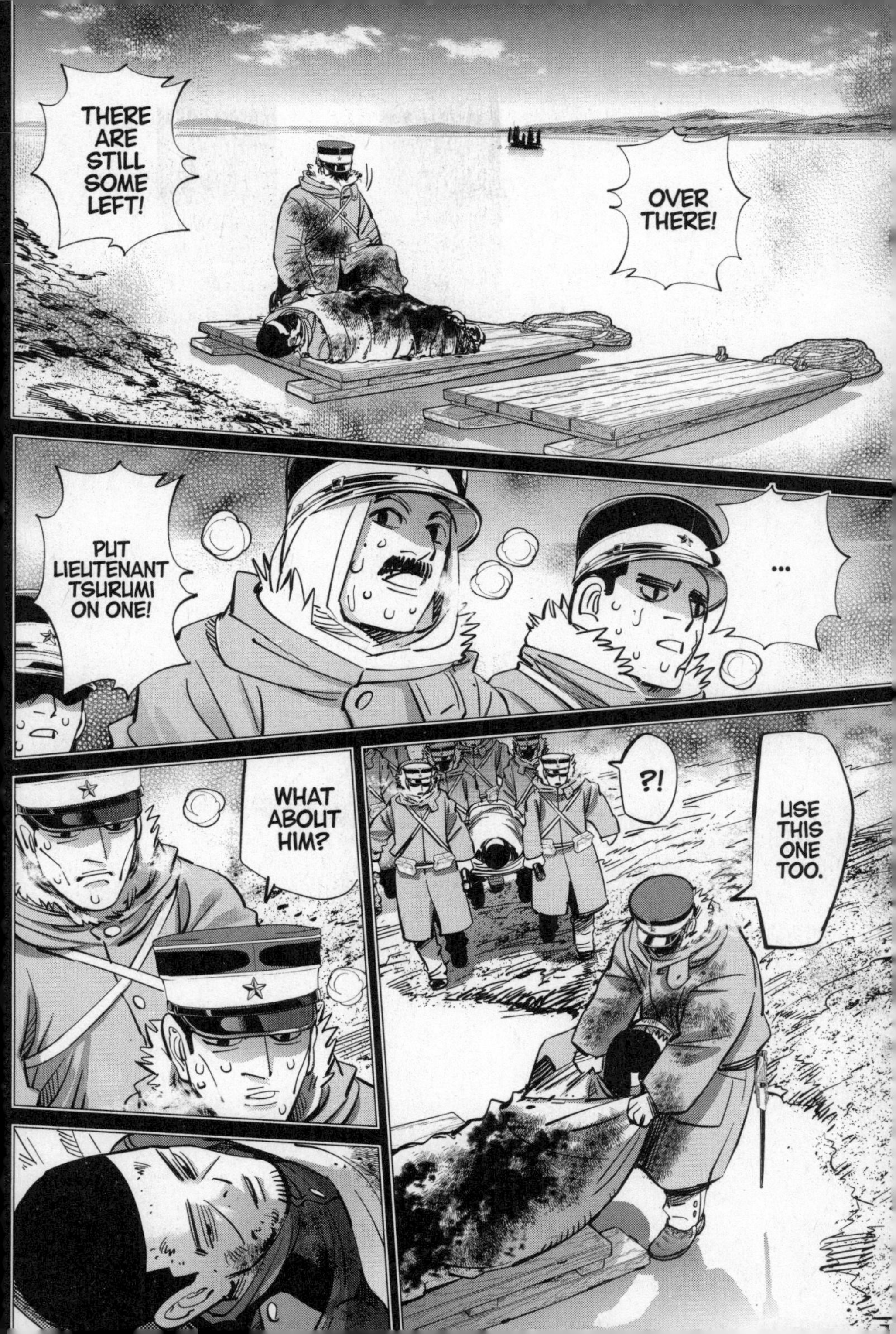
OVER THERE!
THERE ARE STILL SOME LEFT!
...
PUT LIEUTENANT TSURUMI ON ONE!
USE THIS ONE TOO.
?!
WHAT ABOUT HIM?

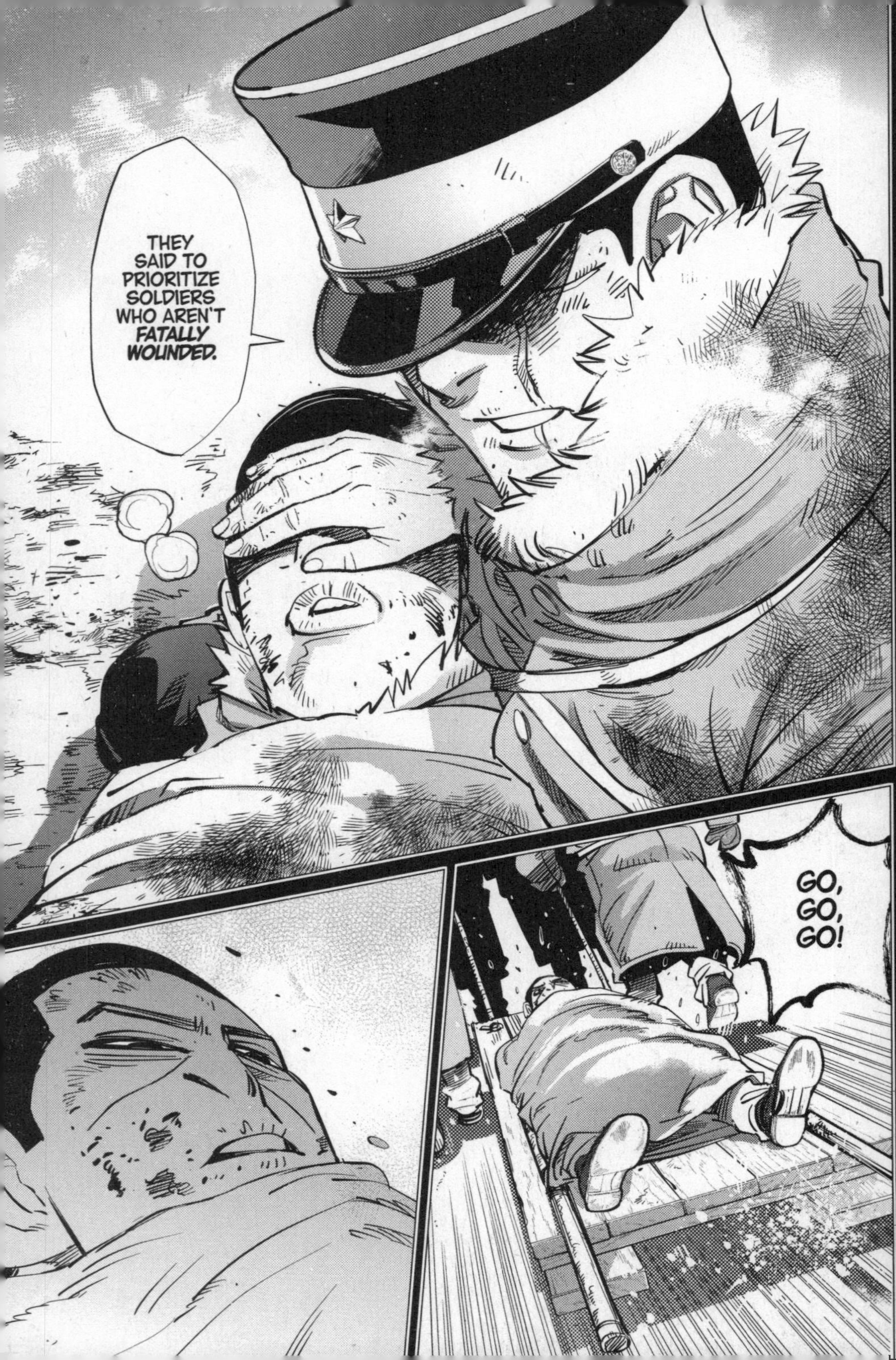
THEY SAID TO PRIORITIZE SOLDIERS WHO AREN'T FATALLY WOUNDED.
GO, GO, GO!

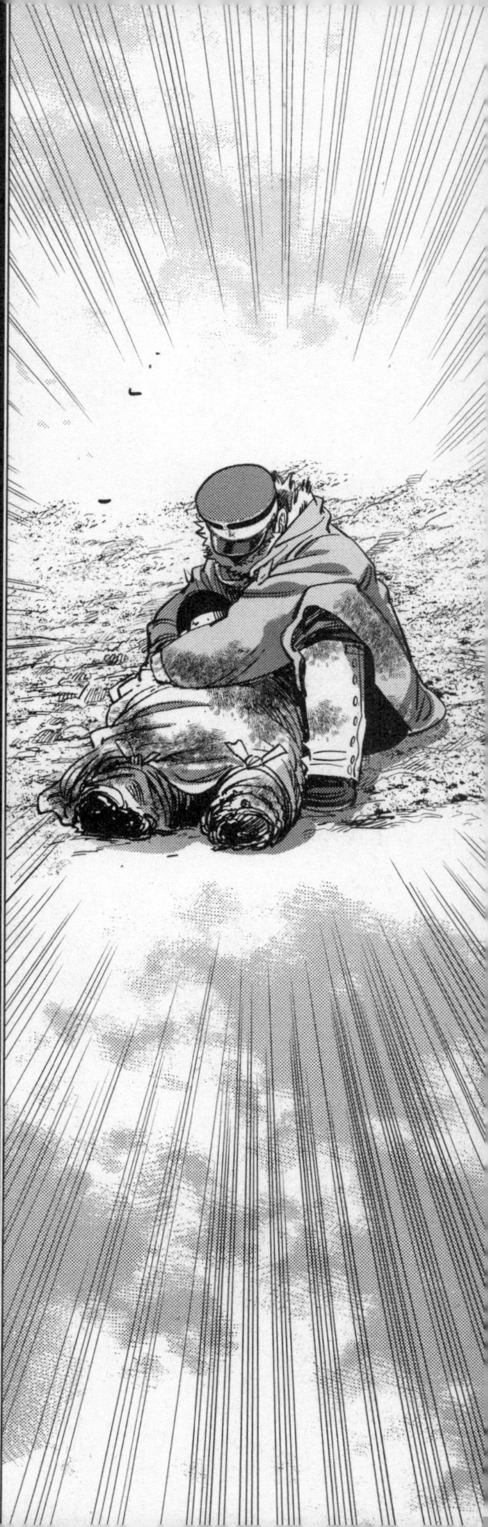
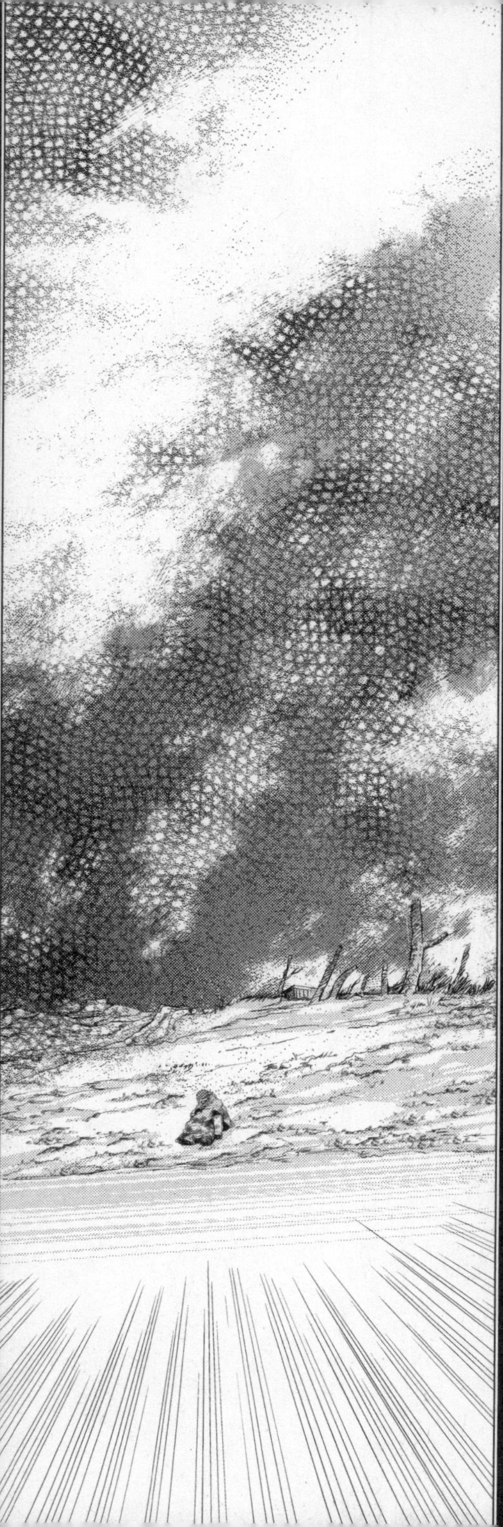

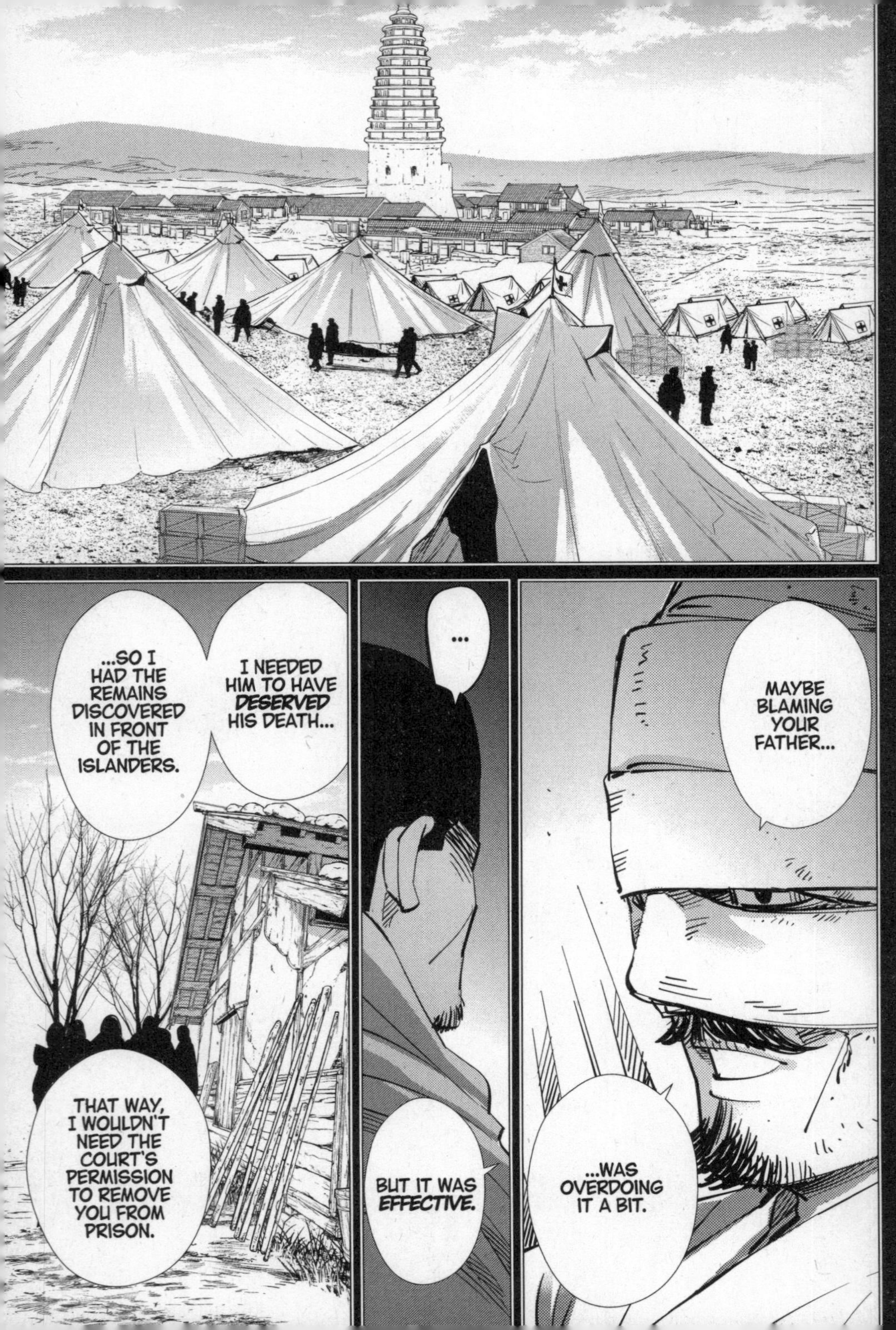
MAYBE BLAMING YOUR FATHER...
...WAS OVERDOING IT A BIT.
...
BUT IT WAS EFFECTIVE.
I NEEDED HIM TO HAVE DESERVED HIS DEATH...
...SO I HAD THE REMAINS DISCOVERED IN FRONT OF THE ISLANDERS.
THAT WAY, I WOULDN'T NEED THE COURT'S PERMISSION TO REMOVE YOU FROM PRISON.

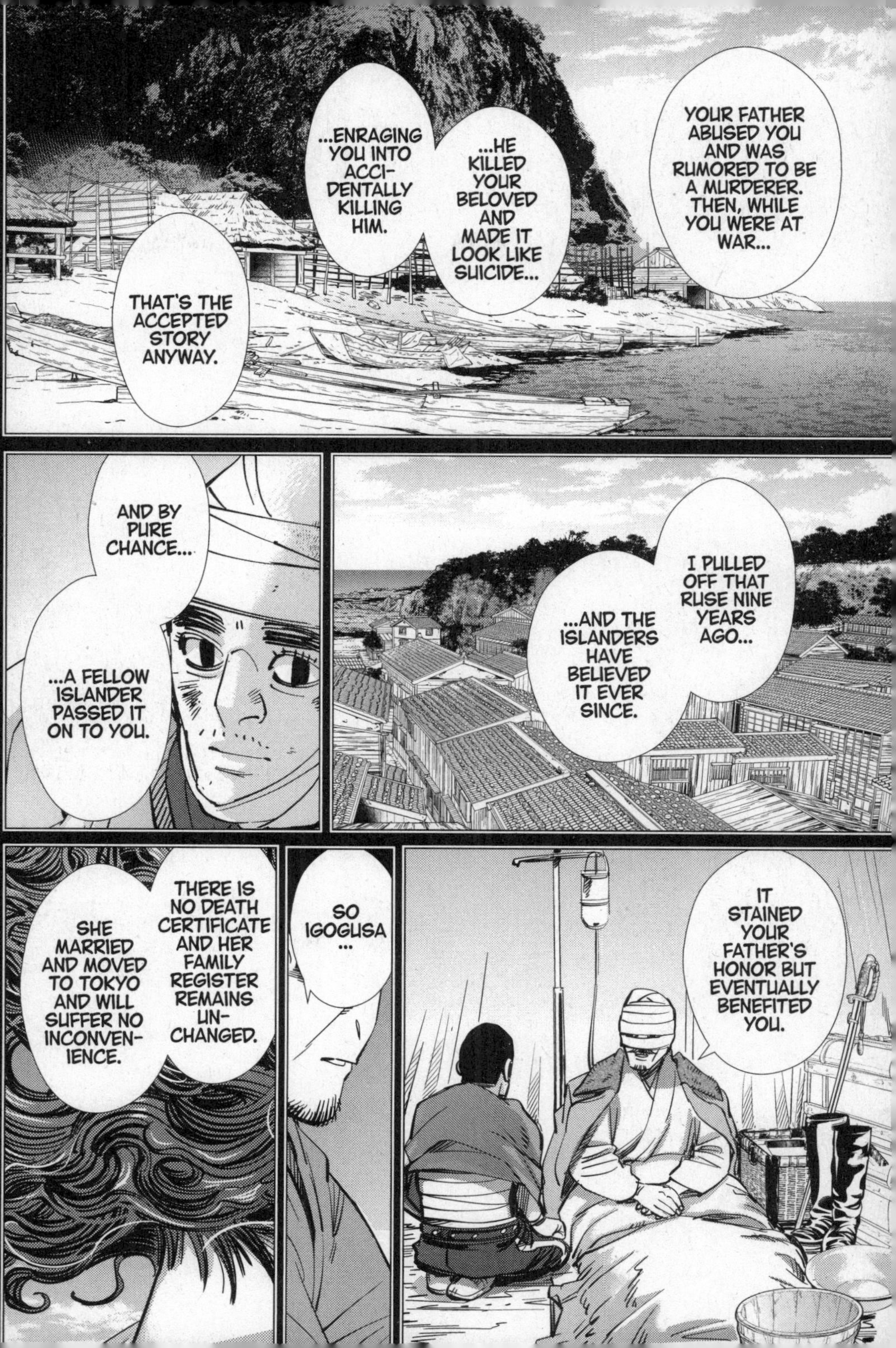
YOUR FATHER ABUSED YOU AND WAS RUMORED TO BE A MURDERER. THEN, WHILE YOU WERE AT WAR...
...HE KILLED YOUR BELOVED AND MADE IT LOOK LIKE SUICIDE...
...ENRAGING YOU INTO ACCI-DENTALLY KILLING HIM.
THAT'S THE ACCEPTED STORY ANYWAY.
I PULLED OFF THAT RUSE NINE YEARS AGO...
...AND THE ISLANDERS HAVE BELIEVED IT EVER SINCE.
AND BY PURE CHANCE...
...A FELLOW ISLANDER PASSED IT ON TO YOU.
IT STAINED YOUR FATHER'S HONOR BUT EVENTUALLY BENEFITED YOU.
SO IGOGUSA ...
THERE IS NO DEATH CERTIFICATE AND HER FAMILY REGISTER REMAINS UN-CHANGED.
SHE MARRIED AND MOVED TO TOKYO AND WILL SUFFER NO INCONVEN-IENCE.

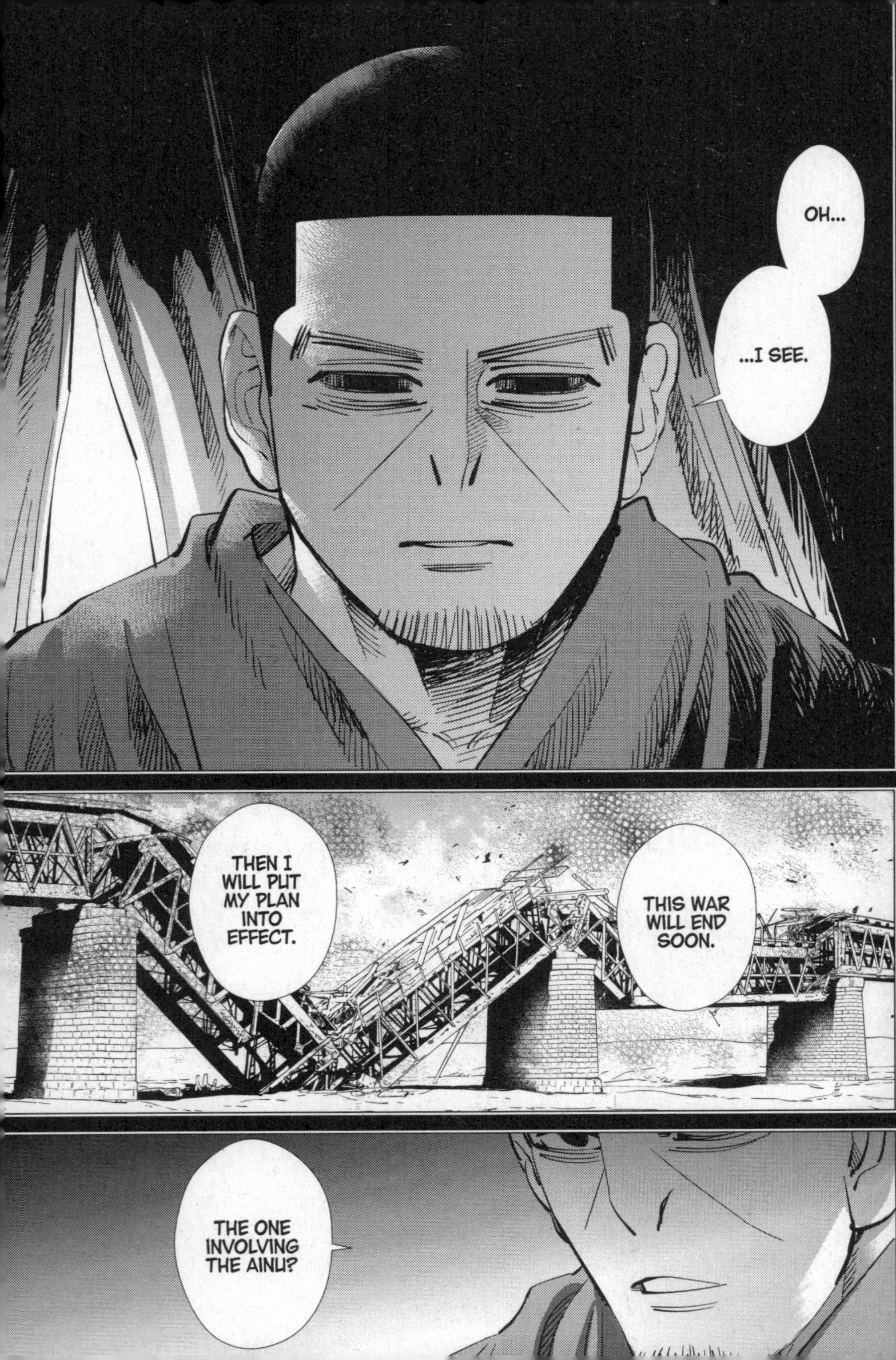
OH...
...I SEE.
THIS WAR WILL END SOON.
THEN I WILL PUT MY PLAN INTO EFFECT.
THE ONE INVOLVING THE AINU?

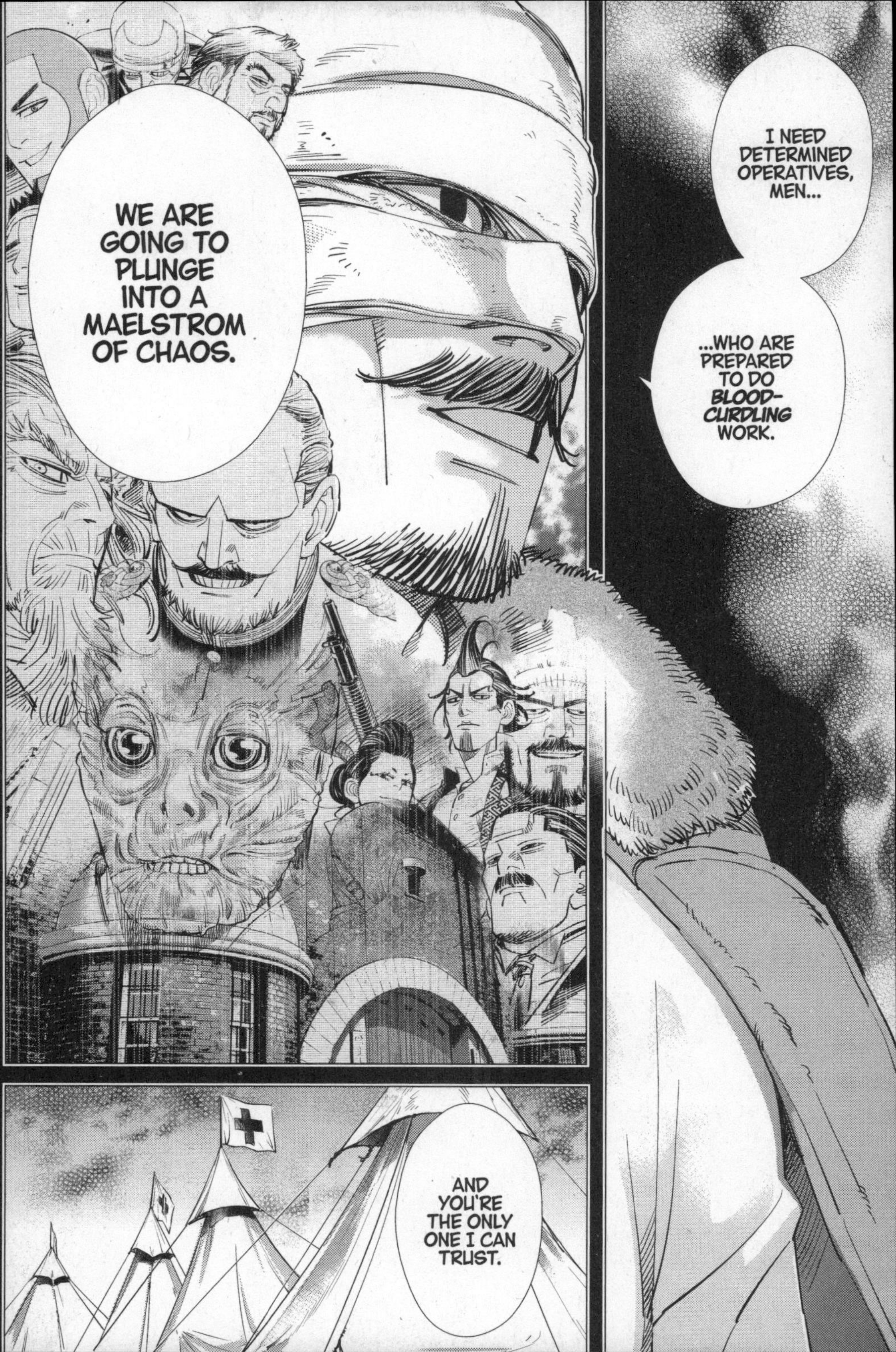
I NEED DETERMINED OPERATIVES, MEN...
...WHO ARE PREPARED TO DO *BLOOD-CURDLING* WORK.
WE ARE GOING TO PLUNGE INTO A MAELSTROM OF CHAOS.
AND YOU'RE THE ONLY ONE I CAN TRUST.

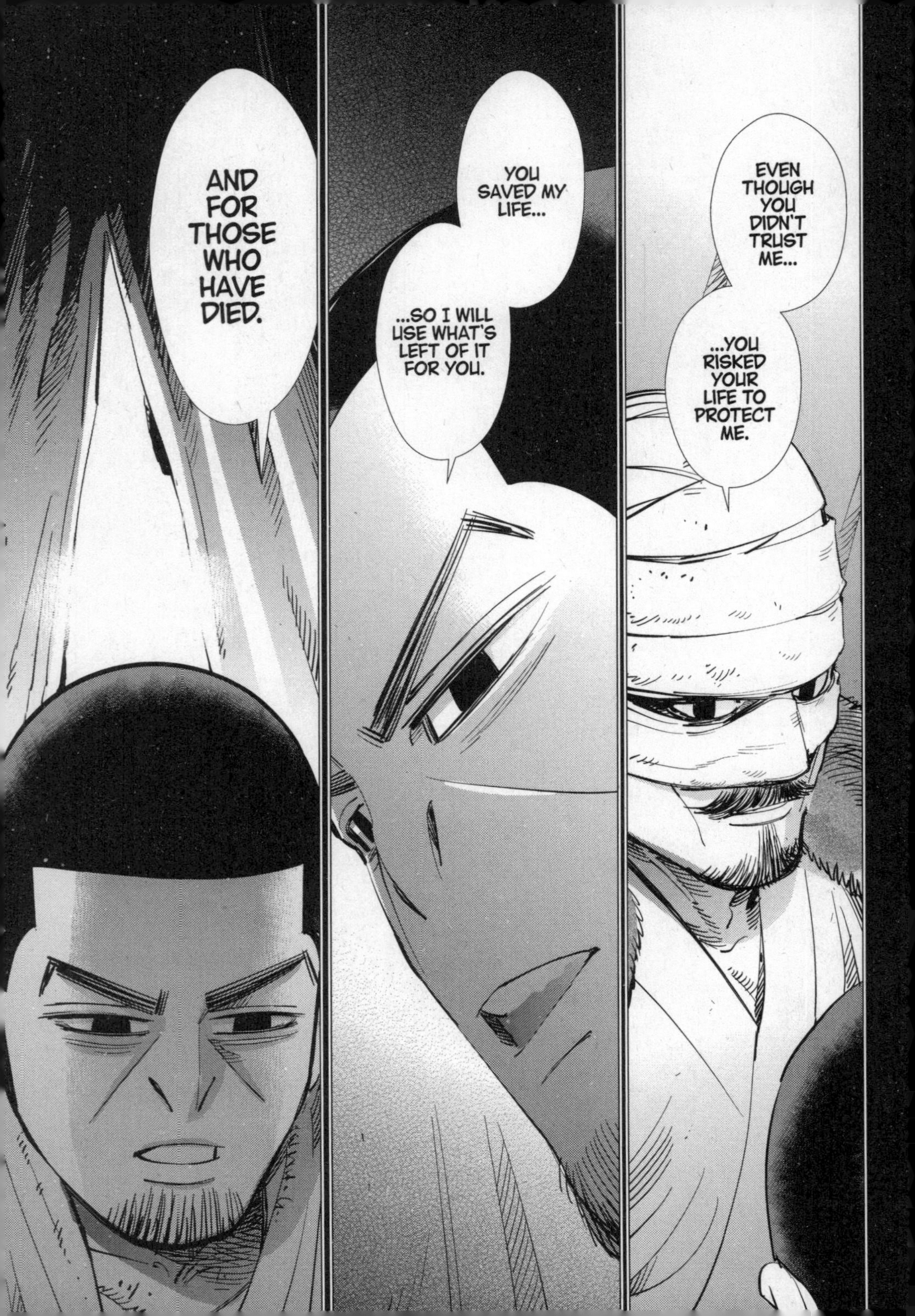
EVEN THOUGH YOU DIDN'T TRUST ME...
...YOU RISKED YOUR LIFE TO PROTECT ME.
YOU SAVED MY LIFE...
...SO I WILL USE WHAT'S LEFT OF IT FOR YOU.
AND FOR THOSE WHO HAVE DIED.

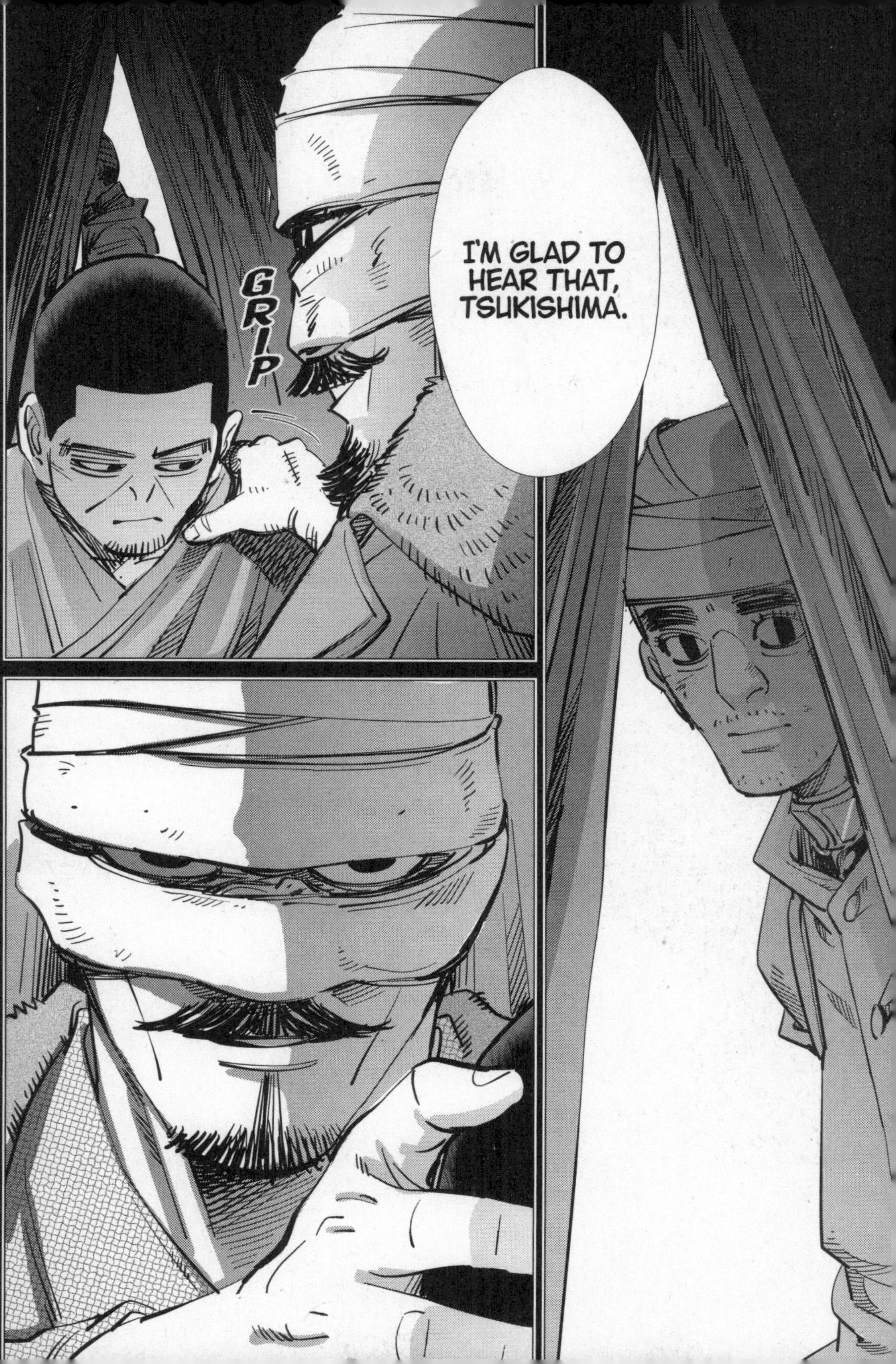
I'M GLAD TO HEAR THAT, TSUKISHIMA.
GRIP

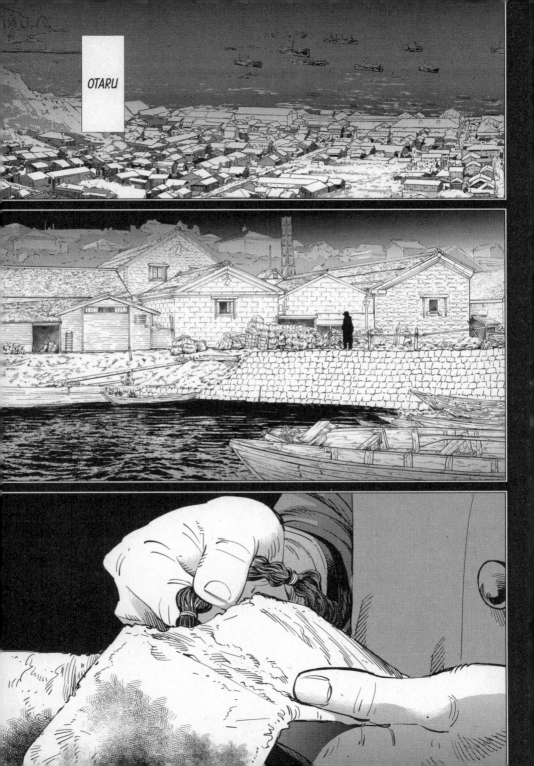

OTARU

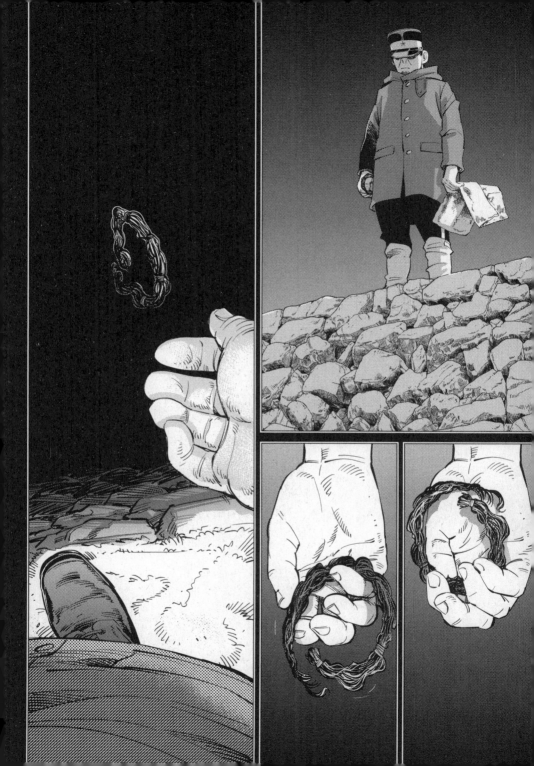

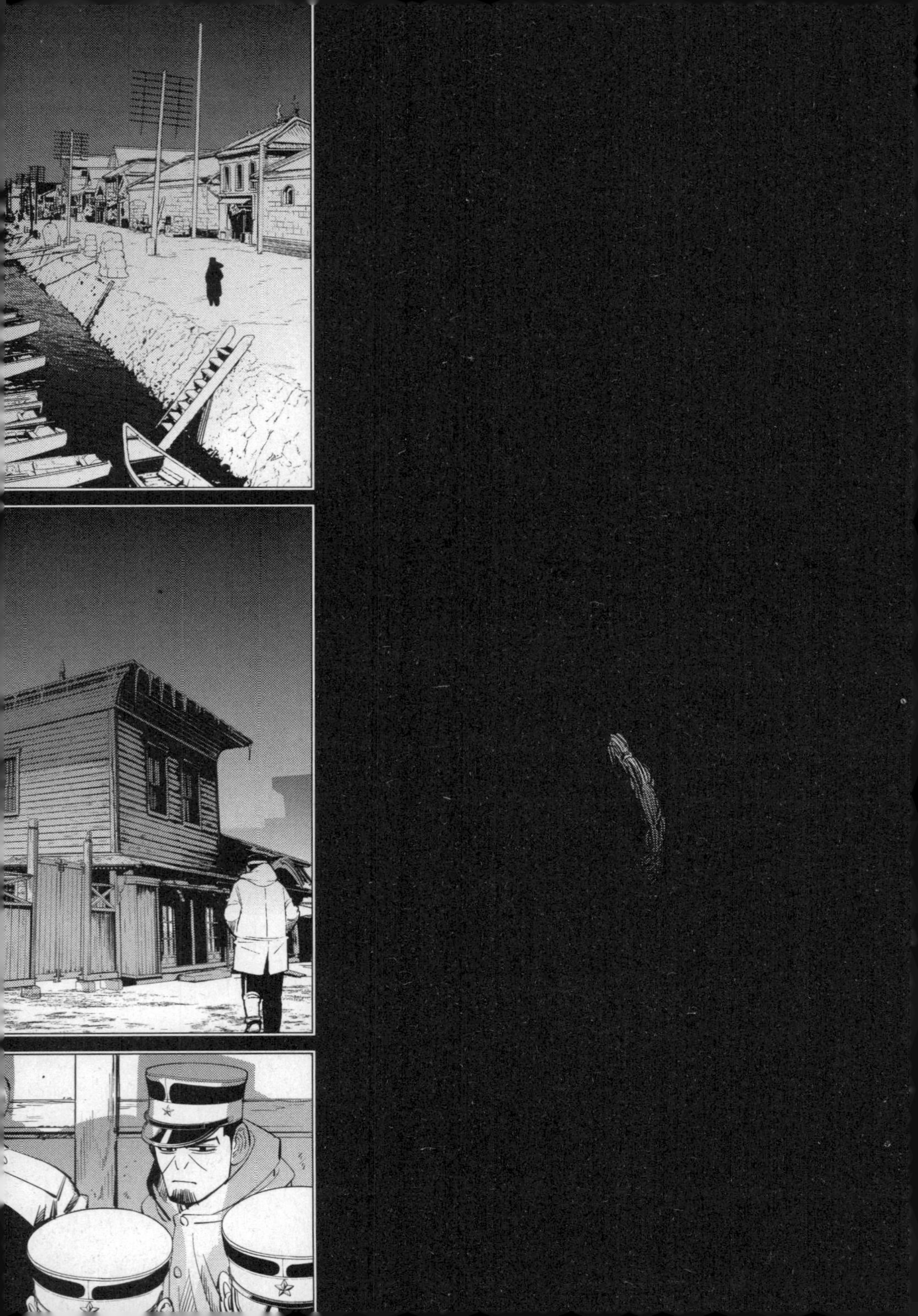

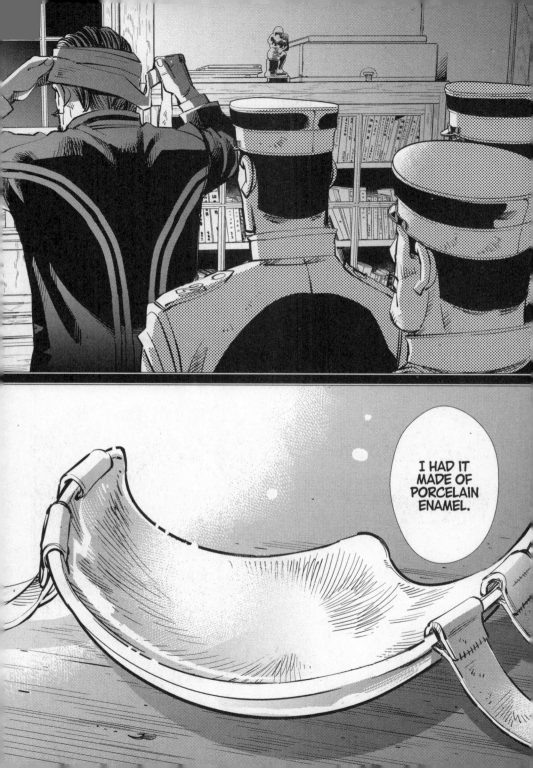

I HAD IT
MADE OF
PORCELAIN
ENAMEL.

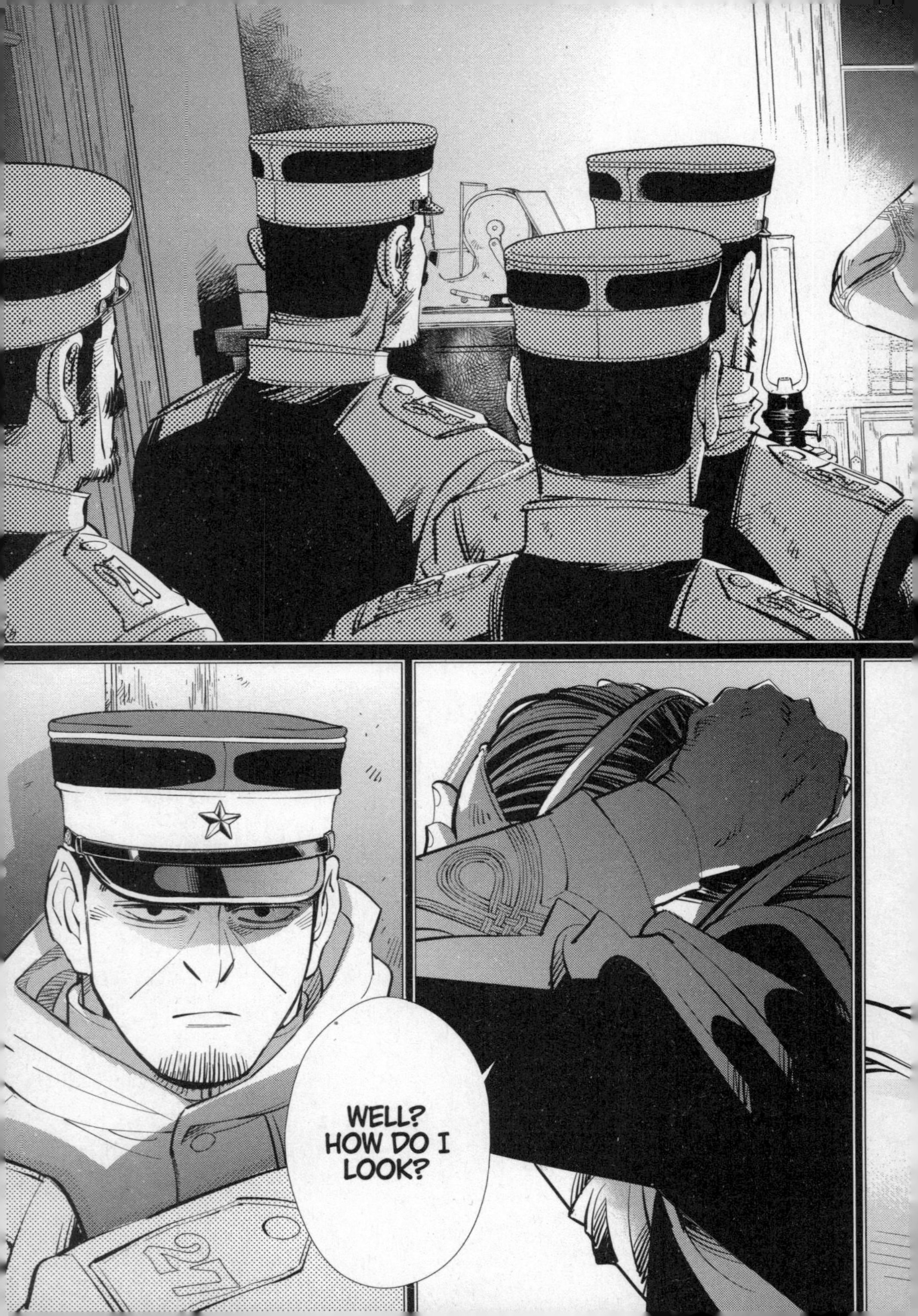
WELL? HOW DO I LOOK?

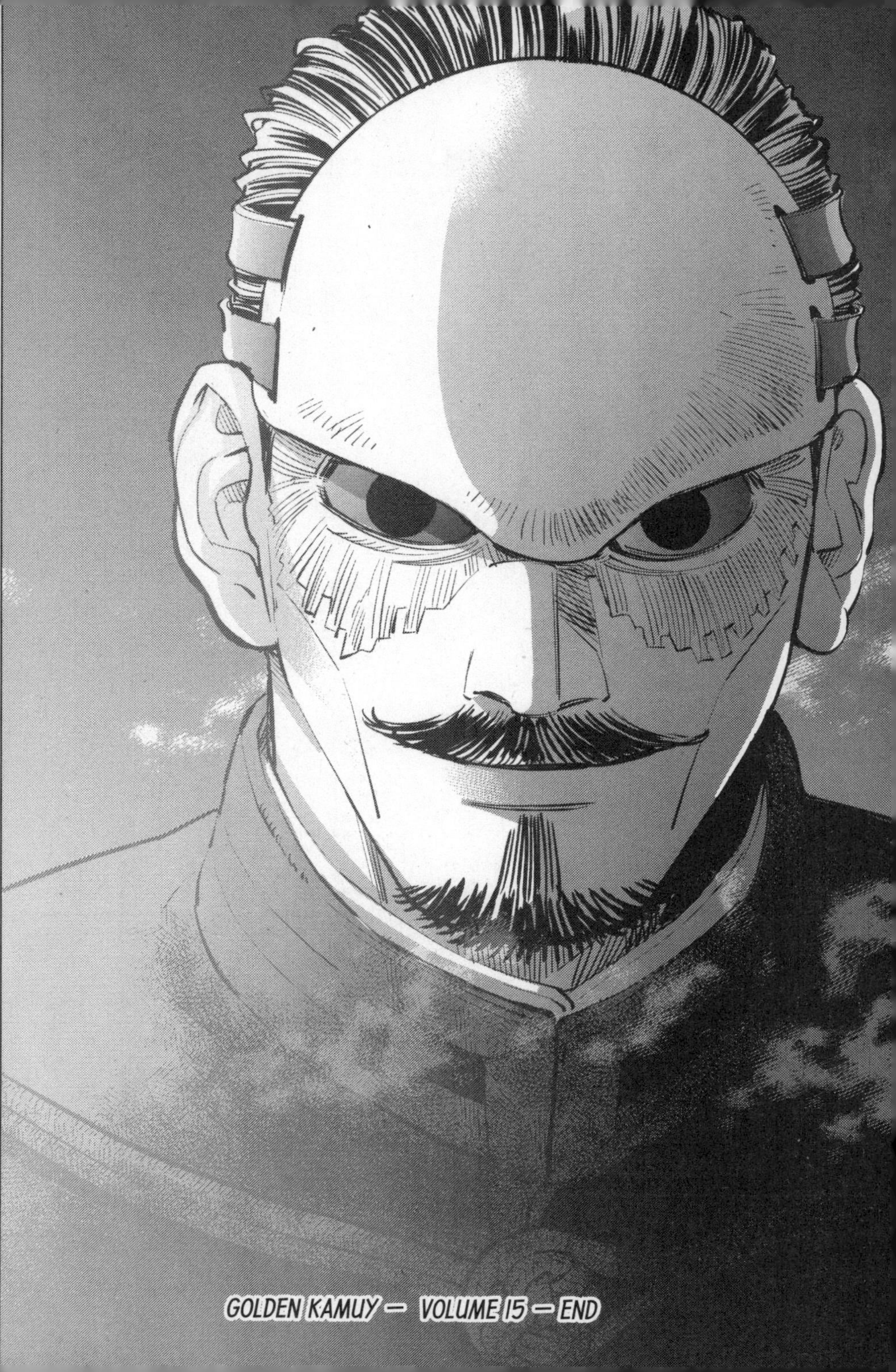
GOLDEN KAMUY — VOLUME 15 — END

Ainu Language Supervision • Hiroshi Nakagaw
Russian Language Supervision • Eugenio Uzhinin

Cooperation from • Hokkaido Ainu Association and the Abashiri Prison Museum • Otaru City General Museum •
Waseda University Aizu Museum • Goto, Kazunobu • Botanic Garden and Museum, Hokkaido University •
National Museum of Ethnology • Nibutani Ainu Culture Museum • The Ainu Museum •
Moon Kabato Museum • Kushiro City Museum • Atsuyo Hisai • Tatsuhiro Tokuda • Shigeharu Terui •
Torpedo boat destroyer consultant: Toshio Yamamoto • All Japan Federation of Karafuto • Tokyo National Museum •
Sakhalin Regional Museum • Shiraishi Hidetoshi • Masato Tamura • Historical Village of Hokkaido

Photo Credits • Takayuki Monma Takanori Matsuda Kozo Ishikawa

Ainu Culture References

Chiri, Takanaka and Yokoyama, Takao. *Ainugo Eiri Jiten* (Ainu Language Illustrated Dictionary). Tokyo: Kagyusha, 1994

Kayano, Shigeru. *Ainu no Mingu* (Ainu Folkcrafts). Kawagoe: Suzusawa Book Store, 1978

Kayano, Shigeru. *Kayano Shigeru no Ainugo Jiten* (Kayano Shigeru's Ainu Language Dictionary). Tokyo: Sanseido, 1996

Musashino Art University – The Research Institute for Culture and Cultural History. *Ainu no Mingu Jissoku Zushu* (Ainu Folkcrafts – Collection of Drawing and Figures). Biratori: Biratori-cho Council for Promoting Ainu Culture, 2014

Satouchi, Ai. *Ainu-shiki ekoroji-seikatsu: Haruzo Ekashi ni manabu shizen no chie* (Ainu Style Ecological Living: Haruzo Ekashi Teaches the Wisdom of Nature). Tokyo: Kabushiki gaisha Shogakukan, 2008

Chiri, Yukie. *Ainu Shin'yoshu* (Chiri Yukie's Ainu Epic Tales). Tokyo: Iwanami Shoten, 1978

Namikawa, Kenji. *Ainu Minzoku no Kiseki* (The Path of the Ainu People). Tokyo: Yamakawa Publishing, 2004

Mook. *Senjuumin Ainu Minzoku* (Bessatsu Taiyo) (The Ainu People (Extra Issue Taiyo).Tokyo: Heibonsha, 2004

Kinoshita, Seizo. *Shiraoikotan Kinoshita Seizo Isaku Shashin Shu* (Shiraoikotan: Kinoshita Seizo's Posthumous Photography Collection). Hokkaido Shiraoi-gun Shiraoi-cho: Shiraoi Heritage Conservation Foundation, 1988

The Ainu Museum. *Ainu no Ifuku Bunka* (The Culture of Ainu Clothing). Hokkaido Shiraoi-gun Shiraoi-cho: Shiraoi Ainu Museum, 1991.

Keira, Tomoko and Kaji, Sayaka. *Ainu no Shiki* (Ainu's Four Seasons). Tokyo: Akashi Shoten, 1995

Fukuoka, Itoko and Sato, Kazuko. *Ainu Shokubutsushi* (Ainu Botanical Journal). Chiba Urayasu-Shi: Sofukan, 1995

Hayakawa, Noboru. *Ainu no Minzoku* (Ainu Folklore). Iwasaki Bijutsusha, 1983

Sunazawa, Kura. *Ku Sukuppu Orushibe* (The Memories of My Generation). Hokkaido, Sapporo-shi: Miyama Shobo, 1983

Haginaka, Miki et al., *Kikigaki Ainu no Shokuji* (Oral History of Ainu Diet).Tokyo: Rural Culture Association Japan, 1992

Nakagawa, Hiroshi. *New Express Ainu Go*. Tokyo: Hakusuisha, 2013

Nakagawa, Hiroshi. *Ainugo Chitose Hogen Jiten* (The Ainu-Japanese dictionary). Chiba Urayasu-Shi: Sofukan, 1995
Nakagawa, Hiroshi and Nakamoto, Mutsuko. *Kamuy Yukara de Ainu Go wo Manabu* Learning Ainu with Kamuy Yukar). Tokyo: Hakusuisha, 2007

Nakagawa, Hiroshi. *Katari au Kotoba no Chikara – Kamuy tachi to Ikiru Sekai* (The Power of Spoken Words – Living in a World with Kamuy). Tokyo: Iwanami Shoten, 2010

Sarashina, Genzo and Sarashina, Hikari. Kotan Seibutsu Ki <1 Juki / Zassou hen> (Kotan Wildlife Vol. 1 – Trees and Weeds). Hosei University Publishing, 1992/2007

Sarashina, Genzo and Sarashina, Hikari. *Kotan Seibutsu Ki <2 Yacho / Kaijuu / Gyozoku hen>* (Kotan Wildlife Vol. 2 – Birds, Sea Creatures, and Fish). Hosei University Publishing, 1992/2007

Sarashina, Genzo and Sarashina, Hikari. *Kotan Seibutsu Ki <3 Yachou / Mizudori / Konchu hen>* (Kotan Wildlife Vol. 3 – Shorebirds, Seabirds, and Insects). Hosei University Publishing, 1992/2007

Sarashina, Genzo. Ainu Minwashu (Collection of Ainu Folktales). Kita Shobou, 1963.

Sarashina, Genzo. Ainu Rekishi to Minzoku (Ainu History and Folklore). Shakai Shisousha, 1968.

Kawakami Yuji. *Sarunkur Ainu Monogatari* (The Tale of Sarunkur Ainu). Kawagoe: Suzusawa Book Store, 2003/2005

Kawakami, Yuji. *Ekashi to Fuchi wo Tazunete* (Visiting Ekashi and Fuchi). Kawagoe: Suzusawa Book Store, 1991

Council for the Conservation of Ainu Culture. *Ainu Minzokushi* (Ainu People Magazine). Dai-ichi Hoki, 1970

Hokkaido Cultural Property Protection Association. *Ainu Ifuku Chousa Houkokusho <1 Ainu Josei ga Denshou Suru Ibunka>* (The Ainu Clothing Research Report Vol. 1 – Traditional Clothing Passed Down Through Generations of Ainu Women). 1986

Okamura, Kichiemon and Clancy, Judith A. *Ainu no Ishou* (The Clothes of the Ainu People). Kyoto Shoin, 1993

Yotsuji, Ichiro. Photos by Mizutani, Morio. *Ainu no Monyo* (Decorative Arts of the Ainu). Kasakura Publishing, 1981

Yoshida, Iwao. *Ainushi Shiryoshu* (Collection of Ainu Historical Documents). Hokkaido Publication Project Center, 1983.

Kubodera, Itsuhiko. *Ainu no Mukashibanashi* (Old Stories of the Ainu). Miyaishoten, 1972.

Kubodera, Itsuhiko (trans.). Ainu Minzokushi (Ainu People Magazine). Dai-ichi Hoki.

Inoue, Koichi and Latyshev, Vladislav M. (coed.). Karafuto Ainu no Mingu (Karafuto Ainu Folkcraft). Hokkaido Publication Project Center, 2002.

Russia ga Mita Ainu Bunka (Ainu Culture as Seen byRussia). The Foundation for Research and Promotion of Ainu Culture, 2013.

Russia Minzokugaku Hakubutsukan Ainu Shiryoten—Russia ga Mita Shimaguni no Hitobito (Russia Museum of Ethnology Ainu Materials Exhibition—Island Peoples as Seen by Russia). The Foundation for Research and Promotion of Ainu Culture, 2005.

The Foundation for Research and Promotion of Ainu Culture (ed.). *Senjima, Karafuto, Hokkaido—Ainu no Kurashi* (Ainu Life on the Kuril Islands, Karafuto and Hokkaido). The Senri Foundation, 2011.

SPb-Ainu Project Group (ed.). *Russia Kagaku Academy Jinruigaku Minzokugaku Hakubutsukan Shozo Ainu Shiryo Mokuroku* (Ainu Collections of Peter the Great Museum of Anthropology and Ethnography\Russian Academy of Sciences Catalogue). Sofukan, 1998.

Yamamoto, Yuko. *Karafuto Ainu—Jukyo to Mingu* (Residences and Folkcraft of the Karafuto Ainu). Sagami Shobo, 1970.

Nishitsuru, Sadaka. *Karafuto Ainu.* Miyama Shobo, 1974.

Kasai, Takechiyo. *Karafuto Ainu no Minzoku* (Folklore of the Karafuto Ainu). Miyama Shobo, 1975.

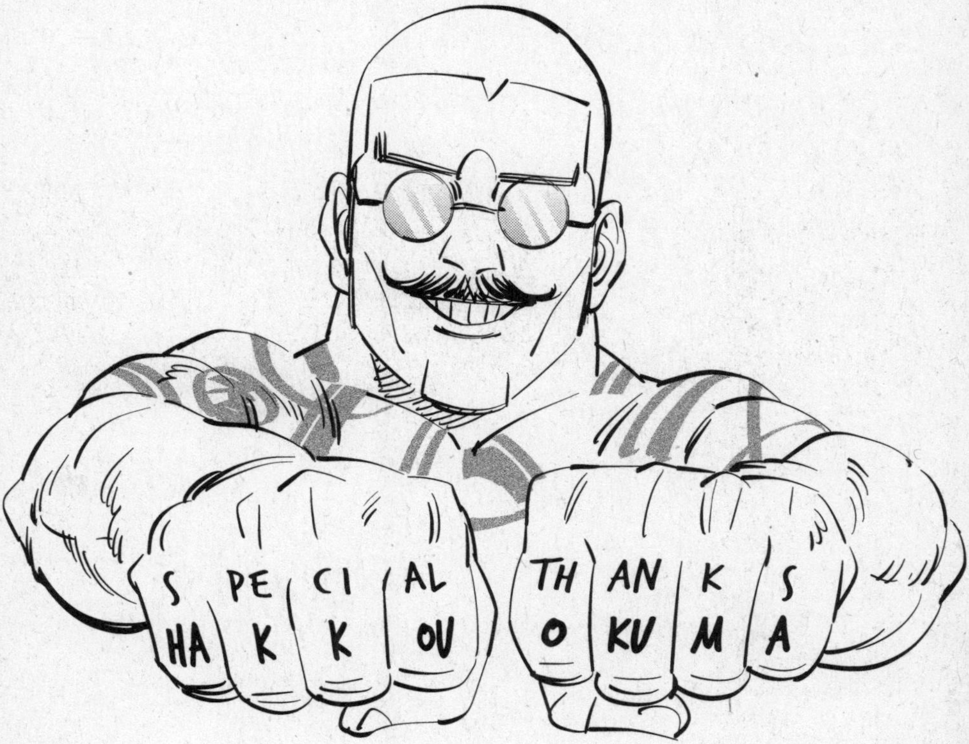
S PE CI AL TH AN K S
HA K K OU O KU M A

Kanto or wa yaku sak no arankep sinep ka isam.
Nothing comes from heaven without purpose. —Ainu proverb

TETARAPE (WEED BARK CLOTHING)

KARAFUTO AINU
CLOTHES MADE FROM
FIBERS OF NETTLES

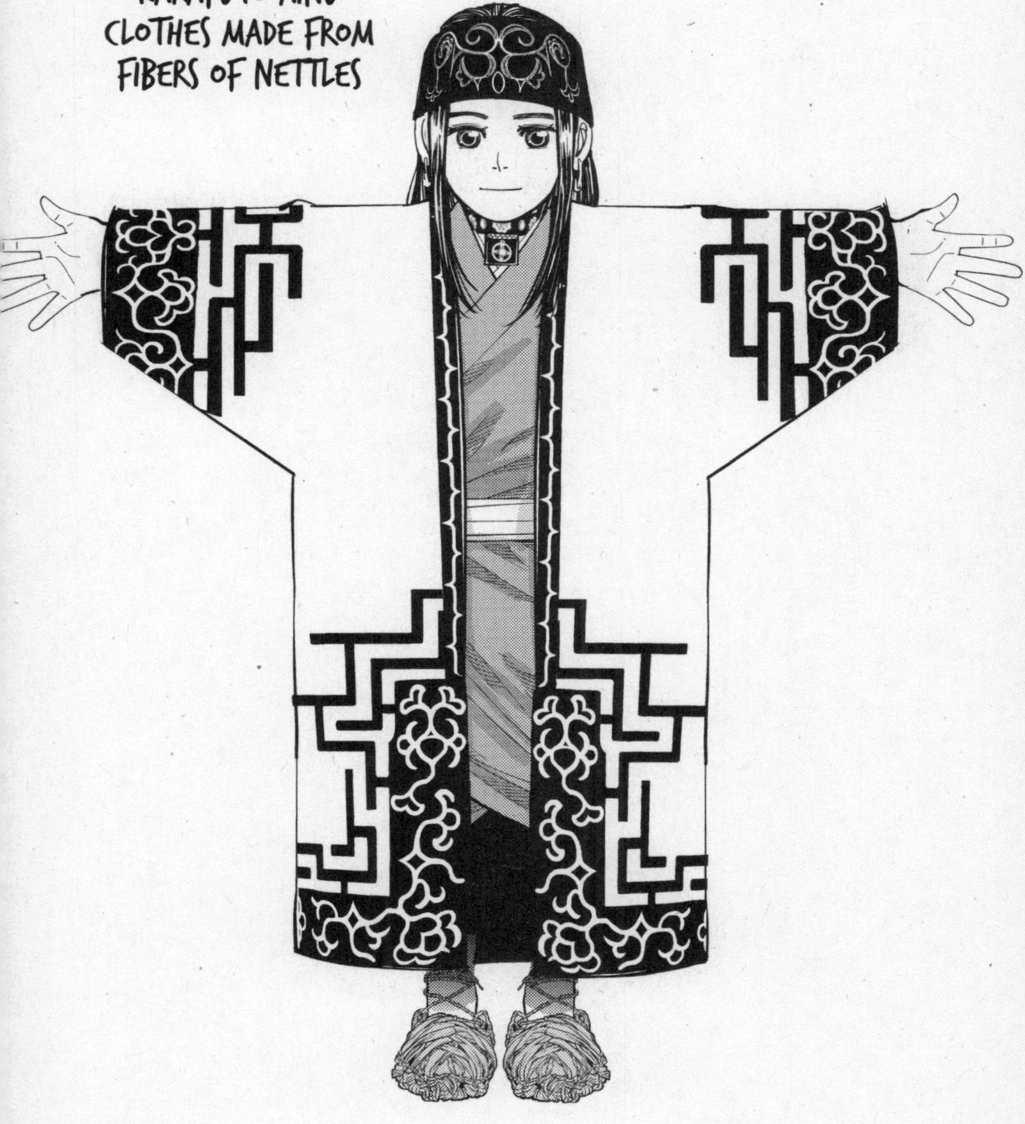